BOOKS BY MARK RUBINSTEIN, M.D.

The Growing Years: A Guide to Your Child's Emotional Development from Birth to Adolescence (with The New York Hospital—Cornell Medical Center)

Heartplan: A Complete Program for Total Fitness of Heart and Mind (with David L. Copen, M.D.)

New Choices: The Latest Options in Treating Breast Cancer (with Dennis P. Cirillo, M.D.)

The Complete Book of Cosmetic Facial Surgery (with Dennis P. Cirillo, M.D.)

The First Encounter: The Beginnings in Psychotherapy (with William A. Console, M.D., and Richard C. Simons, M.D.)

.The
Growing
Years

—◇—

A Guide to Your Child's Emotional
Development from Birth to Adolescence

The New York Hospital–Cornell Medical Center
Department of Psychiatry
with
Mark Rubinstein, M.D.

Foreword by Robert Michels, M.D.
Barklie McKee Henry Professor and Chairman, Department
of Psychiatry, Cornell University Medical College,
Psychiatrist-in-Chief, The New York Hospital

A Fireside Book
Published by Simon & Schuster Inc.
New York   London   Toronto   Sydney   Tokyo

FIRESIDE
SIMON & SCHUSTER BUILDING
ROCKEFELLER CENTER
1230 AVENUE OF THE AMERICAS
NEW YORK, NEW YORK 10020
COPYRIGHT © 1987 BY CORNELL UNIVERSITY
ALL RIGHTS RESERVED
INCLUDING THE RIGHT OF REPRODUCTION
IN WHOLE OR IN PART IN ANY FORM
FIRST FIRESIDE EDITION, 1989
PUBLISHED BY ARRANGEMENT WITH ATHENEUM PUBLISHERS
FIRESIDE AND COLOPHON ARE REGISTERED TRADEMARKS
OF SIMON & SCHUSTER INC.
MANUFACTURED IN THE UNITED STATES OF AMERICA

10 9 8 7 6 5 4 3 2 1 PBK.

LIBRARY OF CONGRESS CATALOGING IN PUBLICATION DATA

THE GROWING YEARS : A GUIDE TO YOUR CHILD'S EMOTIONAL DEVELOPMENT
FROM BIRTH TO ADOLESCENCE / THE NEW YORK HOSPITAL–CORNELL MEDICAL
CENTER, DEPARTMENT OF PSYCHIATRY, WITH MARK RUBINSTEIN; FOREWORD
BY ROBERT MICHELS.— 1ST FIRESIDE ED.
P. CM.
REPRINT. ORIGINALLY PUBLISHED: NEW YORK: ATHENEUM, 1988.
"A FIRESIDE BOOK."
INCLUDES INDEX.
ISBN 0-671-67726-8 (PBK.)
1. CHILD PSYCHOLOGY.   2. CHILD REARING.   I. RUBINSTEIN, MARK, 1942-
II. NEW YORK HOSPITAL–CORNELL MEDICAL CENTER. DEPT. OF PSYCHIATRY.
[BF721.G84 1989]
649'.1'019—DC19

88-26485
CIP

ACKNOWLEDGMENTS

MANY PEOPLE'S CONTRIBUTIONS made *The Growing Years* possible.

Lois Beekman Ehrenkranz conceptualized the need for a book that would help all parents.

Dr. Robert Michels, Chairman of the Department of Psychiatry at The New York Hospital–Cornell Medical Center, graciously made the resources of the department available to me. Participating members of the faculty, psychiatrists and psychologists, added richness, depth, and a most human touch to these pages, as will be evident to the reader. Dr. Aaron Esman coordinated the faculty's participation with equanimity and sensitivity, making valuable suggestions that enriched the book. Judith Hyman of The New York Hospital–Cornell Medical Center helped implement the project at its beginning.

Ronald S. Konecky and Richard Hofstetter attended to crucial details that helped carry the idea of the book to the arena of reality.

Pam Bernstein of the William Morris Agency contributed enthusiasm and energy to the project, helping it become what it now is. Norman Brokaw, as always, was supportive and encouraging, while Mel Berger set the first gears into motion.

Susan Ginsburg, Editor in Chief at Atheneum, quickly recognized the value of this project, and devoted her considerable talents to helping it achieve its potential. Laurie Bernstein, Associate Editor, worked diligently at virtually every aspect of the book's production.

Edith Rubinstein typed countless pages, never faltering; Ruth Pollack and Mona Feldman were added to the typing pool as the book progressed.

My wife, Linda, provided suggestions, insights, understanding, and the most important ingredient of all—love.

Mark Rubinstein, M.D.

CONTENTS

Chapter 4: The School-Age Youngster—Ages Six to Twelve

INTRODUCTION

WRITTEN FOR EVERY PARENT, *The Growing Years* presents a comprehensive developmental journey, beginning with the newborn, moving through all of childhood and through the grade-school years.

In our experience at The New York Hospital–Cornell Medical Center, we see many parents who worry needlessly about their children's developmental progress. We also encounter troubled children whose parents failed to recognize the warning signs of some problems years earlier.

These experiences led us to the conviction that *all parents* could be helped by a book that explains normal behavioral differences as children progress through each phase of their lives. Included would be realistic explanations of *why* children think, feel, and behave as they do, along with practical advice to help parents pinpoint possible trouble spots if they appear.

The Growing Years is divided into two parts. Part I, "Your Child's Emotional Development," has four chapters: *The First Year Of Life, The Toddler—The Second and Third Years, The Preschool Years—Ages Three to Six,* and *The School-Age Youngster—Ages Six to Twelve.* Each chapter begins by exploring the major developmental themes of that period, and is followed by a section that discusses practical issues for that period of your child's life. Finally, in a question-and-answer consultation, a noted Cornell Medical Center expert answers specific questions about that period of your child's development. Throughout each chapter, vivid true-life accounts illustrate the points.

Part II details and explains special situations: the adopted child, when mother works, sibling rivalry, twins, the gifted child, and other topics of concern.

No longer satisfied with myths or hearsay information about raising children, today's parents want sound, practical, up-to-the-minute advice so that they can help their children become mature and fulfilled adults.

Department of Psychiatry,
The New York Hospital–Cornell Medical Center

A NOTE FROM THE WRITER

THE GROWING YEARS is a unique book. While there are other works about child development, few focus on the range of emotional issues from the first day of life through all of childhood. And no other book addresses the controversial topics included in Part II of this volume.

No similar book has ever drawn on the vast expertise of a major university teaching center as this one does. The New York Hospital–Cornell Medical Center's Department of Psychiatry has played an historic role in psychiatric treatment and research for years. The department's efforts helped spur the development of modern drug therapies and have resulted in extensive programs of care and research involving childhood and adolescence.

With two facilities, the Payne Whitney Clinic in Manhattan and the Westchester Division at White Plains, The New York Hospital–Cornell Medical Center's Department of Psychiatry provides services encompassing every aspect of modern psychiatric care. Its faculty includes more than 450 full- and part-time members in what is now the nation's largest psychiatric residency program. The department also helps train 400 medical students each year, along with psychologists, social workers, and other health-care professionals.

The department's Psychobiology Laboratory and the Laboratory of Developmental Processes are nationally respected, while the Bourne Laboratory is internationally known for research into eating disorders. The department's research efforts include the areas of substance abuse, child and adolescent disorders, adolescent suicide, depression, anxiety, and somatic therapies. In 1984 alone, members of the Department's Division of Child and Adolescent Psychiatry authored more than eighty scientific publications throughout the world.

The Growing Years is designed as a readable and practical guidebook for all parents who want information throughout all the years of their children's development. As a physician, psychiatrist, and writer, I am proud to participate in this project. It is my conviction that *The Growing Years* will occupy an important place in the lives of many thousands of parents. It will serve as a rich and valued source of information, guidance, and reassurance for years to come.

Mark Rubinstein, M.D.

HOW TO USE THIS BOOK

THE GROWING YEARS is designed as a complete ready-reference guide for every parent. Each chapter in Part I proceeds from a general description of the child's emotional development to a section called "Practical Issues" in which specific day-to-day parents' concerns are addressed. There follows a section called "A Consultation" in which frequently asked questions are posed to a noted Cornell Medical Center expert. Thus, the book proceeds from the general to the specific.

A complete table of Contents appears at the beginning of the book. Reviewing the Contents before reading a specific chapter will indicate topics of interest or concern to any individual reader. For the reader who wants advice about a particular concern, any section of each chapter can be read alone.

The Growing Years is a comprehensive, systematic presentation of childhood development from birth to adolescence. It can be read for an overall understanding of the child's emotional development, although chapters need not be read in sequence. The book can be used as an informative quick-reference guide about any issue. For instance, if your child is a toddler, you would be most interested in Chapter 2, *The Toddler—The Second and Third Years.* If you are thinking of returning to work, you may then refer to Chapter 7, *When Mother Works,* which is also relevant to your concerns.

The book has many cross-references so that the reader may refer to a related or expanded topic. In addition, the comprehensive Index is designed as a quick guide to help the reader locate any topic of interest. Using the Contents, the Index, and the many cross-references throughout the book, the reader can quickly and easily pinpoint topics he or she wishes to read.

FOREWORD

THE GROWING YEARS is written for parents and other people concerned about raising children. It is written by distinguished experts in
child development and child behavior. Of course, they became experts
by learning from children and from parents. One of the things that they
have learned is that parents often understand far more about their
child's emotional development than they realize. Another is that it is
often helpful to have that understanding systematized, formulated,
related to the understanding of others, and enhanced by what has been
learned from special children—children with unusual difficulties or facing unusual problems. Of course, every child is at times a special child.
Parents should find this book particularly helpful at those times.

The contributors to this book are the faculty of one of the largest
psychiatry programs in the world. They educate many professionals who
deal with children, such as psychiatrists, pediatricians, medical students,
nurses, social workers, and psychologists. More importantly, they work
daily with parents and children, and most are parents themselves.

As Chairman of the Department of Psychiatry of The New York
Hospital–Cornell Medical Center, it is my privilege to present *The
Growing Years.* I hope that it will provide reassurance, advice, and help
for parents, will enrich their relationship with their children, and will
contribute to the health and happiness of all.

Robert Michels, M.D.

PANEL OF CONSULTANTS

Robert C. Ascher, M.D.
Clinical Associate Professor of Psychiatry, Cornell University Medical College; Associate Attending Psychiatrist, Payne Whitney Clinic, The New York Hospital

Aaron H. Esman, M.D.
Professor of Clinical Psychiatry, Cornell University Medical College; Director of Adolescent Services, Payne Whitney Clinic, The New York Hospital

Fady Hajal, M.D.
Assistant Professor of Psychiatry, Cornell University Medical College; Assistant Attending Psychiatrist, Westchester Division, The New York Hospital

Stephen Herman, M.D.
Assistant Professor of Psychiatry in Psychiatry and Pediatrics, Cornell University Medical College; Attending Psychiatrist, Payne Whitney Clinic, The New York Hospital

Margaret E. Hertzig, M.D.
Associate Professor of Psychiatry, Cornell University Medical College; Director, Child Outpatient Services, Payne Whitney Clinic, The New York Hospital

Paulina F. Kernberg, M.D.
Associate Professor of Psychiatry, Cornell University Medical College; Director, Child Psychiatry, Westchester Division, The New York Hospital

Robert Michels, M.D.
Professor of Psychiatry, Cornell University Medical College; Psychiatrist-in-Chief, The New York Hospital

Cynthia P. Pfeffer, M.D.
Associate Professor of Clinical Psychiatry, Cornell University Medical College; Director of Child Inpatient Services, Westchester Division, The New York Hospital

John M. Ross, Ph.D.
Clinical Associate Professor of Psychology in Psychiatry, Cornell University
Medical College; Associate Attending Psychologist, Payne Whitney Clinic, The
New York Hospital

Theodore Shapiro, M.D.
Professor of Psychiatry, Cornell University Medical College; Director, Division
of Child and Adolescent Psychiatry, Payne Whitney Clinic, The New York
Hospital

Miriam Sherman, M.D.
Associate Professor of Clinical Psychiatry, Cornell University Medical College;
Director of Pediatric Consultation Liaison, The New York Hospital

Margaret E. Snow, Ph.D.
Assistant Professor of Psychology in Psychiatry, Cornell University Medical
College; Assistant Attending Psychologist, Payne Whitney Clinic, The New
York Hospital

Ladd Spiegel, M.D.
Instructor in Psychiatry, Cornell University Medical College; Assistant Attending Psychiatrist, Payne Whitney Clinic, The New York Hospital

Daniel N. Stern, M.D.
Professor of Psychiatry, Cornell University Medical College; Director of the
Laboratory of Developmental Processes, Payne Whitney Clinic, The New York
Hospital

Norman L. Straker, M.D.
Clinical Associate Professor of Psychiatry, Cornell University Medical College;
Associate Attending Psychiatrist, Payne Whitney Clinic, The New York
Hospital

Muriel C. Winestine, Ph.D.
Clinical Associate Professor of Psychology in Psychiatry, Cornell University
Medical College; Associate Attending Psychologist, Payne Whitney Clinic, The
New York Hospital

Part I

---◇---

Your Child's Emotional Development

Chapter 1: The First Year of Life

◊ YOUR DEVELOPING CHILD

During the first year of your baby's life, major and dramatic development takes place. This chapter explores these physical, emotional, and intellectual changes, and provides practical advice about this crucial first year.

During the first twelve months, the average baby grows about eight inches, increasing his overall length by about 40 percent. He gains about fifteen pounds, tripling his birth weight. The baby's brain doubles in size, and the nervous system is well on its way to maturing, giving the baby increasing control over his body's capabilities. The infant's body proportions and facial appearance change dramatically, progressing from the newborn's look of "wonderment" to the rounded, responsive, and expressive face of the one-year-old infant.

Over the course of the first year, your helpless and passive newborn becomes a determined, high-energy traveler who rolls, sits, creeps, crawls, toddles, and explores everything, steadily expanding his world. By the end of one short year, the baby—who at first spent the day sleeping, sucking milk, and crying—is preparing to walk and approaches the threshold of true human communication: the ability to talk.

The baby's emotional and intellectual abilities blossom during this exciting first year. From blankly staring at people, he will begin actively participating in your family's social life and its interactions. Your infant will progress from barely being aware of his surroundings to developing a separate identity. Acquiring ever-increasing knowledge about the world, he will learn the myriad differences between people, places, and things, and will learn how various parts of his own body look, feel, and work.

The most human of these developmental attainments are possible because of biological maturation and because of the deep emotional attachments your baby forms with you during this crucial first year of

3

life. During these months, the foundations for all future development are laid down, not only for emotional stability but also for your child's personality and intellectual development. No other period of life will be so completely woven into the fabric of your child's future life and being. No other period of life will more tellingly contribute to the person your child will eventually become.

The Newborn Baby's World

The newborn enters the world with a rich endowment for growth and development. Though not yet a social being, your infant possesses important capabilities for dealing with the world. At birth, the baby will reflexively turn toward a stimulus (the rooting reflex). If you place something in his mouth, he will vigorously suck (the sucking reflex). Because the baby's existence depends on its ability to take in nourishment, these reflexes are crucial for survival.

The infant has additional reflexes, some more useful than others. He will quickly draw away from a painful stimulus and reflexively close his eyes in the presence of a bright light. If you place a finger in each of his palms, he will automatically contract his hands with enough strength to support his body's weight. This "grasp reflex" is sometimes called the "Daddy's reflex" since, some suggest, its main function in humans seems to be to make fathers think the baby recognizes them.

The newborn baby lives in a diffuse world, entirely different from the one we know. Your newborn has no ability to think or to sense himself as someone separate and apart from others. In fact, the infant seems unable to know one part of his body from another. Barely aware of a "self," perceiving vague sensations of relative comfort or discomfort, he lives in a timeless inner world, sleeping approximately twenty hours a day.

The infant's needs at this early stage of life are sleep, warmth, and milk, necessary for rapid growth and development to continue. The baby's entire life seems organized around the feeding experience, and he requires frequent feedings each day. The baby doesn't "know" he's hungry; he doesn't "feel" or experience hunger as adults perceive it. Rather, when his blood sugar lowers, the infant enters into a state of what might be called tension. He has no idea of what causes this; he has no language and can't really think, as we know thinking. And he has no notion of what must be done to alleviate his mounting discomfort. The infant simply uses the one power he has to signal his distress: he cries. This inborn capability is a very powerful tool, usually causing parents to rush to ease the baby's discomfort. While these inborn reflexes are the same in every infant, many differences between newborns can be distinguished even at the very beginning of life.

No Two Newborns Are Alike

Though all are endowed with the same needs and reflexes, newborn infants have inherently different levels of activity, varying sensitivities, different moods (and ways of expressing them), and different temperaments. One baby is easily aroused by noise; another sleeps peacefully. If both infants awaken, one might begin forcefully wailing while the other inquisitively scans the bassinet. Some newborns are active while others are placid. Some infants are naturally "cuddly" and easy to cradle in your arms; others are less responsive, even rigid. Some babies require a great deal of attention; others need less intense care. Newborn babies experience the world differently from one another, and they cause people to respond differently to them. This means that they usually require (and receive) different ways of parenting to satisfy their needs. The early interaction between parents and their newborn will deeply affect the baby's future development and personality.

You and Your Baby: A Nurturing Relationship

Throughout infancy, your child depends completely upon the nurturing care you provide. The very young infant requires food, warmth, bathing, diapering, and frequent care so that she may sleep for many hours each day. During these periods of sleep, your infant's body grows and matures at an incredible rate. The nurturing you provide your baby and the relationship between you and your infant is the dominant theme of this period of development. Yet this developmental period is far more involved than providing mere physical nurturing.

Some years ago, psychologists and psychiatrists studied infants who were reared in institutions. During their first two years, these babies received a different kind of nurturing than that provided to most babies. They were given very little individual attention. Provided with adequate feedings but raised by uninterested caretakers, these infants received little stimulation, no cuddling, and no warm or responsive caretaking. In other words, they were given none of the loving attention that we often call "nurturing."

These unfortunate infants failed to thrive or develop normally. By the age of three months, they showed extreme susceptibility to infections, illness, and even death. By two and a half years of age, very few of these children could speak. In other words, infants who, during the first year of life received only proper physical care but hardly any emotional nurturing, remained unresponsive, intellectually slow, and were late in attaining most of their developmental milestones.

Nurturing, then, means much more than providing your infant with proper physical sustenance. It includes a wide variety of behaviors that result from the warm, loving, and tender feelings you have toward your child. It includes behaviors, thoughts, and feelings not ordinarily considered "nurturing" but that provide your baby with vital emotional feeling.

You probably bring a great deal of nurturing and socializing behavior to your baby without realizing it. You cuddle your baby when nursing; you smile at her, talk and sing to her when changing her diapers. You may bury your face in her belly and gently nuzzle her when you powder her skin, and you kiss her feet and toes. You may hold her at arm's length and lovingly admire her, or you may gently swing her up and down in the air. You coo, rock, babble, croon, and kiss your child as you go about ordinary daily routines such as feeding, cleaning, changing diapers, or bathing her.

Many people think that a first-time mother has some "earthy" intuitive way of knowing how to care for her newborn. Though intuition helps, it isn't everything, and any new parent learns about parenting by being a parent. Though difficult and frightening at first, being a proficient mother or father is something that definitely can be learned.

In time, a parent develops a certain "feel" about establishing a nurturing relationship with a baby. As you care for him, you develop an understanding and feeling for your baby's needs and how to meet them. You learn to sense if your infant's cries are the result of hunger, fatigue, anger, loneliness, or colic. You also learn from his feedback whether or not you have successfully met your baby's needs.

For instance, your baby may have a spasm of colicky pain. Hearing his cries, you may go to the crib to alleviate the baby's distress. Let's say you misinterpret his cries, thinking that he's hungry, and you begin feeding him. He may try to nurse, but after a few swallows will spit out the nipple and resume crying, clearly telling you that you haven't singled out the right need. When the spasm passes and he's more comfortable, the crying will stop and your baby will respond to you with a smile or gurgle. Over time, you will develop consistent responses to your baby's changing needs, whether for feeding, diapering, sleep, relief from loneliness or from colicky pains. Your baby will in turn learn about and respond to your approaches, moods, signals, and behaviors.

Just as each newborn is a unique individual with an entire repertoire of needs and responses, so is each parent-infant interaction a unique and dynamic relationship. Rather than worrying about whether you are a "good" or "bad" mother or father, it's more helpful to consider the mutual harmony that develops between you and your child.

For instance, a mother may have a baby who is a vigorous sucker when nursing. If the mother tends to be active and prefers plenty of give-and-take, she will probably be very pleased with her baby and with this nursing interaction. She and the baby will have a mutual harmony. But if she has a more placid infant who sucks sluggishly and whose sleep cycle is irregular, she may not know exactly when her infant needs to nurse.

Such uncertainty about your child's feeding and sleep cycles could begin to make you doubt your parenting "abilities," even leading to thoughts that you aren't a "good" parent. This feeling could influence the entire tone of your relationship with your baby.

Rather than let this incorrect perception influence you, know that each mother-baby pair is a unique and dynamic one. Some disharmony will occasionally arise, but this doesn't mean you are a "bad" mother. Most new mothers and fathers develop an empathy for their baby's needs. They become more relaxed and comfortable with the routines of baby care as they get to know their baby. Your positive feelings are conveyed to the baby in the way you handle him. Your baby, in turn, "picks up" on your signals and cues, and responds to them. If you are warm and consistently available, your infant will learn that you will do your best to alleviate his tensions and discomforts.

It's a Two-Way Street

You and your baby each contribute to the tone and quality of your relationship. Good parenting doesn't spring gloriously from parents' breasts, and those familiar with newborns know that babies influence their parents, evoking various feelings in them. In fact, you influence one another.

Some parents find it difficult to respond warmly to a new baby. There may be financial pressures or worries. The baby may have arrived at a troubled time in a marriage. Your life setting, expectations, and the feelings you have about being a parent will all enter into the equation.

Carol B. became concerned about her feelings toward her eight-week-old daughter. The mother of a ten-year-old girl, Carol had long thought she would never have another child. Neither she nor her husband had planned on another baby. At thirty-six, involved with her career, Carol had mixed feelings about learning she was pregnant.

For the past few years, Carol and her husband had been having marital problems. Her husband thought another child would cement the marital bonds. Carol decided to have the baby, partly to please her husband, and also to alleviate strains in the marriage. But when the new baby arrived, Carol was surprised at her feelings.

"She's a beautiful baby. She's good, and easy to take care of. But I'm worried. I haven't warmed up to her yet. I don't talk to her, and I don't do any more than I *have* to do. Everything's rush, rush . . . the bottle, getting her off to sleep, like I want to get it over with. I'm not even tender with her, and I know she can tell how I feel. I sometimes wish she was ten years old, right now."

Upset at first by her "mixed" feelings, Carol felt much better a few weeks later when she grew more aware of the sources of her feelings and felt herself warming up to her new child.

Fortunately, most parents find that positive feelings are the rule. They quickly discover a reservoir of loving, tender feelings for their newborn child, and any doubts or reservations seem to fade quickly. Babies have as profound an effect on their parents as their parents have on them. Many a new parent has discovered how parental feelings can run very deep, completely changing one's perceptions. These words were spoken by the father of a three-month-old baby: "Everything's changed. It's not just me anymore, or even us as a couple. We've produced a child, and that changes everything. I'm different now. I'm a father."

About Mixed Feelings

We don't want to idealize the early months of your caretaking experience. Parents of firstborns are sometimes overwhelmed by the profound changes a newborn ushers into their lives. No amount of formal schooling could possibly prepare them for the many accomodations they must make to the physical and emotional needs of a newborn.

The first few months involve feeding around the clock, which may leave you feeling utterly exhausted. A baby's persistent crying may be worrisome and annoying. Bouts of colic may occur, and it may seem that nothing you do quickly soothes your child's discomfort or quells the crying. Bowel movements, mucus, and saliva seem to pour forth endlessly, and the most loving and competent parents can be clumsy and feel overwhelmed.

It's not unusual for the most loving parents to feel resentful at times. There's no need to hide feelings of disappointment or annoyance. The situation can be an emotionally and physically draining one, and resenting discomfort doesn't mean you don't love your baby. Knowing this may help you feel more able to express your occasional resentment of the situation, and your love of the baby.

Parenting at this time is a difficult job, not only because of the sleeplessness and intrusions, but because at first you receive very little feedback from your baby. Not truly recognizing you, barely aware of you, your baby provides you with no heart-warming accolades for a job well done.

When between six and eight weeks of age your baby shows evidence of a dramatic development (described next), the fatigue and troubles quickly fade. Everything suddenly seems worthwhile.

There is no one right way to love a baby. Infants are individuals, needing different kinds and amounts of affection. Parents, too, are individuals and have different ways of expressing their love. Equally important, no parent can totally love a baby at all times and in every circumstance.

Your Baby's Smile

At about six weeks of age (or a little later), a momentous event takes place, one that changes your entire relationship with your baby. At first, the baby demonstrated an innate reflex that involved a kind of "smiling." These first smiles are not in response to another person; they aren't social smiles, but are indications of contentment.

Then, suddenly, your baby begins to smile at you. This smile is not specific for you (although parents delightedly think it is) but is a general reaction to any human face. The baby's perceptions are not yet specific; he'll smile at anything vaguely resembling a face, even two circles painted on a triangular piece of paper. But you will most likely feel delighted at this first indication of your baby's pleasure at the sight of a human face.

Your baby's smile makes you suddenly realize you are living with a real human being, one who experiences pleasure and who actually responds to you. This can be especially meaningful to fathers, who, until this event, may have had little interaction with or feedback from the baby. (Today, fathers generally play a more active role in an infant's nurturing care.) Most parents go to great lengths to make their baby smile; they willingly twist their faces into a variety of grimaces, make abundant gestures, babble inane nonsense, and enter into physical play, providing increased stimulation for the baby. This further cements emotional bonding and attachment between parent and child.

By the age of three months, your baby will begin to smile at you in preference to other people, a crucial development because it indicates that the infant is responding selectively and specifically. Very important changes are taking place in your child's mental and emotional capacities; his responses, at first indiscriminate, are now reserved for especially important people, the parents. Your child is learning to discriminate himself from others and to differentiate various people from each other. The social smile also means that attachment is taking place.

Other Developments

At this time, major changes occur in every area of your child's life. Don't be alarmed if your child is not "on time" in one area. Keep in mind that individual infants vary greatly in their rates of social, emotional, intellectual, and physical development. If your child begins crawling six weeks later than another, this is most likely an insignificant and normal developmental variation.

The newborn drifts in and out of sleep around the clock; hunger seems to be the major thing that fully awakens the infant. Most babies will occasionally lie awake in the crib, apparently enjoying periods of "alert inactivity." But by the age of three months, a major shift occurs; your baby will spend much of the day awake and will sleep through most of the night. While this is generally true, many babies do not sleep through the night; if your infant awakens or has some sleep difficulty, be aware that this is a normal developmental variation and should not be a cause for alarm. Many infants awaken during the night because of hunger or discomfort, and may not regularly sleep through the night until well after the first year of life. Other babies have difficulty falling asleep when first put to bed. (A complete discussion of sleep difficulties is presented in the sections entitled "Bedtime Problems and Discipline," later in this chapter.)

Early morning behavior changes, too: Before this time, the baby usually howls for attention upon awakening. But by four months, he seems to tolerate (and even welcome) a period of solitude after awakening. He may lie peacefully crooning in his crib, scanning his surroundings or playing with his hands. Able to occupy himself, the baby now tolerates your absence far better than before. Keep in mind that some babies innately prefer more stimulation than others and may insist on more frequent interaction with the parents.

At about this time, there is an increase in cooing and babbling, and a genuine laugh occurs in response to your sounds and attentions. This development fosters even more parental delight, and parents do everything in their power to elicit gurgles of laughter from their baby. Again, there are many developmental variations in an infant's attaining any milestone. Babies have different temperaments and some may cry more easily or smile more reluctantly than others.

By three months, your baby's ability to use his body improves remarkably. He now reaches out for things. By four months, he may try to grasp objects, and you may notice that his hand and finger movements are more refined than before. Between five and six months, the baby will actually grasp and manipulate rings and rattles. This allows him to use these objects as toys, and he may occupy himself with these newfound treasures.

At about five months, the baby may sit up with his head supported by your hand. At six months, he may remain seated without support. Babies characteristically assume a Buddha-like posture at this age, but don't be alarmed if while sitting, your baby's torso droops forward until his nose touches the floor. His muscles of posture are still quite weak; independent sitting can be maintained for only a short while. At about six months, he can roll over from back to belly. (Until then, the baby's world has been mostly viewed from a horizontal position on his back). He can also return to the belly-down position by rolling over again.

At this time, the baby can be fed in a high chair. To your combined amusement and chagrin, he will try feeding himself in a clumsy way, creating a complete mess.

By now, he has most likely adapted to your dining schedule, and eats both milk and solids at each feeding. There are, of course, snacks, and for some babies, the bedtime bottle.

During the first six months of life, your child reaches a variety of ongoing developmental milestones—physical, mental, social, and emotional. Babies vary in the speed with which they achieve these important acquisitions.

Attachment

Although the newborn is not a social creature, over the course of the first year he becomes capable of many complicated social interchanges. The phenomenon of attachment is a crucial key to developing sound social relationships, emotional well-being, and intellectual capabilities. Attachment refers to the very powerful emotional bonds that develop between you and your child, and that, over time, your child will extend to other people.

As a parent, your attachment may begin with an upwelling of powerful feelings the moment you see your newborn. For the baby, attachment evolves gradually, growing slowly out of an infinite variety of close interchanges with you (or with other family members and parenting figures). It grows from an ongoing relationship with someone who is responsive, who satisfies the baby's needs, reduces tensions, and is nurturing and loving, or with a number of such people.

Attachment is vitally important for many reasons. It is the basis for your child's capacity eventually to feel affection for people outside the immediate family. It provides the foundation for the process of socialization and fosters a baby's willingness to be disciplined. It gives your baby a secure emotional base from which to turn his attention to the outside world. And your baby uses attachment to you as a base from which he can eventually strive toward independence.

Attachment to a parenting person may vary, because there are socially and psychologically different styles of nurturing. In our culture, one person, usually the biological mother, provides most of the early nurturing interaction with the infant. But other parenting styles also allow for successful development. Nurturing may be shared by many women (or men), such as on a kibbutz or in a large, extended family. In other situations, most of an infant's care is provided by someone other than the biological mother, such as the European nanny or nursemaid. Today, many young couples divide child care between mother and father. When both parents work, increasingly common today, an infant is usually cared for part of the time by a baby-sitter or caretaker, possibly with input by grandparents.

All these arrangements can work well. An infant need not receive care from only one caretaker, although a primary mothering figure prevails in most arrangements. The most important element is that responsive interaction consistently occur over a long period of time. (For a complete discussion of surrogate care, continuity of caretaking, the effects of multiple caretakers, working mothers, staying home with a newborn, and quality time, see in this chapter the brief section called "A Working Mother" and the larger "Consultation" section, and see Chapter 7, *When Mother Works.*)

Regardless of the way an infant is raised, he will develop a specific form of attachment to the person or persons most involved in the caretaking. The quality of those early relationships and the kind of attachment your infant develops will ultimately have a profound effect on the kinds of relationships your child develops later in life. Much more than physical nourishment or simple conditioning is involved in the baby's evolving attachment toward the parental or nurturing figures. Your responsive social involvement with your baby is the key contribution to her growing attachment. Through various games and social play, you and your child come to know one another and cement attachment.

Early in your child's first year, you may play various games with your baby. Most parents don't even have to think about this play. You soon find yourself starting rounds of This Little Piggy, counting games, Peekaboo, Hide-and-Seek, Show Me Your Nose (Eyes, Ears, etc.), and a variety of games that involve laughing, bouncing, rocking, swinging, and cuddling your baby. Games with warm give-and-take are fun for you and your baby, and help the baby learn about her body (Show Me Your Nose . . .) as well as helping her learn how the world works. (For a complete discussion about making physical contact with baby, the best times to play with baby, intense stimulation, play periods, and extra emotional and intellectual input for your newborn, see "A Consultation" in this chapter.)

Stranger Anxiety

We know that your baby is becoming increasingly attached to you when we see another dramatic development in the way he relates to people. Between six and nine months of age, your baby will very likely begin showing discomfort at the approach of unfamiliar people. This is called stranger anxiety. At the approach of an unfamiliar person, the baby may scream, clutch at you, and begin crying. Even acquaintances and relatives whom the baby accepted during the early months may elicit this reaction. Grandparents, aunts, uncles, and friends cannot understand why this happens, and you may worry, however irrationally, that they will somehow be offended at your child's wariness of them.

Because of repeated exposure, your baby has built up a stable mental image of familiar people. He compares them to strangers, who don't match his framework. This reaction to strangers is a sign of your child's increasing ability to distinguish himself from you, and you from other people—an important intellectual achievement. Above all, it indicates your baby's anxiety about the possibility of parental absence, which is what stranger anxiety seems to be all about. This is actually evidence of increasingly strong attachment to you.

The Beginnings of Separation Anxiety

Sometime during the second six months of life, we begin to see another important sign of attachment: separation anxiety. This is a form of distress your child feels when she is shut off from you for any length of time. A hallmark of this era in life, separation anxiety will remain a powerful issue for the first two years of life.

You can see separation anxiety at work as you watch your baby's increasing abilities to move around the house. Somewhere between six and eight months of age, she will begin crawling. At first, she will stay close to you. Then she moves a short distance away, quickly returning to make physical contact by grabbing your ankles. Soon, she moves about the room and the house, returning at frequent intervals to make contact or to gaze at you for reassurance. The urge to move away and explore an ever-expanding world is competing with the wish to remain in close contact with you.

Eventually, the child becomes more adventurous, staying away for longer periods of time. She may not need direct visual contact, but rather may be content to hear your voice from the next room. The theme of this period—from about ten months to two years—involves your baby's progressive separation from you and her burgeoning sense of independence.

Your child may struggle with separation anxiety in a variety of ways. He may play certain games that make things go away and then come back. Peekaboo helps children with separation anxiety. He makes you disappear—momentarily, of course. And then, with a flick of his hands, you come back! This causes giggles of delight. In a psychological sense, by playing this universal game, your child controls your comings and goings. He takes charge of your very existence.

The same theme occurs with Hide-and-Seek, which children begin to play at this time. Your child may crawl behind a door while you carry out a diligent search, calling the baby's name and pretending you have no idea of his whereabouts. As you approach, the baby betrays his hiding place by giggling, and when you suddenly "discover" him, a great deal of hugging occurs, accompanied by the child's gurgles of delight.

Be aware that suspenseful games such as Hide-and-Seek should not go on for too long. Your baby delights in suspenseful evasion but for only a brief time, since prolonged suspense about your disappearing can actively evoke the child's separation anxiety. Suspense can soon escalate to terror.

Drop-and-Pick-It-Up is another favorite game at this time. While in her high chair, the child drops a cup or spoon to the floor, listening for the sound of impact. Peering down, she searches for the "lost" object. When you retrieve the spoon and return it, she giggles and throws it down again. You hand it back, only to have this scenario repeated, as the baby discovers that getting you to pick up the spoon is great sport. The same game may be played by dropping a favorite doll or toy from the crib to the floor. Since it may be the one toy your baby needs to go to sleep, you retrieve it, only to have it flung to the floor once again.

While wearisome for you, this game accomplishes some very important tasks for your child. By repeating a new experience until it is mastered, she is learning about space and distance, an important intellectual achievement. This game allows your child to "control" you in a way that bolsters her confidence and builds mutuality. And the child is trying to master separation anxiety; by tossing the toy or spoon overboard, she is trying (with your cooperation) to bring back something that has been "lost." At heart is the idea of keeping the parent (mother or father) with her at all times. Since this is impossible, the game is an important way for the child to play out symbolically losing you and then having you return.

We will discuss practical problems concerning how to deal with separation and your child's anxiety about it in the sections entitled "Practical Issues" and "A Consultation," later in this chapter.

A Linus Blanket

The struggle with separation anxiety extends over a long period of time. Slowly, your child begins to move away (emotionally and physically), but anxiety accompanies these steps toward independence. With walking, your child develops new capabilities and a new impetus for exploring the world as a separate person, away from you and other people.

Children have various ways of dealing with the inevitable anxiety that accompanies separation. Toward the end of the first year, your child may become intensely attached to a favorite toy, blanket, or other object that accompanies her everywhere. Linus, of the comic strip "Peanuts," toddling around with his ever-present blanket, is probably the best-known image of this nearly universal phenomenon. Your child may cling to a teddy bear, a favorite doll, or some other highly treasured toy or object.

This beloved toy is called a transitional object. The blanket or doll has certain qualities that remind your child of you. It's warm, soft, cuddly, or may have taken on a specific feel and odor. Trying to wash or replace the blanket with another only upsets your baby, who wants it to remain exactly as it is. Providing the child with a form of emotional security, it helps her make the transition from deep attachment and dependence on you to more independent functioning.

The need for a link to you will remain for years and may intensify at any time of separation. The one repeated instance of separation for your baby is going to sleep each night. Being in a darkened room, lying alone, and falling asleep mean losing touch with you, and many children need (and should have) a transitional link to mother (or a mothering figure) at bedtime. This may be the very same bottle, blanket, or stuffed animal your child hauls around during the day.

The transition may be made in a more direct and less symbolic way: actually having you present at bedtime, which can help the baby slowly overcome separation anxiety. The child may insist on your staying in the room while she falls asleep. She may prefer that you sing to her or that you gently pat her back or buttocks as she drifts off to sleep. An older child dealing with such separation anxiety may ask for a glass of milk or request a bedtime story. These requests reflect your child's anxiety about losing touch with you by going to sleep. This is normal, and it can be very helpful to provide your child with this additional contact (patting the buttocks, staying with the baby, singing, or simply remaining in the child's room until she falls asleep). All these activities will help your baby overcome separation anxiety. (A complete, practical discussion of bedtime behaviors and problems and how to deal with them is presented in the section called "Bedtime Problems," in this chapter. Also see "A Consultation" for a practical discussion of baby-sitters, sleeping arrangements, bedtime rituals, separation issues, prolonged crying when parents leave, and how to deal with these problems.)

Your Child's Evolving Mind

The newborn has innate reflexes to help it survive outside the womb. At the beginning of life, his world is a primitive one, governed by simple reflexes such as sucking and grasping. Through experience over the first year of life, a series of actions and reactions come to be mentally "mapped" by the baby. He becomes capable of primitive thinking. His ability to gather new information and assimilate it into a body of knowledge gradually becomes more sophisticated. However, your child's inner world during the early years of development is a very different place than the one grownups take for granted.

From the age of one month to four months, the infant coordinates and refines early reflex behaviors, such as sucking, grasping, listening, and looking. For example, he learns to coordinate sucking and grasping, and brings these two behaviors together, so that when nursing, he may hold onto the bottle or breast as he sucks.

From about four to eight months of age, the baby delights in repeating activities that he has accidentally set into motion. For example, if given a rattle, he will at first be startled by the noise made when he shakes it. Soon he will repeat the shaking for the simple pleasure of repeating the sound. The baby slowly learns that he is no longer governed only by reflexes and coordinating or refining them. In a sense, the baby begins to actively explore his world and tries to make things happen.

From about eight months of age until the end of the first year, the child's activities become increasingly purposeful. He learns about various objects (rattles, toys, pillows, the crib) and learns about space and spatial relationships (the room, the next room, and sounds coming from one room to another). He becomes more aware of the world around him and how it works. For instance, he comes to realize that two toys cannot occupy the same place at the same time. He learns that a square peg will not fit into a round hole, or realizes that when he lets a spoon fall from a high chair, it drops down, onto the floor. The child must learn these basic workings of the world by repeating long processes of trial and error.

A major intellectual development begins at about eight months. Until this time, the child seems unaware that something continues to exist after it has passed from view. For instance, if you place a bottle in front of a six-month-old baby, he will reach for it. But if you cover the bottle with a cloth so he cannot see it, his expression goes blank and his gaze then drifts away. He makes no attempt to retrieve the bottle, not realizing it's beneath the cloth. The bottle no longer exists for him.

But at eight months, he begins to learn that an object (the bottle) exists, even if it is no longer visible. At some point, he will remove the cloth and discover the bottle. But when you move the bottle from beneath the cloth (with the baby watching) and place it beneath a cushion, he will return again and again to the cloth, still attempting to find the bottle. It will take some time before he realizes that he must now look beneath the cushion to find the bottle.

This slowly developing capacity to retain a mental image is very important. By the time he is two years old, the baby will develop what is called object permanence, the capacity to know that something (or someone) still exists, even though gone from sight. In other words, the baby develops the ability to maintain a stable inner mental representation of a bottle (or person), no matter where it's located.

The capacity for object permanence is important in understanding the young child's separation anxiety. Before the age of two, she may grow anxious when you are gone, not only because of attachment, but because she is uncertain that you *still exist*. For the young child, a parent's going out for an evening may conjure up doubts that the adult will return.

Emotionally meaningful people such as parents usually become "fixed" in the baby's mind earlier than other, less meaningful people. But still, until your child's sense of object permanence is solidly fixed, her limited knowledge of the world may cause her to fear forever losing you simply because you've gone out for a few hours.

Basic Trust

A crucial issue during infancy is the baby's ability to slowly develop a sense of basic trust. If as parents you've provided reliable, consistent, and loving nurturing, if you've been sensitively responsive to your infant's needs, your baby will in time develop basic trust. He will feel that when he needs something (such as food, attention, or just cuddling), you will reliably provide it. He will feel that you are available and responsive to him. These feelings will slowly develop over the course of the first year. First centering on you, they will later be generalized for your child, becoming his view of the world at large. A trusting baby feels good about himself and comes to see the world as a satisfying, manageable, and fairly predictable place.

An infant who does not receive adequate nurturing, on the other hand, may never develop feelings of basic trust. He feels a profound mistrust about whether his basic needs are going to be met. Such a baby feels helpless and sees the world as a source of uncertainty and misery.

One word of caution: meeting your child's early needs doesn't mean always giving him whatever he wants. A reasonable delay in feeding (such as the few minutes required to warm or prepare a bottle) or in cuddling your baby after he wakes up from a nap isn't going to "damage" the baby. In fact, by the age of four months your baby can probably wait (while very eager) for a feeding. Actually, a balance between frustration and gratification is necessary for sound emotional development. Some delays help your baby learn to put off and anticipate gratification, a vital emotional attainment since ordinary life is filled with frustration and delay.

Most parents intuitively reach a balance between gratifying and frustrating a child's wishes. They get a sense of how long their infant can wait before being held or fed; they learn how long a delay their child can tolerate. (A complete, practical discussion about feeding is presented in the sections entitled "Feeding: A Balance Between Depriving and Giving," "Breast or Bottle?," "Weaning," and "A Good Nursing Experience," later in this chapter.)

Some parents, unable to tolerate a child's frustration, rush to satisfy his needs even before he makes them known. This may be the parent who, as soon as the infant makes a sound, slips the nipple into his mouth, even though he lies peacefully in the crib and hasn't communicated a wish to be fed. Overanticipating the baby's needs, this parent limits the baby's ability to develop the capacity to delay gratification. The result may be an overindulged child who can never wait to satisfy any need.

Only when gratification is consistently delayed for very long periods of time will the baby develop doubts about the world. But remember that a baby has very little perspective, and if very long delays are the rule, a seed of mistrust may be planted.

As important as meeting the baby's needs is the *way* in which they are met. If a parent is impatient or hostile, if the baby is handled in an anxious, perfunctory, or abrupt way (recall Carol B.), the infant will eventually sense these feelings. Then feelings of doubt and mistrust will color the child's perceptions.

Your baby needs handling and attention that express love and responsiveness. Given such basic emotional nurturing, he can tolerate reasonable delay, especially at first, when you are learning the skills of parenting. Many first-time parents wonder "how much" attention a young infant requires; they grow concerned about how long to hold or play with their baby each day. There is no firm rule about this, however; as long as your infant is alert and responsive to your attentions, sensitive handling and interaction (such as cuddling, cooing, holding, patting, rocking, talking) can be given. This can occur during the day or evenings, and may occupy many hours each day. (See later in this chapter, "A Good Nursing Experience," "Physical Contact with Baby," "The Best Times to Be with Baby," "Intense Stimulation" (playing), "Intense Play Periods," and "Extra Input for Baby.")

Trust and attachment overlap. Attachment is the foundation upon which trust is built. Basic trust then is generalized into the broader outlook of optimism and a sense that people can reasonably be trusted later in life. The child who learns basic trust feels that the world is essentially good and right.

The Beginnings of Language

Although infancy is the time in life when a baby cannot talk, you and your infant do many things together that help your child develop language.

Most parents routinely talk or sing to their babies as they go about the day's chores, contributing to the baby's eventual talking and conveying to him that the voice is a primary means of communication. Over the course of the first two months, the infant's cooing and crowing give way to a variety of sounds that become a babbling. At about six months, she may make sounds that begin to sound like ma-ma. Many parents are convinced that the baby is now calling them by name. It may be some months, however, before she truly calls your name.

In virtually every culture, children make early babbling sounds that signify mother or father. It may be ma-ma, da-da, ba-ba, or la-la. Parents throughout the world respond with delight to these first indications that the baby is "calling" them by name. It seems that people of every language have chosen certain sounds to signify mother and father; they are universally two syllable, repetitive sounds that babies can easily vocalize (such as ma-ma and da-da). These sounds are eagerly reinforced by the parents, who are joy-struck at their baby's apparent recognition of them. By late infancy (around nine months), the babbling begins to take on the intonations and rhythms of the baby's native tongue, and by the child's first birthday, his babbling has become an indecipherable version of his parents' language.

Games of imitation feed importantly into your baby's language development. Most parents playfully imitate the sounds their babies make, and later on, babies end up imitating sounds (and eventually language) that their parents make.

A game that promotes your child's learning of language involves asking for the names of things. Your baby points at something with a questioning sound or gesture. You nod and supply the name. The child then gives an indication (usually a grunt or smile) of acknowledgment. A variation of this involves the baby's correctly responding to your request to show you his features. Show Me Your Ears (Eyes, Mouth, etc.) becomes a game in which the baby explores his body while enhancing his familiarity with language. These games should be encouraged because they provide abundant social interchange between you and your baby, in addition to helping him acquire language. The game also indicates your baby's awareness that things actually have names, a vital discovery for categorizing the world, and an important element of intellectual development.

When more advanced, but still unable to actually talk, your child may communicate by means of concrete behavior. She may hand you her coat or sweater when she wants to go outside, or point to the stroller. She may point to a book, indicating a wish for you to read to her. (Reading to a child is a wonderful way of interacting and socializing, and of promoting language development.) Although the baby cannot yet speak, language learning has definitely taken place. Your positive reactions to these developments (smiling, encouraging words and gestures) will promote even more communicative behavior and language use by your baby. The child has developed receptive language: the ability to understand a great deal of what she hears. Your baby will respond appropriately to key words or phrases that signal important routines: "It's bedtime"; "It's time for a bath"; "Do you want the bottle (cookie, doll, boat, whatever)?" and other emotionally loaded phrases ("loaded" because they refer to objects or situations that the baby craves or eagerly anticipates).

Generally, the child won't use productive language (actual talking) until sometime beyond the end of the first year. The time at which a child begins using words, phrases, and sentences varies greatly from one child to another. Many parents worry unnecessarily that their child is not yet speaking by the age of thirteen or fourteen months. Then suddenly, words and phrases begin pouring forth in a torrent. Keep in mind that many children do not talk well until they are two and even three years old. (For a more complete discussion of language development, see "Emphasis on the Intellect," later in this chapter. Also see in Chapter 2, "Your Toddler's Speech," "Influence of Speech Problems," "Hardly Speaks," and "Reading to a Child.")

Awareness of the Self

At the very center of your infant's developing self-awareness is basic trust. This means the child feels good about people in relation to his self and feels good about the self in relation to others. The sense of a separate self requires that the baby gradually detach himself from the diffuse identity of early infancy in which he could barely distinguish himself from his caretaker. In other words, he must slowly separate from you to develop a sense of himself as an independent person.

Of course, during the first year of life, a child's capacity to have an awareness of "me" as a person is quite limited. A young child cannot truly understand that the same situation can appear and feel very differently to different people with varying outlooks. But by the end of the first year, he has already made enormous strides toward having a sense of himself as an individual in a world of other people.

The newborn infant barely seems aware of his own body. A month-old child may gaze at his own hand as though a foreign object is floating into view. Slowly, over the course of the next few months, the baby discovers his body, part by part and region by region. By four months, the baby's developing body image and memory enable him to wait for a feeding. It's an active kind of waiting, with the baby eagerly anticipating the breast or bottle. He may even begin sucking on a finger in an effort to momentarily relieve his inner tension. This behavior demonstrates that your baby has a conscious awareness and a mental image of you and the forthcoming bottle. This means he has begun accurately to define the barriers between "me" and "not me." He knows and anticipates that someone "outside" himself will eventually gratify his needs. This capacity to delay indicates memory, and the beginnings of an awareness of himself as a separate self.

As the first year draws to a close, the baby has discovered most of his body, part by part. At about one year, he discovers his genitals. This may happen earlier in a boy than a girl, probably because his penis is more easily visible than a girl's vulva. The boy often discovers his penis while taking a bath. The girl must discover her genitals as part of the slow exploration of her body. In either event, most infants will fondle their genitals by about one year of age. This usually happens at bedtime but may occur during the day as well. You need not worry about this behavior; it's an expected and normal part of self-exploration. We shall discuss this further in the section " 'Bad' Habits," later in this chapter.

While discovering his body, the child is also developing a vital sense of himself as a *person*. He learns by your actions and reactions to him to sense himself as worthwhile, loved, and lovable, or as unlovable and not worthwhile. The child who has a sense of being truly loved easily gives and receives affection, feels reasonably self-assured, and actively explores the world around him. Loving, attentive, and consistent nurturing will help your child develop a sense of himself as a valuable person. This is very much bound to and part of his developing basic trust.

Those First Steps

As your child grows and develops, she expands her repertoire of physical activities. Foremost among them is her increasing ability to move from one place to another, which has enormous implications for further emotional development.

Somewhere around eight months (but anytime between six and twelve months) the baby will pull herself to her feet. She may not quite know how to get back down, and her newfound posture may frighten her into howling with alarm until you pick her up. Very soon, though, she will learn to simply let go and plop onto her seat, a short drop that causes no harm.

About a month later (between seven and twelve months) she may walk with some adult help, cruising in side-stepping fashion while clutching for support at coffee tables, chairs, a sofa, or any reachable object. By about eleven months (ranging from nine to about sixteen months), she may stand alone.

And then one day it happens. Already standing, she may raise her hands for balance, stay rigidly in place, gaze at you, and then toddle a few steps forward into your waiting arms. This momentous event occurs at about one year (with a range of about nine to seventeen months). As we will see in the next chapter, your child's ability to walk ushers in a new developmental era and radically changes certain aspects of her relationship with you: because she can easily move away from you, walking helps solidify and expand the child's growing sense of a separate identity.

◊ PRACTICAL ISSUES DURING THE FIRST YEAR

In this section, we will explore a variety of practical concerns for the first year of life. Each issue is not only important when it arises but has profound implications for your child's future emotional growth and development.

Feeding: A Balance Between Depriving and Giving

The first responsibility of new parents is the feeding of a newborn baby. Many first-time parents become concerned about nursing, whether by breast or bottle. They often worry about when to feed, and how to respond to a hungry baby's cries.

First, it's important to realize that your baby may cry for reasons other than hunger. He may cry because he has colic, because of heat, because of discomfort caused by soiled diapers, and for other reasons. In time, you will learn your baby's signals and cues and be better able to correctly identify his tension states. Yet there's no doubt that the most frequent cause of crying in very young infants is tension caused by hunger.

Most pediatricians and psychiatrists agree that demand feeding is probably best for the very young infant. Because your baby cannot possibly "understand" scheduling and can't be expected to regulate his needs according to a schedule, it makes sense to feed the baby when he indicates that he's hungry. This may mean that at first you will be very busy with frequent, even around-the-clock, feedings, which can be trying. By four months (often younger), most babies can wait four to five hours between feedings and can sleep through the entire night. By about six months, your baby will probably adapt to your eating schedule.

However, this may not always be the case. Many infants take longer to adapt to a feeding schedule and require feedings more frequently than every four to five hours. There may be physiologic reasons for this, as some infants with smaller stomachs cannot take in large amounts of food at one time and may therefore require smaller but more frequent feedings.

Temperamental differences may also account for an infant's not being scheduled by six months of age. It is perfectly normal for a baby to require frequent feedings (even during the night) up to the age of one year. This simply reflects an individual baby's preference and temperament, and the baby will eventually adapt to your eating schedule. As with so many issues in a child's development, individual variations between babies are very common.

Your baby's feeding experiences are part of his earliest experiences in learning about the world. While the newborn has a biological tension state that we call hunger, this is not the same as the hunger adults know. Rather, it is a vague, diffuse state of discomfort that causes the infant to make his needs known by crying.

When your newborn cries hungrily, he doesn't quiet down when you first enter the room. He has no way of knowing that the preparatory steps (such as your entering the room) are a prelude to his tension being relieved. He continues crying as you prepare the bottle or breast, and even when you pick him up to begin nursing. He may cry so frantically that at first he doesn't realize the nipple is in his mouth, and he may not suck.

But some weeks later, when you enter the room, the baby's crying begins to subside. When you pick him up, he may stop crying completely. A few weeks later, your simply entering the room may be enough to quiet him completely. The baby has learned to anticipate an entire repertoire of experiences (the rattling of a pan, the sounds you make, your voice, your entering the room, his being picked up) as part of a process that will eventually relieve his discomfort. His earlier feeding experiences have allowed him to slowly build up a mental image of the feeding experience and of the relief it brings.

The fact that your infant must *wait* between his first pangs of hunger and actually getting the bottle or breast is very important. This delay helps him develop a mental representation of the experience, which is really a representation of the outer world. The baby's anticipation of the bottle or breast allows him to develop a sense that relief will soon be provided. Through his earliest feeding experiences, he learns that, while not immediate, relief from discomfort will consistently be provided, that the world is good and right, but not perfect.

Some mothers have difficulty allowing an infant to wait. They cannot bear the sound of their baby's cries. They anticipate all his needs, trying to satisfy the baby even before he makes them known. They may end up gratifying the wrong need: baby may have colic and not want to nurse. Worse, such a mother inhibits her child from developing the capacity to wait. A child treated this way never gains the ability to control his tension. He may grow up into an adult who is impulsive, impatient, immature, and who cannot tolerate frustration or delay.

On the other hand, some mothers rarely meet an infant's earliest needs, forcing the baby to wait an intolerably long time before hunger and other needs are satisfied. The infant isn't fed or held until he's frantic, or until his hunger cries are stifled by exhaustion. This infant may develop into a sad and pessimistic adult who expects little of life.

For a balance between gratification and frustration, you don't have to set up frustrations. They will take place naturally and inevitably in countless ways. During the course of any ordinary day, your baby must wait until you finish another chore and approach the crib. He will have to accomodate to the reality that there will be an interval of time between his first hunger pangs and your picking him up to feed him. You cannot be instantly ready to nurse your baby.

Good caretaking doesn't mean ever-present attention with no frustration for your child. It need not mean instant indulgence of every need. Keep in mind that consistent, responsive nurturing, which includes some frustration, will help your child develop vital abilities he will need for dealing with the world. It will also help him develop confidence that when he *truly* needs something, you will be there for him.

Breast or Bottle?

The first decision you must make as a new mother is whether to breast-feed or bottle-feed your baby. The choice is a matter of personal preference.

The nutritive value of human milk is unsurpassed. Less likely to produce allergic reactions than cow's milk, your own milk contains antibodies that help protect your baby against infections. And you needn't worry about hygienic factors. Many mothers find that breast-feeding provides them with an "earthy" and intimate connection to the baby, one they feel they can't duplicate with a bottle. Some mothers find the infant's sucking to be an intense, even sensuous experience that promotes attachment and cements bonding.

On the other hand, a bottle can be given to your baby with the same physical closeness as the breast; this includes holding, as well as visual and vocal stimulation of your baby. And a bottle can be given by the baby's father or by an older sibling, so the nursing experience can be shared by family members. Bottle feeding allows you to avoid possible problems with irritated or sore nipples and may be more convenient than breast-feeding.

The choice depends on a variety of physical and psychological reactions. Some women incorrectly feel that bottle-feeding implies that they aren't "good" mothers. They feel obligated or duty-bound to breast feed. This can create unnecessary tensions for you and your baby. Some mothers, frightened by the intensity and sensuous quality of the breast-feeding experience, may wisely choose the bottle instead. Other mothers may be repelled by what they consider the "animal" quality of breast-feeding and feel more comfortable with bottle feeding.

Physical and emotional factors can complicate your decision. You may produce insufficient quantities of milk and may have to supplement nursing with a bottle or even abandon breast-feeding. Ideally, this can be accomplished without making you feel "inadequate." If your infant sucks sluggishly, you may find yourself feeling, however irrationally, rejected by the baby. It may be best to discontinue breast-feeding if it creates more tension than pleasure.

In short, there is no one right way to nurse your baby. If you feel satisfied by breast-feeding, then it's perfectly fine. If the experience is difficult or makes you uncomfortable, then don't do it. The decision is yours and should be based on what works best for you and your baby.

Weaning

Weaning involves the transition from nipple (either breast or bottle) to drinking from a cup. It also means making the change from a purely liquid diet (of mostly milk) to solid foods (really, strained and mushy foods). In the past, weaning was considered a major frustration and source of emotional trauma for the child. It may be that weaning was once thought to be traumatic because until recently it was done at an older age, and before "solid" foods had been gradually introduced to the baby at an early time.

Weaning is the first of many steps your baby will take throughout infancy and childhood, steps in which he must slowly separate from you and begin to function more independently. Nursing is one of the earliest shared experiences between mother and child, and perhaps the most intimate of nurturing activities. Because weaning means "letting go," some mothers, as well as infants, may be reluctant to make the transition from breast or bottle to other foods.

Because weaning means giving up the nipple and sucking, it may cause your baby to increase the frequency of thumb-sucking. This is to be expected and shouldn't cause alarm.

Trying to make the baby's transition easier, some mothers provide the baby with a nighttime bottle. They then find that he insists not only on having the bottle at bedtime, but also "needs" it to fall asleep. A bottle supplied in this way becomes symbolic of mother and of the earlier nursing relationship. The bottle becomes a transitional object your baby needs to quell his separation anxiety about going to sleep. Knowing this should make you less concerned if your baby insists on keeping his bottle as a bedtime comfort device well beyond the first year. A nighttime bottle causes no harm and may help a baby fall asleep.

Although most baby-care books include practical advice about weaning, we will provide general guidelines based on sound psychological principles:

- Weaning should be a slow transition, not an abrupt experience for your baby.
- Make certain not to combine weaning with any anticipated separation. The overlapping separation and deprivation of the nipple (which has elements of separation) may prove to be overwhelming for your baby.
- Begin giving your baby tastes of solid food early (at two to three months) so that the experience of new food isn't an abrupt one for the child. Most babies can drink from a cup (with help, of course) at about six months.
- If you breast feed, you may find it helpful to provide your infant with one bottle-feeding each day so that the transition from breast to bottle isn't a difficult one.
- When first trying solid foods, don't give them at the beginning of the meal, when your baby is hungriest. Let the baby satisfy his initial hunger; he may then be much more interested in a new taste and consistency.
- At times of stress or anxiety, your infant may revert back to the nipple; this provides emotional comfort. Don't be surprised if this happens, and be willing to give in to it. When your child feels better, he will resume his new regimen.

• Be gentle and consistent. Remember that weaning is part of your baby's early nurturing experience. It doesn't have to be abrupt or traumatic.

One word about prolonged breast-feeding. Some mothers, reluctant to give up breast-feeding, cite certain primitive societies that allow breast-feeding until a child is two or three years old. These mothers, convinced that such a "natural" method is best, may prolong breast-feeding well beyond their child's second year. Such a mother may be motivated to excessively prolong breast-feeding for many reasons: She may have a great deal of difficulty separating from her baby, fearing that the child's weaning is akin to "losing" the baby. Or she may derive a great deal of pleasure in feeling so "needed" by her baby. While there is no great harm in this, it seems unnecessary. Such prolonged nursing occurs in very few societies, and may be little more than a means of natural contraception.

Bedtime Problems

During early infancy, eating and sleeping are intertwined, as the baby spends long periods of time sleeping and wakes for nursing. At about three months, the baby may sleep through the night, providing welcome relief for parents who have tended to her around the clock. While some babies begin sleeping through the night at this time, others do not. Many infants awaken during the night. This may be due to physical causes such as hunger, gas, or colic, or because of discomfort caused by urine or stool in the infant's diaper. Some babies awaken because of individual differences that determine their sleep cycles and rhythms.

Whatever the reason for an infant's awakening, he may cry and require some kind of middle-of-the-night attention such as change of diaper or cuddling. More than likely, he will require a feeding in order to return to sleep. It's helpful to have a division of labor in this area: father can tend to nighttime attention to relieve a mother who stays at home during the day. If both parents work (see Chapter 7, *When Mother Works*), a divided schedule of nighttime feeding can be devised so that mother and father share equally in these responsibilities. This can be done even if a baby is being breast-fed, as there are breast pumps available for the extraction of milk that can then be saved for a nighttime feeding. Parents who work together with each other and with their baby will eventually find a pattern that works for the entire family.

The baby's developing a distinct sleep pattern may usher in a difficulty between you and your child: her resistance to going to sleep. Before this, there may have been some brief fussing at bedtime, but the baby drifted off to sleep. She now seems aware that bedtime means the end of socializing, play, and attention. This may lead to a powerful protest in the form of screaming.

This event indicates your infant's growing awareness of herself as separate from you, and is evidence of bedtime separation anxiety. You will see other forms of separation anxiety throughout the next two years.

The baby's bedtime screaming isn't indiscriminate or prolonged crying. Instead, she yells for a few seconds and then stops, as though listening for your reaction. If you start toward the crib, she quiets down. If, hopeful she's falling asleep, you start for the door, a series of howls arises, calling you back to the crib. This may be the baby's first purposeful use of her voice for communication.

Parents often try several methods to ease this problem, with varying results:

One is to leave a soft night-light burning in the baby's room. This eases her transition to darkness and sleep, lessening separation anxiety. Another tactic is to give the baby her favorite toy or stuffed animal, or a bedtime bottle (all are transitional objects) to ease her off to sleep. However, this may transform the bottle into a required part of the bedtime routine for a long time to come.

Some parents let the baby fall asleep amid adult company, and move her to the crib once she's asleep. A problem with this method is that the baby may become used to falling asleep in the middle of everything and be unable to drift off when the house is quiet. Or she may wake up while you are moving her to the crib, starting a new series of howling protests.

Another approach involves staying with your baby after she has been put to bed. You may pat her back, singing softly until sleep comes. Of course, this may take a long time and can evolve into a wearisome, fixed ritual lasting well beyond the second or third year, ultimately creating more problems than it solves.

There may come a time when, having exhausted all rituals, you will simply have to leave your baby alone and, if necessary, let her cry herself to sleep. This may require some fortitude on your part, since it's difficult for a parent to bear such tempestuous crying. But at some point, you must draw a line between playtime and sleep. In a few evenings, your baby will get the message that crying is of little use, although each moment of her howling may seem like an agonizing eternity to you. Be reassured that such crying will pass, will not physically harm your child, and will leave no psychological scars. Much to your relief, once the baby comes to terms with the fact that she must go to sleep, she will eventually do so. She will also greet you in the morning without a shred of resentment.

Bedtime problems may be your baby's first encounter with discipline. She must learn that she cannot always get what she wants, and that there are times when you simply can't be with her. This is one step in helping your child overcome separation anxiety.

When she is sick and discomfited, you will, of course, go to the baby during the night. Once the illness passes, she will have to relearn the lesson that bedtime means going to sleep, not playing and more attention.

Baby-Sitters

Many new parents are reluctant to leave a young child, even in the hands of a skilled and experienced baby-sitter. Most parents recognize intuitively that their baby has an immature sense of himself as a separate person, and feels threatened by separation anxiety when he's out of contact (or at the threat of loss of contact) with a loving and familiar parent. Because of this reaction, many parents curtail various social activities during the first year of their child's life. Others take the baby to restaurants and various adult settings, providing it's workable for them and (one hopes) for other adults as well. But, as with the bedtime experience, a point arrives when your baby must tolerate a separation and learn that you will return.

The very young baby's ability to retain stable mental images is fairly shaky. He may not recognize you because you are dressed up for an evening out. He may fail to recognize you if you wear makeup. A sudden change in your appearance may provoke stranger anxiety. His anxiety may worsen when he realizes that being dressed up is a prelude to your leaving. All this may provoke an outburst of frantic crying. Such a reaction may occur with each leavetaking and can continue well beyond the first year for some children.

Because of this reaction, it's a good idea to have a steady baby-sitter whom your baby knows and likes. This person, a parental surrogate, becomes partly a transitional "object," a link to you. With repeated exposure, your baby will become less inconsolable at the threatened separation when you are leaving for an evening. If an unfamiliar sitter must be used, have that person arrive at least an hour before your departure. This affords time for the new sitter, in your presence, to get acquainted and establish a relationship with the baby. Diminishing stranger anxiety, it also allows the new sitter to take on certain "transitional object" qualities in your child's mind. This makes your leaving as distress-free as possible.

There is the occasional child who seems unable to "accept" a baby-sitter. This is the child who, no matter how familiar the sitter, becomes frantic and throws a tantrum the moment the sitter appears at the door. Basically, the same principle applies as when putting your baby to bed: at some point, parents must bid farewell and, despite the baby's howls of protest, take leave of the child. While this is difficult for many parents to do, it must eventually be done. Some parents try vainly to avoid such separations by not going out, or by attempting to take the baby with them everywhere they go. This is a mistake because it allows the child to effectively manipulate parental activities, and it only postpones the inevitable. Eventually, you must take occasional leave of your baby. (See "Nervous About Leaving Baby with a Sitter" and "Baby Cries When Parents Leave," later in this chapter. Also see in Chapter 2, "Baby Goes Everywhere.")

If you must be away from home for an extended period of time—such as a stay in the hospital—the same principle applies. Unless the parent at home is free to take over completely, he or she must arrange for a full-time baby-sitter who will act as a surrogate parent. When you return, don't be surprised if your baby greets you as though you're a stranger, remaining coolly aloof for a few hours or even days. (On the topic of hospitalizing a baby, see Chapter 19, *When a Child Goes to the Hospital*.)

In a step-by-step way, your child must eventually learn to separate from you. Even if separations such as hospitalization can be avoided, there will be situations during your child's first year (bedtime and baby-sitter experiences) where meaningful separations must take place. They provide your baby with early lessons in life, lessons that, while they can be delayed, must inevitably be learned.

"Bad" Habits

Many parents grow concerned about baby behaviors they term "habits," which seem always to have "bad" connotations. Two common behaviors are thumb-sucking and fondling of the genitals.

Sucking is an essential behavior for your baby's survival from the very first day of life. It begins as an innate reflex and takes on deep meanings for the infant. During early infancy, it becomes associated with the gratification of nursing and means being close with mother. For physical and emotional reasons, sucking becomes pleasurable in its own right. Watching an infant sucking on his finger gives an insight into the pleasure sucking provides. You can see that the infant is engaged in an activity that is much more than simply a "habit."

Babies who don't get enough sucking during nursing or who are being weaned may begin sucking on other things: a pacifier, part of a blanket, the corner of a sheet, or, most often, the thumb.

Sucking—whether on thumb, pacifier, or bottle—comforts a baby, especially at bedtime when insecurity and separation anxiety may surface. The child who sucks may fall into a dreamy state, and sucking seems to help shut out contact with the baby's surroundings. This may ease his drifting off to sleep. Other bedtime habits accompanying sucking may be fingering a blanket or curling a lock of hair. Or your baby may clutch a favorite stuffed animal or other transitional object that helps him fall asleep.

Fondling of the genitals is a baby behavior that is often disturbing to parents, who may view it as a sign of perversity or moral depravity. It's nothing of the sort. It's part and parcel of the baby's slow discovery of his body and often occurs at about one year of age. Providing pleasure, it seems also to comfort the baby, helping ease him to sleep. Try not letting your baby's fondling upset you. A baby who has loving attention and plenty of activities during the day won't become preoccupied with masturbation.

"Spoiling"

Some parents believe that giving an infant too much attention will "spoil" the child. They fear that the baby will become insatiable in his demands for attention, or that he'll become unendingly demanding. In a misguided way, such parents may, from the beginning of the first year, try to cultivate the baby's capacity to "rely on himself."

When your infant cries, it's because she needs something, or because something is wrong. She may be hungry, hot, have a spasm of colic, or be uncomfortably wet. She is crying for human contact and attentive care-giving, and it should be given. The older child may seek attention because of boredom or loneliness, and there comes a time when she must occupy herself with toys, a book, or some other self-reliant activity. In time, your child must learn to tolerate delay and understand that you have more immediate concerns that must be taken care of before such attention can be given.

But during infancy, your baby needs responsive caretaking, and it should be generously provided. This is not spoiling. Some form of "spoiling" may begin during infancy when a mother is overly concerned about her baby's possible discomfort, rushing to gratify every need, even before the baby expresses it. Such a mother may unwittingly stifle the baby's capacity to tolerate delay or frustration, which is an inevitable part of life.

Discipline

Your infant is not born with self-control. Nor is he innately able to delay gratification. He can't understand the consequences of his actions and can't truly know how you or other people feel about most things. In other words, a baby's abilities to use sound judgment, to anticipate how his behavior affects others are very limited. Therefore, any control over the infant must at first come from the parents.

If your baby has received sensitive nurturing, he develops strong bonds of attachment and a solid sense of basic trust. These qualities are the underpinnings for many things: the ability to eventually become more independent, the willingness to communicate, and the capacity to be disciplined.

The issue of discipline—better described as control—is not prominent during the first year. The infant hardly understands most things and demonstrates very little behavior that must be controlled. These issues become more important as your baby's ability to move about the house increases, that is, once the child masters toddling, generally after one year of age. Although discipline is an essential topic for the second and third years, a few general points can be made now.

Some parents fear that disciplining a child means stifling his initiative and curiosity, or scarring the child in some imagined way. Nothing could be farther from the truth. Children need and often want control. The parent who doesn't provide sensible controls and limitations paves the way for a tyrant who knows no limits and who lacks consideration of others.

Discipline simply means exerting some control over your child's impulses so that every "need" isn't instantly gratified. Discipline is not the same as punishment. Most often, the baby's first encounter with "discipline" is the issue of bedtime limitations. Though the baby may protest with a series of ear-splitting howls, once he learns that he must go to sleep and cannot always have you present, he falls asleep. The baby has learned an important lesson in life; he cannot have every wish indulged or granted. He must come to terms with this reality of the world.

Toys

Play is vital for the infant and young child. Social play and its important meanings were described earlier. Good caretaking is related not only to social interchanges with your infant but also to making available to your baby a variety of inanimate playthings. It also means taking an interest in your baby's toys, responding to her playing with them, and encouraging such play.

Playthings are important for your child's intellectual development. The child uses them in a variety of ways: touching, manipulating, tasting (this is very important during infancy), spinning, dangling, throwing, pushing, pulling, and other activities that help the baby learn about size, shapes, consistencies, relative distances, and other physical properties of the world.

The first playthings are often soft and cuddly: a blanket, stuffed doll, or teddy bear. These transitional objects, which often have a feel or smell that is very comforting, remind the baby of one or both parents.

Mobiles hanging over the bassinet or crib are fine for a young baby; most dangle or spin and can be grasped and manipulated when the baby is capable of doing so. (See "Toys" in the "Consultation" section of this chapter.)

Your baby will make use of a variety of objects that aren't toys in the strict sense of the word, but that are routinely found in the home. Kitchen utensils seem to be favorites: pots, pans, plastic containers, and an assortment of objects that can be banged, slammed, spun, and tumbled across a floor. As annoying as you may find it, your baby may enjoy playing with her food. She may squeeze, mash, spread, and smear everything she can get her hands on, and may pour liquid from a cup onto the floor for the pleasure of watching it pour.

Once the baby is bathed in the tub, an endless variety of playthings can be found. Some will float, others won't. All can make a splash. And all make the bath a pleasurable and greatly anticipated time of play for your baby.

Besides household objects, various toys can be purchased, but homemade playthings are just as good. There's no need to flood your child with expensive or complicated toys purchased at a store.

Your baby will discover a host of objects on her own: soap, toothpaste, bottle caps, toilet paper, tissues, dishes, boxes, buttons, foods, knobs, drawers, and other household items. Of course, you must carefully consider the potential for these items to pose a danger to your child. Close supervision must be provided, and a child should not be allowed to play with sharp, hard, or very small objects that can be swallowed. Naturally, you must be cautious and keep your baby away from caustic materials or potential poisons and other dangerous substances. In time, when your child is really toddling, you will have to baby-proof your house. All these playthings will provide your baby with an opportunity to gain control over her motor skills, and will help her learn how things work. Taking an interest in your child's playing and playthings will foster social exchanges, and will help your baby discover the world.

The Premature Baby

It was once thought that the premature baby would remain "behind" and would have abnormal or distorted development through childhood. This simply isn't true. Providing there are no abnormalities at birth, the "young" or premature newborn, although needing extra care at first, usually develops perfectly well.

Years ago, the premature baby was regarded as though it was a fetus rather than a baby. Left in the hospital and given little individual attention or loving handling, the infant received little of the usual care that other newborns received. It is now recognized that premature babies need the same stimulation and care that full-term babies require. Today, premature babies are given regular care and handling by their mothers, although the infant may have to spend extra time in the hospital or in an incubator.

Formerly, it was common for a mother to return home while her premature baby remained in the hospital for weeks, if necessary. Such separation at the outset of a newborn's life could delay the process of attachment between mother and infant, although attachment proceeded once the baby came home. Today, with a more enlightened approach, such early separations are avoided or minimized. Adequate time and effort are given to ensure that a new mother and her premature baby have opportunity for attachment to form at the very beginning of the newborn's life.

A Working Mother

Increasing numbers of mothers are joining the work force each year, many with babies under one year of age. In fact, working mothers are rapidly becoming the norm rather than the exception. This topic is of such importance that Chapter 7, *When Mother Works,* is devoted to it. At present, we will make some general points about a working mother's relationship with her very young infant.

Just as there is no "one" way to love a baby, there is no single or "correct" way to rear your child. Every child needs attention to basic physical needs, as we've described. In addition, your baby needs loving and responsive caretaking to promote sound emotional (and physical) development. There is, however, a great deal of latitude in the way good care-giving can be provided.

Many experts feel that attachment to a specific and stable mother figure is crucial to a baby's sound emotional development. Some parents grow concerned, worrying that this means that only one caretaker can provide consistent "mothering" to a young infant. Some parents fear that if a mother isn't always present, she may deprive her child of the opportunity to cement attachment and develop normally. This simply is not true.

As a working mother, you can remain a stable and primary figure in your baby's life, though you will have to give up certain opportunities for contact with your infant. How this occurs will vary, of course, depending on your job, the possibility of working part-time or at home, and many other factors. It depends, too, on the arrangements you and your husband make (with each other and at your respective jobs), and on the availability of good surrogate caretakers, who must become a crucial ingredient in this equation. Fine care-giving can be provided by a relative or by a hired nanny, assuming the surrogate is a warm, responsive, and sensitive person. Arranging for your child's care to be assigned even to multiple caretakers doesn't prevent you from being of primary importance. Your baby's care may be responsibly spread out among various people. This need not be a deprivation for your baby.

Children with multiple caretakers (such as kibbutz children) may indeed have an advantage: they rarely develop stranger anxiety. Exposed to many people and caretaking styles at an early age, these children have valuable contact with a variety of people and different styles of human interaction.

Children of working mothers may have advantages over children of at-home mothers. Working mothers, it seems, foster increased self-esteem, maturity, and a sense of responsibility in their children. A mother who remains at home may do much more than is necessary for her child, delaying the child's ability to become independent.

Attachment to a specific caretaking person, especially the mother, is formed by about six months. This means that during the first half of your infant's first year, you have plenty of latitude and time to arrange for the best surrogate-parent care available. Evidence indicates that the quality of infant care (not necessarily the overall time spent by any one person) is the most important factor for ensuring attachment and good emotional development. This also means that a mother can return to work as early as six weeks to three months after delivery and still be the primary caretaker of her infant.

Experts vary in their opinions about other-than-mother care. The final verdict may not be in for years, but the facts indicate that more and more mothers will be joining the work force in the next few years. This means that business, government, and all of us must adjust our views and programs to respond to a new generation of parents who seek solutions to a very complex issue. In the future, this may even require that business and government provide some form of joint financial support for families of working mothers. (See Chapter 7, *When Mother Works*, for a complete discussion of all these issues, including working full- or part-time, when to return to work, how to choose a surrogate caretaker, quality time, nanny or private day care, and other important concerns.)

◊ A CONSULTATION—QUESTIONS AND ANSWERS

Our consultant about the first year of life is Daniel N. Stern, M.D. Dr. Stern is Professor of Psychiatry at Cornell University Medical College, and is the Director of the Laboratory of Developmental Processes at the Payne Whitney Clinic of The New York Hospital.

Recognizing Mother

When will my baby know that I'm her mother?

Dr. Stern: A fetus hears rather well during the last trimester of pregnancy. While the uterus and amniotic fluid distort sound, the fetus can clearly hear the mother's voice and learns to recognize it. There is evidence that a newborn baby presented with a sound pattern approximating mother's voice will recognize that sound at birth, and there is every reason to believe that a baby recognizes its own mother's voice at birth.

There's also good evidence that a baby can recognize its mother's face at about one month of age, or perhaps at six weeks. By two or three days after birth, a newborn baby recognizes the odor of his own mother's breast milk.

Keep in mind that your baby will not recognize you in the same way that we adults recognize someone. For the very young infant, recognition is a diffuse series of sensory events occurring in the baby's somewhat undifferentiated world. These events involve auditory, visual, and olfactory modalities by which your infant recognizes you very early in his or her life.

A Good Nursing Experience

My baby is adopted and I can't breast-feed her. How can I make her nursing experience the best one possible?

DR. STERN: I'm concerned by what may be the premise of your question. As a mother, you need not "make up" for anything to your baby. If you and your baby got together by adoption, it's a perfectly fine way for you to have come together. Also implied in your question is concern that breast-feeding is the preferable way to feed your baby.

There is no evidence that breast-feeding is preferable to bottle-feeding. While breast-feeding provides certain advantages, there are advantages to bottle-feeding, too. It may be easier to regulate your baby's feeding with breast milk, which is an advantage. Of course, you cannot see the amount of milk you are delivering to your infant by breast-feeding, which is a disadvantage.

The important consideration is that both methods of nursing your baby are fine. If you cannot breast-feed because your baby is adopted, or for any other reason, you need not be concerned that you will give your baby a "second-rate" nursing experience.

As far as I'm concerned, "a good nursing experience" means the baby gets enough to eat and is made comfortable. During the first month or two of life, not much else is going on, and the main task is to provide your baby with proper nourishment. In other words, the baby must be fed. He must be held in a comfortable position (for the infant *and* for you); there should be a comfortable room temperature; and the baby must be calm enough so he or she will want to nurse. Once your baby is actually nursing, your task is simply to get sufficient quantities of milk into the infant, keeping him as comfortable as possible.

Physical Contact with Baby

How can I increase contact with my baby? Is there a preferred way, physically, of holding her for more contact and warmth?

DR. STERN: First, one must ask what the contact is for. If your baby needs comforting, the best way to do that is skin-to-skin, holding the baby's belly against your own. If you want social interaction or want to have fun with your baby, then a position with the baby in your lap, with some distance available, is best. This allows you to look at each other so you can have more interaction. Actually, the positions that are probably most comfortable and provide most contact between mother and child are those we see in various baby pictures seen in advertisements and the media.

The most important consideration when we talk about contact is the emotional fueling that you and your baby provide for each other. It's really important that you feel good about having and holding your baby, and that you express warmth and a loving feeling for your child. This is the essential groundwork on which contact is built. If you feel loving toward your child, you will make the most and the best contact with your baby. If you have genuine loving feelings for your baby, you won't have to worry about technique. It will simply happen.

Sleeps in Parents' Room

Because of limited room, our newborn infant will sleep in our bedroom. I've been told that this is a bad arrangement. Please advise me.

DR. STERN: If there is no alternative, then there's no issue. I don't think it's terrible for a baby to sleep in the parent's room during the first year of life. In most societies, and for the vast majority of the world's population, a baby and its mother are hardly ever separated throughout the entire first year of life. In these societies, mother carries the baby with her everywhere, even if she's performing manual labor or working in the fields. Quite often, babies in these societies sleep with the parents in their bed throughout the night. This is probably the environment in which human beings evolved from the beginning of history, and it seems to be the way most so-called primitive cultures go about it.

I think in some ways it's easier to have the baby in your room during the first three months, until he is regulated. It can actually be easier both for parents and child, if it doesn't drive a couple crazy.

Of course, parents may be reluctant for the baby to sleep in the bedroom out of concern that the infant should not witness sexual intercourse. (Anyone who's concerned about this issue is unlikely to have intercourse in the baby's presence anyway.) Keep in mind that for many thousands of years different cultures have reared children in various ways, and there's little doubt that since human history began, infants have witnessed parental intercourse. There's no reason to believe that this is as important an issue as we sometimes are led to believe it is. The issue may really be more in parents' minds than in the baby's mind.

Sleeping in the Same Place Every Night

How important is it for my baby to sleep in the same place each night?

DR. STERN: Having your baby sleep in the same place every night is a good idea. It's important to provide a great deal of ritual around the major cyclic events in your baby's daily life, events such as sleeping, eating, and waking up. Infants use external cues to help trigger diurnal cycles, and therefore the ritual surrounding bedtime is very important. Putting the baby down, sitting on the bed in the same place, leaning over the baby, singing a little song, then leaving the room—all are very important.

While each parent does this differently, I think it's crucial to have some regular and predictable sequence of events at the baby's bedtime. Your baby can enter a synchronized rhythm with this sequence, and it can be useful as an aid to going to sleep. Any ritual that lends predictability can be used to cue your baby into a regular pattern of sleeping.

Toys

When should I first get my baby some toys?

DR. STERN: Toys don't seem to matter very much until the baby is about four months old. Many parents place a mobile over a baby's crib. While it certainly won't hurt the baby, I'm not convinced it's going to help much either. In the beginning of life, babies are designed to be interested in and to have plenty of human stimulation, rather than stimulation from inanimate objects. Most toys or devices given to a very young infant are not of any great help.

A child will be receptive to, and benefit from, toys at about four to five months of age. This is the period of time when the baby begins to develop hand-eye coordination. At this time, manipulatable toys can be helpful to your child. The baby will begin seeking out such toys in addition to human stimulation, although the need for human contact never subsides during the first year. Toys are only part of the general stimulation surrounding an infant during the first months. They can be used to greater advantage by your child sometime after the age of four to five months.

Toys don't have to be very fancy. In fact, most objects serve perfectly well as toys during the first year: stimulating things, such as rattles; kitchen utensils such as pots and pans; and any other manipulatable or interesting objects. While the toy industry would have us believe otherwise, elaborate, store-bought toys are not very important, and should not be primary in providing a young child with appropriate stimulation or as instruments to promote hand-eye coordination.

The Best Times to Be with Baby

If I have limited time, is there a best time to spend with my baby?

DR. STERN: There are generally two best times to be with your baby: one is the best time for the *baby*, and the other is the best time for *you*. Since babies are more flexible than adults, perhaps the best time to spend with your baby is the time that's best and most convenient for you. If it really comes down to a choice, you would want to spend time with your baby when you are most free and available.

There is no specific time of the day when it's best to be with your baby, but researchers have noticed that infants seem to be most responsive in the morning. They tend to "bottom out" later, in the afternoon. This may simply be an artifact because many studies seem to indicate that the observers or the parents become fatigued by afternoon, and may themselves be the ones who "bottom out."

Emphasis on the Intellect

Can too much emphasis be placed on intellectual development right from the beginning—such as getting all the right toys, and so on?

DR. STERN: There can be far too much emphasis based on intellectual development, and this can sometimes be a problem because many parents seem to overvalue the idea of intellect. Infants don't need to learn anything during the first six months of life. In fact, there's nothing you can teach a baby during this period of time. The most helpful situation for an infant at this time is a sensitive, interactive environment with the parents.

For instance, if you decide that you want your baby to speak excellent English, and you speak nothing but perfect diction to an infant, he will have a terrible experience. A baby is geared to listen and respond to baby talk, not to perfectly spoken English! The moment you begin to "teach" a baby anything, you have a problem because you lose spontaneity. Most things that are valuable to an infant occur spontaneously and involve both the parent and infant in having fun! Any activity that provides fun for you and the baby will have more value and provide more "information" for the baby than any attempt at formal teaching. Attempting to teach an infant is counterproductive.

At about six to eight months, when a baby is playing with an object, you can begin to help structure a task so the infant can do it better. You can show the baby alternative ways to do things. When the baby gets older and becomes verbal, you can help her learn alternative ways to say things. Instruction *is* important but has very little value during the first six months of life.

It's important to realize that when a parent attempts to instruct an infant younger than six months of age, the baby is going to learn very little. When a parent is having *fun* with a baby, the parent is most probably instinctively tailoring his or her behavior in a way that's more readily accessible to the infant in terms of learning. Having fun should be a parent's primary objective with an infant. You simply cannot rush an infant's intellectual development by overstimulation. An infant's intellectual capacities unfold according to a maturational timetable, one that moves at its own rate and that cannot and should not be "rushed." A parent can only respond to this progressive unfolding.

If a parent plays with a baby, if she attempts to have fun, there is a natural playing out of a particularly appealing theme in one or another variation. This occurs naturally and intuitively. A certain act is performed; it's then repeated again and again, eventually working up to a "punch line." Any of the repetitive ritualistic infant games, such as Three Little Piggies, is a good example. This is a natural, spontaneous teaching format, one that cannot be recreated in a formal or structured way by attempting to instruct. If a parent overvalues formal educative tasks, a baby will actually learn less.

In the beginning of life, a baby must "learn" that there is an exchange of communicative signals between itself and mother, and that various emotions come into play. The baby must learn what it's like being with someone who loves and enjoys being with the baby; what it's like to be played with; what it's like to be stimulated, and when necessary, comforted by the parent. These things can only be learned in a nonplanned, interactive sequence, one that unfolds on its own, in a loving and natural way between parent and child. Actually, an infant is quite protected against all this intellectual stuff, because it cannot speak. An infant's primary task is to become involved in and learn from these crucial emotional exchanges. Language and formal teaching would only get in the way.

Intense Stimulation

I've heard about various programs where parents of infants learn how to provide intense stimulation by rocking, bouncing, patting their babies, and other activities. Will such practices increase my baby's intellect?

DR. STERN: I don't really know why a parent would want to provide such stimulation for an infant. During the course of an ordinary day when a parent holds the baby, cuddles the infant, soothes or feeds or talks to a baby, a great deal of physical stimulation is provided. It's important to realize that there are temperamental differences between infants. Some babies must be protected from high levels of stimulation, while others may seek it out and require high levels of it. Such variations in babies are very important and preclude an indiscriminate approach involving a great deal of physical stimulation for every child.

The systematic stimulation of an infant is not the way most cultures have evolved in terms of early infant care. In fact, many cultures have realized that babies are probably more alert and take in more of their environment when they're at a relatively *low* level of stimulation. For instance, certain cultures have traditionally swaddled their infants. This is done for many months during the first year of life, and these babies seem to be far more alert than babies who receive a great deal of physical stimulation and whose legs are completely free. While there may be some circumstances in which it's necessary to arouse a baby for an important interaction such as feeding or playing, there's no need to purposely go about physically stimulating an infant in a systematic, programmed way.

Intense Play Periods

I've heard that I should spend two or more distinct periods of time with my baby giving her intense stimulation. Is this true?

DR. STERN: There's no question that playing with your baby is a good thing to do. But I really don't know where the idea of two or more distinct periods of time comes from, and I don't exactly know what is meant by intense stimulation.

Play is a vital component of your baby's life at this time. If your interaction is relaxed, then you're probably playing with your baby most of the time. It's difficult to imagine what would comprise "nonplay" with an infant. Aside from ordinary functions such as getting the nipple into a baby's mouth, or perhaps changing diapers, you are probably playing with and stimulating your baby more than you know. Many parents— even when changing an infant's diapers or when involved in these routines—end up playing with the baby.

I'm a bit concerned that you may really be asking about "teaching" your baby instead of playing. There are so many opportunities for play that there doesn't have to be a program. In a fairly typical feeding situation, the baby will nurse for a few minutes, then become less focused on the nipple and engage the parent. The baby becomes more alert and interactive; mother will usually stop the feeding for a while and begin to interact playfully with the baby. Then they resume feeding. These play sessions, if you want to call them that, can last anywhere from ten seconds to ten minutes, or longer. The baby's readiness is the primary thing initiating the play and interaction. Most mothers are exquisitely responsive to their baby's signals and eventually become rather expert at defining when the baby is receptive for play and interaction.

This is probably the most sensitive way to go about finding out when to play with your baby. It's far more productive than trying to program your baby into distinct play periods. Again, keep in mind that enormous individual variations exist between infants. Some infants fall asleep immediately after eating, while others become more alert and interactive. Some babies prefer playing as soon as their hunger edges off, perhaps one minute into a feeding.

Most parents eventually fall into a pattern with a baby; they evolve certain periods during the day when playing with the baby takes precedence over other adult activities. There's nothing wrong with such an arrangement; it can even help structure the baby's day, but still, it has a rhythm and fluidity of its own.

The issue of what constitutes "intense" play or stimulation cannot be decided unilaterally by a parent, nor can it be decided in advance. Intensity is relative to how receptive your baby is to stimulation or playing. This is determined by your baby's temperament.

Nervous About Leaving Baby with a Sitter

I'm nervous about leaving our six-month-old baby with a sitter. I'm concerned that she'll have trouble handling the separation. Is this normal?

DR. STERN: Characteristically, babies begin to become upset by strangers at about six or seven months. It's best to have someone who is not a total stranger and with whom the baby is familiar for any baby-sitting situation. There's nothing wrong with leaving your baby with a sitter, providing it's not a complete stranger. This of course depends on a number of issues: how long you're going to be gone, whether it's for half an hour or perhaps for dinner. Obviously, the situation is different if you are going away for a weekend.

It's generally easier to leave your baby during the first six months, prior to her developing stranger anxiety. However, that's not the way it usually works out. Most parents find it very difficult to spend time away from a baby during the first six months, although the baby has yet to develop stranger anxiety. The real question is, how do parents leave an infant for a while and manage to keep all parties sane? After all, an occasional evening out is a perfectly natural thing.

The most natural way to keep everyone sane would involve an available extended family with people to take up any slack and act as surrogate parents for the baby. Of course, in our society today, we rarely see such extended families, which is why we have problems and questions about surrogate care for babies. The most sensible thing is to approximate the extended family as best you can. A baby-sitter for your child should be someone who is familiar to the baby. If for some reason you must have a complete stranger or new baby-sitter, it's best to have that person come an hour or two before you leave, so your baby can become accustomed to this stranger, who may then take on some qualities of a transitional object for your baby.

Baby Cries When Parents Leave

Our nine-month-old screams just as we're about to leave for the evening. Our sitter told us that he stops soon after we leave, but I'm not sure. I have trouble with this situation each time. What should I do?

DR. STERN: There's not much that you can do. Your baby will not change this particular pattern of behavior. You must decide if it's sufficiently important for you to go out for the evening. If going out is important, then you should leave and not return because of the baby's crying. The crying should not manipulate your activity or evening. Your baby's crying is a natural response. If the baby's behavior successfully holds you at the door or prevents you from leaving, a situation will develop in which his behavior effectively manipulates you. This will receive reinforcement by your not leaving, and your baby will end up crying even longer. Remember, the baby is truly upset by your leaving, and you must accept that. But then—there are leavetakings in life.

Staying Home with a Newborn

How long should I stay home with my newborn before I return to work?

DR. STERN: If you have a choice and enjoy being at home with your baby, it would probably be ideal to stay home for about one year. The first year of life is the time when your baby has the most need for and the most concentration on a parent. It's not essential that you stay home for a full year, and today most women who do stay home remain for three to six months. You're better off staying home with your baby for a longer period of time, providing you're happy about this arrangement.

However, if a woman feels she is losing ground in her career and begins to resent this situation, or if she finds it boring to perform caretaking tasks, then staying home for a long time helps neither her nor the baby. There's no magic number to denote how long is best to stay home with an infant. Paradoxically, most women return to work during the second six months of the baby's life; this is when the baby is most sensitive to separation, having developed stranger anxiety. But most babies seem to do reasonably well despite the difficulties of any particular method.

Of course, many mothers have no choice and must return to work soon after having had a baby. The biggest issue determining the success of this arrangement is the quality of care given by a surrogate parent in the natural mother's absence. As the primary parent, you are still the major influence on your baby, even if someone else provides a major portion of the caretaking. You need not be present all day for a great deal of meaningful interaction to take place and to remain the primary figure in your baby's life. However, good-quality surrogate care is needed to assure your infant's sound emotional development during this first year.

We often hear the phrase "quality time" used to denote that the crucial element in a parent's interaction with a baby is the quality of warmth and responsiveness, even if the actual time spent with the baby is minimal. This concept cannot be faulted, given the reality that many women must work and spend relatively little time with their infants during the work week. In fact, a parent and baby may very well be aroused for, or "get up" for, the times when they can be together.

Work with children of the kibbutz experience in Israel has demonstrated that nobody ever truly replaces the primary parents. In fact, the primary parents always occupy a position of enormous influence and importance in a baby's emotional life. Although a parent may not be able to spend as much time as he or she would like with the child, there's no doubt that a parent still remains a major and significant figure in a baby's emotional life. (See Chapter 7, *When Mother Works.*)

Effects of Many Caretakers

We have an extended family with parents, grandparents, and sisters living together. As a result, our baby has different people providing for him. Although I'm his primary caretaker, is having all these people an advantage, or can it confuse my baby?

DR. STERN: I suspect that this arrangement is a distinct advantage for a child and will not confuse him. It's important to have one primary caretaker, and the identity of that primary figure is usually quite evident to everyone involved. As long as the presence of a primary caretaker is stable and not in question, then auxiliary people can only be an advantage to your baby, providing they are good caretakers and reasonably loving.

It does appear that babies who have multiple caretakers develop less stranger anxiety than those with only one primary caretaker. Stranger anxiety should not be viewed as a bad development. It's merely an indication that an infant is learning to discriminate different people from each other, and that there is a world of the familiar and unfamiliar. Whoever is in the world of familiars will remain so, and those outside that world will be strangers to the child. There may be some advantages to having many caretakers since this arrangement exposes a baby to different styles of interaction with different people.

Extra Input for Baby

I would like my infant to have as much sensory input as possible. Will having a television set next to the crib be helpful?

DR. STERN: Some parents may want to provide a baby with as much stimulation as the infant can tolerate or as much as technology can provide. An adequate level of stimulation must be determined inevitably by the baby's response. There's no reason in the world to put a television next to a baby's crib. You don't need an electronic baby-sitter. Such "input" would not teach your baby anything and is poorly adapted to the baby's needs because it isn't responsive or interactive with the child. Infants seem not to be terribly interested in television. While doing some experiments with three-month-olds that involved television, we noticed that the stimulus of greatest interest to them was the white snow on the TV screen. The more static and the poorer the reception, the more interested the babies were!

Worries Baby Is "Slow"

My nine-month-old seems not to be developing as quickly as his brother did at the same age. He's not robust, and isn't standing yet, while his brother easily stood at this age. Am I wrong to be concerned?

DR. STERN: Your nine-month-old baby is simply not developing as quickly as his brother did at the same age. There are enormous developmental differences between babies, and there's nothing wrong with one baby reaching certain developmental landmarks earlier than another. It doesn't mean that the slower baby is retarded or isn't developing on time. It's simply a matter of variation from one infant to another.

In this situation, we're discussing physical development, which along with mental and emotional milestones, can vary greatly from one baby to another. While your second son may be a bit behind in standing, his developmental timetable may be far ahead in many other ways. Simply let him be who he is going to be.

If for some reason you feel there are major problems and that he is developmentally slow in a number of obvious ways, it's wise to consult with your pediatrician. But it sounds as though your baby falls within the normal limits of variability for a nine-month-old. You must simply accept the fact that your second baby will become a different kind of person than your firstborn child.

You cannot rush a child's development. Maturational milestones—sitting up, walking, talking, and other major developmental feats—march progressively at their own pace. You can talk to a baby until you're blue in the face, but you'll probably never really hasten the point at which the baby begins speaking on his own. The baby's maturational timetable determines his rate of physical, mental, and emotional development, and very little can be done to alter it. An infant needs human speech and responsive interaction to "prime" the system and make the baby more accessible to the eventual acquisition of language and other developmental milestones, but still this is largely determined by a maturational timetable.

A certain tribe in Africa greatly values the baby's ability to walk at an early age. Early developmental progress in this area makes life easier for members of the community. This group of people spends a great deal of time giving infants walking exercises from the very beginning of life.

The baby's legs are exercised, various motions are practiced, and so forth. After this prolonged and intense effort, they successfully advance the onset of walking in their tribe as compared to other tribes, by a period of about ten days! This small advance seems hardly worth the intense effort and extraordinary amount of time devoted to this task.

There's no need to worry about the rate at which a baby achieves various developmental milestones. There are physical, emotional, and cognitive variations between and among babies. These differences must be respected and allowed to play themselves out, so that each baby eventually develops into a unique person.

A Baby's Erections

My five-month-old son gets erections quite often, especially when I'm cleaning him. Is this normal?

DR. STERN: Yes, this is perfectly normal. In fact, whenever a baby has REM sleep (a period of time during sleep characterized by rapid eye movements), there are erections. This is a completely normal phenomenon. It is neither good nor bad. It simply is. It's the way your baby works. This is nothing to become concerned about, and should not become an issue. If you find that this disturbs you, then perhaps you are dealing with some internal problem or conflict of your own. However, as far as your baby is concerned, it is perfectly normal.

Nervous Mother

I'm the mother of a two-month-old baby, my first child, and I'm still nervous about how to hold her. I haven't yet built up the confidence that I'm doing the right thing. I don't want to be too tentative because I'm concerned my baby will sense it. Are these normal feelings?

DR. STERN: I think that, at first, uncertain feelings are not only normal, but are probably inevitable for any new mother. In our society, fewer and fewer women have had previous experience in handling babies, because we no longer have extended families. In fact, most first-time parents live somewhat isolated lives, away from relatives or an extended family that could be helpful. Many women today must learn about basic caretaking on their own, which can be difficult to accomplish. It's an awesome feeling to realize that for the first time in your life, you have ultimate responsibility for another human being's life! This brings not only self-doubt, but natural anxiety into any first-time mother's life.

Generally, by about two months, most mothers feel quite a bit more comfortable about these issues than at first. By six to eight weeks, when the baby begins regulating his patterns, most mothers begin feeling comfortable with their interaction with their infant. At this point, most mothers seem to realize that they're doing things "right," and they may not even know how or why.

If you don't have a sense of confidence, and still feel uncomfortably tentative with your baby, you may generally lack confidence in yourself. This could be a characterological trait of yours throughout your life at large. You might want to consider visiting a professional for a consultation if you feel that your confidence is very shaky.

The most confidence-inspiring infusion available to new mothers can be contact with other mothers, whether they are experienced caretakers or novices. Mothers learn quickest by modeling; by watching other mothers do what they do. The playground or park bench grapevine is probably the most effective way of inspiring confidence and of teaching child-rearing techniques to new mothers.

The professional world, in my view, has largely failed mothers of young babies. We have not explicitly answered questions that are difficult for new mothers to pose. There have been some teaching successes with postdelivery and parenting classes, where learning how to diaper babies and prepare formulas are readily taught. But there are other issues such as the question posed here, namely, worries about a lack of confidence, or advice about handling a baby in a way that conveys a sense of love, caring, and security to the baby. New parents often find it embarrassing to ask these questions. It can be helpful to see other people with similar questions because this can validate your own concerns. Groups, whether informal or otherwise, can be very good "therapy" for new parents.

An Overview

First-time parents are best off if they consider their experience with their baby to be an open-ended process of discovery. There is no road map, and you cannot know exactly what's going to happen. If something works for you and your baby at the present time, you must be prepared for the inevitable fact that it may not work in two weeks' time. This occurs because a baby develops beyond the present point; the infant enters another stage, so you must alter the way you handle your infant.

Parents who feels they must have a completely predictable routine at all times will undoubtedly become frustrated by the child's developmental changes. These changes must be negotiated as they arise. Parents who seem happiest are those who can view their first child-rearing experience as though it's a new and exciting journey, a journey to different places where decisions must sometimes be made on the spot, and where you must learn to trust your judgments and feelings. This happens in relation to a baby's sleeping, with the infant's nursing, eating, playing, locomotion, and with other activities. There will never be a preset "program" to completely suit you and your baby at all times. A parent must remain open-minded and flexible, able to adapt to a baby's ever-changing needs and developmental progress. Change is a byword of the first year, change that may occur in small daily increments or that takes place in great leaps.

This doesn't mean you can't have structure in your relationship with the baby. While structure and predictability are essential, you must remain flexible and ready to alter the structure as the need arises. I've mentioned various structures, such as ritualizing bedtime, patterning the baby's feeding schedule, or patterning how and when you play with an infant. All this should be encouraged, but it isn't etched in stone. What works well today may no longer work three weeks from now. At that time, you must once again discover what works best. Hopefully, all this occurs in the context of a sensitive, loving, and care-giving relationship with your baby.

In a way, the relationship with your baby at this time comes closest to what in this culture we recognize as the initial phase of a romantic relationship. At this time in a relationship, you don't fully know the other person. You're first exploring who the person is—what that person likes or prefers—and each of you works at learning how to go about being with and enjoying the best of each other. This initial phase of a romance is a process of discovery. That's the way the first months of a baby's life should be, before certain things become ritualized. Hopefully, your relationship with your child will, as in romance, always retain a sense of wonder and discovery.

Chapter 2: The Toddler—
The Second and Third Years

◊ YOUR DEVELOPING CHILD

At about fifteen months of age, your child enters the period called toddlerhood. Lasting some two years, this phase is marked by crucial developmental themes. Your child makes dramatic progress in upright walking (toddling, at first), begins acquiring language, and strives (with some difficulty) toward separating from you.

In the beginning of the second year, your child will practice becoming more self-sufficient. This effort will be given enormous impetus by his newfound ability to walk and speak, allowing him an active role in choosing how close or distant he remains to you. The toddler has what has been called a "love affair with the world," eagerly exploring it and practicing at temporarily distancing himself from you.

By about eighteen months, the child will truly be a more separate person, with a greater sense of his distinct identity. He may become temporarily frightened by this newly discovered separateness, occasionally rushing back to you for emotional "refueling." To your child, the world contains innumerable dangers; your help and reassurance in facing these obstacles (as well as temptations) will play a vital role in how he masters this phase of development and the others that follow.

The young toddler is still very much a baby; every new object is seized, pulled, hauled, squeezed, turned, and then stuffed into the mouth. The toddler of fifteen or eighteen months may rely more on his rapidly expanding motor skills than on his still primitive verbal abilities, but this will change as he approaches twenty-four months. By about two years of age, the toddler is a whirling wonder of nonstop talk, much to the delight (and sometimes embarrassment) of his parents.

Your Child Walks: How This Changes Everything

A variety of important changes occur at the beginning of the second year. Although unsteady at first, your toddler's newly acquired skills improve with amazing speed as she learns to navigate through the house. (Walking may begin as early as seven to nine months or as late as sixteen months.) Laboriously making her way at first, she soon becomes steadier, learning to pivot on one foot, making quick turns, and mastering combinations of complex movements. Before you know it, she's trotting about, pushing a wagon, climbing onto chairs, slipping under tables, and slowly making her way (backward) down a flight of stairs.

Practicing constantly, the young toddler derives enormous pleasure from mastering the new challenges of walking, climbing, and navigating everywhere. A toddler delights in trying everything. She negotiates her way into an adult-sized chair by climbing up onto her knees and then slowly twisting herself about in the proper direction. She slowly makes her way up a flight of steps, one step at a time, pulling her second foot up to the level of the first. At about two years of age, your child may be able to walk downstairs while tightly clutching your index finger. She likes nothing better than to constantly move about: running, trotting, climbing, falling, getting up, and then running once again.

The ability to stand and walk occurs earlier in girls than in boys, because girls' nervous systems mature somewhat earlier. For the same reason, girls also tend to use language earlier, although this varies from child to child. It's helpful to know that while one child may seem "behind" in terms of walking or climbing, she may be "ahead" in other areas. And while "behind" today, she may display a previously unshown skill tomorrow. Remember, no two children are alike.

Hurtling here and there, exploring one room or another, your toddler may empty drawers, open closets, scale heights, and make a mess of everything. An expensive ashtray may fall victim; a crystal vase may tumble to the floor. She may dash headlong toward the precipitous edge of a staircase; she may dart with incredible speed toward a traffic-filled intersection or a lake's edge. She could climb onto a windowsill or poke at an electric wall socket. Exploring the underside of the kitchen sink, she may discover a brightly colored bottle that can be readily opened. Heedless of danger, she may find the temptation to taste its contents overwhelming.

Your toddler's rapidly increasing mobility and expansive curiosity, along with her growing sense of independence, present you with a momentous challenge: for the first time in her life, you must set limits on your child's activities, by actually saying "no." This means that you must protect your child, as well as her surroundings, and the word "no" becomes an important hallmark of this era of development.

The Concept "No"

Imagine your toddler's world. He sees everything from its underside: tables, chairs, the kitchen sink, appliances, and counters. Boundlessly curious, filled with restless energy and enthusiasm, exploring new textures, colors, and shapes, he wanders everywhere. Never having known real limits, the whole world is truly his oyster. Then, approaching the top of the stairwell, he suddenly hears the word "no."

In a very real way, "no" introduces an entirely new level of communication to your child; it is very possibly the first negative warning you've ever verbalized to him. Equally important, it's the very first abstract intellectual concept you've ever conveyed to your child. The first no ushers a new era into your child's life.

"No" can end up meaning many different things to the child, depending on how you present this concept. You may not actually say no, but you must begin to convey the idea of prohibition to your child. This can be done in a number of ways: you can remove the ashtray (vase, cigarette lighter, etc.); you can bodily remove your child from the tempting or dangerous situation; you can divert his attention to a more acceptable object or situation; you can bark a sharp "No!"; you can simply shake your head and gently say "No."

You say no to protect your unsuspecting toddler from harming himself or the things with which he comes in contact. Your child, however, cannot understand these potential dangers and your prohibitions. He simply wants to explore his expanding universe of intriguing places and things. He's trying valiantly to separate from you and become more independent, though he rushes back and clings to you for reassurance when the going gets rough. But from his unsophisticated point of view, your warnings, prohibitions, and restrictions are utterly incomprehensible. Exhilarated by the wealth of objects waiting to be discovered, touched, and manipulated, your child and you enter a period of time that can be difficult for both of you. Keep in mind that much of the toddler's "contrariness" is really a matter of his curiosity more than a genuine desire to frustrate a parent. Knowing this may help you remain level-headed even as your toddler seems to defy you.

All Those No's

By the time your toddler is two years old, "no" becomes a way of life for parent and child. Your child seems to say no automatically. He may seem contrary, impossible to handle, constantly opposed to anything you say or do. This is actually one way your child has of both being *like* you (identifying with you) and of asserting his autonomy and independence. By imitating your no, he is being very much like you. At the same time, his no is a way of saying, "I'm on my own, and I can do what I want to." It's part of the process of separating from you and can become a battle of wills. With good reason, many people call this period in a toddler's life the terrible twos.

Two words form the battle cry of the two-year-old's struggle for self-assertive autonomy, "Me!" and "No!" "Me!" means, "I want to do it myself!" The no's aren't always verbal: your toddler may go limp, refusing to move from whatever object or situation intrigues him (an ashtray, a windowsill, a sharp object, a lamp cord). He may kick willfully and then freeze in a rigid pose. He may run from the room and throw a temper tantrum. Reacting strongly to such displays only reinforces them; ignoring the outburst usually weakens this negative (and sometimes deafening) reaction. As one mother of a two-year-old said: "I soon discovered that the best way to quiet Jason when he threw a tantrum was to ignore it. He would lie on the floor and scream, so I'd walk into the next room. He would follow me, position himself on the floor and pick up where he'd left off. Within a moment, I'd leave the room again. He would follow, but his screaming would become softer. And it wouldn't last very long. When I moved away again, he would whimper a few times and then become quiet. Then would come a sort of sulking silence, and before long, all was well."

Sometimes a strenuous battle of wills occurs. When this happens, you must be prepared to carry out your restriction with complete assurance and authority, especially if your toddler insists on doing something dangerous or destructive. You may find yourself forced into carrying a wildly kicking, squalling child away from the temptation. Afterward, it's best to ease the bruising weight of your parental authority with some extra affection or attention. If not, your child may feel diminished and humiliated, which can lead to his having self-doubt and even a sense of shame.

You may sometimes notice that your child's opposition is little more than playacting, an attempt at trying out another no, seeing how it feels to defy you. Even though he shouts "No!" when confronted with the proposition of going to bed, the time comes, and he's tucked more or less willingly into bed. Despite an avalanche of no's, he lies still while you calmly slip his shoes onto his feet. Despite a torrent of verbal objections to eating, he remains seated, even opening his mouth while you imperturbably feed him, and the succession of no's dwindles to less than a whisper. If you fail to detect the not-so-secretive playfulness in some of your child's disobedience, you may unwittingly become a partner in an unintended crisis of wills. Such a battle need not always exist.

Contrariness is normal at this age. Some experts consider negativism and all the no's during the toddler years to be an essential ingredient in your child's developing a fledgling sense of self-assured independence. If you can prevent these contrary flare-ups from becoming major confrontations, your child may actually gain something from the defiance in the long run, becoming more autonomous and self-assured. This, of course, requires a level head and a sense of humor on your part. If your toddler has plenty of opportunity to explore things and practice getting to know the world on his own—balanced, of course, by proper support and by certain restrictions—he can develop a sound sense of his own abilities and limitations. This will provide him with a readiness to face the world and a capacity to struggle successfully with new problems as his life goes on.

The way you set limits for your child can have enormous meaning in terms of his later emotional development. Many experts view the crucial issue of toddlerhood as whether a child develops a sense of autonomy or becomes mired in shame and doubt. Autonomy means your child eventually develops the capacity to sense himself as being in charge of his life, able to make reasonable decisions and carry them through. Your toddler is faced with new possibilities each day, and he wants to try them out for himself, with very little help (however well-intended) from you. When successful in gaining pleasure from his own activities, he feels satisfied, competent, develops a capacity for initiative in his later life, and is launched toward true autonomy and a sense of self-sufficiency.

The toddler whose mother always shouts "No!" is at a great disadvantage. The child who never gets to touch *anything* may eventually have problems feeling free enough to *do* anything. The toddler who faces a constant barrage of overstated limits has a difficult struggle indeed. In later life, he may have difficulty forgetting his mother's anxious repetitions: "Don't go there!"—"Stay near me!"—"Stay away from that!"—"Stay away from everything!"—"You'll hurt yourself!"—"Shame on you!"—"Don't open that!"—"I *knew* you would hurt yourself!"

Such a child, immersed in imagined dangers, constantly warned and hearing dire predictions of harm, one whose parents predict failure at any attempt at mastery, has his sense of autonomy slowly undermined. He may eventually develop feelings of shame and doubt: doubt about taking charge of anything, shame for his own strivings, and even shame about his own body. Such a child may develop into an adult who feels worthless and incompetent.

Your toddler has both competences and limitations. He may overestimate his abilities, not truly appreciating his limitations. Your role as a parent is to allow your child every reasonable opportunity for self-testing and exploration. This doesn't mean *no* limits; such promiscuous freedom can lead to "spoiling," and can foster a child who never learns reasonable boundaries, or one who is seriously injured.

On the other hand, you may find yourself making Herculean efforts to keep from being overprotective. This is important, but at the same time you must prevent your toddler from undertaking foolish or dangerous activities. It helps if you can be ready to provide comfort and reassurance when your child overestimates his capacities and fails at something, or when things simply go wrong. The key is balance: a reasonable measure of sound limit-setting but without stifling your child's strivings for competency and independence.

Remember, your toddler may quickly vacillate between a bold autonomy (running toward a playful dog on the street) and a clinging dependency (crying for you to ease the pain of his scraped knee). In the midst of self-assertive insistence on doing something for himself, he may suddenly give in to your wishes, or seem very much a baby, wanting to be carried, coddled, and kissed.

No toddler achieves full autonomy. But, if during infancy your child has acquired a sense of basic trust, a sense of confidence that his basic needs will be lovingly met, his new powers of mobility and language, coupled with his self-sufficient strivings, will help him attain a better sense of himself as an individual. He will demonstrate healthy initiative, be willing to explore new things, and become a competent person in his own right.

The Seeds of Conscience

With limit-setting, your toddler is learning the do's and don'ts of life. By imitating and identifying with your role of setting limits, your toddler begins to internalize these rules. She begins to develop a conscience. This development begins in a rudimentary way, but it's vitally important.

Ellen, a curious two-and-a-half-year-old, was discovered by her mother after she had emptied three drawers of her parents' bedroom bureau. Ellen's mother reacted a bit harshly; she was upset, both at the mess, and at what she felt was her toddler's invasion of parental privacy, since Ellen had quietly gone into her parents' bedroom while her mother was busy in the kitchen.

Scolding Ellen, her mother yelled, "No! No! These aren't your things!" and then gently slapped Ellen's hand before replacing the contents back into the drawers.

Some twenty minutes later, Ellen's mother, again in the kitchen, thought she heard her daughter's voice coming from the bedroom. Moving to the bedroom doorway, she saw her daughter standing at the same bureau with one drawer open. Curiously peering inside, Ellen, who had no idea that her mother was quietly watching, seemed obviously aware she was doing something wrong. Ellen's mother waited, stifling the impulse to rush angrily into the room. As Ellen's hand neared the contents of the open drawer, Ellen slapped it and in a sharp tone similar to her mother's said, "No! No! These aren't your things!" Looking as aggrieved as her mother had twenty minutes earlier, Ellen closed the drawer and shook her head.

This kind of behavior is more than mere imitation. By identifying with do's and don'ts, your toddler is setting up an internal control system that will be used to modify and influence her own behavior. Because your child wants more than anything to be loved and craves your approval, she will in time internalize your values, learning those behaviors she knows you approve and those that meet with your displeasure.

This developing conscience is crucial for every child. A solid sense of right versus wrong (which takes a long time to develop) is essential for your child's capacity to get along reasonably with other people, who must live in a world where certain things are truly prohibited. While at first your toddler will refrain from behaviors only because she fears losing your approval, she will eventually internalize this system of do's and don'ts. She will know that something is right or wrong because it feels that way, not because she fears being caught and then punished.

Because the toddler is constantly changing, the do's and don'ts of daily life must change with his increasing skills and abilities. Something disapproved of today may be perfectly fine three or six months later. The twenty-month-old who toddles to the head of a flight of stairs hears a resounding "No!" from his mother or father. He learns that this is "wrong" and unacceptable behavior, and curbs his impulse to head down the stairs. However, when he's two and a half, the prohibition no longer applies because he is capable of negotiating the stairs by himself. The value system that the toddler is internalizing must remain somewhat flexible if it's going to apply realistically during the child's future life.

Toilet Training: An Exercise in Love or a Battlefield?

The two-year-old child struggles for mastery and a sense of control, valiantly trying to separate himself from his parents, particularly mother. He may occasionally have temper tantrums and be contrary. He must constantly decide whether he wants to do what is "right" (things meeting your approval) or whether he wants to be a "bad" child, doing things that are "wrong" (things of which you disapprove).

At about this time, many parents decide that their child should learn to control his bowel movements and use the toilet. When this occurs, important developmental issues—of mastery, control, of doing the "right" or "wrong" thing, and of pleasing or displeasing you—may come to focus on your child's body, specifically on his willingness or ability to control his bowel movements.

The problems of toddlerhood may unfortunately narrow down to an intense focus on toilet training, especially if you attempt to train your child too early. Early training may impose demands on the child that he cannot easily understand, much less master. Premature attempts at toilet training (premature means before the age of two or two and a half) may confuse your toddler. Toilet training asks that he "produce" or "give" in order to please you; at other times, he must "hold it in" or not "give" so as to please you and thereby be "good." Control is asked of the child just at the period of time when his developmental struggle with self-control is likely to be greatest. Premature attempts at toilet training may ignite the issue into a relentless struggle; the toilet becomes a battlefield, a war of wills for mastery over your child's body and who controls it.

Many experts feel that there is no reason to attempt to toilet train your child before he's two and a half years old. They suggest that patient waiting, rather than prematurely stressing toilet training, brings fine results. Many children, if given time and the opportunity to decide for themselves, will eventually express a wish to use the toilet. They actually want to follow the example of other family members, feeling that such grown-up activities are good and desirable. They may learn to use the toilet with minimal encouragement.

If toilet training is properly timed and and made into a positive, rewarding experience that can be shared between you and your child, there is little likelihood that it will escalate into a major issue. Instead, it becomes a part of your toddler's path toward eventual self-sufficiency, providing him with healthy feelings of accomplishment and mastery. We will discuss some important practical aspects of toilet training (and its emotional components) in the "practical issues" section later in the chapter.

About Mixed Feelings

Your toddler has mixed feelings about his push toward autonomy. While striving for competency and undertaking new challenges, he also longs for the safety of parental ministrations. When in a supermarket, the toddler may daringly charge ahead to explore the exciting wonders of the next aisle, only to burst into babyish tears when he realizes he's momentarily lost. Or a child may delightedly anticipate her weekly visit to the play school, only to protest tearfully when her mother departs. Generally, strivings toward autonomy and mastery prevail, but along with a good many doubts and anxieties.

Parents, too, have mixed feelings about a child's growth and development. They delight in their infant's first smile, applaud her first steps, are thrilled by her first day in school, and are glad when she tackles new developmental milestones that mark emotional and physical progress. Yet they may be racked by doubts and misgivings, and by concern that they are pushing too hard or expecting too much of the child. Many parents worry that they are losing their baby. Some parents, overwhelmed by fear or concern, unconsciously actually thwart the attaining of such milestones, unwittingly sabotaging a child's healthy move toward independence.

As a child develops, your role in his life must change. Your infant's dependency during the first months of life and your protectively nurturing ways are very appropriate at that time. But your extreme involvement must slowly give way as your child reaches toddlerhood and begins trying out the world on his own. (See " 'Losing' Her Baby," later in this chapter.)

Awareness of the Body and the Self

Toddlers still have an incomplete ability to tell the difference between some aspects of themselves and the rest of the world. For a two-year-old, something broken may actually seem a threat to his own body. A toddler may become upset by the slightest break in a toy or other object, demanding that you fix it. He may refuse a broken cookie while eagerly grabbing at a whole one. Some children will refuse to play with a broken doll, even after it's been repaired.

Your toddler's running commentary on his own activities, his constant self-reminders of your prohibitions (saying to himself, "Don't touch" or "Not yours") indicate awareness of himself as distinct and separate from you, but occasionally these distinctions are blurred. The child is still struggling to define himself as a separate and individual person. This may suddenly become apparent when your two-year-old becomes fiercely possessive about her belongings: toys, clothing, and playthings of all sorts. Don't be shocked if this occurs. Such possessiveness is important in helping the toddler define what belongs to her and therefore define her own identity.

Your toddler can name the features of her face and various body parts, although this can sometimes confuse a child. A special area of confusion may arise in naming the genitals. This partly results because parents are anxious about sexuality when it applies to their children. Some parents mistakenly avoid this issue completely.

Childish euphemisms about the genitals may further confuse your child. You wouldn't tell your child that his nose was a "smeller" or that his mouth was a "taster" or a "chewer," yet in naming genitals, many parents avoid using proper anatomical terms. The penis or vagina becomes a "pisser," a "sissy," a "wee-wee," or other words that describe the function rather than the organ's name. One little girl was told that her buttocks were a "heiny" and that her vulva was a "little heiny." Such evasive and euphemistic naming of the genitals may lead to confusion, especially for a young girl.

Toilet training and simple exploration of the body may focus your child's attention on the anal-genital-urinary area. Cleaning of the child's genitals (whether before, during, or after toilet training) produces pleasurable sensations for the child. He or she begins exploring the area while alone, partly out of curiosity and partly because it feels good.

The boy's penis is external and accessible both visually and by touching. He can clearly distinguish between moving his bowels and urinating, and easily finds pleasure in touching his genitals.

The little girl cannot so easily see her genitals and is less likely to explore the region, especially inside her vagina. The fact that she remains seated both to urinate and defecate may add to her confusion about her organs' functions. In fact, many three-year-old girls have the distinct fantasy of there being only one opening through which everything passes (urine, feces, and a baby) although sometimes they think the baby comes out the stomach. Parents may contribute to such anatomical and functional confusion by naming the vagina for the urinary function (a "wee-wee"). Or they may simply designate the girls' genital area as being "down there," or tell her that it's *all* her "bottom" (which is where "business" comes from). This global designation of the entire area may come to mean for the little girl that one organ contains a vagina, rectum, urethra, and a clitoris, that everything (urine, feces, babies) come from this opening.

This can cause a girl to develop vague ideas about her genital anatomy. The toddler who was told that her vagina was a variation of her buttocks (called a little heiny), was only vaguely aware of the differences between her vagina and her rectum until she was in her preteen years. In fact, as a grown woman, she was overly concerned with fears that her vaginal area was "dirty" and foul-smelling, since she had transferred her notions of rectal functioning onto her vagina. The point is that making clear, unembarrassed distinctions between the rectum and the vagina, between where urine or feces or babies come from, will help your little girl gain a clearer idea of herself and her body.

Your toddler defines himself by his body, and by the things he owns (which can be an extension of himself). Self-definition at this age also comes from the arduous process of the child's separating from you and by his achieving competency at a variety of daily tasks such as using eating utensils, playing, climbing up stairs, and other activities that involve using the body in a competent and goal-directed way.

Self-awareness and self-definition also evolve from your child's perception of how you regard him. You can make your feelings obvious by praising him for his accomplishments: using a spoon, drinking from a cup, or successfully negotiating a flight of stairs. Feel free to use words and phrases that indicate your proud awareness of your child's accomplishments. "You're such a big boy, now"; "Aren't you a big girl, just like Mommy?"; "We're so proud of you"; "We're happy that you can be so grown-up," all said with smiles and warm and encouraging tones and gestures, will make your child feel proud of himself and very much loved and appreciated. Equally important is the more enduring quality of tender affection you consistently convey to your child, no matter what happens at any given moment. When a toddler is loved, he or she knows it, even though you may occasionally scold or be upset with the child. On the other hand, the child who feels continuously rejected, or who is made to feel unwanted or unimportant, will feel little self-satisfaction, even when he is occasionally praised.

Your Toddler's Speech

Although the beginnings of speech occur at the end of the first year, most children do not speak well until they are about two years old. Before then, there has been infant babbling and the baby has developed receptive language: the child understands what is being said before actually using words. (See in Chapter 1, "The Beginnings of Language.") The first "word" a child utters is often a sound derived from early babbling: "ma-ma" or "da-da," which comes to signify the person(s) closest to the baby.

The toddler not only understands certain language but actually begins using words. Your child's early language is limited mostly to the naming of objects. There is no continuity of phrases, no understanding or verbalization of abstract concepts, and very little linguistic complexity. Instead, the child learns to associate a particular object with a sound, which is repeatedly reinforced by his parents or caretaker.

When you hand your toddler a cookie and say "Cookie," it won't take him long to make the connection between the object in his hand and the sound you have spoken. When he repeats the word "cookie," you will undoubtedly smile with delight. You use positive reinforcement to help your child learn his earliest words and phrases. It is largely through the mother (or mothering figures) that your child's language begins and expands.

Your toddler's early one-word utterances usually compress an entire sentence (or thought) into a single word. "Up" means, "I want to be picked up." "Car" means, "I want to go to the car." "Mommy," spoken while the toddler points to a pocketbook, means, "This is Mommy's pocketbook." Children learn certain key words quite early: "hot," "up," "out," "more," and others that become "loaded" with special meanings for them.

At this time, your child's quest for new words is insatiable, and he seems absolutely intent upon compiling a vast catalog of names as he trots around the house labeling everything in sight. He may name something with a definitive tone of finality, such as "Dog!" and then smile at you. Or he may say "Dog?" while gazing inquisitively, as though asking you to confirm that his label is correct. It is natural and easy to provide the necessary reinforcement—a nod and a smile—to help the child acquire an expanding vocabulary.

He will soon progress beyond one-word sentences, beginning to speak a gibberish that is interlaced with actual words. The entire production, on the verge of being comprehensible, mimics the sounds, cadences, and tones of adult speech. The practiced listener will decipher, from the context and from the interspersed real words, just what the child is saying. You will learn to decipher your child's gibberish and to provide the toddler with crucial building blocks for language development.

Once your toddler has a basic stock of words, her vocabulary grows at an incredible rate, and soon words are joined into two-word phrases. "Rachel, lunch" may refer to a number of ideas, depending on the context in which this communication is used. This may mean that Rachel wants her lunch, that she is eating her lunch, or that she has finished eating lunch. Though primitive, two-word phrases express a variety of things—activities, wishes, thoughts, feelings—and can, in their way, describe a variety of situations.

Your toddler's sentences will increase in length over the next few months. Sentences may have little regard for standard word forms or order, and the grammatical features of your child's speech may be simply awful. Pronouns may be incorrect; words may be spoken out of order or transposed; tenses may be wrong; and plurals will sometimes sound delightfully funny. In short, all the rules will be broken, but your toddler will effectively make known most of his wishes, needs, thoughts, and feelings, and be well on the way to mastering the art of human communication.

Joshua, a robust twenty-one-month-old toddler, was visiting his grandmother, who owned a small dog named Bosco. Fascinated, Joshua ran to Bosco, wanting to play. The dog, however, was startled by the child's sudden (and noisy) approach, and let out a warning bark. Joshua's enthusiasm turned suddenly to fear, and for some hours he kept repeating the phrase "Bite *you?*"

Although his use of pronouns was incorrect, everyone knew that Joshua was asking, "Will the dog bite *me?*" While poor Bosco never bit Joshua, he kept a healthy distance from the exuberant toddler, who busied himself emptying out Grandma's linen closet.

Over the course of about one year, your child acquires a sizable vocabulary and begins combining words to express a variety of ideas. And this occurs with very little help from anyone. Your child will sometimes ask for the names of things, but he learns most words simply by listening to people talk. Bear in mind that many words do not name actual objects (such as "chair" or "table"); rather, they apply to concepts such as "like," "remember," or "know," abstractions that cannot be seen or touched. Other words apply to actions, such as "go," "leave," or "come here." There are words for direction, temperatures, and feelings, and many others more complex than the names of concrete objects. Your child eventually learns them all.

As your child progresses in language development, he adopts the standard sentence patterns and constructions heard throughout his daily life. He develops a sense of the constructions that sound and feel right to him, given his family, neighborhood, and culture.

Your child learns language by hearing it spoken in a meaningful context of objects, situations, places, relationships, and feelings. Learning the rules for construction, syntax, and grammar, he also extracts from what he hears, tones of voice and various emotional nuances: anger, disdain, sarcasm, sympathy, humor, disbelief, doubt, annoyance, and a wide range of subtle (and not-so-subtle) indicators of human feelings. He will also learn to echo mannerisms and affectations of speech, much to the embarrassment of many a parent who sees himself reflected in a toddler's exaggerated turn of phrase. And your child may demonstrate an uncanny knack for the appropriate (though uncomprehending) use of expletives and curse words!

Language codifies and organizes an entire world of experience for the child, solidifying whatever he's already learned while creating new opportunities for intellectual and emotional growth. Acquiring the capacity to communicate, first with mother, then with other family members, and finally with the rest of the world, is a vital step in your child's increasing independence. (For more about speech and language, see "Influence of Speech Problems," "Hardly Speaks," and "Reading to a Child," later in this chapter.)

The Toddler's Mind

From the point of about one year until eighteen months, the toddler engages in purposeful trial-and-error explorations of everything. The child learns that one thing can lead to another or can be a purposeful means to obtaining something else. For instance, a child may reach from his playpen toward a toy truck but not be able to reach it. After a while, instead of crying for mother, he may learn that he can retrieve the truck by pulling at the rug on which it is resting.

By two years of age, your child has the ability to represent things through symbols. The foremost demonstration of this capacity is your toddler's expanding use of language. Another is the appearance of symbolic play. A child may pick up the telephone and begin talking as though carrying on a conversation. She may pretend to wash her hands with an imaginary bar of soap, or pretend that she is a dog, scrambling about on her hands and knees while making barking sounds.

A major intellectual achievement by the age of two years is the acquiring of complete object permanence; that is, the toddler now realizes that something exists even though it may not be present at a given moment. Despite this well-developed capacity, your two-year-old may not yet appreciate that one object cannot be in two places at the same time.

While walking on the street with her mother, two-year-old Melissa noticed a woman whose ski jacket was the same color and design as her mother's. Visibly upset, Melissa pointed at the other woman and cried, "Mommy's coat!" and then burst into tears, thinking the woman had taken her mother's jacket. She seemed oblivious of the fact that her mother was wearing the very ski jacket that the other woman had "stolen."

Between two and three years of age, your child's verbal abilities expand rapidly. She wants to know the name of everything she sees, and those objects whose names she already knows are pointed out with a self-assured satisfaction that shows the delight any young child experiences in mastering the world. Her sentence structure becomes more correct and more complex; she employs subjects, objects, and a verb, rather than the two-word phrases she used when she was two years old.

Between two and three years of age, the toddler begins understanding certain abstractions. She knows that "two" shoes are more than "one" shoe; that "three" cookies are more than "two," and she appreciates distinct differences in quantities. She also begins to understand certain time-related words like "day," "night," "now," and later." "Tomorrow" and "soon" take on real meaning, indicating her increased ability to conceptualize and tolerate reasonable delays. She may parrot your "Not now," "In a minute," or "Soon," and at some point, it becomes clear that she understands these somewhat abstract concepts.

Another important language development is your child's capacity to use pronouns properly. By the age of three, she speaks about "I," "you," "he," "she," "we," and "they," clearly showing that she now makes distinctions between herself and others, as well as appreciating differences between people.

A toddler knows how to make a great many things happen. He can make faucets work, turn light switches on and off, switch on the stereo, television, and VCR, adjust the television's volume or picture, and is generally aware of cause-and-effect relationships in a variety of practical situations.

The toddler knows the house and backyard, and is very aware of many familiar regions. He knows the locations of various household items, the layout of the house or apartment, the backyard and how to get there, knows the way to a friend's street or to Grandma's house. Although he can navigate to and from specific (familiar) locations, the child has very little idea of how these areas are related to each other in a coherent, unified whole, and his orientation can be somewhat tenuous. He can get from one place to another, providing he's taken a certain route before, but has trouble inventing an alternate route, and will get lost if he deviates even slightly from a customary path. This is easily seen in a grocery store where the child may have a certain familiarity with the aisles and shelves, having been there many times before. He may even ask for a specific location, the "cookies" or "desserts," and eagerly anticipates a favorite treat (whose package he will instantly recognize). Despite his knowledge of the store, should he wander down a different aisle and lose sight of his mother, he quickly becomes disoriented and panic-stricken.

Your child may call her grandmother "Nana" or her grandfather "Pop Pop," but she has no real appreciation of the relationships that bind members of the family. She cannot fathom that "Nana" is your parent; she can't conceive of your even *having* a father or mother. Nor can she appreciate that your sister and you share the same parents. Although she has a powerful appreciation that close people (within the family) have special bonds to one another and form a distinct group, she has no real understanding of kinship terms and their meanings. Only when she nears five or six years will she make some sense of terms like "grandmother" and "grandfather," "aunt" and "uncle," "brother" and "sister," or "cousin," truly understanding the biological, social, and emotional ties that these people have with each other. Until then, words like "grandpa" are mere labels affixed to certain close people.

Approaching three years of age, the child begins categorizing everything. Each object or person he sees must have a name and belong to some group. It must fit into a whole, be categorized as shorter or taller in comparison to something else. It must be bigger or smaller, this way or that, red or green, dark-haired or light-haired—the comparisons and compartmentalizations are endless. The three-year-old is structuring, ordering, and systematizing his expanding world. All this is vividly reflected in his rapidly enlarging vocabulary and his increasingly sophisticated use of language.

Though his capacities are growing, the three-year-old has important intellectual limitations. At this age, a child is impressed by something that is visible and tangible; he has little sophistication in making subtle judgments about the relationships between things. For instance, you may show a three-year-old a tall, narrow container that holds a pint of liquid. If you then show him another that is shorter but wider, having more volume (it holds one quart) and ask the child which container holds more water, he will choose the taller one. He cannot yet grasp the concept that volume is determined by *both* height and width. To his one-dimensional way of thinking, taller means more.

And the child's sense of certainty about himself is still tenuous. For instance, a three-year-old girl knows that her name is Helen; the name Helen defines her. If you tease her by saying "You're not Helen, I'm

Helen," she will become anxious and insist that *she* is Helen, not you. Her entire sense of herself is challenged by your assertion that you are who she thinks *she* is. By challenging her name, you unwittingly challenge her sense of herself and her very identity.

Play and Activities

Much of your toddler's daily life is taken up by activities we generally call play. This is serious business for the child, helping him get to know the world. A distinctive feature of a two-year-old's play is that it has no real goal other than the pleasure derived from the play itself. The young toddler is happy banging two pots together, shredding paper towels and stuffing them into a box, turning the handle of a coffee grinder, or performing any other manipulative and repetitive activity. The child is not oriented toward achievement and doesn't need to see a final product or end result of his play. He will readily abandon one activity for another, not feeling that the first project is "incomplete" or requires more attention. The toddler is satisfied with merely mastering and perfecting a variety of skills.

When young toddlers play near each other, they may be virtually unaware of each other's existence. Wrapped in his own concerns, the child busily pushes a truck, bangs a peg into a board, or scoops sand into a pail, having no real interaction with the other child. In other words, there is a minimum amount of socialization between young toddlers.

The toddler loves virtually any activity. In a park or nursery-school playground, she loves to ride on a swing, bounce up and down on a seesaw, dig in a sandbox, attempt using jungle gyms and sliding boards, wheel about on a tricycle, and play at anything involving exuberant body movement. Adults are often amazed at the boundless energy of toddlers: the typical child is described as tirelessly moving everywhere and getting into everything. While this is often true, toddlers have their quiet moments, too. Your child may love gazing at picture books or listening to music, and may watch television with rapt attention. Parents are often awed by the ease with which a two-year-old can memorize a variety of television commercials, and they are amazed at the skill with which she can recall specific songs on a record album.

Between eighteen and twenty-four months, the young toddler will begin playing out ordinary scenes from household life. Such dramatic play indicates that your child is now capable of symbolic thinking and can represent one object or action by another. A child may play with dolls at this age, feeding them, scolding, cleaning and rocking them, reenacting various scenes from everyday life. He may invent scenes, too, usually modeled on what has been seen, pretend to talk on the telephone (don't be surprised to see and hear a caricatural version of yourself), pour coffee into a cup, shave the face (girls do this, too), and engage in other activities that indicate that he hears and sees much more than you ever thought.

Some games from infancy will remain part of your toddler's repertoire: Peekaboo, Hide-and-Seek, and other individual favorites. Your child will also enjoy snuggling up to you with a book and will especially enjoy hearing a favorite story (over and over again). Lap-sitting is a favorite toddler pastime.

At about three years of age, your child may join one or two others in joint play, where the children cooperate in a game or project. As children age, the play becomes more goal-oriented, moving from a beginning, through a middle, to an end. They may play school or build a sand castle, and there will be varying degrees of cooperation at different points. Even though tentative at first, this kind of social play indicates a growing awareness of others, and an increasing ability to socialize and play with other children.

Kids This Age Can Be Awful Liars

Along with social behavior, your child develops an increasingly rich fantasy life. As language and the child's capacity to conceptualize develop, she enjoys using these new abilities. The child begins daydreaming (fantasizing), making things up in her mind that she cannot do in reality. The child's inner world becomes a richer and more exciting place as fantasy provides outlets for feelings and wishes that cannot be gratified in reality. A three-year-old can easily slip over the line between fantasy and reality, and does so virtually every day.

A child of three may suddenly seem to be an awful liar. Constantly fabricating stories, she tells tales about where she went and what she saw while she was in some special (nonexistent) place. Or she may tell an obvious lie: someone else (a friend, or an imaginary companion) spilled the glass of milk. Most of these tall tales are ridiculously transparent, involving elements that make parents want to laugh, but they can sometimes be worrisome.

A toddler this age can believe that his parents are omniscient, that they see and know everything, including what he thinks and feels. But he isn't really certain, and a well-timed, outrageous fabrication can be your child's way of testing to see if you really know the truth. He's not lying with the intent of duping you. Nor is he necessarily trying to cover up a misdeed, even if he denies that he spilled the milk and accuses a friend (who isn't even present) of having done it. He's merely testing your powers of observation and your parental perceptions.

There's no sense in becoming righteously indignant at all these "lies." They're the child's way of testing how much you do and don't know, and they're a result of his still not having completely defined himself as a separate person from you. After all, if you know what he's thinking, then the lines that separate you from your child are somewhat blurred. You don't have to pretend to accept these outrageous fabrications. Instead, you can joke about them, saying something like, "Uh-oh, Paul's telling us another one of his imaginary stories again." Coupled with a sly smile and a hug, this kind of response will be immensely reassuring to your toddler.

An Imaginary Companion

For some children, imaginary play and fantasy take on a specific form, one that can sometimes be troubling to parents. Your child may invent an imaginary companion who accompanies him everywhere. As many as 50 percent of three-year-olds and slightly older preschoolers have imaginary companions, a perfectly normal phenomenon at such a time.

The companion may be human or animal, or a toy that the child treats as though it's alive. This playmate may live in your child's mind with extraordinary vividness, and you may find yourself indulgently setting an extra place at the table for this omnipresent friend.

The imaginary companion may serve as a ready-made playmate for a lonely child (firstborn children have many more imaginary companions than other children). Or the companion may become a model or a scapegoat for a child who wishes to blame any misdeed on the hapless friend. If juice is spilled, this friend is the culprit; should an expensive cut-glass vase break, the imaginary friend is at fault. This companion, existing only in your child's mind, may become a figure onto whom all your child's unacceptable feelings, thoughts, and actions are projected, and the child may try to deflect any possible criticism from himself onto this friend. An imaginary companion can take on any form and can serve many useful purposes for your child.

Philip, an exuberant three-year-old, was briefly hospitalized for a hernia repair. His mother remained with him during the hospital stay, and brought his favorite toy, a stuffed bear named Teddy. All went well, and some days later Philip returned home, having had the operation.

But something had changed; Philip now called Teddy Stitches, and the cuddlesome animal accompanied Philip everywhere. Stitches sat with Philip at the dinner table, shared his food, went to bed with him, and was a faithful companion, taking on a wide range of imaginary qualities. In addition, each night before going to bed, Philip tended to Stitches's groin area, removing the bear's imaginary sutures and comforting his little friend.

It was very clear to Philip's parents that Stitches was a convenient way for their three-year-old to playact his recent hospital experience, and that Philip's relationship with Stitches helped him deal with the anxiety evoked by his surgery and hospital stay.

Whether or not your child's imaginary companions serve as useful a purpose as Philip's did, they are an exercise in your child's use of his expanding capacity for fantasy. It makes little sense to try to "convince" your child that the companion doesn't exist. Above all, don't be critical of your toddler and don't react to his outrageous tales as though he's willfully lying or malevolently contriving to dupe you. It's best to maintain a sense of humor about these "companions," even though that they will occasionally be used by your child as a way of saying things that would otherwise be unacceptable. (See in Chapter 3, "Uses Bad Language" and "Impolite 'Playmate.'") Imaginary companions may stay on the scene for weeks or months, or they may arrive, do whatever they do, and then quickly disappear. They may run away, die in a plane crash, or simply fade away. This is a normal part of your child's fantasy life at this age, and may continue well into the preschool years.

Boys and Girls Together: The Differences Between the Sexes

By the end of toddlerhood, sharply defined differences in temperaments, interests, and play patterns exist between boys and girls. Experiences from the moment of birth on contribute to these marked and meaningful differences. The first question parents often ask the obstetrician is, "Is it a boy or a girl?" Before then, the baby was an ambiguous being, neither a "he" nor a "she." Once you know your child's sex, an entire constellation of thoughts, feelings, and attitudes about the baby comes to the fore, and your infant's role in life begins taking shape.

How are ideas about masculinity and femininity transmitted to an infant who barely knows it exists, let alone that it has physical characteristics that forever make it a boy or a girl? While obvious and important biological differences exist, these endowments are not the only factors entering into the baby's eventual ideas about being a boy or girl? These basic dispositions are in large part transmitted by parents to their child.

They are packaged as sets of expectations, feelings, and attitudes, about which the child slowly becomes aware. As a parent, you treat your baby girl differently than your boy because you've acquired from your own parents and from the culture at large a gender-related value system, including various expectations and behaviors that encourage a boy or girl to behave one way or another.

Most of us have stereotyped ways of thinking about things as either masculine or feminine. While a baby boy seems inherently (biologically) more aggressive than a girl, other vitally important elements come into play. From the very beginning, a little boy is picked up and handled differently (more roughly) than is a little girl. Most parents handle a girl more gently and protectively, which will eventually encourage more subdued, "girlish" behavior. Studies indicate that mothers' voices are remarkably different when babbling or talking to a little boy than to a girl. Interestingly, animal studies show that mother monkeys behave differently with their male infants than with female infants.

From the outset, early caretakers respond to the baby's gender. Without being aware of it, you express your expectations of a baby through the ways you talk with and handle your child, in the manner and colors in which you clothe the baby, and through the kinds of toys you provide and toward which you direct the child's attention, shaping or reinforcing his or her interests.

Parents enmesh a child in a complicated social and emotional environment, which eventually begins dictating how the child thinks, feels, and responds. They unwittingly direct the child into a certain sex role, reacting delightedly to "sex-appropriate" behaviors, while expressing clear dissatisfaction when a child behaves "inappropriately." For instance, a father may smile with delight when his three-year-old son begins climbing a chain-link fence but will rush to rescue his three-year-old daughter when she does the same, for fear that she may be harmed. Both boy and girl notice their parents' reactions and begin to internalize them.

Children of eighteen months (and even younger) already identify themselves as boys or girls. While they may not have any notions about or interest in genital differences, they are developing very clear pictures of what is masculine and what is feminine. Your two-year-old knows that one playmate is a "girl" and that another is a "boy," even without an anatomical inspection. Your child has already formed what is called a core gender identity.

Much early patterning is based on very evident sex-bound roles, behaviors, and expectations. If father works all day while mother stays home caring for (and disciplining) the children, a child's view of masculinity and femininity is bound to be affected. This evolving sense of one's self as a boy or a girl will be experienced in terms of how the parents are perceived. Your child models himself or herself on the significant people of early life in the home. Today, with more mothers working than ever before, some role distinctions may not be so clear-cut as was once the case. Changing cultural patterns of parenting may eventually affect children's emerging attitudes about female and male roles.

On the other hand, it is clear that a child increasingly chooses to imitate and play the role of the parent of the same sex. Father drives a car, so the little boy plays with cars and toy trucks. If mother is the primary caretaker, a little girl eventually plays with dolls. If mother is a physician, the girl may play with a stethoscope.

Whether this identity is boy-truck or girl-doll, the important thing is for your child to identify with other people of the same sex. If you are a single parent with a child of the opposite sex (for instance, a mother with a young boy) your child still has ample opportunity to identify with members of the opposite sex. Male figures with whom your child can identify include close relatives such as uncles, a grandfather, and the child's father (who visits him regularly). He will also be influenced by cultural expectations as indicated by the media and people with whom your child has contact. Self-definition and an emerging separate identity are the major concerns of toddlerhood, and at three years of age this issue can have enormous meanings to your child. If you say to a three year old girl, "You're not a girl; you're a boy," she will become visibly upset and vehemently insist that she is a girl.

Anatomical and biological differences are just one factor involved in boys and girls differentiating themselves from each other. Some people believe that "anatomy is destiny," while others believe that a child's gender identity is completely determined by society and the child's identification with parental attitudes. Something can be said for each position, but neither alone is completely correct. We know that a child's genetic endowment is a crucial component. But we also know that family and societal factors can have an enormous influence on a child's sense of being either a boy or a girl, sometimes even overriding biology. In certain rare circumstances, children have learned to experience themselves in a sex role that completely contradicts their biological endowment.

Although attitudes may slowly be changing, boys are still treated like "boys" and girls like "girls." These differences may not be very great during infancy, when both boy and girl babies are given stuffed toys or cuddlesome dolls as comfort devices. But certain distinctions between the sexes become more pronounced during toddlerhood. By the time he is a toddler, a boy may be told, "Boys don't cry," or he may be told not to be "sissyish." A girl who acts aggressively may be told, "Nice girls don't do that! Act like a little lady."

When a little girl wants to play baseball, she may receive a bemused smile of tolerance from her parents but is rarely encouraged to follow through. A boy however is exhorted to participate and compete vigorously, at some point even defining himself (partly) by how well he plays. Should a boy older than three years of age express interest in dolls or carriages, he may be shamed for playing with "girls' things," or for "acting like a sissy." Interestingly, parents always seem more concerned about a boy's masculinity being affected by "feminine" influences than about a girl's masculine interests eroding her femininity. A tomboy is usually more acceptable to parents than a "sissy." It seems that mothers and fathers alike consider masculinity something that is quite fragile (it isn't), something easily undermined by as simple a thing as a doll.

Today, many parents are concerned not so much with a child being encouraged to assume a specific sex role, but with the way a given sex role is defined. Such parents are concerned that a child may be directed into or away from certain traditionally sex-bound interests, even though these activities are not necessarily "male" or "female." Parents worry that a child's options may be narrowed to those interests or careers arbitrarily deemed appropriate for a boy or girl. They also worry that a child may develop certain lifelong attitudes that narrow his or her opportunities to experience the world. Roles today are far more flexible than they were some years ago. Girls can become astronauts and physicians, boys can become airline attendants, and career choices in general are no longer as sex-bound as they once were. A child of either sex is best off being encouraged to play with various kinds of toys (dolls and trucks) and should be allowed to participate in games of all kinds, regardless of their traditional associations with one sex or another.

It's important to avoid telling a small boy that any display of emotions is "sissyish" or inappropriate. Boys as well as girls have feelings, and it's healthy to show them, whether they're feelings of affection, sadness, or other universal human emotions. Similarly, a small girl should not be discouraged from exhibiting "aggression" or assertiveness; she should not be told that such displays are not the ways "a nice girl" reacts. Rather, she should be encouraged to show a wide range of thoughts and feelings even if they are occasionally accompanied by anger or "aggression." Your little girl should learn early in her life just as the little boy does that competition and self-assertion are important components of effective functioning as a person.

Boys and girls are best off when provided with opportunities in every possible direction. In the long run, only a woman can be a mother and breast-feed a child, and only a man can father a child. Biology and gender, though influenced by the family and the culture, seem somehow largely to take care of themselves.

◊ PRACTICAL ISSUES FOR THE TODDLER

A variety of practical issues and problems may arise during the toddler years. These usually involve the major developmental themes of this period, such as setting limits, discipline, temper tantrums, toilet training, and other issues involving a child's evolving sense of autonomy. This section explores them, providing specific advice about handling them.

Discipline

Discipline is necessary during any phase of a child's development. Discipline means necessary control; it's not the same thing as punishment. While each developmental phase calls for a different kind of discipline, certain general principles apply, whether dealing with a toddler, a preschooler, or a school-age child:

- Use sensible timing when teaching controls to your child. A child who is not physically or mentally ready to deal with your wish that he control certain behaviors cannot comply with your wishes. For instance, because a child of seven months cannot control his bowel functions, it makes no sense to begin toilet training.
- When teaching your child some new behavior (or prompting her to control herself), do so gradually. Avoid an abrupt transition from one situation or expectation to another. And don't expect immediate results. A child needs time to make necessary adjustments. For instance, expect toilet training to take weeks, even months. Gradual progress will be punctuated by occasional setbacks, part of your child's attempt to master new situations and sets of demands.

  Most children will cooperate if they are introduced to something new with reasonable patience and sensitivity. Rushing a child can be self-defeating, because it often provokes resistance. Remember, each child has an individual style and tempo that works best for learning and practicing new behaviors.
- When asking your child to do (or not do) something, the best way to get results is to use positive reinforcement. More than anything,

your child wants to be loved and to please you. Using encouragement, smiles, and genuine praise for a desired behavior, instead of scolding, yelling, and hitting for undesired behaviors, is usually the best and most productive method.

- When exercising authority, be firm and act with self-confident decisiveness. Indecision or inconsistency about asserting authority gives a child mixed and confusing messages. Be secure in your belief that you love your child and are doing what you genuinely believe is best.
- Don't preach or moralize. Righteous indignation will get you nowhere with a toddler who doesn't truly understand anything about "badness" or being "naughty." A toddler may try your patience to the limits, and even though you've said no ten times, may still open a bureau drawer and empty it out. Preaching is useless. Firm, gentle control will be more helpful, and far more successful.

As your child grows older and truly learns right from wrong, he or she will do what is right for its own sake. Even then, moralizing is not the best way to get a child to do something. An older child will respond positively to a loving parent who is a good model, who cares enough to set reasonable limits, and who has firm but sensitive expectations of the child.

Setting Limits

Setting limits (restrictions) on your toddler is an important component of your relationship. Restrictions are essential to protect your child, and to protect objects from the potentially destructive reach of a toddler. Sometimes limits are necessary simply to preserve other people's rights.

Your toddler is an eager explorer, an experimenter whose mobility far outstrips his capacity to appreciate danger. He may imprudently pull on a lamp cord or scale a footstool onto a tabletop or kitchen counter. He may naively wave a fork or some other sharp instrument near his eyes. Within one second, the most innocuous activity can become a cause for alarm. One particular danger involves any body of water: ocean, lake, pool, or pond. Toddlers seem unable to appreciate the danger that water poses, and may trot right in. Constant vigilance is imperative at the beach, and near lakes, ponds, and swimming pools.

When you find it necessary to set limits, be gentle but firm. Your child won't understand subtlety and will actually feel most secure knowing exactly what he can and cannot do. Don't be tentative. A well-defined command is far more effective and easier for a toddler to deal with than any attempt to "explain" why he can't carry a crystal glass across the room.

The toddler's mobility and indomitable curiosity may force you to baby-proof your house or apartment. Actually, it's impossible to live with a toddler without some attempts to limit the damage she can do to herself and to household valuables. Baby-proofing basically involves removing fragile or dangerous objects from your child's reach. Some dangerous items are used every day: kitchen knives, utensils, various dishes and other items. These should be grouped together (if possible) and kept out of the child's reach. Once you have limited the number of taboo items or areas you must protect, your house is not mined with forbidden objects, and you avoid having to hurl never-ending noes at your child. However, you still must be vigilant; your toddler may display more ingenuity than you ever imagined possible.

Because of the toddler's unending curiosity and ability to get "into" everything, it's often necessary for parents to take various extra precautions. Electrical outlets may have to be plugged or blocked; favorite knickknacks and antique treasures must be relocated and removed from access, or stored away for a year or longer. Fences or barriers of some kind must often be installed at the heads of stairwells and across doors that lead to potentially dangerous objects or places (such as access to a busy street). Some parents must literally "undecorate" their homes during their child's phase of toddlerhood.

Your child will quickly learn the objects and areas that are off-limits. This doesn't guarantee that she won't actively pursue a particularly intriguing item: a scissors, favorite classical record, or treasured antique. Prolonged silence from another room may be the first warning of some forbidden exploring that could cause injury or damage.

No matter how well you set limits, your child will occasionally reach for a forbidden item, sometimes right before your eyes. A firm no usually discourages the attempt. If your child again reaches for the item, the no will have to be repeated more sharply. Some parents are concerned that their no may be barked and sound too prohibitive or even threatening, but no harm comes to a child who hears a sharp, resounding "No!"

Keep in mind that your toddler may reach for a taboo item again and again, not so much because she is contrary (although this can occur) but because she may want to test how serious you are about a particular taboo. It's best to remain firm and consistent, forbidding your child to touch or handle something that could cause injury or be damaged. Two ways to deal with such testing (besides repeating no's) are to deflect your child's attention by giving her some permitted toy to replace the forbidden item, or to move the child to another, safer area of the house.

No matter how well you set limits, a certain number of minor cuts, scrapes, and bruises are inevitable by-products of any toddler's explorations. These can sometimes be valuable lessons for the child, provided the injuries are minor. And certain household items will inevitably fall victim to the toddler's curiosity. Try to take these material losses in stride. (See "Difficulty in Setting Limits," later in this chapter.)

Temper Tantrums

In response to certain restrictions, a two- or three-year-old may have a temper tantrum. The one general rule is simple: Don't reinforce a tantrum by giving it more attention than it warrants. If your child learns that he can get whatever he wants by howling, he will howl whenever he wants something badly enough. Once temper tantrums are reinforced as a viable method of achieving satisfaction, they will become part of your child's "currency" for dealing with you. This can be difficult behavior to change or eradicate.

There is only one way to handle a temper tantrum in a public place such as a restaurant: fairness and consideration for others dictate that you quickly remove your child to a private place and spare everyone else. Don't lecture or moralize; simply convey gently but firmly that the display is useless, and do your best to ignore the crying. It will eventually stop.

Toilet Training

Although toilet training should be a normal developmental process, this subject causes many parents a great deal of worry. It's striking that so many parents become concerned about toilet training at an inappropriate time in their child's development: either too early, when the baby is six or seven months old, or quite late, when the child is past three years of age.

Toilet training usually comes at a time when the child's major concerns are a sense of autonomy versus feelings of shame and doubt. These issues can unfortunately become connected to the toilet if training is improperly timed or undertaken. If the child feels you are taking control of his body, he may resist, and a battle of wills can follow. This can bring about negative, contrary behavior, which—whether focused on the toilet or something else—can become part of a child's personality, influencing how he relates to other people later in life. On the other hand, successful toilet training can make a child feel more mature and fosters feelings of competence and self-confidence.

TIMING.   During the first year, your baby has no voluntary control over his bowel movements. Some parents start training during this first year, achieving a kind of reflex conditioning, but this is not cooperation, and the child is not really toilet trained.

After eighteen months, a child begins to be aware of his bowel movements. He first becomes aware that a movement *has* taken place. Then comes an awareness that a movement *is* taking place. At some point (usually around two years), he becomes aware that a bowel movement *is about* to occur. This is when toilet training can be most effectively undertaken; the child has both the physical and emotional capacities to deal with the demands of training. To start earlier risks repeated failures, which can make a child begin to doubt himself.

It's important to recall that despite a two-year-old's contrariness, your approval and praise are powerful rewards to the child. Wanting love and acceptance above all, the child also wants to emulate adult members of the family. At this age, he understands the meanings of praise, is proud of his accomplishment, and has regular bowel movements. As in most developmental matters, your child's physical *and* emotional readiness are essential for a challenge to be mastered.

TRAINING.   When you decide to begin, bring out the potty chair. This device fits over the regular toilet seat or can be placed on the floor. The floor type is preferable because the child can sit on it with her feet securely on the floor. This is reassuring, since many toddlers are fearful of the height of a toilet seat and frightened by the sight and sound of a flushing toilet.

It's a good idea for your child to have some word to refer to her bowel movements (whether "doo-doo" or another), so she can use it as a signal when she recognizes a bowel movement coming. It's also a good idea for her to get used to the potty chair before actually using it to defecate. She can sit on it with her clothes on before she begins training.

When you decide that it's time to start the training, place her on the potty chair as soon as she gives you some signal that a movement is about to occur. Initially, there may be a period when nothing happens. Try keeping her amused, giving her a toy or a book to look at. Be encouraging and optimistic. If she becomes restless and wants to get off the chair, don't force the issue. Let her get off. If she has a bowel movement some minutes later, take it in stride and wait for the next opportunity. Don't make her feel guilty or that she's disappointed you in some way.

During the period of toilet training, it's a good idea for the toddler to feel that the potty seat belongs only to her; a sense of ownership may contribute to her pride in being able to control her bowels. Once training has begun, it's also a good idea to reserve the potty seat for bowel movements only (or a serious attempt); don't allow her to play with the seat or treat it as a plaything. This helps convey to the child your seriousness (though gentle and nonconfronting) about her controlling her bowels.

When she's successful at moving her bowels into the potty chair, give her plenty of praise, telling her how proud of her you feel. Emphasize the fact that she now goes to the toilet like a grown-up. After wiping and cleaning, give her a hug and kiss, making the entire experience a rewarding one for the child.

Don't hurry to empty the potty into the toilet to flush the feces away. Keep in mind that a young child's sense of his body isn't well-defined; he may not completely know where the body begins and ends. A child thinks that feces are actually part of the body and may feel that when he moves his bowels he loses part of himself into the bowl. It can be upsetting for him to see "part" of himself suddenly flushed down the toilet.

A child doesn't view his feces as foul-smelling or disgusting. Such a view is learned from parents. When you coax him to move his bowels at the proper time and place, you are asking your child to give something over to you. The child may actually come to view his feces as a kind of gift to you. If you were a two-year-old who willingly had complied with your mother's urgings to move your bowels, and if your mother applauded, obviously delighted in what you produced for her, but then made a face (of revulsion) and flushed your "gift" away, you would probably be very confused.

Basically, your child has very little interest in being toilet trained. He feels that he is surrendering (or giving up) something to you. To do this, he must feel that he gets something in return. That something is your love and approval, which are vital to his sense of being worthwhile and loved. As with most issues during a child's emotional development, you will get much better results by using your child's wish to be loved than by exploiting a fear of punishment.

Don't punish, chastise, or yell at your child if at first she is unsuccessful at toilet training. Never shame her about the toilet or her body. Rather, be patient, encouraging, and consistent. Above all, exhibit a loving attitude, have fortitude, and let your child know that you will not give up once the process of toilet training has begun. If you do, you may have to start all over again, which will confuse the child.

Very few children can be toilet trained in a few days. A gradual process, toilet training usually takes a few months. If at the outset your child begins making an issue out of training, and the process begins to interfere with her need to feel independent, put it off for a few weeks. When she feels more self-sufficient and confident in herself, there is less possibility that toilet training will become a battle of wills.

Remember, each child is different, and no hard-and-fast rules apply to all children all the time. Most children are trained by the time they are two and a half, but some toddlers have a bit of difficulty, and may not be trained until the age of three years. Don't feel guilty, and above all, don't make your child feel guilt or shame about it. It makes no sense to feel that either you or your child has "failed" in this milestone. The rate at which your child becomes toilet trained is neither a reflection of your skills as a parent nor an indication of your child's "willfulness" or "badness." It may simply reflect a rhythm or tempo that works best for you and your toddler.

When you've had some success with training, you may want to take your child out of diapers and put him in daytime training pants. Help him feel proud to be taken out of diapers, and let him know how happy you are about this achievement. Use encouraging phrases such as "Now you're like Mommy and Daddy," or "Now you wear clothes just like a grown-up. You don't have to wear diapers."

SOME TOILET-TRAINING DIFFERENCES BETWEEN BOYS AND GIRLS.   Differences between boys and girls can make for different styles, patterns, and rates of mastery and development. This can be especially true with toilet training. A girl's nervous system tends to mature earlier than a boy's. The girl is more able to control her sphincter at an earlier age than a boy. She may find it easier to recognize the signal of her own internal stirrings, make her needs known, and even be more willing to let her pants down for the potty than a boy. In addition, a boy is usually more active than the girl, and you may find yourself in general saying no more often to a boy than to a girl. At this age, a boy tends to have more conflicts with his mother than does a girl. With the boy, the stage may be set for a certain amount of built-in resentment and defiance to center on the toilet.

When you train your daughter to use the toilet, she remains seated for urination and to move her bowels. Young boys are usually started the same way, seated, whether for urination or defecation. This may strike the boy as strange because he sees his father urinate while standing. This can create further conflict for the boy, who may very much want to be like his father. Your boy may resist urinating while seated, and it's best if the father or a familiar adult male is available to teach him how to urinate from a standing position.

A girl may want to urinate from the standing position, too, if she has seen her father urinate. She may wish to imitate him, despite explanations about why this will not work. She may have to learn by trial and inevitable error that she is best off urinating from the seated position.

BLADDER TRAINING.   Successful bowel control often results in some control of urination as well. It may not be necessary to do much about bladder training, and often a child can control his urine soon after he has learned to control bowel movements. With a little girl, be prepared for some resistance to urinating while seated, if she has seen a brother or her father urinate in a standing position. Sad, wet experience will teach her that she must sit to urinate.

Again, boys may be quite a bit slower than girls in establishing control over their urine. As may happen with bowel training, accidents occur until the child is three years old. Nighttime bladder control usually follows daytime control after a delay of several months. If your child's nighttime control is taking very long, after he's achieved bowel and daytime bladder control, you can awaken the child before you go to bed and let him urinate in the toilet. Full nighttime control is achieved sooner or later. Time usually takes care of any minor problem.

An important point to remember is that even a very well-trained child will have an occasional lapse of bladder control. During the day the child may become too excited by a game to notice the warning signals of urination. Or he may simply put off going to the toilet because of involvement in an activity. This shouldn't become a major issue or something about which the child is made to feel ashamed. Nighttime bladder control may be lost when a child is ill, or if a situation of special importance arises. Any situation of excitement, tension, or unusual stress may cause a temporary loss of nighttime control. Even an older child may revert to bedwetting under severe stress.

When a New Baby Arrives

Toddlerhood is a time when a child may have to deal with the arrival of a new brother or sister. This can pose problems for any child, but especially for a firstborn one, who may suddenly feel his position usurped by the new arrival.

You can forestall or minimize your toddler's jealousy toward the new baby. If the child is old enough, perhaps two and a half, you can tell him in advance that a baby is coming, so it isn't a complete surprise. A toddler can be made to feel that, as part of the family, he has a share in making preparations for the newcomer. In this way, the new baby belongs to the child as well as to the parents. In telling your toddler about the baby who will soon arrive, it's best not to convey the notion that everything will be different or that there will be major changes when the new arrival comes. But no matter what you do, it's doubtful that you can completely prevent your child from becoming jealous of the intruder.

Judy was twenty-eight months old when her parents told her that a new baby would be arriving. Judy was excited by the prospect, and the family frequently talked about the baby and how things would be when it came. Interested in her incipient sibling, Judy was nearing three years when a baby boy arrived.

Her parents felt gratified by Judy's response to her little brother. She showed an avid interest in him, asked questions about him, and wanted to help with the baby's care. Her parents felt that their telling Judy in advance about the baby had been wise, since Judy had time to adjust and had accepted her baby brother.

Three weeks after her brother's arrival, Judy turned quizzically to her mother and asked, "Isn't it time to send him back to the hospital?"

Toddlers may show jealousy in any of several ways. Some may actually try to injure the new arrival, which of course cannot be permitted. Such a child must be restrained and told that this is not allowed. This is a matter of discipline, with limits being set about permissible and impermissible behavior. If it becomes necessary to discipline in this way, avoid moralizing to your child; don't treat him as though he's "bad" or "wicked" because of his jealous wishes. Keep in mind that the toddler is fearful of being displaced and of losing your love. There will be times when the new baby will require the lion's share of attention (such as when he is ill or colicky), and your toddler may indeed feel like a second-class citizen. This may heighten her jealous feelings about the baby. Instead of actually trying to harm the baby, she may express obvious wishes about getting rid of the newcomer: flushing it down the toilet, throwing it away, taking it back to the hospital, or giving it away.

Your toddler may show her jealous wishes for more attention by regression, that is, by returning to infantile ways of behaving. She may uncharacteristically cry at imagined slights or whine as a way of getting things. She may become clingingly dependent, no longer being able to do things she could, only weeks earlier, easily do for herself. She may want you to undress her at bedtime, or put her to bed and sing to her, or she may want to sleep in your bed each night. Her speech may suddenly become more babyish, in rare instances disappearing for a short time. She may begin to stammer or develop tics. She may sulk or have temper tantrums at the slightest provocation or may lose bladder control. All this behavior indicates that she feels (or fears) being left out, or that she's worried about losing your affection. She has concluded that the only way to ensure getting her share of attention is to be as babyish as the interloper.

If your child shows these signs of regression, there are a few simple measures to take. First, don't try to "shame" her into acting more like a grown-up; this will only worsen matters by feeding into the issue of self-sufficiency versus shame and doubt. It's best to give her extra attention, making her feel special and making sure she knows that you love her as much as before.

Equally important, gently tell her that it's safe for her to act her age, that you love her as much as ever, and that part of the reason you love her is precisely because she *is* bigger, older, and more mature than the new baby. This will help foster pride in herself, and will allay her concern that she has become (or will become) a second-class citizen, especially if before the baby's arrival she was the only child.

Jealousy and rivalry may intensify if a toddler feels that the new baby's arrival has compromised your love for her. If this happens, the child may feel she can regain your love only by fighting, by regressing, or by doing everything possible to get back whatever she feels she has lost. The best way to avoid or minimize this reaction is to help your child feel that she's lost nothing with the arrival of the new baby. (For a more complete discussion of sibling relations and problems, see Chapter 5, *Sibling Rivalry.*)

Eating Problems

Problems with feeding may occur during the toddler years and are one of the primary reasons why mothers consult pediatricians about their two-and three-year-old children.

Eating can become the main arena in which the struggle for mastery and independence takes place. A child may learn that eating (or not eating) is a powerful tool in any battle, especially one in which he is trying to assert his independence. He can refuse his food, turn his head away, refuse to open his mouth, play with his food, or even vomit it up if he's been forced to eat. Fussing or dawdling with food can quickly get mother's attention if a child feels neglected or insufficiently loved. Dawdling over food can be the most powerful (and maddening, for parents) way in which a child makes feeding a struggle.

Assuming that a child is reasonably hungry, he quickly learns that food must be eaten if dawdling with it results in its being taken away. It's best to let the child's food remain on the table until everyone else has finished eating. You must use good judgment here; mealtime is usually a social occasion for both parents and child, and it's unreasonable to expect your toddler to eat without some playfulness or delay at the table. The point is that you can prevent food from becoming too much of a plaything or a vehicle by which a child expresses his dissatisfaction.

Dawdling is not the only table issue that can trouble parents. Your toddler may suddenly "not be hungry" for a day, or even longer. He or she may suddenly begin eating very lightly for a day or two, or longer, and this may arouse some concern that the child has a cold or flu, which in fact may be the case. At other times, for reasons having to do with anger, annoyance, spite, or other feelings, a child may be conveying messages by poor eating, dawdling, or simply refusing food.

Some children are characteristically "picky" eaters; others may have consistently robust appetites, enjoying most foods they are served. Again, temperamental differences between children become obvious in many areas; one of them concerns food and the willingness to explore new tastes and eat most foods. Nearly every child of any age has some food favorites, and most children demonstrate "quirky" preferences for particular foods. Unless a child's preferences or tendency to reject foods place the child in jeopardy of being undernourished, such preferences and peculiarities are not a cause for alarm.

If your child refuses to eat or delays eating, you may find it useful to make the act of eating a positive and interactive one, rather than scolding or expressing your displeasure. This can be done with simple games such as the time-honored "airplane going into the hangar" or the "train entering the tunnel," which have been successfully used by parents for years. The one danger is that such playful interaction may become the mealtime rule, and a cunning child may soon learn that mealtime becomes a period when he appropriates all parental attention. Most parents find that such indulgences have no untoward effects when they're provided sensibly and don't become the major vehicle of mealtime interchanges.

Keep in mind the likelihood that a child will not recognize a particular food in all its forms; if your toddler "hates" apples, he may "love" applesauce. The child who refuses boiled or baked potato may eagerly await mashed potatoes. Therefore, it's best to remain flexible in regard to your child's tastes because most foods can be presented in different and virtually unrecognizable forms. It doesn't accomplish anything for a parent to insist that a toddler eat everything exactly as prepared.

Nearly every toddler develops certain favorite foods; such cherished preferences may hold sway for weeks or months only to fade and be replaced by others. Most toddler-age children will, for a while, insist on having a certain food (for instance, tomato) with every meal, no matter what else is served, and will become upset or uncooperative if this specific food is missing. Simply provide that food.

An important point to keep in mind is that the toddler's major struggle is that of autonomy and control. This applies to meals as well, and it's best not to let the family meal become a battleground. Your child's body possesses a certain innate "wisdom" and over time, if left to pick and choose those foods that are appealing, your child will more than likely eat a well-balanced diet. Even if your child insists on having spaghetti and carrots (or any combination of "odd" foods) at almost every meal, it may be wise to accommodate him. Over the course of time he will be well-nourished, despite his seemingly "weird" and unappealing preferences.

The notion of specific mealtimes where everyone gathers around the table is a social concept and is not truly linked to your child's bodily or biologic needs. Your toddler simply may not be hungry at the times you designate as "lunchtime" or "dinnertime" and in some instances it's best to allow your child's appetite to determine when he is fed. By the time your toddler becomes a preschooler, it's likely that he will conform with the family's mealtime social mores.

This all assumes that you haven't allowed food to become a major symbol of love. Some parents mistakenly convey to a child that eating is an expression of love, that a child must eat to show his love. Such a pattern can last for years, and some mothers actually interpret a child's not wanting to eat everything on his plate as an indication of rejection. Such a mother piles food onto a plate (doing this to adults, too) and insists that every last morsel be eaten. This mother is saying, "This food means I love you, and you can show that you love me by eating it all."

Even more troublesome can be the mother who, because of her own emotional needs and insecurities, feeds her child to take care of every discomfort. As mentioned earlier, this is the mother who rarely allows her infant to cry or express needs but who resorts to immediate feeding. Such a child has difficulty learning the true physiological signs of hunger and may barely establish in his mind the relationship between hunger and the act of eating. Rather, food becomes a way of coping with anxieties or with unhappiness. Such a child can grow into an adult who unfortunately thinks that eating is the solution to all of life's problems. (For additional discussions concerning eating problems, see "Food as a Weapon" and "Makes a Mess," later in this chapter. Also see Chapter 14, *The Overweight Child.*)

◊ A CONSULTATION—QUESTIONS AND ANSWERS

Theodore Shapiro, M.D., provides the consultation about toddlers. Dr. Shapiro is a Professor of Psychiatry at Cornell University Medical College, and is the Director of Child and Adolescent Psychiatry at the Payne Whitney Clinic of The New York Hospital.

Influence of Speech Problems

My two-and-a-half-year-old daughter spends lots of time with our neighbor's kids, ages three and five. They both have speech problems; they pronounce words a bit differently than most other children their age. Will this daily exposure affect my child's speech development?

DR. SHAPIRO: In a general sense, children's speech patterns adapt to the larger community. The larger community's local accent supersedes the specific accent of a particular family. For instance, adults who are foreign-born and who speak English with an accent do not raise children who speak with an accent. Rather, the children learn to speak English in a way that's compatible with the larger community.

Your daughter can play with virtually anybody, even children who speak another language, and the dominant manner of speaking in your locale will come through. This would be the case even if someone in your own home had a problem with articulating certain words or sounds; your daughter would learn to speak English in the manner approved by the community at large.

In fact, articulation problems are quite common in childhood. Typical mispronunciations are "wabbit" for rabbit, or "fing" for thing. These common errors of early childhood sometimes become what I call "cutisms." Parents take these unique pronunciations as being cute and rarely correct them, whereas they will correct errors of fact that child makes.

There is no need to worry that your daughter will be adversely influenced by the mispronunciations she hears. Despite the neighbor's kids, her speech will develop normally.

Aggressive Two-Year-Old

Our two-year-old daughter often bulls her way into her four-year-old brother's toys. She's much more aggressive than he is (or was at her age) and our son is a little afraid of her. What can we do?

DR. SHAPIRO: First, you must be aware that children in the same family may be very different. And even if they had similar temperaments, a four-year-old is very different from a two-year-old; a child's developmental stage affects his capacity for socialization. Your two-year-old is less socialized than your four-year-old, and that's quite appropriate. The two-year-old has not yet internalized certain standards of "Don't," "Do not," "I must share," "I must take turns," and so on. These are the issues that nursery schools begin to concentrate on when a child is three or four years old, and these concepts slowly become part of the process of socialization.

You must also consider that your four-year-old may very much feel intruded upon in this situation. In a sense, you must protect your older child from the younger one by creating circumstances in which the younger child's barging in isn't totally disruptive to the older child's play. You must take the time and effort to protect the older one while understanding that the younger child has needs. You can do this by setting up various barriers in your home, such as a gate at the entranceway of a room. You can also distract your daughter when the temptation to bull her way into her brother's toys is very great. Usually, verbal no's won't work very well for a two-year-old, and you must sometimes physically restrain her.

On the other hand, there ought to be some time when your younger child can be with her older brother so he can learn to appreciate the presence of the younger child and learn tolerance as well. This is something of a balancing act, but during all stages of your child's development, you travel a course between too much restriction and too much permission.

A Single Mother Toilet Trains a Boy

I'm a single mother of a two-year-old boy. I'm beginning to toilet train him. Many books suggest letting a boy watch his father, but there's no man in the house. Will this affect my son's toilet training?

DR. SHAPIRO: Many children are brought up by opposite-sexed parents so that imitation of a same-sexed parent is not possible. In general, over the course of time, your son will be sufficiently exposed to men so that he will learn what a man is about, and he will begin to take this into account.

In terms of toilet training, a woman can help her son by showing him the differences between standing and the sitting position for urination. You don't have to personally demonstrate this to him.

Keep in mind that many little boys begin their toileting experience by sitting both to urinate and defecate because these functions are accomplished simultaneously. The boy learns to urinate in the standing position sometime later. This is because of some practical considerations, such as poor aim and the tendency to urinate on the floor. It's also partly because a boy is directed toward bowel training at first, with urinary training coming as a secondary accomplishment. In a general way, your son's toilet training won't be compromised because there's no man in the house.

Because so many children are brought up by single parents these days, some parents do private things, such as toileting, with the door open, not closed. There really is no need for this kind of exposure. Toilet functions should involve some privacy in a household; I think this is ultimately important for the child's socialization.

A Toddler's Growing Independence

Our two-year-old is a typical toddler—into everything and going everywhere. My wife gets very nervous and runs after him, making him stay nearby when he plays. This makes sense up to a point, but I think she goes too far. She seems to be threatened by his growing independence. Can you help us?

DR. SHAPIRO: The two-year-old period can be troublesome in some households and smooth in others. Part of this is due to the way two-year-olds act, and part is due to what their reputation has come to be. In some ways, designations such as the terrible twos and the period of "no" have given two-year-olds a bad reputation. In fact, many parents find this period of a child's life vibrant and delightful because of the freedom with which these children act, as well as their growing awareness of themselves as separate individuals from their parents. For many parents, a child's trials at independent action are rewarding and exciting.

If your wife's concern about your child's activity is centered around practical issues such as your apartment being furnished with antiques, you should rethink your furnishings in terms of the presence of a two-year-old. If her concern is centered around her incapacity or unwillingness to let go of your son, then we are dealing with a question that has major developmental implications. The central question in such an issue is when to let go, how to let go, and how to slowly accomplish the letting go according to your child's capacities and your anxiety about his ability to take care of himself.

In a biological sense, the human infant needs a parent as a buffer, simply to survive. The question of how long such buffering should be extended is one that permeates childhood development. A two-year-old has achieved certain developmental landmarks that permit some independence. He has plenty of mobility and can make clear distinctions between himself and others. He is beginning to speak and has sufficient language to get along in various ways. All these achievements can give the child a foolhardy sense of his capacities while he gradually learns how much and how far he can wander. Kids of this age will often run ahead of their parents, laughing as though they wish to be chased; they may then spin around and dash back to mother, in a kind of emotional refueling.

Central to your concern are the different parental styles of you and your wife. It is possible that you are critical of your wife, for either valid reasons or other, more personal, reasons concerning your own past and feelings about a mother's hovering attitude. Or you may be correct in seeing your wife's behavior as overly anxious and genuinely wish to correct it. The answer to your question must involve a careful weighing of various considerations: What are your individual attitudes as parents? Are they reasonable? What are the child's capacities? And what are the realistic dangers in your child's daily environment?

Hardly Speaks

My eighteen-month-old's speech hasn't really flowered. He points at every-thing, grunts, and says only a few words. His sixteen-month-old cousin is far ahead. Is my son behind in his development?

DR. SHAPIRO: There is a great deal of latitude in the developmental course of children, especially during the early years. The area of language is one in which, while landmarks are generally achieved at about the same time, there is still a fair range of normal distribution.

You may read that a twelve-month-old says "mama" and "dada" and some other words, an eighteen-month-old child may have a vocabu-lary of twenty-five to fifty words, and a two-year-old may speak in short, two-word telegraphic sentences. These landmarks have a broad latitude in regard to when they actually occur. In fact, the best way to gauge your child's landmarks is not necessarily the language he produces but his comprehension of language.

The fact that your child says a few words, that he grunts and seems to comprehend things, would generally indicate that he's developing on time. He's not developing faster than his sixteen-month-old cousin, so you might have to say that he's "behind" the sixteen-month-old child. But that doesn't mean that it's not normal for your child. Each child has an individual maturational and developmental schedule and range.

To more fully assess your child's language development, you might want to know a number of other things. Did his siblings develop their language a bit later? What does your mother or mother-in-law say about your and your spouse's developmental schedules? Are your child's motor landmarks on time? Does he seem to comprehend things? Does he hear well? Is he interested and responsive to spoken language? It sounds as though he is doing quite well in these areas.

You should know that some intellectually well-endowed people began talking *very* late in childhood. There are some highly cultivated and very bright members of our own faculty here at The New York Hospital who are said not to have spoken until they were four years old. And some people say that they've made up for that delay ever since!

If you are worried about your child being retarded, such a problem would show itself in the language area, but it would also emerge across the board in a wide-ranging array of behaviors. Comprehension would lag; pointing would lag; motor landmarks would often lag as well. In the absence of any of these rather global signs of "slowness" or retardation, I think you ought to relax and enjoy your child's very individual development and growth.

"Losing" Her Baby

Our daughter began walking at fifteen months. Now, at eighteen months, she tries going everywhere and won't let me help her. She seems independent— she won't even let me turn the pages of a book for her. I almost feel like I'm losing my baby. Is this normal?

DR. SHAPIRO: The toddler often feels a kind of exuberance as she achieves new developmental landmarks. This may lead to a strong sense of independence. Your eighteen-month-old daughter may be a little ahead of schedule, since we often see this kind of behavior at about two years of age. These newfound landmarks can permit your child to do certain things as though she is the world's only center of will and control, as though she's omnipotent. There really *can* be a "love affair with the world" at this stage, and your child's exploration of everything becomes paramount. Anything that interferes with such active, inquisitive exploration seems to be an intrusion to the child. Of course, there will be a rude awakening for any child, because her activities must be curtailed for her own safety, and for other reasons as well. Once the child registers this reality, she may have a more cautious and somewhat less exuberant approach to the world. Then she won't appear so negativistic.

A parent's attitude about all this becomes central to the outcome of this developmental stage. That is, how much room can a parent permit a child and allow her to show such independence? I think there was an erroneous approach during the 1920s and 1930s when many parents thought that their children would be better off never being curtailed or frustrated in *any* way. We now know that this is not the best approach. It's useful for children to know that they are *not* the center of all things, that there are other wills in the world, and that their parents have rights, too. The relationship between parents and a child is not quite a democracy, and there must be some restrictions on what a child does and on how easily and in what ways she is gratified.

I'm concerned about your feeling that you are "losing" your child. A parent who feels this way may really want a passive and sedentary lap baby; once the baby becomes a toddler, such a parent has trouble letting go. I would suggest a consultation with a professional so you can discuss your developing child and better understand how her emerging sense of independence affects you.

Comes into Bed

Our two-and-a-half-year-old daughter started coming into our bed at night when she was sick a while ago. Now we can't break her of this habit. We put her into her own bed, but she ends up in ours. What should we do?

DR. SHAPIRO: This is an area where for years professionals were categorical in their responses, saying, "Get the child out of your bed before it becomes a habitual practice!" Modern thinking takes a somewhat more relaxed view about this issue, although the eventual outcome may be very much the same. Namely, it's best to eventually get the child back into her own bed.

Keep in mind that the notion of a child having her own bed, own room, and own space is an upper-middle-class, Western concept. In many homes throughout the world, because of lack of space, children sleep in the same room with their parents, share a bed with siblings, and may even crawl into bed with their parents. A large proportion of the world's surface is populated by children who sleep in the parental bed. In fact, a certain movement with a fairly zealous following espouses the "family" bed.

The situation with your daughter is quite common. Most parents are more indulgent of a child when she's ill. When the regression that occurs during an illness persists beyond the illness, something of a habit has developed. My experience with these situations usually reveals that one or both parents tacitly encourage this behavior in the child or that the effort necessary for the change is not made. I think you must ask yourselves how much you want your child to be out of your bed, and how much effort you are willing to make in this regard.

The longer this arrangement persists, the more likely it is that it will become a habit that will be difficult to break. It will take a few nights of one parent walking your daughter back to her own bed, perhaps staying with her until she falls asleep, for the old (and presumably preferable) pattern to be reestablished.

Many Fears

My two-and-a-half-year-old has lots of fears. He's afraid of loud noises, of dogs and cats, and he's afraid of the toilet. I've been told that children this age have fears, but is this normal?

DR. SHAPIRO: Fears in two-and-a-half-to-four-year-old children are a dime a dozen. Fears of these sorts are part of the usual dozen and are commonly described by parents. In fact, these fears are nearly universal.

Consider the eye-level view of a two- or three-year-old. A hairy giant might actually be a dog or a cat with shining eyes. Similarly, the toilet, which makes a sudden loud noise, is added into the picture because children this age usually go through toilet training. A great deal of magical animism goes into the child's experience: Are feces animate or inanimate? Are they parts of the body or are they separate? At this age, a child's comprehension is limited, and when parents encourage a child to be toilet trained, they make a great fuss over his passing stool into the potty or toilet. And then—they flush this treasure away! This can be confusing and even frightening to a child, and adds to fears concerning the toilet bowl. All your child's fears are quite normal at this time. Eventually, they will pass.

Can't Stay Away When Baby Cries

Our baby is nearly two years old and doesn't yet sleep through the night. He cries, and though I'm determined to let him cry himself to sleep, I can't do it. My husband gets annoyed with all this. Can you advise me what the baby is crying about and how to handle it?

DR. SHAPIRO: There is an important element in this question. You make it fairly clear that your baby has never slept through the night. If your child had formerly slept through the night and is now having a recurrence of night wakening, I would say that this is normal, because somewhere between eighteen months and two years of age kids once again begin waking and have trouble sleeping through the night.

With the advent of advanced sleep research, it's now known that sleep patterns, once established after the first year of life, approximate the adult picture. So the adult pattern becomes established quite early. Also, children with sleep difficulties have been extensively studied, and it has been found that most problems in falling asleep and maintaining sleep are not physiological, but are related to habituation and parental handling. Most of these studies clearly indicate that someone in the family must become the "heavy" by helping the child fall asleep. This is done by a parent's not creating too much arousal for the child when he awakens. It means not being permissive and being willing to help the child fall back to sleep. In other words, it simply means breaking a bad habit and getting the child to learn a better way of staying asleep.

When a child has *always* slept poorly, there may be parental problems in patterning the child to get to sleep. This may occur at the very beginning of a child's life. There may be too much time taken with the 4 A.M. bottle, or the parents rush immediately to the crib when the child stirs in the night. Or they may be too willing to comply with the child's wish to play just before bedtime.

Of course, some children need less sleep than others. There are ways of regulating this; you can alter the time or length of the child's nap during the day, or the time the child goes to bed. By altering these patterns, you may find that your child does much better, and sleeps through the night.

Masturbates Frequently

Our son is nearly three years old and has begun masturbating frequently. He's been fondling his genitals whenever he seems upset or anxious. Can you advise us?

DR. SHAPIRO: I think the word "masturbation" has taken on such broad meaning that almost any genital touching is called masturbation. In many people's minds, masturbation calls forth images of purposeful genital manipulation associated with erotic and other fantasies. Yet this is not, I am quite sure, what your son is doing. In fact, early investigators of infant development noted that one of the indicators of healthy development was a child reaching for his genitals, beginning at about the second year of life. This usually occurred when the child was being diapered and was considered a sign that good mothering was taking place.

A child will fondle a pleasurable body zone and will tend to repeat the pleasure during times of altered states of consciousness, during periods of drowsiness, when he is preoccupied, or when he is tense or anxious. These are perfectly natural occurrences. I wouldn't be so concerned about a child fondling his genitals; rather, I would be concerned that tension and anxiety are prominent in his life and occur too frequently. I don't think it would be helpful to prohibit the fondling at this time. Some general issues of appropriateness and socialization may come up: Is he fondling himself in public? Is he exposing himself rather than fondling himself through his clothing? These are issues of socialization, and don't mean that the masturbation itself is a problem. To my mind, frequent masturbation may be a symptom of underlying difficulties.

Ready for Preschool?

Our daughter is nearly two years old and we're thinking of sending her to a preschool. Is she old enough for this experience, or should we wait?

DR. SHAPIRO: Preschool means that parents can be relieved of certain child-care burdens. It also means that a child may receive additional socialization, which is very important. If a child of two is able to tolerate such separation from parents, a preschool situation can provide valuable contact with others (children and adults) outside the family. In our culture, the idea of a preschool nursery setting, or a day-care center, is fraught with mystery and difficulty. This is a fairly recent development, and recent reports about sexual and physical abuse have raised additional concerns about some preschool settings where personnel are not properly qualified and licensed.

The question about whether your child is too young for a preschool cannot be answered on grounds of biological maturity or on a developmental basis. It must be answered mainly on culturally relevant grounds. Most experts agree that if substitute caretaking is good, the preschool arrangement is probably a good one for both mother and child. It frees a mother to work and can lessen the burden of child-rearing for a particular parent, thereby reducing the resentment that so often arises when a parent feels the need to work as well as be a parent.

In the end, you must know your own situation and must judge for yourself whether a preschool arrangement is going to work for you and your toddler. (See in Chapter 3, "Preschools and Day Care.")

Should Mother Work?

I'm the mother of a two-year-old and I would like to return to work. Is this a good idea?

DR. SHAPIRO: The concept of a mother's returning to work at some point after the birth of her baby is a rather recent historical development in Western urban society. Much of this is related to the women's movement and to changing attitudes about women's roles in the home and elsewhere in our society.

A good deal of data suggest that mothers' staying home with a baby is an artifact of the Victorian period. In fact, in many cultures mothers have always worked. They simply strapped babies to their backs or placed them in caretaking situations with a surrogate parent. The central issue is really how a child will be cared for in the absence of a mother. Most experts today feel that if good, sensitive, and consistent surrogate care is available for a child, there is no danger of the child feeling emotionally deprived. In fact, studies indicate that parents are regarded by the child as the primary caretakers even when surrogate caretaking has been used from a very early period in the child's life.

If as a parent you feel the need to return to work but do not do so out of concern that it will somehow "harm" your child, there will undoubtedly be a buildup of resentment in such an arrangement. Such a resentment-filled situation is best avoided, and many experts point out that the mother who truly wishes to work and does so actually ends up spending "quality" time with her child instead of feeling "locked" into a situation that breeds resentment. (See Chapter 7, *When Mother Works.*)

Food as a Weapon

Our toddler is nearly three years old. Whenever he doesn't get what he wants, he won't eat. This upsets my wife and she gives in just to get him to eat. How should this be handled?

DR. SHAPIRO: Three-year-olds can sometimes be cunning. The linkage between getting one's way and not eating is not usually quite so apparent with many children. It's a linkage that gets established through practice, habit, and through a particular family's way of handling the rather "loaded" issue of food.

Such a situation may arise when at first it was a linkage of happenstance. But then the behavior is reinforced because it elicits reaction from the child's mother. Once it becomes reinforced, it develops into a regular, patterned behavior.

Feeding behavior and eating become representative of intimacy, and can be interpreted as the giving and taking of love. By not eating, your child is saying, "If you won't give something to me, then I won't take your love, or give my love to you. Refusing to eat takes on a symbolic meaning at this level. Remember that all eating behavior, especially nursing during the earliest time of life, is a center for socialization. Later in life, when people wish to socialize with each other, they eat together. Eating is a powerful and important reference point, both for socialization and for symbolic statements of attachment and generosity, especially concerning caring and love.

On a more practical level, you must be able to accept the notion that some things are not as important as others, and that some frustrations are more important for a child to endure than others. Your child's refusal to eat should not be viewed as a punishment or deprivation to you. It would probably be helpful if you could deemphasize the importance of eating or not eating; in other words, don't allow your child to reinforce this kind of behavior. Unless he is not maintaining a healthy weight for his age and height, food should not become the arena for arguments or for a battle of wills.

There seems to be a great deal of complex interaction between you and your wife. It may be helpful for you both to meet with a professional to discuss this and see if you can come to some agreement about how best to approach the problem. But however you put an end to this appeasement and to the issue of food as a weapon, this unproductive cycle must be "broken."

Cries When Parents Leave

Our daughter is two and a half. Whenever we get ready to leave for an evening out, she has a tantrum. The baby-sitter tells us that a half hour after we've left, the baby is exhausted and falls asleep. How can we handle this tantrum?

DR. SHAPIRO: At an earlier developmental state, separation anxiety is a healthy sign that a child has become attached enough to a specific caretaker to object to that person's leaving. At certain points in development, there is a revival of the anxiety, and this can be used by a child in a manipulative way. By having a tantrum, a child may force parents into gratifying her wishes. On the other hand, a child may have a genuine concern about separation, and a parent must have a certain amount of empathy for what a child feels and experiences. Your two-and-a-half-year-old's ability to understand that you will return, and her comprehension of time spans, are imperfect. For her, your leaving may momentarily signify abandonment.

So long as you are certain that the baby-sitter is kind and considerate, you can probably feel confident that this is your child's own variation of a very common occurrence. Her crying for a half hour is a bit unusual. Most often the child calms down and begins playing with the baby-sitter as soon as the parents depart. On the other hand, some children find it very hard to stop crying once they begin.

As a matter of course, I would look for other signs of anxiety or conflict. Is your child worried that you may leave her during the day? Is she having difficulties sleeping through the night? Does she have trouble going to bed? This behavior will probably pass or become less intense after four or five times, and your daughter should eventually accommodate to your leaving for an evening. If it doesn't pass, it may warrant a consultation to determine if separation problems are causing this behavior.

Baby Goes Everywhere

Our son is nearly three years old and we've never left him with a baby-sitter. We've taken him everywhere, or we just stay home. This is not only limiting to us, but I think it's bad for our child. My wife disagrees. Can you advise us?

DR. SHAPIRO: There are some parents who try to shield their child from ever experiencing anything that may be frustrating, or that may provoke some modicum of anxiety. I think that these parents misunderstand the nature of child development. Some parents seem to believe that as a child develops, he will learn more control. These parents believe that with achieving control, the child will want to be mature and will then give up various gratifications. In other words, some parents actually believe that development will take place because of a natural maturational thrust, or because a child *wants* it to occur. Up to a certain point, there's some truth in this thinking, but only some.

The reward for giving up some things is love, which can be a very powerful motivating force in life. Your child must ultimately give up the gratification of having a constant parental presence. Your child will eventually be forced to separate from you. This might not have been the case if the family lived in a frontier life-style in which the grown child lived with the parents or nearby, and joined father and mother in the fields or milking cows. When we had a cottage society and didn't have schooling outside the home, the family was more cohesive and remained more intact than it does today. But even then, young people left home, eventually separating from their parents.

The answer is not so much which parent is right; it has much more to do with the kind of child you wish to raise. If you want a more independent youngster, it's best for him to begin practicing separation at an earlier age. But there is no critical period of life when this issue must be addressed, and your child may still become quite independent even though he spends so much time with his parents throughout these early years.

You and your wife are obviously having a difference of opinion. Such differences have a way of getting across to a child and may become the focal point of various manipulations or of family tensions and difficulties. It would be best for you and your wife to decide how you wish your child to develop and how you intend to accomplish this. You should also discuss the various needs and satisfactions you each have in relation to your child, and to each other.

Reading to a Child

We spend a great deal of time reading to our two-year-old. I've been told that this can stimulate his interest in books and that it may increase his reading ability. Will it help him learn to read earlier?

DR. SHAPIRO: In one sense this is true. Let me illustrate this in the following way. At one point in my own child's development, the question came up about music lessons. I recall the music teacher asking me if we had a great deal of music in our household. "Do you or your wife listen to music, or do either of you play music?" he asked. "If you don't, the lessons alone may not be sufficient to stimulate your child's interest and abilities in music."

Books are similar. If you want your child to be a reader, reading to your son becomes an important part of the experience leading up to his eventually reading on his own. If your child sees you only watching television or going to ball games, and never sees you with a book, reading will not be emphasized as an important activity in your household. That message will sink in. One part of the early identification would be reading to your child, but another would be to create circumstances in which your child will want to do whatever you are doing. If reading is part of your repertoire, then it will most likely become important to your child.

One fly in this ointment, however, is that later on, if your child realizes that you want this *too much*, he may react against it and do exactly the opposite of what he knows you want. So the secret is—as a real-estate broker might say—you can't want that house too much or you won't get it at the right price.

I am sometimes asked by parents if reading to a young child somehow stimulates or facilitates some neurological pathway, or if such early activity has some biological influence that makes for ease with reading or language, or helps a child master these functions earlier. I answer this question by quoting Jean Piaget, the great Swiss psychologist who studied intelligence and the ways in which children learn. He said that when he came to the United States, he was frequently met by what he called "the American question." That question is: "When can we do it *earlier?*" His answer was, "A chimpanzee of three months of age is far more advanced than a human infant, but the chimpanzee doesn't go much further."

I think we may be too preoccupied with accomplishing things at too early an age. We must realize that a maturational schedule is appropriately fixed in most human babies and children. We're probably teaching reading at the right time with most children. That doesn't mean that there aren't some kids who learn to read very early, and who can do it very well. Some exceptional individuals demonstrate very early capacities of one kind or another. But I don't think that teaching reading at a very early age facilitates specific neuronal pathways. Such activity may encourage the habit of reading, which could lay the foundations for a child's later behavior and attitudes about reading. It's important that the child read well when he or she learns to read, but earlier isn't necessarily better.

Again, I think that the reading situation between a parent and child is a very important model for later development and attitudes about books and about reading as a desirable activity. But this is based on identification with a parent, not on some specific organic stimulation.

Makes a Mess

Our eighteen-month-old makes a mess whenever he eats. Everything flies everywhere and I get upset. How should I handle this?

DR. SHAPIRO: I think that you must question the reasons for being so upset by this behavior. At eighteen months, your child cannot be socialized when it comes to eating habits. He's simply too young and developmentally immature. He has few inhibitions and a very imperfect sense of what is right or acceptable as opposed to that which is unacceptable. In addition, he has imperfect motor control and has not yet had sufficient practice in performing the various maneuvers involved in eating. At this time of his development, your son is practicing and learning, and cannot perform these tasks very well. A mess is the natural outcome.

You might want to hold back on allowing your child to feed himself until he's more developed and has better motor and social skills. Unless you do that, you simply cannot expect to have a neat house or kitchen.

As a parent, part of your task at this stage of your child's development is to make the part of your house in which your child lives as child-proof as possible. If he messes while he eats, you might get into a jogging suit or don an old raincoat, so you can get involved and enjoy your child at this time in his life. You need a sense of humor in all this. If you can't do this or find it intolerable, you may simply have to get someone else to feed the child, so long as you don't feel you are losing contact with him. Or get someone else to do the cleaning up, if possible.

Or you might want to plan the baby's bath immediately after eating. But keep in mind your child's limited capacities at this time, and his need to practice at using the materials of the world. All this inevitably means he will make a mess.

You must be realistic about your child's capacities and skills at this age. To expect him to keep clean, to want him to have internalized controls and to know right from wrong, is only setting the stage for endless noes on your part. This can make household life an ongoing source of frustration and conflict for both you and your child.

Too Many Toys

Whenever our three-year-old does anything right, my husband buys him a toy. It seems like a bribe, and we've discussed this many times. I question the role of toys and think that they can be given for right and wrong reasons. Can you advise me?

DR. SHAPIRO: The issue of toys raises many points and questions. Many toy manufacturers have survived by purporting that their toys promote a child's emotional or intellectual development, or that certain toys are "educational." Very often, the promotion of toys for children over the age of three is based on a sensationalistic value. A good deal of the thriving toy market is based on the fact that unsuspecting children are exposed to television advertisements, and depends also on children comparing their own toys to those of the other kids.

Toys can be very useful for a child in learning about the physical aspects of the world. They can also promote fantasy and spur a child's imagination, although any piece of material can be used by a child to represent something else. In fact, parents are often dismayed when they present a child with an elaborate toy, only to discover that the child is far more interested in the packing crate than the toy! And of course different toys appeal to different-aged children. There are age-related toys; a child of one particular age may find a specific toy babyish, but it may be appropriate for a younger child. Another toy may be too advanced for a younger child.

This situation does sound very much as though your husband is in some way bribing your son. This is not useful. Certainly, positive reinforcement is helpful when you want a child to learn something, but such reinforcement need not be a toy. If toys are given for no good reason and a child comes to expect such presents, this is a poor arrangement. Wanting your child to have everything creates problems; it can lead to a child becoming jaded. Certainly, many children are overindulged; as they grow older, the gifts and toys become increasingly more expensive.

Such a toy no longer feels like a reward to the child, and he quickly becomes bored by an item so easily obtained.

In fact, it's important during development for a child to want something for a while before getting it. It's healthy for a child to mentally play with a toy, anticipating it, fantasizing about it, and even longing for it. For a child to then obtain what was longed for can lead to greater appreciation of it and to far greater satisfaction. This of course becomes a matter of individual psychology and has a great deal to do with how a child learns to strive for and attain various things.

Difficulty in Setting Limits

Our two-year-old son is into everything. We've tried telling him no, but it doesn't stop him. He goes right back to doing whatever he wants. We find this exasperating and don't know what to do. Is there a better way to let him know that there are limits?

DR. SHAPIRO: The concept "no" is a new one to a two-year-old. A child of this age hears "no" all the time, and identifies with you when you say no. Your child reflects all the no's in his negativism, that is, by doing just the opposite of what you want him to do. How do you set limits and how does a child internalize the limits so that they become a useful deterrent and prevent him from doing whatever you don't want him to do? That's the trick of bringing up a two-year-old.

Most two-year-olds go through this phase. They eventually learn the no's and become more socialized. The best advice to parents during this stage is: Don't despair. Sooner or later, your child will get the point and learn where he is or isn't allowed. He will come to know the things he can and cannot touch, and will learn various limits. If your child is not listening to the verbal no's, you're probably best off removing him from the situation and trying to divert his attention. I see nothing worthwhile in trying to make these prohibitions reasonable to a two-year-old. In other words, don't explain too much to a child of this age. You can't explain to a two-year-old that by running out into the street he may endanger his life. That's too rational a contingency for a toddler to grasp completely. Simply say no and be ready to intervene physically should the need arise.

Faced with all this, many parents question whether or not to hit a child when prohibiting certain things. The general advice of most experts is to try to avoid punishment by physical abuse. However, many parents find their anger welling up at such a rate that they finally erupt and hit the child while in a rage. A well-placed and mild spank or reprimand much earlier on is far better. I think that if a parent knows himself or herself, and knows that there is a tendency to erupt, it's probably better to exercise earlier restraint over the child than to let the situation get to the point of an emotional eruption.

I'm often asked about a parent shouting or yelling at a child when things go too far. If we had to make a hierarchy, yelling is better than hitting, but on the other hand, habitual yelling is not a comfortable environment for a child. In fact, many children who have grown up with shouting parents will tell you that they learned very early in life to ignore, tune out, or not listen to their parents. Yelling is simply another sign of a parent's frustrated rage and of a frustrated sense of power. It's the sign of a frazzled parent.

Chapter 3: The Preschool Years –
Ages Three to Six

◊ YOUR DEVELOPING CHILD

Around the age of two and a half or three, the child grows beyond being a baby to become a preschool child. During the next three years, he passes through one of the most difficult and life-altering phases of his developmental journey. As a baby and very young child, he enjoyed an intense and special relationship with mother, one that was the bedrock of his early life. But now, for his emotional interest to shift beyond the family—to playmates, school, and the world at large—your child must relinquish part of this early attachment. Though accomplished with a great deal of emotional pain, this shift is critical to any child's developing independence and eventual maturity.

These three years are often called the Oedipal phase because a child of this age develops romantic feelings about the parent of the opposite sex, along with competitive feelings toward the same-sexed parent. (The Oedipus myth is of Greek origin, and tells of Oedipus, who unwittingly killed his father and married his mother.) During this period of emotional struggle, your child gains an appreciation and acceptance of himself or herself as a boy or girl, achieving a firm sense of sexual identity.

A great deal of emotional development occurs during this critical period. Because your child makes the transition from a primary relationship with mother to an intense relationship with both parents, he is forced to restructure his views about himself and the world at large. He must come to terms with and accept certain indelible truths about himself, about life, and about love. In doing this, your child's conscience is solidified. He comes to know right from wrong, and learns his own prerogatives and his limitations. In addition, he must adjust to the reality of siblings and the competition for attention and affection that a brother or sister may bring.

During this time, your child must develop and refine the mental tools and the emotional stability needed to deal with an expanding world, one that will go far beyond the somewhat narrow confines of the family. He will enter a complicated world of other children and will learn how to socialize and play. These three years bring enormous emotional shifts that help prepare your child for the school years, when he must free his attention and energy for the process of learning.

The Social Life of Three- and Four-Year-Olds

The preschool child's world expands to include a variety of people outside the home—teachers, surrogate parents, and other children. As an infant and toddler, your child's identity was closely interwoven with the family. While the family remains the primary frame of reference and emotional force for years to come, a three- or four-year-old actually moves out into the world. She is now exposed to new ideas, and to an expanding community of people, problems, and roles. This requires a restructuring of your child's view of herself and of the world at large.

A child who has spent time with a variety of people—grandparents, a nanny, older siblings, other relatives, sitters—may have a temporary advantage in social skills over a child with less experience in dealing with people other than parents. For a child of this age, the parents continue to represent all that's good and wise in the world, and the child comes to view new adults as parent surrogates. With children her own age, however, your child must work out an entirely new set of social relationships.

Playing with Peers

By this age, your child can care for herself well enough to play with other children. During this period, fantasy is uppermost. While your child is not yet ready to accommodate the harsh demands of reality, she can change a situation by imagining it to be different. She can be an astronaut one moment, a nurse the next, or an enormous horse by simply wishing it. If she doesn't like the way a particular game or scene is going, she may simply undo it by playing it once again, assigning to herself (or another child) a very different role, or changing the course of action. She may be so absorbed by the play that she forgets it's a game, and she may blur the boundary line between fantasy and reality. Later in the preschool years, she will have learned to draw a distinct line between make-believe and reality; she will know that actions have consequences for herself and for others.

Despite the dominance of playfulness, there's an earnestness in the child's activity at this time. She tries out new roles as ways of gathering experience and learning about different aspects of life. As with the toddler, play at this age is serious business; it's one of the many ways your child learns about her world.

A child this age craves the company of other children, both for companionship and for playing various roles and games. If you listen to two children "conversing" at this time, you will quickly discover that the conversation is not really for the exchange of information or ideas; rather, its aim seems to be pleasure in simply verbalizing with another.

One child speaks and waits for a reply. When the second speaks, his response has little connection to what the first child said; most often, he uses the first child's words as a springboard for some new line of thought. This dual, or collective, monologue allows each child to voice his preoccupations or fantasies. Here's a sample of two 4-year-olds holding a conversation:

> ROBERT: I saw a horse yesterday. It was big and brown, and far away in the grass.
>
> ANDREW: I saw a dog named Sidney. He was black, with a beard, and mustache, like my daddy's.
>
> ROBERT: It was in Wilton, where they have lots of them.
>
> ANDREW: And I fed him . . . Sidney . . . right from my hand. It was dog food. Yucky!
>
> ROBERT: I wanted to ride him, but he was big, and far away. Were you ever in Wilton?
>
> ANDREW: Do they have dogs there? I love dogs. And Sidney was the smartest dog I ever saw.
>
> ROBERT: Like a horse. With a long tail.

Children's conversations are not always such dual monologues. At times, the child tries desperately to give information, but the attempt may be filled with illogical sequences of thought and non sequiturs, making it difficult for an adult to follow the child's meaning or know what's really being said. (A parent or someone familiar with the child stands a better chance at guessing the child's meaning.) The trouble is that a young preschooler's thought processes are egocentric; he simply doesn't recognize the need to provide enough information for the listener to understand what he's trying to communicate.

As mentioned earlier, the toddler gradually begins playing near others. He may be immersed in his own activity, side by side with another child, and there may be almost no interaction between them. This is called parallel play. Eventually, it becomes *associative play*, in which children do things in groups, although there isn't yet a true integration of activity for a well-defined purpose. You may see a group of children digging together in a sandbox (often at cross-purposes), cavorting in a wading pool, or swarming over a jungle gym. Sometime later, having learned to coordinate their activities, children enter into cooperative play, in which true interaction and cooperation occur. Roles are assigned, and the play has purpose and direction.

During the preschool years, children engage in dramatic play. They take on roles, and scenes from domestic life are played out. Later, these scenes reflect life in the world at large and are liberally mixed with fantasy.

Dramatic play involves dressing in adult clothes, playing doctor or nurse, mother or father, policeman, fireman, airplane pilot, gas station attendant, truck driver, grocery store clerk, gardener, and an endless list of other roles taken from home and the world at large. These roles allow your child to learn about other people and to be like them. They allow the child, through the magical power of fantasy, to take part in the world beyond the household. The roles that most appeal to the child are visible ones, and have purposes, ways, and means that are clearly defined to the child. It's quite rare to see a four-year-old playing attorney, accountant, or stockbroker.

As children learn to communicate more easily, their games become more complicated, and a variety of social traits come to the fore: cooperation, leadership, and, quite often, aggression.

Cooperation becomes more obvious as children play at games that require the child's coordinating her activities to take part in a collective game. Some preschoolers begin to show leadership qualities at this time. One child may successfully identify with adults and lead a group of children quite authoritatively. Another may become "bossy" in an attempt to overcome insecurity and win the respect or attention of the others. Another may try to rule by sheer force of physical power. There are countless variations, and a child at this age may become a leader or a follower as the circumstances warrant.

Aggression makes its appearance in the play of preschool children. Younger preschoolers quarrel over possessions. Later in the preschool years, social issues become the main source of conflict: who dislikes whom, who will play with whom, who will be included or excluded. As a rule, friends and enemies change quickly in any group, and loyalties can shift with amazing speed. It's quite usual for one or two children to be generally admired and liked, while one or two unfortunate ones may be disliked or picked on by others.

Boys and girls have different patterns of conflict. Physical aggression becomes more common in boys, whereas girls quarrel less during the preschool years. When they do argue, they generally use words rather than physical force. (For a complete discussion of bullying; scapegoating, and being left out, see Chapter 17, *The Bully and the Victim*.)

Occasionally, a child may resort to the company of an imaginary companion who, by definition, is less competitive than other children. As mentioned earlier in the chapter on toddlers, having an imaginary companion can be a healthy and adaptive part of your child's fantasy life, provided it doesn't become your child's only form of social contact. Here, too, a transitional object such as a favorite stuffed doll or toy may become emotionally important to your child, taking on attributes of an imaginary companion. (See in Chapter 2, "An Imaginary Companion.")

Fantasy and Reality

As your child approaches two and a half or three years of age, his ability to speak fluently and to maintain some degree of self-direction and control become impressively apparent. By age three, some children are nonstop talkers, and because much of what a child says may be "cute" or clever, it's easy to overestimate a child's mental and emotional capacities at this time.

An important development during these years is the gradual ability to delineate fantasy from reality. Only after a long period of time does the boundary line become sharply drawn for the child; even then, wishes, fears, and fantasies color and distort a child's perceptions to a great extent. Although a preschool child understands a great deal about the world, though she recognizes people, places, and things and can properly sort out the do's and don'ts in many situations, fantasy, and magic abound everywhere.

A young preschooler can escape reality with the mere thought of being elsewhere. Completely absorbed by a fantasy role, she can actually become someone else in another time; a princess in a faraway kingdom, or a magic horse that can fly. An imaginary companion, whether conjured up in the mind or embodied by a stuffed doll, can assume a powerful reality for the child, one that can sometimes upset or worry parents.

A four-year-old child thinks the people she sees on the television screen are real, actually inside the set. The magical transformations that she sees on the screen, especially in cartoons, are taken to be very real. The child thinks the voices coming from the radio or stereo speaker are those of real people, and she may wonder how they got inside.

A nighttime dream may assume frighteningly realistic proportions for the child, and a roaring lion may remain, even during waking hours, a continuing threat to her safety and well-being. A child of four may think she can be changed into a boy, or that a boy can somehow become a girl. She may think that mother somehow "forgot" to give her a penis or that she had her own cut away. She may believe that fathers give birth to boys, and mothers to girls. She may think that a new baby arrives because the parents bought it at a store, or that mommy went to the hospital for an operation, which is how the baby got "out." It will take years before the facts and realities of life are accurately sorted out and freed from the influence of fantasy and imagination.

While your child's intellectual abilities and verbal skills expand between three and six years of age, it's important to be aware of his limitations in thinking and understanding. These limitations and gaps in logical thinking are pervasive. Knowing about them can help you understand how your child's fantasy life can profoundly influence this critical phase of emotional development.

The Child's Abilities and Limitations

At this period of your child's development, the blossoming capacity for symbolic thinking makes its appearance. Your child begins to use mental symbols, such as words and images, to represent real events in the world. Other forms of symbolic thinking are dramatic play and representational drawing, by which a child reproduces or represents some real object by using materials on paper. All symbolic thinking, whether using words, drawing materials, or engaging in dramatic play, involve deferred imitation, the ability to perceive something, store it away in memory, and then later reproduce it in word or action.

Your child's thinking at this age has certain features that limit him from fully understanding events around him. His thinking at this time is very egocentric: He sees things only from *his* limited viewpoint and from *his* own narrow perspective. He cannot appreciate that another person may see and think about something in a way different than his own. If you ask a four- or five-year-old what another person sees, he will describe what he himself sees. A child this age, when repeating a story or retelling an event, has difficulty relating it so that another person can understand it. The child actually believes that other people (and animals, as well as inanimate objects) are motivated in the same way that he is. For instance, the dog barked because he was hungry (it's a short time before the child's dinnertime) or the bus goes fast because it wants to go home to its mommy and daddy.

Another limitation is the child's inability to take into account more than one feature of a situation at a time. As with toddlers, when a container of liquid is poured into a new, differently proportioned container, the preschool child cannot grasp that the quantity of liquid remains the same. The child is overly impressed with one feature, the height, and defines the taller container as containing more liquid than the wider and shorter container. He cannot shift from one conceptual framework to another.

Your child's reasoning about how the world works has other limitations. Most important is how he barely understands cause and effect when trying to explain things. The preschool child takes for granted that things happen, without conceptualizing that one thing leads to another. For the child, the world simply works, and it doesn't matter how.

Because he hasn't yet mastered his perceptions of cause and effect, any two events that coincide may have some causal connection in the child's mind; either one can be the cause of the other. For instance, a five-year-old's mother told him it was going to snow in a few hours (she'd heard the weather forecast on the radio). He waited anxiously at the window, and when the snow began falling, he excitedly attributed this event to his mother's words. She had said it would snow, and so it did! One event led to another.

Animism is another characteristic of your child's thinking during this period. Humanlike feelings, thoughts, and purposes are attributed to everything: animals, plants, and inanimate objects. A flower can't be picked because to do so will hurt it. Walking on grass is wrong because the grass doesn't like being stepped on. Flowers close their petals at night because they are tired and want to go to sleep. The moon hides behind the clouds because it's scared or because it's shy. The birds sing because they're happy; the train whistle blows because the train is looking for its mommy (especially if the child wants *his* mother).

Helen, six years old, stared sadly at a four-story town house wedged between two very tall buildings. "The little house is so sad and unhappy," she said mournfully. When her mother asked her why this was so, Helen replied, "Because it sits alone in the shadow of the other houses. It never gets any sun."

Your child's mind can shift from reality to fantasy, and then back to reality again, all in a moment. She may shower love and compassion upon a broken doll, ministering to its wound, soothing the doll's pain, only to unconcernedly toss it aside when something else captures her attention.

During this time, your child assumes that everything can be explained by some human force, one that wills things to happen for its own powerful purposes. Everything has human purpose, motivation, and designs. When walking through the woods, she may ask, "Who put all the leaves on the trees?" or "Who made the sky blue?" Or she may ask, "Why do oranges have skins? We throw them away, so why do they have to be there anyway?"

Your child has difficulty understanding that there are different kinds of reality or that something may seem very real but not be so. For instance, dreams have a certain reality (for the dreamer, when they are being dreamed), but are not part of everyday life. Yet your child may believe that her dreams have a tangible existence in the bedroom, that they are outside herself. She may believe that her dreams actually exist for others—they can see and experience her dreams—or she may think she can experience other people's dreams. A lion lunging for her in a dream may come to inhabit the bedroom, or the monster dreamed about last night may still be lurking silently beneath the bed.

Because she hasn't yet solidified her sense of herself, your child's ability to view herself as separate and apart from others is tenuous. She may think you (or any adult) can know her thoughts, that adults are all-powerful. This may provoke her into lying or conjuring up fantastic tales as a way of testing your omniscience.

The young child's sense of time is poorly framed. The four- or five-year-old has no real knowledge of her own past, and the future is a vague abstraction with little meaning. When she learns certain key words having to do with time, she doesn't have a true understanding of the concepts involved. Time doesn't exist as a continuum for the child, and a true understanding of yesterday-today-tomorrow may not exist until she begins school, even though at four or five she struggles to understand that time passes. A child this age may know the names of the days of the week or the months. She may know the seasons and the major holidays. But she most likely cannot tell time and will not be able to do so until she reaches school age.

A preschool child is often hungry for some knowledge about her own unremembered past. She may ask you to tell her about "when I was little" or about things "from a long time ago, when I couldn't remember," and she may love looking at her own baby pictures. In gazing at these photographs, she might as well be looking at some disembodied representation of herself; there is little sense that she is actually the same person as the unremembered figure in the picture.

Although she may begin forgetting the past as soon as she lives it, a child at this age can remember many isolated facts and incidents, much to her parents' amazement. She may remember the details of a house near a lake one summer years ago or may recall the names of two playmates from that summer, even being able to describe these other children. However, she has no true continuity of memory; she has little overall context in which to place the isolated memory of the event or the person she remembers.

Your child may struggle with the notion that you yourself were once a child. To him, it seems absurd that you could ever have been so small and powerless, that you had to listen to your mother and father, or that somewhere in prehistory, you yourself had to go to bed at an appointed hour. The concept of time is fluid, as is the notion of changing roles over the course of time; your child may simply not believe that you weren't always the way you are now. He may find it difficult to appreciate that roles can shift as life goes on. He may find it impossible to fathom that time differences remain constant; that you will always be twenty-five or more years older than he is. He may actually express the conviction that he will someday "catch up" with you and marry you. Or he may tell you, "Someday, when I'm grown up like you are, I'll be big and drive a car just like you. And you'll have to go to bed early, like I do."

With all their mental limitations, preschool children can occasionally impress adults with their abilities and mental skills. Roger, a six-year-old boy, despite the intellectual limitations typical of a child this age, knew the entire line-up of his father's favorite baseball team. He could identify each player by his uniform number, and could appreciate the differences between team players, their batting stances and batting averages. He also knew the differences between the home team and other teams. An avid baseball fan, his father provided the boy with positive emotional and mental reinforcement for acquiring and displaying this prodigious amount of knowledge.

During this period of development, your child may amaze you with both complex and primitive ways of thinking, each existing beside the other.

Worries About the Body

Beginning at about the age of three, your child may show heightened interest in his body. While some exploration of the body has occurred all along, at this point the child's interest intensifies and focuses on the genitals. He may begin fondling his genitals with obvious pleasure. Many parents are worried by this normal process; they are especially embarrassed if the child touches his genitals in public or when other people are visiting.

You may notice that both boys and girls now show another form of interest in the body, one concerning the possible loss and replacement of various body parts. She may express fascination with a doll's anatomy, wondering aloud if the doll's arm will grow back if it's removed. She may wonder about the doll's genitals and may shred the doll apart in an effort to learn what's "inside." (A boy will do the same thing.) The child may suddenly begin expressing enormous interest in the workings of the body, asking countless questions about losing an arm, an ear, or about having an "operation."

Questions abound about how the eyes function, about where babies come from, about being deaf or blind, or about losing some vital organ or bodily part. Your child may express amazed interest in the fact that both halves of a worm remain "alive" after the creature has been cut in two. In addition to such abstract concerns, more personal ones arise. The child suddenly runs to you with a host of minor bumps, bruises, and scrapes, each requiring examination and treatment (usually, a kiss and a Band-Aid suffice). A boy who, before this time, willingly went to the barber is now terrorized by the mere mention of getting his hair cut. The conversations of three- and four-year-olds bubble with threats of bodily mutilation and dismemberment. "I'll cut you into little pieces," or "I'll chop off your arms and legs and feed them to the sharks," or "Your bottom will fall off " are commonly heard from children at this age.

THE BOY'S WORRIES. At three years of age, the boy finds touching his penis to be an intense source of pleasure. He also views his penis as something very valuable and wants very much to show it off. As a result, many a three-year-old has walked completely naked into a room filled with adults. The boy's pride in his penis is part of his wanting to be like his father, with whom he is identifying more and more as time passes. A boy of this age is very impressed by size; he may boast proudly about his father (who seems to him the biggest and strongest man in the world), about his older (and bigger) brother, or about an uncle who epitomizes all that is big, manly, and admirable. Part of the boy's concern with maleness and with size makes him feel proud of his penis and thus want to show it off.

In his egocentric way of thinking (which is very normal for a child this age) the boy assumes that everyone's body is quite the same as his, since he has no real knowledge of the anatomical differences between the sexes. At some point, he will see the difference, and his assumption about people's bodies will be completely shattered. It may happen when a baby sister is born, when he sees his mother or another woman naked, or when he is bathed with a little girl. He will discover that the little girl's body is not the same as his. To his amazement and consternation, he will see that instead of having a penis, the little girl has a slit.

In his primitive and egocentric way of thinking, the boy will very likely conclude that the girl once had a penis, but she lost it. He then concludes that he too may lose *his* penis.

For a three-year-old boy, this seems a threatening danger. The sudden realization of the anatomical differences between boys and girls can seem so overwhelming and frightening that he cannot believe what his eyes clearly see. He may conclude that the girl actually has a penis, but it's hidden inside her body. This can turn the three-year-old into a precocious surgeon, eagerly pulling apart a doll; he's searching for its hidden penis. Remember, a child of this age has very limited knowledge of the world and of the body. The notion that the lost penis is really hidden inside the girl holds a certain alluring plausibility for the three-year-old boy.

He may conclude that while the girl's penis is gone, this loss is only temporary. Her penis will somehow, magically, return (just as a starfish's leg will grow back after it's pulled off). This implausible conclusion is reinforced by countless television cartoons in which a character suffers outrageous bodily insults without really being harmed.

The fantasy of regenerating body parts is very common in three- and four-year-old boys, and you may notice this idea played out in a particular game at this age. The boy delights in hiding his penis between his legs (erect or not) and laughs happily when it pops out, whole and completely visible. He is reassuring himself about his penis. What he cannot see is not forever gone; the loss is only a brief illusion.

No matter how he deals with this worry, your three- or four-year-old will try to reassure himself that his body (especially his penis) is healthy and intact. He may pretend that the girl's penis is still present; he may convince himself that it's hidden inside her; he may take solace in the fantasy of regeneration; he may worry about every part of his body *except* his penis (all the scrapes, bumps, and bruises—and all the Band-Aids); or he may decide that little girls are somehow dangerous and must be avoided.

Remember, in his magical way of thinking, the child's fantasies can run rampant; he may believe that to be touched by a girl is somehow to have his body's integrity threatened. Keeping this in mind, it shouldn't surprise you to encounter a four-year-old boy who is reluctant to have anything to do with girls.

No matter how he tries to reassure himself, the four-year-old boy's worries about his body (and penis) are very important. This ongoing struggle will take years to resolve and can cause your child to experience a great deal of anxiety. When your four-year-old holds his penis (he may do this with maddening frequency), it's not only because doing so feels good; touching his penis is important reassurance that it is still there, whole and intact, even though there are other people in the world whose genitals have vanished.

THE GIRL'S WORRIES. As does the boy, the three-year-old girl assumes that people's bodies are all very much alike. There is virtually no appreciation that boys and girls are constructed differently. Rather, the distinction between boys and girls is based largely on superficial characteristics such as hair length or clothing.

Three-year-old Donna watched her cousin Tracy, a two-year-old toddler, cavorting naked in a wading pool. When asked if Tracy was a boy or a girl, Donna replied, "I don't know. It doesn't have any clothes on!"

At some point, the little girl discovers the anatomical difference between boys and girls. It may occur when a younger brother is born, when she sees her father or an older brother naked, or when she's bathed with a little boy. At some point, to her complete mystification and shock, the three- or four-year-old girl discovers that the boy has a penis, while she does not. She may react to this discovery in a number of ways.

She may have a similar reaction to the boy's, suddenly growing concerned about bodily harm or injury. She may feel that she's been damaged, or even mutilated. Concluding that she once had—and lost— a penis, she may grow concerned about the rest of her body, and worry that it too will be damaged, torn apart, or mutilated. She may decide that she wants a penis, too, and, as the boy did, may fantasize that it's hidden inside of her. She may become engrossed in her doll's anatomy, displaying prodigious surgical skill in her search for the doll's hidden penis. She may develop the notion that somehow her own hidden penis will someday materialize, and she will then be like the boy. Or she may conclude that having a penis isn't terribly important since mother doesn't have one, and someday she will be like mother.

WANTING TO BE LIKE EACH OTHER. It's not at all unusual for a girl of three or four to express wishes about having a penis. It's important to realize that the four-year-old boy may be envious of female anatomy; he may express the wish to have a baby (just like mother), and many four-year-old boys wish they had breasts. However, these envious wishes are generally discouraged by parents because a boy isn't allowed to be "sissyish" or to express wishes to be a girl. Parents are often more tolerant of the little girl's wishes to be like a boy; they may tacitly approve of her playing with guns or of her acting tomboyishly, while they react negatively to the boy who expresses wishes to be a girl and have breasts or babies.

The point is that it's perfectly normal for your little boy to express wishes to be a girl, as it is for your girl to want to be a boy. Such envious wishes are transitory and nearly universal. All children have these wishes, and they often play them out in various roles and fantasies. These fantasies are normal, natural experiences, necessary for your child to develop a sound sense of being male or female. They are vital in helping your child learn societal roles and expectations.

Don't be shocked or critical if you discover your four-year-old daughter playing with "boys'" toys or playing some "masculine" role such as cowboy, policeman, or fireman. Such playacting and fantasies about being a male won't impair her sense of being feminine. They won't prevent her from becoming an adult woman who can become a wife and mother. Similarly, there's no need to worry if your four-year-old boy occasionally plays nurse or wants to give a bottle to his sister's dolls. Such "feminine" behavior and game-playing won't impair his sense of being male. Nor will it interfere with his eventually taking on a man's role as a husband and father. Provided that you present yourself—man or woman—as a good model with whom your child can identify, he or she will become a man or woman based on the healthy model that you present.

The Oedipal Phase

Most of any child's first three years of life have centered on an intense relationship with mother. At this critical stage of development, an important change occurs; the child shifts from a relationship primarily focusing on mother to one involving both parents. This intense, triangular relationship is very easily seen, and most parents know that between the ages of three and six the child develops many powerful feelings about both parents.

During the Oedipal stage, the child develops "romantic" and possessive feelings toward the parent of the opposite sex. With these wishes, rivalrous feelings toward the same-sexed parent arise. This is complicated by the fact that despite the rivalry with the same-sexed parent, loving and affectionate feelings continue to exist. In other words, your child encounters conflict between these intense feelings. This conflict must eventually be resolved. Virtually every child, boy or girl, develops some unique version of these powerful feelings during the years between three and 6, and this phase of development profoundly influences your child's future.

Balancing these feelings and heavily involved in the relationship with each parent, he or she will traverse this developmental phase, making emotional shifts that are crucial for a growing sense of sexual identity, for eventual independence, and for progress beyond the confines of the family.

THE GIRL'S OEDIPAL ROMANCE.   Beginning at about the age of three, your daughter will begin to turn toward father with increasing interest. The intensity of her wishes concerning him may vary depending on how she has reacted to her discovery that she doesn't have a penis. She may be perfectly happy with her female anatomy and decide that she would like to be like her mother and possess what (and whom) her mother has. If she feels deprived about not having a penis, she may magically "blame" mother for her imagined deficit. After all, mother makes the babies, and the child may question why she was made differently. She may then turn toward her father so she can feel compensated for what she doesn't have.

Your daughter's first step toward having relationships with men in later life is this crucial turning toward father. A father's reaction to his daughter's interest in him is vitally important, and for the most part, fathers find it easy to show affection toward a daughter as compared to a son. During this period, your daughter will want father completely to herself. Hoping for his exclusive attention, she may unwittingly express the most callous designs. She may ask, "Daddy, can you and I get married, just like with mommy?" Or she may inquire, "Mommy, when are you going on a trip so I can take care of daddy and the house?" She may even wonder aloud when mother will die so she can then take over her position in the household.

What does your little girl want when she flagrantly expresses such outrageous wishes? What does her wish to "marry" her father really mean to her? Remember, the child's thinking is magical and not nearly so sophisticated as adult logic and the adult's capacity to use reason. Basically, your daughter wants the same loving attention from her father that mother already has. She fully knows that her parents have a private life together; she wants to take part in that life and have father to herself.

She may want daddy to kiss her and hold her, and, whatever her fantasies are about what her parents do in the privacy of their bedroom, she may want to have a baby with her father. Keep in mind that she has no true understanding of what having a baby entails. Instead, she fantasizes about what it would be like to have a baby (and therefore be very much like mother), based on her life's experiences and whatever information she's been given about how babies are made and born. Even then, she will conjure up the most fantastic notions about how babies are produced.

No matter how she perceives the roles of mother and father, the child will, in some way, want to have father exclusively to herself. This wish will cause her to feel some rivalry with her mother. This is an ambivalent situation for the child, since during the entire three or four years of her life, she has been intensely attached to mother, who has been either her primary caretaker or at least at the very center of her emotional life.

Over the next few years, the child comes to realize that she will never really have father to herself, that she's too young and cannot realistically compete with mother for father's attentions, and that father, though loving and even fostering his daughter's flirtations, has never really taken her wishes seriously. The little girl must eventually come to terms with her unrealistic notions, knowing at some point that her childish wishes are doomed to frustration. Realizing this, she decides to no longer risk angering or alienating mother; she instead decides to become as much like mother as possible. She will someday become a grown woman and marry a grown man, who will be like father. By this identification with mother, she solidifies her sexual identity, learning how to become (and live like) a woman, so she can some day have a relationship with a man like father.

This long, slow process doesn't come to a sudden end when a girl is six years old. Your daughter may continue to have an intensely romantic relationship with father throughout childhood, one lasting well into adolescence and, in some ways, even into adult life. Many a young girl has a somewhat flirtatious relationship with her father, wanting to be special, even being "daddy's little girl" far beyond the time of her being "little" or a "girl." This is quite normal. We all know that some women carry this even further, marrying men who are fifteen or twenty years their senior. We often say that such a woman married a "father figure," and this is one acceptable variation of a woman's working out her romantic attachment to her father.

During this period of development, in addition to identifying with mother, your daughter internalizes certain parental values. She develops a set of ideas about how best to please you and how to avoid displeasing. "Mother likes me to be this way"—"Daddy likes a girl who speaks softly"—"Daddy and mommy would like me to behave like a young lady"—"I shouldn't be nasty or use certain language"—"I should be polite." Learning to avoid certain ways of behaving, she takes on others, making them part of her way of being.

These values become part of an inner idea of the kind of person she should be. Solidifying a sense of right and wrong, your child slowly develops a conscience. Although the seeds of conscience were formed during toddlerhood, by the end of her Oedipal phase, your child's conscience is far more mature and deeply ingrained. She refrains from wrong doing because it feels good to do something she inwardly knows is right. Doing wrong will cause her to feel guilt, an inner sense that she's done wrong or that she has been bad, whether she is caught or not. Over the next few years, her conscience will become more firmly established and mature, as she identifies with other significant women such as teachers, counselors, and other adults who play a meaningful part in the child's life.

Your child can resolve these powerful Oedipal feelings in various ways. One girl may decide that she will eventually marry a man and have a baby, becoming very much like mother. This identification will take form and become elaborated as the years pass. Another girl may make a similar identification, but as she grows up, will choose not to marry, but will have a career instead. Or she may eventually decide to have both a career and a family. Her life-style and the ways she eventually defines her femininity depend partly on her childhood experiences, on the attitudes and expectations that were part of her early emotional environment, and on the opportunities available to her as an adult. All this takes place in a crucially important social and cultural climate that may foster or hinder the expression of what is considered to be feminine at a particular time.

Today, many people question the role model of marriage-household-baby that once predominated and with which the young girl usually identifies as a preschooler. Many more potential pathways for success exist for today's child, and young girls grow up knowing they may choose careers as well as marriage and motherhood. It's important to recognize that there are many possible variations for a young girl's successfully negotiating this phase of development; there is no one "right" or "best" way to fulfill the richness of one's potential.

Various complications may crop up for a girl as she goes through the Oedipal phase. A little brother may be born at precisely the time the child most intensely seeks closeness with her father. Suppose this particular father favors a son and, in response to the newcomer's arrival, lavishes all his attention on the little brother. Feeling envious and deprived of her father's love, this girl might conclude that father's attention could only be captured by a boy. This child might then tend to feel "devalued" and "inferior" as a girl, sensing that she is a disappointment to her father, a view of herself that she could carry with her throughout her life.

If parents divorce or separate when a daughter is three or four years old, at the very height of her wishes to have a close and intense relationship with father, father has a less direct influence on the child's life than would otherwise be the case. She might wonder if she possibly did something to cause father to leave the house or distance himself from her (remember the child's magical and egocentric way of thinking at this age). This girl's course of development will vary, depending on whether or not an uncle, a grandfather, a new husband, or some other man is available as a focus for her Oedipal attentions at this critical period of development. While such a male figure cannot easily "replace" father, he can become an intense focus of the little girl's Oedipal interests. Her course will also depend on her father's continuing interest in her (even if he remarries and has another child with a new wife), and on her mother's willingness or ability to set aside any bitter feelings she may have toward the child's father. All these variations and possibilities will enter into the equation. Separation and divorce is such an increasingly important and common phenomenon that a chapter is devoted to this topic in Part II. (See Chapter 6, *Separation, Divorce, and the Child.*)

Other important variations will influence a young girl's development during this time. A child may be the oldest of four siblings, and be the only girl. Or she may be the youngest, with both boys and girls as siblings. She might be an only child. A little girl's mother could die, leaving her as the only one to replace her (depending on the number of daughters) and "take care" of daddy. The death could leave the child with profound and unresolved feelings of guilt, especially if mother's death occurred precisely when the child most wished to replace mother and have father to herself.

Some women, though adults, never outgrow this developmental period. Such a woman, though in every respect a grown-up, actually feels she is still a child wanting father completely for herself. She wants a man, just as the little girl wants her daddy. She may wish to be held and loved but fears a true sexual relationship. Seductive and easily able to arouse a man's interest, such a woman has little capacity for an adult sexual relationship. She has identified with mother and turned toward a man for a certain kind of love but has not really progressed beyond her original attachment to her father.

There are countless variations in negotiating this developmental phase. Each can bring about a healthy resolution of the little girl's wish to rival her mother for her father's attention. And each can lead to partial resolutions of the conflicting feelings during this period in a young girl's life. Each child negotiates this crucial developmental phase in her own way, depending on her parents' lives and conflicts (individually and as a couple), on the child's position in the family, on the family's situation in society, and on the society's standards for becoming a woman.

THE BOY'S OEDIPAL ROMANCE. At about three years of age, the boy begins feeling possessive about his mother and moves into a competitive relationship with his father. He longs for his mother's companionship, wanting to have her for himself. He would like to be bigger and stronger than daddy, and have everything father has. While admiring and still loving his father, he also wishes he would go away. One five-year-old, watching a sanitation truck pull away from the house, said to his mother, "What would we do if daddy was put in the garbage?"

When father returns home from work, the boy greets him with a hug but may also want to wrestle. He has loving feelings as well as feelings of hostility. In other words, the boy's feelings toward his father are ambivalent. This complicated set of feelings is fraught with danger for the boy, who thinks in childishly magical and unrealistic ways. Remember, a four- or five-year-old child actually believes that a parent can know his thoughts. Though wishing his father would "disappear," the child must consistently tolerate the presence of this very powerful man, and he comes to the disturbing conclusion that father knows precisely what he is thinking. To make matters worse, the little boy convinces himself that when father becomes aware of his hostile wishes, he will angrily retaliate.

This concern about retaliation takes on a very specific tone at this time. Although he fears he will be injured in some general way, the boy's fear now focuses on a specific body part: his penis. He grows worried that he will lose it. Why should this happen?

First, recall that the boy only recently became aware of the fact that the girl has no penis; in the child's primitive thoughts and with his magical reasoning, this is ample proof that a penis can indeed be lost. Second, at this age, the boy's penis is a source of considerable pleasure. He enjoys fondling and touching it, and it becomes the focus for fantasies of being as big and powerful as father. The child's anxieties about competing with father condense into his penis, which in the boy's mind becomes the body part that offends his father.

This is a very conflict-filled and anxiety-ridden time for a small boy, and he is likely to show the effects of this period for a long while. A six-year-old boy will commonly avoid girls and may even refuse to hold a girl's hand when asked by a teacher to form a circle. The boy responds as though something about the girl is utterly frightening. What frightens the boy is the thought of the girl's genitals—a reminder both of his fear that he could lose his penis and of the period of conflict he has just traversed.

When he is six years old, a boy is enormously concerned with masculine activities and role models; he plays at being an astronaut, football player, baseball player, or soldier, male roles he assumes with virtually caricatural intensity.

Over the course of this period, he realizes that he cannot successfully compete with his father for his mother's affections. Despite his ardent wishes, he must face the sobering reality that as much as his mother loves him, she has never taken his romantic notions seriously. As the girl was forced to do with mother, the boy identifies with father, deciding that the best way to resolve this conflict is to become like father. In accomplishing this task, he internalizes the role of masculinity, hoping to become a man and someday have a woman like mother.

In doing this, he also internalizes a set of values and prohibitions: it's fine to say or do this, but I should never say or do that. The child internalizes a conscience. His conscience is immature, absolute, and very strict, as is the conscience of the six-year-old girl. For instance, one of the boy's beliefs may be that he must completely renounce interest or pleasure in any contact with mother. He may go so far as to think he must have no interest in girls. If he is going to be able to enjoy a mature relationship with a woman in his adult life, the boy will have to modify his very strict and childlike value system as he grows older. As happens with the girl, his conscience matures, becoming somewhat more flexible as the years pass. This process is facilitated by the boy's having contacts with other male figures—teachers, relatives, and counselors—and by his identifying with them as he grows older.

As with girls, a boy may experience many variations in his resolution of the Oedipal conflict. These will vary depending on the personalities of his father and mother, on their relationship with the child and with each other, and on the little boy's position in the family.

One boy's father might be the sort of man who overwhelms the child, belittling him and implicitly threatening the boy for his childish notions and romantic wishes. Such a father can never tolerate his son's competitive feelings and feels compelled to "defeat" the boy at every turn. Feeling he could never compete with such a father, the boy may completely renounce the notion of attempting to be like him. So threatening a father could cause the child to retreat in his development; the boy could grow up to be a passive, submissive individual with very little ability to be self-assertive.

A father may, for any number of reasons, be absent. Or he may himself be very passive, not providing an adequate role model for the boy's developing sense of masculine sexual identity. A child in this circumstance might have difficulty developing a sound, healthy sense of himself as a man.

A boy may negotiate the Oedipal phase without completely resolving some of his childish anxieties. Some men have never outgrown their fear of women, remaining much like the six-year-old who must devalue and deprecate women because of the implicit threat that they represent. Because of an unresolved anxiety about their maleness, which emanates from the Oedipal period, certain men need reassurance about their somewhat tenuous sense of masculinity. Such men must renounce any interest that they define to themselves as being even remotely "feminine." Absorbed by competitive sports and work, they pride themselves on being "rugged," shunning music, theater, literature, or any other "feminine" activity.

When this man marries, he spurns housework, never touching a dish or a broom. Should he become a father, he avoids taking part in his child's care. Without knowing it, he is burdened by a fear that such activity somehow reflects poorly on his shaky sense of masculinity. Reminiscent of the six-year-old who has gone through the anxieties of the Oedipal period, this man adopts a caricatural, supermasculine posture toward everything.

Other complications may arise. Suppose the child's parents separate or divorce when the five-year-old boy's romantic and rivalrous wishes are at their peak. To his egocentric way of thinking, the child could conclude that his wish for father to disappear magically came true. Because he also loves and admires his father, a boy in these circumstances could easily feel guilty for his imagined misdeed of having wished to be rid of his father.

Other events—a death in the family, a change of jobs, the birth of a sibling—may alter the triangular relationship between the child and his parents. Just as with the girl, the boy's position in the family—oldest child, youngest, only child, only boy among sisters, or another—partly determines the emotional tone of this period and influences your child's eventual development into an adult who takes on a masculine role in his life.

Because he fears injury to his body, the boy's passage through this phase can be quite tumultuous, and he is forced to renounce dramatically his unacceptable Oedipal wishes. This period of development comes to an abrupt end for the boy. We rarely see a boy's lingering romantic attachment to mother as clearly as we encounter a girl's attachment to her father, which may last into adult life. While a young woman's romanticized involvement with father or with a "father figure" is quite common, a young man's involvement with an older woman is uncommon, and we hardly ever see a man marrying a much older woman.

THE OEDIPAL PHASE AND THE ONE-PARENT HOUSEHOLD.   Many things can interfere with or complicate the usual "triangle" formed by a child and his or her parents. Such events include the birth of a sibling, the birth of twins, the death of a sibling, family discord, divorce, death of a parent, or any disruption in a family's unity. Today, with high divorce rates, many preschool children must negotiate the Oedipal phase of development in a home with one parent; this is usually the mother.

Discord or disruption in the family's structure will complicate a child's emotional life, and at this age will influence how he or she deals with the Oedipal phase. Such family difficulties add to an already conflict-filled time for a child, but need not prevent the youngster from successfully negotiating this crucial developmental phase.

If the girl's father is available to visit and has some regular, loving role in her life, she can still focus her Oedipal longings on him. The child's course is somewhat more complicated and fraught with conflict (depending on how both parents deal with the situation) than if father was consistently available in a home relatively free of conflict. Other men may also be available as objects of the little girl's romantic fantasies; these include uncles, a grandfather, other relatives, and perhaps other men with whom mother may have relationships.

Similarly, while the boy's Oedipal phase is somewhat more complicated in a one-parent household, the youngster usually has some meaningful contact with his father and can form a variety of Oedipal fantasies in this way. In addition, other male figures are usually available; relatives, family friends, and, later, teachers and counselors become figures with whom the boy can identify.

In truth, life, with two parents or one, is never ideal, and complications of many kinds arise for most children. While a one-parent household is less-than-ideal for any child, it does not prevent a successful resolution of the Oedipal phase of development. Such an arrangement can complicate an already conflict-filled time, but it is one of many variations in living in a less-than-perfect world.

The Preschool Child's Conscience

Your child will emerge from the preschool years very much transformed. As compared with the three-year-old toddler, the six-year-old child has radically changed how he relates to each parent, and how he sees himself and his options in life. One of the cardinal events of this period is the child's taking on the parents' ideals and prohibitions. The child makes their basic value system part of his own mind, developing an inner idea of those things he should not do (the prohibitions) and of those things he should want and aspire to do (the ideals).

In attaining this conscience, the child acquires an internal regulator of his thoughts, feelings, and actions (or potential actions). Any unacceptable wishes or feelings (those that his parents would disapprove of and which now meet with the child's own disapproval) will be opposed by his rather strict conscience. The child is now capable of feeling guilt, an inner sense that he is doing (or thinking or feeling) something that is unacceptable.

At the age of six years, a child's conscience is quite harsh and inflexible. He may rigidly adhere to certain internalized prohibitions, completely avoiding temptation of any kind. This is completely normal for a six-year-old and should not be a cause for alarm. If his conscience does not eventually become more flexible, if it remains rigidly strict and overly punitive as he grows older, he will feel inappropriately guilty for virtually *any* wish, no matter how benign it may be. This can become a crippling burden for a child, one that destroys initiative and dampens the child's willingness to become actively involved in new activities.

It is usually easy for a parent to determine if a child is burdened by an excessively harsh conscience as he enters the school-age years. If your child seems unwilling to engage in new activities, if he seems constricted in his interests or unwilling to meet new people or try new things, he may suffer from a very strict conscience. The child with an excessively rigid code of morals will blame himself for feeling or thinking about anything he deems to be "wrong" or that seems unacceptable. Such a child may habitually confess to "misdeeds" or be all too ready to blame himself for many things, even for imagined "wrongs" or "sins."

You should be concerned if your child develops rituals that become excessive; such rituals are set into motion in an attempt to ward off unacceptable thoughts and feelings. The child with excessive rituals and compulsions may begin to excessively wash his hands (more than five times per day) or may develop elaborate bedtime rituals such as having to say the same thing or go through complicated routines (again, possibly excessive hand-washing) before going to bed. (For a complete discussion of rituals and compulsions, as well as a description of a troubled child, see in Chapter 4, "Magic and Ritual," "Compulsions," "Counseling and Child Guidance," "Signs of Trouble," and "What a Parent Can Do.")

The child's conscience usually matures with time. He retains a sense of deeply embedded morality without having an overly critical conscience. He takes pleasure in learning new things, enlarging his repertoire of experiences, and identifying with various adults throughout the rest of childhood and adolescence. His values and conscience become modified, and he discovers outlets for initiative and ambitions.

Dealing with an Oedipal Child

During this period, your child may express unbelievable fantasies. Don't be surprised to hear the most outlandish suggestions sometimes spoken casually, sometimes declared with an emphasis so earnest that you will have to smother the wish to laugh. Your daughter may proclaim that she intends to marry daddy, or that she wants to keep house for her father. She may encourage her mother to take a very long trip, or suggest that she, the child, and daddy go on a vacation together, without Mommy.

Your son may make similar proclamations, stating his intention to marry Mommy or to take care of her when daddy goes away. In addition, he may make provocative or challenging statements to his father, and may even make physical gestures of thinly disguised hostility.

Keep in mind that your child, boy or girl, is struggling with intensely ambivalent feelings. He or she loves, admires, and competes with one parent, trying to win the affections of the other. Yet throughout all this, your child feels he or she needs both parents and can become anxious at the intensity of these feelings and magically tinged wishes.

During this period, your role, whether mother or father, is to be a consistent and affectionate role model for your child. It's best not to belittle your son's preposterous suggestions about marrying his mother. Nor should they be taken seriously. It's best to simply explain to him that you (mother) love him dearly and to tell him that someday he will grow up to be a man who will marry a grown woman his own age. As a father, it's best to avoid taking too seriously your son's statements about replacing you. When facing such ambivalent and hostile gestures from your son, you can say, "Someday you'll be big and strong like me, maybe even bigger." You can then engage him in playful wrestling or competition, making certain not to physically overwhelm or overpower him. To do so each and every time is to provide the not-so-subtle message that he can never "match up" to you. Remember, as much as your son wants to "get rid of" you, he admires and wants to become an adult version of you. Don't deride or belittle the child's romantic or aggressive notions, whether the child be a romantically or competitively inclined son or daughter.

During this phase, remain consistent and tolerant of your child's intense (and sometimes frightening) feelings. As an adult model, you ultimately help your child realize that it's necessary to become an adult, which, among other things, means moving beyond these intense family attachments. As a parent, you are your child's first object of true love; to a very great extent, the way your child experiences this first great "love affair" in life will partly determine how he experiences future relationships.

As a single parent, your task is more complex. In a sense, you must play, to some extent, the roles of both mother and father. If you are divorced, your child should have ample contact with your spouse; such visits should be free of strife, discord, or recriminations. Allow your child to have sufficient exposure to your spouse and to other same-sexed individuals for Oedipal fantasies, strivings, and identifications to form. This issue is so important that a chapter is devoted to it in Part II. (See Chapter 6, *Separation, Divorce, and the Child.*)

Whether you have a two-parent or one-parent household, avoid being overly seductive. While your son or daughter may want very much to join the parents in their bed, this can be occasionally permitted as an expression of family warmth and togetherness but should not become a regular pattern. Ultimately, you must frustrate your child's romantic feelings, which means the child cannot have all that he or she wants. To some extent, this is a balancing act, since you don't want to reject your child. It's usually easier for a father and daughter to have a romanticized relationship with each other than it is for a mother and son; our culture permits some variations of this. Remember, though, your ultimate role is to help your child achieve a self-identity as a boy or girl who will eventually become a man or woman, one who will find an appropriate partner outside the family.

◊ PRACTICAL ISSUES FOR THE PRESCHOOL CHILD

Many practical issues and problems arise during the time between three and six years. Many such difficulties arise from the conflict-filled fantasies of the Oedipal phase, while others have to do with the child's expanding world of peers and exposure to others such as occurs in the preschool setting. Some are limited to this period, others may crop up before or after this time, but they are all important. This section explores them.

When There Are Too Many Monsters

During this period, your child may develop a host of fears—of bogeymen, monsters such as Frankenstein or Dracula, of ghosts, ghouls, and goblins, of imagined creatures, and of inexplicable terrors in the darkness. The child may develop fears of robbers or pirates, or some irrational fear of lions, tigers, dogs, or insects.

Recall that the child—let's say a boy—has ambivalent feelings about his father. Wishing the father were gone, yet wanting to be like him, the child is also burdened by the notion that the father might just know exactly what he's thinking. What might father then do? Torn by conflicting feelings of love, hostility, and admiration, and fearing the possibility of the father's reprisals, how can the child deal with all this?

It would be intolerable for him to live in the same house with someone whom he so intensely fears. If he displaces this conflict onto some other person or thing, the boy is no longer forced to struggle with these feelings about his father. He may suddenly fear that a giant dog will bite him on the street. Or he may become terrified that a huge gorilla will carry him off and devour him. He may have trouble sleeping because he imagines some dreaded monster lurking in the darkness. Without knowing it, the child has displaced his fear of his father's reprisals onto something (or someone) much easier to avoid. While he can't avoid the father, he can easily bypass the neighbor's dog or avoid visiting the zoo. Or he can insist that mother remain with him as he waits for sleep to come, thereby avoiding some imagined monster. By avoiding the thing onto which his conflicting feelings have been displaced, the child makes the conflict far more tolerable.

Nightmares and fears will occur as part of your child's attempt to deal with intense feelings of conflict at this time in development. One symptom usually disappears after a short time, only to be replaced by another fear that runs its course and then, too, disappears. Should your child develop an intense fear of someone or something, there is little cause for concern. Simple reassurance will usually help him overcome it or deal with it until it passes. It isn't necessary to "show" him that his fear is irrational by taking him to the zoo or by bringing a dog into the house. With a little time, the fear will subside and disappear.

There may be an occasion when your child encounters the dreaded dog or cat at close quarters. In such an instance, the key is to remain calm and not show evidence of alarm; to frantically rush to your child to "save" him only reinforces his fear of the animal. Nor should you attempt to "desensitize" your child to the situation by coaxing him to pat or "make nice" to the dog. Calmly and simply escort him away from the situation, saying, "I know you're scared, but there's really nothing to be frightened about. Nobody wants to hurt you." Remember that in time, such childhood fears disappear.

Usually, the feared thing is easily avoided; that's the point of the symptom in the first place. For instance, if your child fears dogs (it may be a specific dog living nearby), he can avoid the object of his dread by simply not going near that dog. However, should he become afraid of leaving the house to go to school or the playground for fear of encoun-tering that (or any) dog, the child's normal functioning is being con-stricted. If such a situation persists, he should be given the opportunity to understand and overcome the fear. Psychological counseling would then be appropriate. For the most part, however, nightmares and fears are transient, do not interfere with the routines of daily living, and are normal experiences for a child this age.

Fear of Death

Many children develop an irrational fear of death during this period. This fear isn't rooted in some abstract notion or knowledge but stems from the child's knowing that people die, as well as that something could happen to him. Your child's fear of death may focus either on himself or on you. He may anxiously ask, "Mommy, when am I going to die?" Or, "Daddy, will you die soon?" He may ask, "When will you die, Mommy?" These questions will be asked with genuine anxiety, and they are of considerable concern to your child. (See "Worries About Older Dad," later in this chapter.)

Whether asking about his own or your mortality, your child's fear of death is part of the unresolved issue of separation anxiety. Although this was a primary issue during infancy and toddlerhood, separation anxiety must be dealt with throughout every phase of life. During the preschool period, in addition to fear of separation, your child's anxious concerns about death may be part of the way he deals with his ambiva-lent wish to be rid of father (or mother), with whom he feels some competition for the other parent's affections. Your child may be "undo-ing" the *wish* that you disappear or go away (which is similar to dying) by developing a *fear* that this will happen to you. In other words, the wish becomes a fear.

Although it's difficult for a child this age to imagine or understand the finality of death, this fear can be an important one. In a sense, when asking about mortality, your child is really asking, "Are you going to leave me or go away?"

Simple reassurance that you are not about to die can be very helpful to your child. She wants to know that you will not leave, that you will love her and be available to her despite her powerfully mixed feelings during this period of development. The subject of helping children deal with death is very important. A chapter is devoted to it in Part II. (See Chapter 8, *Telling Your Child About Death.*)

Where Do Babies Come From?

The origin of babies is one of the foremost mysteries of childhood. Sooner or later, usually when a new baby is about to arrive, your child will begin incessantly questioning you about where babies come from. A simple explanation for a three-year-old child will usually suffice: explaining that the baby grows inside the mother and comes out through a special opening will satisfy your child for some time. A detailed anatomical explanation is beyond a three-year-old's ability to understand.

No matter how much or little you tell a young preschool child about the facts of life, she is likely to create fantastic theories and notions about it. She may think that a baby is bought at the store. She may develop the idea that since mother goes to the hospital to have a baby, an operation is necessary for it to be born. This can be very upsetting for a young girl, who may conjure up disastrous consequences to her own body if and when she decides to have a child. This can be even more anxiety-provoking to the young child who already thinks she's been mutilated because she has no penis.

Other childlike theories abound: a baby is slowly assembled at the baby factory; the baby is born by mommy's eating a seed that grows inside her and comes out through the rectum; the baby grows inside the stomach after you eat a certain food (usually something containing seeds); mother's egg has a shell, like a hen's egg; and an imaginative variety of other fantastic distortions.

It's a good idea to tell your child as much as she can possibly understand. When she wants to know more, she will ask. It's helpful to teach the child the correct names of genital anatomy; euphemisms and "cute" terms aren't necessary and may cause additional confusion. It's wise to communicate to your child that there's nothing shameful about the body and how it works. Your explanations should be given in a relaxed way, without conveying anxiety or concern to the child. These are absolutely normal questions; do your best to answer them simply, in terms your child can understand.

Remember, your child's thinking is magical and unrealistic during this period of development. Don't be surprised if, no matter how logical and accurate your explanation, your child independently arrives at the most fantastic conclusions about where babies come from. Most important, convey to the child that a baby's birth is the natural consequence of a mother and father's loving each other and wanting to have a baby. Given in a relaxed way, the information you provide will help your child feel that when she wants to know more, you will be ready to explain as much as you can.

Lying

As was the case for the older toddler, the young preschooler's imagination may run rampant. The child's world is a strange mélange of the real and the fantastic. Many parents, not realizing the limitations and influences to which a child's mind is subject, become upset and concerned, thinking their child's fantastic tales are signs of a pathological liar. Actually, there are different kinds of lies; some are quite harmless, while others may signal trouble.

The young preschooler's lies seem little more than an effort to remake reality into something more desirable. A child may fantasize heroic powers or may tell of wondrous exploits, all designed to win your admiration and attention. In small doses, these tales and fantasies may be cute and are harmless. Should they get out of hand and become a major part of your child's mental life, your child may be telling you he isn't getting enough attention. Such a child needs more praise for his everyday achievements so he won't be driven into fantasy for such attention.

A young preschooler is likely to think that his thoughts are known by or are perceptible to adults. The child actually thinks that it's only a matter of time before an omniscient adult actually picks up on these thoughts. Sometimes, in an effort to test your parental powers, your child will purposely distort the truth in the most obvious way. He didn't write with a crayon on the wall, someone else did; he *did* wash his hands before dinner (despite the fact that they are filthy); and other obvious misstatements of fact. By the end of the preschool years, a child may be able to fabricate plausible accounts designed to gain credit for himself or to discredit another. By this time, the child has a serious expectation of being believed.

Your reaction to a lie is important, and may set the tone for your child's dealing with future relations with friends, teachers, and other people. When you know that your child has lied, treat the matter as casually as you can. Tell him that you doubt he's telling the truth, that you favor truthfulness, and that you're certain he *does* tell the truth most of the time. Moral outrage at a lie is never helpful; it calls the child's *entire worth* into question rather than dealing with the specific issue at hand.

If your child confesses to a lie or confesses to having done something wrong, punishment is the wrong way to react. Punishing your child for confessing a misdeed simply teaches him to become a better liar to avoid future punishment. Tell him that you're glad he decided to tell the truth, and explain why he was wrong in doing whatever he did.

An occasional lie is inevitable. It's part of living, whether as a child or grown-up. Only if your child's lying becomes pervasive should it be a cause for concern. The child who constantly distorts the truth may be living a very barren reality. He may feel neglected or unwanted, or may not feel himself worthwhile. To compensate, he may feel the need to exaggerate and distort the truth, even wanting to be caught in a lie to gain a modicum of attention. Such a child may benefit from psychological counseling.

Masturbation

Masturbation, the pleasurable fondling of the genitals, is common in children of all ages. A child may masturbate with or without erotic fantasies. It provides pleasure and is reassuring for the boy who may be worried about the fate of his penis.

A girl discovers her genitals as part of her self-discovery and growing awareness of her body. A young girl's masturbation may not appear as frequent or as obvious as the masturbatory activities of a boy, but she does obtain pleasure in touching her genitals.

For the boy, masturbation may have both pleasurable and painful aspects. An erection may occur even when the child prefers it does not. It may persist to the point of discomfort, and the child may become upset, fearing he has lost control of his own body since his penis may remain erect despite his wishes to the contrary.

Recall that your child, whether boy or girl, is concerned about the genitals. There are fantasies about what has already happened or about what may happen to the genitals, about castration and mutilation. Therefore, never threaten dire consequences to the child by saying "It will fall off," or "You'll get sick," or other warnings about masturbation.

There's no need to worry about your child's masturbation unless it becomes a very frequent form of behavior in which he or she engages continually, every day, and in public. You can try diverting your child's attention when masturbation occurs. You may feel embarrassed by your child's fondling his or her genitals when visitors are present, and you may decide to discourage the child from masturbating in front of them. You can tell your child that people outside the family may not like such activity, so it's best to confine it to situations when visitors aren't around. See "Masturbating," later in this chapter, and in Chapter 2, see "Masturbates Frequently.")

Bad Language

A child this age may suddenly begin using "bad" words. These are usually terms having to do with the toilet, with feces, with superficial anatomy and with bowel movements, and is often called "toilet talk." Some years later, a child may begin using sexual terms that are very upsetting to parents.

Although your preschool child has very little knowledge about the meaning of these words, she knows very well that they can cause enormous agitation for a parent. Expressing outrage at your child's use of these terms will only intensify their value and meaning to the child, reinforcing her use of the terms whenever she wants to shock or surprise you.

You may want to limit your child's use of various bad words. This is best done by telling her that words of this sort are used only in certain places, at limited times, and only in front of certain people. While you don't have to approve of your child's vocabulary at all times, it's best to avoid becoming agitated since this will serve as an unwitting reinforcement for the child to use these words with maddening frequency. (See "Uses Bad Language," later in this chapter.)

When Baby Talk Persists

Baby talk is absolutely warranted and expected when your child begins talking. Once she is well on the road to speaking, it's best to use standard, adult English rather than the "cute" and babyish pronunciations that were at first delightful for both you and your child.

During the preschool years, the child's language becomes refined, elaborated, and consolidated. You may occasionally notice your child having some problem pronouncing certain words or having articulation problems of one kind or another. The great majority of such "defects" are simply due to immaturity, and your child will no doubt correct such minor pronunciation mistakes as she matures.

Some parents grow concerned when a child persists in using baby talk long after other children the same age have abandoned such speech patterns. The continuation of baby talk may result from parents unwittingly encouraging its use. If you notice such a pattern, you must ask yourself if you are encouraging baby talk, and if you are somehow making babyhood too attractive to your child.

Occasionally, a child may revert to baby talk after having abandoned it some months earlier. This may be a sign of regression because of emotional pressure or stress—such as the arrival of a new baby—although any new challenge can cause a child to regress and begin using baby talk.

If your child uses baby talk or has resumed using it after having been launched toward more standard speech, don't attack it directly. Don't chastise your child for "being a baby," and don't tell her, "Speak like a grown-up, not like a baby!" This minor and transient speech problem is best corrected by providing your child with a good speech model. Use adult pronunciation consistently, and your child will soon get the message. (See in Chapter 2, "Influence of Speech Problems" and "Hardly Speaks," and later in this chapter, "Enhancing a Child's Language.")

Bedtime Problems

It's very common for a child this age to resist going to bed. There are several reasons for such resistance. First, he may be fearful of having a nightmare or may fear a "monster" or some other terrifying creature he's conjured up. Fears and bad dreams are quite common at this age. Deal with them by simply knowing that in time they will disappear.

Your child may come into your bedroom during the night, insisting that he sleep with you for fear of a nightmare or a monster. Avoid letting this behavior become a consistent pattern. This will only encourage more sleepless nights and fearful approaches. At this age, your child is struggling with powerful Oedipal wishes; allowing the child into your bed may introduce an erotic element into the wish to be near mother (or father, as the case may be) and may foster further sleep difficulties. Remember, part of your role as a parent is to help your child negotiate this phase of development, allowing him to develop the mental and emotional tools eventually to find satisfactions beyond the family. By allowing your child to sleep with you, you may unconsciously but seductively foster greater romantic interest in his parents, which won't help his move toward interests and eventual attachments beyond the family.

Calm reassurance usually helps a child get to sleep, despite monsters, robbers, and other fearsome creatures of the night. If your child insists that a dim hall light be left on, it's a reasonable request, and a light may help him feel less anxious. Remember, too, your child may still be struggling with separation anxiety. Going to sleep means that the child must leave the familiar routines of family life behind. Allowing him to sleep in your bed, staying in the child's room until he falls asleep, and other measures that prolong contact, can delay your child's mastering of separation anxiety.

Of course, there may come times when you must be somewhat flexible about your child coming into bed with you. During times of illness or stress, the young child may regress and come into your room, wanting to climb into bed. Or it may be necessary for you to accompany your child back to bed and remain as a reassuring presence until he or she falls asleep. As a general rule, prolonging contact, whether by allowing your child into bed with you or by staying at the child's bedside, can and should be done only during a stressful period for the child. Such periods may include illness, returning home from a trying visit to the doctor, returning from a hospital stay, following the birth of a sibling, or any other situation that temporarily upsets the child's emotional equilibrium. (See Chapter 19, *When a Child Goes to the Hospital*, and Chapter 5, *Sibling Rivalry*.)

Many children this age take a favorite toy to bed. Such use of a transitional object may continue in one form or another, even into the school years. (See "Wants to Share the Bed," later in this chapter.)

Bed-wetting

Bed-wetting (technically called *enuresis*) can cause enormous concern for parents. Although bed-wetting is not itself harmful, it can lead to many problems for a child. Family life can be changed as inordinate attention is focused on the child who wets, and the child may become an object of anger, of scapegoating, and of the family's need to keep a "secret" from others outside the family. For the child, bed-wetting can lead to anxiety about parents' reactions, to impaired or constricted relationships with friends, and lowered self-esteem.

Enuresis is the involuntary discharge of urine after the age when bladder control was (or should have been) attained, usually between three and five years of age. The frequency of wetting required for a child to be considered enuretic is somewhat arbitrary, ranging from estimates of once per month to as often as three times per week. Each child's situation must be considered individually, but it's probably reasonable to consider bed-wetting a problem if it occurs once per week or more frequently. Of course, this definition varies; some parents (and experts) would find it problematic if a child wets as infrequently as once per month.

A distinction is made between *primary* enuresis, meaning that a child has never achieved bladder control, as opposed to *secondary* enuresis, which means a child resumes wetting after a period of dryness, usually some three to six months after the child has achieved full bladder control. Daytime wetting is not nearly as common as nighttime enuresis.

Bed-wetting occurs two or three times more commonly in boys than girls. It is difficult to give accurate statistics about this problem since so many families keep a child's bed-wetting a well-guarded family secret. Between 12 and 25 percent of children up to four years old are enuretic, while 10 to 13 percent of children up to six years of age wet their beds. Nighttime enuresis is not a rare symptom and may be even more common than we think. It decreases with age (dropping to about 2 percent of children by age twelve). For a very few, it may continue into adolescence.

CAUSES OF BED-WETTING. Although a great deal of research about enuresis has been done, a comprehensive understanding of its cause does not exist. There are probably a number of causes: genetic, medical, psychological, and involving sleep disorders, and these causes can occur alone or in combination.

- *Genetic causes* may play some role. Up to 75 percent of enuretic children have parents who were both enuretic as children. About 44 percent of enuretic children have one parent who was a bed-wetter as a child.
- *Medical causes* sometimes play a role. In a few cases, bladder infections and various bladder abnormalities cause or promote enuresis. Bed-wetting may be one of the first symptoms of childhood diabetes mellitus and other diseases.
- *Developmental immaturity* may contribute to bed-wetting in some children. Certain enuretic children have decreased bladder capacity, and enuretic children of both sexes are often shorter and less developmentally mature than nonenuretic children.
- *Sleep disorders* are thought to play some role in bed-wetting. Parents often describe the child who wets as a very deep sleeper. At one time, scientific findings seemed to support the theory that some enuretic children may have a sleep disorder, but recent evidence casts doubt on this explanation.

• *Psychological reasons* are very important in certain children who wet. Some psychiatrists feel that primary enuresis may follow premature, coercive toilet training, or overindulgent toilet-training methods. These physicians feel that the bed-wetting is the child's retaliation against the parents, and indicates an infantalized relationship of the child to the parents. However, most experts do not consider primary enuresis to be caused by psychological factors.

Secondary enuresis (the return to bed-wetting after bladder control has been attained) is more often considered to have psychological causes than primary enuresis. It can be understood as a symptom following any stressful event such as a hospitalization, parental divorce, the birth of a sibling, the family's moving to a new neighborhood, and any other psychological stress.

EVALUATING THE CHILD WHO WETS.   The initial evaluation of a child who wets is usually done by a pediatrician. Your doctor may feel that a psychiatric consultation would be helpful. The child's complete history must be reviewed and as much as possible learned about the onset of the wetting, its relationship to stresses or family changes, the ways the symptoms present, and the family's reaction to the bed-wetting. In addition, a thorough physical examination (along with appropriate medical laboratory tests) should be done to rule out any possible urologic or medical reasons for the enuresis.

DEALING WITH THE CHILD WHO WETS.   There are a number of general approaches for dealing with the child who wets. None of them require risk or expense, and they are frequently useful alone or in combination.

• Remember, many children have episodes of bed-wetting. This symptom is very common, occurring occasionally in nearly all children. Use common sense. The child who has a rare accident (once every six weeks) is not truly having a problem. Occasional bed-wetting is quite common, occurring in nearly 25 percent of children up to four years of age.
• The percentage of children who continue bed-wetting declines as age increases. The overwhelming chance is that your child will stop nighttime wetting as he or she grows older. Very few problems persist until adolescence.
• Your child is not purposefully or willfully wetting his bed. There is no reason to view bed-wetting as something under the child's control or as something he's doing for attention. Avoid making the wet

bed a battlefield. Such discord actually increases the frequency of wetting.

- Avoid making this problem the central or focal issue of your relationship with your child. Under no circumstances should you shame or punish your child for wetting. This won't change the problem and will only serve as a means to make the child feel devalued and demeaned.
- Reduce or eliminate any fluids before bedtime.
- Consider waking the child to urinate after he's slept for several hours (just before you go to bed).
- Consider encouraging a child who can write to keep a "journal" in which he records nights when he's wet the bed. When doing this, avoid any display of disapproval if bed-wetting occurs. Such displays provoke feelings of guilt and shame. A journal can serve as a powerful reminder to the child of an event he might prefer to forget, and may help ensure his feelings of active participation in dealing with this problem.
- Be optimistic and encouraging. You don't have to cover up that you would prefer your child to have bladder control, and that you want him to make every effort possible in that direction. Reward him for dry nights, commenting positively on his achievement. This is positive reinforcement.
- Determine if wetting began during or after some stressful situation or crisis (this applies in some cases of secondary enuresis). Typical conflicts in which bed-wetting appears as a symptom involve situational reactions (for instance, the birth of a sibling) or a separation problem in which the wet bed serves as a battlefield for parents and child (for example, when wetting begins one month before the child is scheduled to leave for summer camp). In such cases, psychological counseling can be helpful.

OTHER TREATMENTS.   In certain severe cases of enuresis in which the child has never achieved bladder control, the symptom can become an unfortunate focal point in the relationship between a child and his parents. Some parents, no matter how they try to do otherwise, have such negative feelings about bed-wetting that the problem dominates family life. In such cases, when there is no clear psychologic precipitant, you may wish to consider two other methods of dealing with enuresis.

Both conditioning and medication can be effective approaches to the treatment of long-standing and resistant bed-wetting. You must consult with your child's pediatrician when seriously considering using either of these methods.

Sometimes doctors prescribe a behavior modification, or conditioning, technique based on the theory that enuresis is an undesirable habit stemming from faulty learning. The most common method uses a bell-and-pad device: The first drops of urine on a mattress pad complete an electrical circuit, triggering an alarm to sound. The child is awakened and goes to the bathroom to urinate. Before using this method, any medical or physical problems must be ruled out as a cause of enuresis.

Conditioning can be helpful if the child actively participates in using the apparatus and isn't afraid of it. Parents must be thoroughly familiar with the apparatus and its use. Frequent contact with the therapist for both child and parents (a form of psychotherapy) is essential to make certain that the treatment is progressing properly. Treatment usually lasts about five to six weeks, and results can be impressive.

A psychiatric medication named imipramine (an antidepressant) has been found to be useful in certain cases of bed-wetting. The medication acts on the nerves supplying the urinary bladder, helping the child retain urine during the night. While this approach has been successful in some resistant cases, any medication can have side effects. In addition, caution must be exercised when dealing with young children. You must keep in mind the possibility of an overdose for either the child being treated or a younger sibling who may ingest the medication. One drawback of using medication is that the child (or parents) may view the taking of medicine as an indication of disease, which has negative connotations.

Television

Television is a fact of life, and it's here to stay. Many parents worry about the effects of television on their children. There's no doubt that television can be a source of knowledge, can influence how children think and feel, and can present various models for children's behavior. Keep in mind that a young child's ability to separate reality from fantasy is still tenuous; a child may deeply believe that what she sees on the screen is actually happening.

As can happen with any important information medium, television can become a constructive or destructive force in your child's life, depending on how you and your child use it.

Extensive television-watching by a young child may limit the time she spends actively exploring the world on her own. It can limit healthy interactions with other people, which is one of the primary ways your child discovers the world and learns how to deal with people. Many preschool teachers and sensitive parents grow concerned when they notice a young child's play reflecting and imitating something seen on television rather than playing out a product of the child's own experiences or fantasy life.

There is some evidence that watching television can facilitate a child's learning to read. A child can have sensory input of both seeing and hearing words presented on the screen; this is thought to promote association between the spoken and printed word. On the other hand, a child who has had a steady diet of television throughout the years may later watch television rather than read.

Many parents worry about the possible connection between violence on television and the possibility of violent behavior resulting from such exposure. A number of studies have been done, with inconclusive results. However, the consensus seems to be that watching violent television programs can provoke violent behavior mainly in people who are already inclined to behave violently.

Some parents are content to allow their children free access to several hours of television every day, using the television set as an electronic baby-sitter. The important consideration is that television can both expand and limit your child's experiences, depending on how you use it. There is little doubt that to some degree television can expose a child to a variety of otherwise unavailable experiences. With judicious use, television can be a positive force in your child's life.

Rather than allowing a child unlimited access to the television, you might consider making your child's time in front of the set a shared experience. Up to a point, television can be a family activity that you and your child share together.

We feel that you must, to some extent, ration or limit the time your child spends watching television. The images, sounds, and worlds that television presents can be seductive, and your child's motor development requires physical activity during the preschool years. If for no other reason, television, a sedentary activity, should be limited for the sake of your child's healthy motor development. While television can be a positive force, it's best for your child to spend as much time as possible *actively* participating in sensory, intellectual, and motor experiences, rather than passively taking in preformed images on a television screen.

Preschools and Day Care

Most children can benefit from a group activity, beginning at the age of two or three years, until formal schooling begins. While a preschool experience isn't necessary for every child, it can be particularly valuable for a child whose daily experiences with other children are limited, an only child, or a child who lives in a city apartment and has limited access to other children. By the age of three, a child should have the company of other children the same age, both for activities and to learn how to get along with other children.

An additional benefit is that preschool exposes a child to adults other than the parents. Some parents feel that sending a young child to school is helpful when the child is too attached to the parents. For the growing number of families in which both parents work outside the home, a good preschool functions as a surrogate caretaker, as well as offering an educating and socializing experience.

As of this writing, families in which the parents must work face a significant problem, because of limited governmental funding of pre-schools that provide good curricula and well-trained staff, and maintain good facilities. Private schools are expensive, and families with limited financial means who need care for their young children are often faced with difficult decisions. There is no doubt that government, and possibly businesses and other employers, must play a more active role in funding good day-care centers and preschools for parents who want and need them.

DAY CARE.   Day-care centers were first formed to accommodate the growing numbers of families with working mothers. Unlike traditional nursery school, day care spans a wider age range, from infancy through the preschool years. Since the purpose of a day-care center is to provide surrogate care, the hours are longer than nursery-school hours, typically running from 8 A.M. to 6 P.M. to accommodate usual working hours. In a sense, day care is a form of long-term baby-sitting. An entire range of physical and psychological care must be provided: meals, toileting, play, naps, and many social and intellectual activities.

Ideally, day-care-center teachers should all be highly trained, li-censed, and qualified as nursery-school teachers, but this is rarely the case. More often, supervisors have the proper qualifications and oversee other personnel. Many day-care centers use volunteer parents, neighbor-hood adults, and high-school and college students to assist with the daily running of the centers. (See Chapter 7, *When Mother Works,* for a discussion of day-care centers and surrogate care of children.)

NURSERY SCHOOLS.   The decision to have your child attend a pre-school (or nursery school) is one of the most important you make, since it may be the first organized experience your child has with other children and adults. Ideally, a good preschool should deal with all aspects of a child's development, while remaining sensitive to each child's individual interests, talents, and level of development.

A good preschool can provide a variety of valuable experiences: social play, dramatic play (both alone and with other children), playing with blocks, finger-painting, clay-modeling, construction with various materials, drawing, listening to music, singing, dancing, outdoor activities of many kinds, and a variety of social, creative, and intellectual activities to help your child grow in many ways.

HOW TO EVALUATE A PRESCHOOL.   Once you have decided that your child will benefit from a preschool experience, you must decide which school is best suited for the child's needs. Today, most preschools have deemphasized the force-feeding quality of preparing children for the formal aspects of education beginning at age five or six. Preschools today emphasize socialization and intellectual exposure without being "preparatory" for formal schooling.

When considering any preschool, you must learn as much as you can about the school's program and program philosophy, and about its staffing and facility, so you can intelligently decide. The following practical tips will help you locate and evaluate a preschool that is suitable for your child.

- Get suggestions and recommendations from other parents. This can be helpful, especially if the information comes from parents you know and trust. It's also a good idea to have had some exposure to their children.
- Ask your pediatrician for a recommendation. He or she may know of excellent schools.
- Visit the school for a firsthand view of the facility and its program. There is no substitute for an in-person visit. It's probably best to make several visits, even making one unannounced visit to observe how things are done.

WHAT TO LOOK FOR AND ASK ABOUT.   When visiting a preschool, you should observe and inquire about the following aspects of the school's facility, staff, and program:

- Are the physical facilities adequate? Is there plenty of space (indoors and outdoors) for a wide range of activities? Is the facility safe and clean? Are there large common areas for group play and games, as well as areas where a child can be alone for a while?

- Are there sufficient materials? A variety of learning (which means playing) materials is very important. Are there books for various-aged children? Is there a phonograph? Is there a piano or some other musical instrument? Are there toys and objects that allow for dramatic play: household objects (from the kitchen and elsewhere); adult clothing for children to dress up and for playacting; blocks; finger paints; and a variety of other stimulating objects that can serve as a springboard for play, exploration, and for widening your child's exposure to, and knowledge, of the world? Remember, play is serious business for children; it's how they get to know more and more about the world.
- Although not mandatory, it's best if the school has some animal and plant life, which can serve as a source of endless wonderment for children, promoting questions about life and about living things. Pets would include a dog, cat, hamsters, gerbils, tropical fish, or other animals that will vary depending on whether the school is located in the city or the country.
- Observe the level of activity. Are the children active and supervised while playing, or are they unsupervised and doing very little? Although activity is fine, there should also be periods of relative quiet to balance the activities.
- Inquire about the school's curriculum. Is the program organized, yet flexible? Do the activities balance action with occasional inactivity, boisterousness with quiet play and opportunities for children to explore things reflectively on their own? Is there individual instruction and attention? Are several groups engaged in different activities, or is the approach inflexible, forcing all children to participate in one activity at a time? Are there special events and festivities such as Christmas and Easter parties? Is there an occasional field trip for interested children? Is there room for individual variation and for different children to express and satisfy different interests?
- How many children are there for each teacher to supervise and deal with? A well-organized program should have no more than seven or eight children per teacher.
- Does the school require that all children be immunized against common childhood diseases? A facility that takes its public health responsibilities seriously will require you to show proof of your child's vaccinations.
- What are the professional qualifications of the teachers? Can you assess the teachers' personal attributes? While personal qualities are difficult to assess in a single visit, it's important to know that a good

preschool teacher must be confident and mature, and, above all, likes working with children. You are best off making several visits and watching the interaction between children and teachers. Are the teachers friendly and outgoing? Do they spend time with individual children, responding to requests for help in a warm and interested way? Do they allow the children to express individual creativity, or are they mechanical in their approach? Do the children seem relaxed and comfortable with the teachers? Can you make a judgment about the general atmosphere of the school?

WHEN TO START PRESCHOOL OR DAY CARE.   Some preschools start with two-year-olds. This may be fine if your child is fairly independent and doesn't experience a great deal of separation anxiety. But many two-year-olds simply aren't ready; they cling dependently and are frightened by any separation from mother, especially for an entire day. This is worse if the class is large and the teacher must pay attention to nine or ten children throughout the day.

A two-year-old may have to become slowly accustomed to the idea of preschool, and you may have to wait until your child is three years old before he is ready to leave home for part of the day.

SOME ADJUSTMENT PROBLEMS.   An outgoing three- or four-year-old may find the first days of preschool smooth sailing. Occasionally, a child is very attached to a parent and has difficulty adjusting to being away from home and mother. This child may cry inconsolably on the first day and then refuse to return the next day. Or the child may reluctantly return but cling fearfully to the parent. Separation anxiety makes itself obvious within the first few days and can be a difficult problem.

If your child has trouble making the transition to preschool, you may find it helpful to introduce him gradually to the situation. Discuss this with the teacher, who has probably seen similar situations before. A brief transitional program may be worked out in which you accompany your child to school and stay with him for an hour, then take him home. On the following day, you remain for an hour and a half, and the next day for two or three hours, each time remaining in the background. This will allow your child to slowly build some attachments to the teacher and other children, preparing for the time when you will leave him at school for the entire time.

A child may slowly accustom himself to the school, but may then get hurt or for another reason suddenly become fearful and want you back once again. Discuss this with the teacher, deciding if it's wise for you to return for another day or two, again remaining in the background.

Occasionally, a child may remain fearful of returning to school even though the teacher is warm and understanding. It's best to tell such a child that everyone must eventually go to school. It's wise to remain firm, doing your best to help the child make this transition. Such resistance to attending preschool can be so great that you may have to abandon your plan at that time and simply wait until your child is a bit older and has more fully mastered separation anxiety. Eventually, dependency and clinging must be overcome. If a child remains fearful and refuses to attend school, you may have to consider psychological counseling for the child.

Even after a child makes the transition, you may encounter an episode of regression. For instance, your daughter may have some initial reluctance to attend school, but after a shaky start (with or without you present), she makes the transition and adjusts well. A family vacation later interrupts school, allowing a few weeks with both parents. When vacation ends and normal routines begin, your daughter may again have to make the transition back to school, dealing with some separation anxiety. The experience may be reminiscent of when she went for the very first time, but generally, she will readapt to the preschool setting more quickly than she did the first time.

Your relationship with your child's teacher is an important one. Feel free to discuss your child with the teacher. Many parents express surprise when a preschool teacher describes an aspect of a child's behavior that parents have never seen or known about (aggression, hostility, selfishness, whining, whatever). Remember, the teacher has the opportunity to see your child in a variety of settings: playing with toys, dramatic play, on field trips, and in different situations with and without other children. All this occurs away from parents, where the child may be testing limits. The teacher's unique perspective allows for many valid observations of your child's behavior, alone and with others. This in turn can provide valuable information about your child's abilities as well as any potential problems.

◊ A CONSULTATION—QUESTIONS AND ANSWERS

Our consultant for a discussion about preschoolers is Paulina F. Kernberg, M.D. Dr. Kernberg is an Associate Professor of Psychiatry at the Cornell University Medical College and is the Director of Child Psychiatry at the Westchester Division of The New York Hospital.

Spanking

Our four-year-old is incorrigible. I often end up yelling and occasionally I've even spanked him. Is there a better way to discipline him?

DR. KERNBERG: I am frequently asked this question. The major thing wrong with spanking is that it can become so intense that the child is brutalized by a parent who loses control. That's one extreme; another extreme is that nowadays, many parents are afraid to acknowledge that they even think of spanking a child. This brings up the central question concerning discipline: how do you get a child to do what you want him to do, so that physical force is not necessary as a method of discipline?

It's general knowledge that most children will do what they can do easily. They will do whatever they enjoy doing, and will do whatever results in parental approval or reward for their behavior. It is equally important to realize that a child enjoys activities that provide him with a sense of competence and with a feeling of being genuinely appreciated. Awareness of these important general principles will help you motivate your four-year-old to do the things that you wish him to do. In this way, you will not have to resort to nearly as much discipline as has apparently been the case so far.

If a child must be spanked, it's best if he truly believes that the spanking was done for his own sake and not because of a parent's inner turmoil. Even a very young child can sense when a parent has simply lost control and that a spanking occurs because the parent has gone into an uncontrolled frenzy.

Discipline is important in any child's life, and parents must communicate to a child that certain boundaries exist. A child should know that limits and structures prevail, and that the parents hold certain convictions. Over the years, I've become very modest about providing an opinion concerning how children should be raised. It's difficult to say there's only one right way, but certain principles do seem to make a good deal of sense.

If a parent is quite consistent and has definite convictions about right and wrong, and if the parent communicates what the child should and should not do, things will generally work out well. In fact, children actually prefer such a parent and unquestionably dislike a wishy-washy or unprincipled way of disciplining. Many of today's first-time parents in their thirties and forties seem to feel they can't even ask their child to go to the toilet! This is of course a bit of an exaggeration on my part, but I do think there's an element of truth in it. Many of today's older parents are more permissive, in part because they are concerned about "traumatizing" a child by requiring certain behaviors of the child. There is no doubt that a child is reassured by a parent who has convictions about right and wrong, who makes certain reasonable demands of the child, and who really means what he or she says. In my experience, the parent who frequently spanks a child is one who has not set proper limits, is a parent who has probably not clearly defined the do's and don'ts, and is one who is uncertain about his or her own convictions in matters of discipline.

Wants to Stay Home

Our four-year-old son has been in preschool since he was two, and now he wants to stay home. My husband and I both work, and I can't stay home with him. Besides, I'm not sure it's the best thing to do. Please advise us.

DR. KERNBERG: If, during the course of the first three years of life, a child has not developed the sense that he can reliably count on mother, he may begin exhibiting some regression when he finds himself facing the specter of separation. Many mothers find it difficult to appreciate the quality of a child's regression when the child is sent to school, or when she is placed in a situation where mother will be less accessible than before. Many parents simply want their child to be "independent." Of course, we all want our children to be independent, but the best way for a child to develop independence is to first be *dependent* and, in the process, slowly develop the conviction that mother is available and accessible, and can ultimately be relied upon. Only then can a child truly progress toward developing independence.

I often see this problem in children of various ages, not just at four years. Parents of older teenagers often ask advice about the very same issue, although on the surface the situation appears to be different. Actually, it's the same conflict when a seventeen- or eighteen-year-old doesn't want to go away to college after having been seemingly independent all the years before.

There is one other crucial element in this equation—namely, the nature of your relationship with your child. This can be a very complex issue, and far more may occur than meets the eye.

Only yesterday, I saw a mother in consultation. Her six-year-old daughter is a bright, creative, energetic child who has always seemed robust and independent. She suddenly became frightened of going off to school. Upon exploring the situation with the mother, it became apparent that for the last few months she had been subtly conveying to her daughter her own anxiety about the child's going off to school for the first time. The daughter had picked up on her mother's anxiety and was merely reflecting it. I began gently pointing out this mother's ambivalence about "losing" her child, conveying to her that it would be important to view her daughter as a child who is striving toward independence and not as an extension of herself.

I cite this example to indicate how complicated certain separation issues are for both child and parent. Separation is a crucial issue throughout all of development, and occasionally a parent may be more reluctant than a child to see the child leave the family setting. Children may be little, but they must be viewed as separate persons who will eventually separate away from their parents and live lives of their own.

In your situation, you must make certain that your own ambivalent feelings are not at play. If they are not, you can provide your son with additional reassurance, but he should continue with the preschool program he has been attending for the last two years. You might wish to explore why he is now presenting a wish to remain home. Is there some stress or difficulty at school that is contributing to this regression? Perhaps a talk with his teacher will shed more light on this question.

Masturbating

My three-year-old daughter masturbates whenever she's bored, tired, or anxious. She does this so much she's irritated her skin. I tried to ignore it, thinking it would stop, but now I'm concerned.

DR. KERNBERG: While you are concerned about your daughter's masturbating, the masturbation must be viewed as little more than a symptom. I think it's most important to focus on whatever is making your daughter bored, tired, or anxious. She is conveying that the only effective means by which she can deal with fatigue, boredom, or anxiety is self-stimulation. It's important to discover the circumstances in your daughter's life that lead to these frequent states of mind.

Masturbation is a perfectly normal activity and should be private and pleasurable for a child. It should not be an antidote to boredom, anxiety, or fatigue. Unpleasant emotional states such as anxiety or boredom should not enter into the situation.

Between the ages of three and six, a child should not experience a great deal of fatigue or boredom. At this age, a child is the epitome of joy and energy. It often makes adults feel wonderful just to *look* at a child of this age! When a child is frequently bored, anxious, or fatigued, something in the child's life must be explored. I would recommend a professional consultation to explore your daughter's difficulties. I say this because it appears that this pattern has lasted for some time and, as a parent, you are concerned about this.

A consultation means exactly that: a visit to a professional who will listen to and talk with you, helping you understand your child's behavior. The psychiatrist need not actually see your child, but rather can understand your child's difficulties by merely hearing your recounting of the situation. You will then be in a better position to understand and help your child deal with the unpleasant feeling states that you have described.

Uses Bad Language

Our four-year-old son has suddenly been using the most outrageous profanities. We try to ignore them or at least not make a big deal, but sometimes it goes too far. How can we handle his cursing?

Dr. KERNBERG: Some years ago, a twelve-year-old patient I was treating came in reciting a list of profanities that took up most of a forty-minute session. He cursed on and on, and finally he paused. I smiled at him and said, "Well, now that you've had your say, shouldn't we get on to what's really bothering you?" Having finished his performance, he too smiled, and we went on to talk about other things.

It's important to understand that when children curse, they often want a reaction from an adult. A child wants to see whether or not a big person will become upset or disturbed by all the bad language. Instead of throwing stones, the child has words. The most useful thing a child may have at his disposal is something so simple as the "right" word.

One of the predicaments for children of this age is that they are quite smart, and realize how small, powerless, and vulnerable they really are. They must give in to an adult's whims and conform to a parent's expectations. Cursing can give a child an enormous sense of power, and, in a way, this is a positive aspect of such language. Your child is using profanities not to be "dirty" or "obscene," but to have a sense of power by uttering things that are ordinarily forbidden and thereby to elicit a reaction from a parent.

You can deal with this by accepting the situation, but do not encourage profanity. You can basically say to the child, "OK, I've heard you. That's enough. Now let's go on to something else." Paradoxically, the more negative your reaction to a child's cursing, the more you will encourage the cursing. The child, after all, is simply flexing his verbal muscles and delighting in the reaction that follows.

Wants to Share the Bed

Our five-year-old son gets into bed with us and then wants his father to leave and go into his bed. I know this is related to the Oedipal period, but I never thought it would be this blatant. How should we handle this?

DR. KERNBERG: This is a very frequent question. First, be aware that only in the Western world's middle and upper classes do children sleep in their own rooms and have their very own beds. In many areas of the world, families share beds, and this does not present problems.

Sharing the parents' bed can become a problem if it interferes with a couple's intimate sexual life, or when the child's presence in the bed becomes an excuse for a parent to avoid sexual relations. Some parents covertly or unconsciously encourage a child to come into bed with them, and their sexual life is then compromised.

A child's occasional presence in the bed can be fine. This can be an expression of warmth, tenderness, and the family's being together. The traditions and values of various families may indeed be different and must be respected. There are many families in which this activity is encouraged and can be pursued in a healthy way. However, it is crucial that if a child is permitted in bed with the parents, it should be in the interest of family warmth and intimacy, and not as a way to deal with or avoid the parents' marital or sexual tensions.

In this situation, your son wants to replace father and have mother and the parental bed to himself. He is really saying, "Father should be the small one; I should be the big one." You should kindly and simply tell your child that he will someday grow up and have someone his own age to sleep with. But at this time, daddy and mommy are together, and the bed is theirs. It can be difficult to empathize with a child, but you must do the best you can.

Is No Preschool a Disadvantage?

My four-year-old son has been home with me since he was born. I'm worried that he'll be disadvantaged next year in kindergarten because he hasn't had any preschool experience. However, he has played with other children. Will this be a problem?

DR. KERNBERG: The crucial aspect of this situation is that your son has had play experience with other children. A child who has had no play experience with peers is indeed at a disadvantage. When first entering preschool, children learn cognitive and intellectual skills through play, through fantasy, and through gathering experiences in the world. This is most often accomplished by playing with other children. A child who has engaged in these various activities, with or *without* a preschool, is likely to do quite well. Your son's not having been to preschool will not be a disadvantage to him, since he has had experiences with other children.

Impolite "Playmate"

Our five-year-old son has an imaginary playmate. I'm concerned because this "friend" tells our child to say things we disapprove of, such as swear words, and tells our child to act in an impolite way. What can we do?

DR. KERNBERG: For various reasons, a child may not have a great deal of access to other children. In such a situation, a resourceful child may conjure up imaginary playmates, since a child needs companions. When friends are inaccessible, he may create them in his own mind. Your child's imaginary playmate is not a problem and should not cause you great concern.

Your child has found a solution to the problem of cursing. It is not he who is saying the bad things or acting impolitely but his "friend." I would take the same approach with him as I would take with the child who curses. I would acknowledge the imaginary friend as part of your child's personality, and I would listen to what this "bad" imaginary child is saying. I would then encourage him to talk about other things, but without becoming upset, which would only create more impetus for this "friend" to tell your son even more. I would also acknowledge that he is very resourceful and creative!

Part of a parent's task is to empathize with a child and understand what his fears, wishes, and conflicts may be. In addition, a parent is best able to help a child by appreciating the positive aspects of his behavior and by acknowledging whatever is positive. In that context, you can then correct that which is negative, namely, this "friend's" cursing. Once you empathically acknowledge a child's feelings, you are in a better position to get him to renounce the unacceptable language. (See in Chapter 2, "An Imaginary Companion.")

A Jealous Pest

Whenever I have friends over, my three-year-old son gets very jealous and makes a pest of himself. Why does he do this, and what can I do about it?

DR. KERNBERG: Mothers vary in their capacity to provide a child with attention, or with the feeling of adequate attention. I was recently observing a mother of two 3-year-old twins. This woman had the talent of making *each* twin feel that she was uniquely interested in *that* child.

She went back and forth from one child to another in such a way that each one felt very much attended to. This is a great talent, and some mothers can do it very well. Others can only concentrate on one child at a time; if there is a second child, the older gets very jealous. Or, as in your situation, should mother have friends visit, the child grows envious and becomes disruptive.

We often see this, even with children as young as one or two years of age; mother gets on the telephone, the child begins playing with a socket, or does something that demands attention. The child may cry or whimper, or in some way indicate that she needs contact. Some mothers have the talent, even while talking to other people, of looking at a child in a certain way, of acknowledging the child's presence, and making the child feel content or very much a part of the mother's mental and emotional life.

I am convinced that you can learn to do this, or improve your capacity to somehow acknowledge your child's presence, even while paying attention to others. It's really a matter of making your son feel that you empathize with his need for attention. It does not necessarily mean you will drop what you are doing and rush to his side. Simply glance at your child; smile or nod; practice acknowledging him in many small but meaningful ways. He will no longer feel forgotten or ignored. If you can learn to do this, I think you'll see a remarkable change in your child's capacity to tolerate your attention being divided between himself and other people.

Worries About Older Dad

I'm fifty-two years old and the father of a five-year-old boy. He makes it clear that he knows I'm much older than the other children's fathers, and he often asks me how long I'll stay alive, and other questions that show his anxieties about this. How should I deal with this?

DR. KERNBERG: We must view this situation from the perspective of both child and father.

Lets look at the child first. Your son may in fact be dealing with some very hostile and competitive urges toward you, and may express these urges as a fear. I very well remember when I was five years old. An uncle of mine owned a pencil that I very much wanted; it was an amazing device that could write in many different colors. I once asked him, "Uncle, when will you die so that I can have this pencil?" So a fear can be a wish as well as a fear, and a five-year-old boy's feelings toward his father can indeed be very mixed.

Now let's examine this issue from the perspective of the parent. It may very well be that you yourself are concerned about your age. Many middle-aged parents realize, especially with the birth of a child, that their options in life are limited and that they do not have "forever." I think that some of this worry about your age may be your own, and your son is picking up on your concerns.

I see a similar situation with some older children who, in their late teens and early twenties, are getting ready to leave the house. They suddenly begin feeling very guilty, as though they are "throwing their parents into old age," since their leavetaking will create an "empty nest" for their now-aging parents. When one explores this issue in some depth, it may become clear that the parents are giving a subtle message to the son or daughter, one indicating their concerns about the empty house and about growing older. In your situation, I would recommend an honest self-appraisal in which you truly question if you yourself are overly concerned about death and are somehow conveying this to your child.

A Boy Plays with Dolls

Our four-year-old son sometimes plays with his sister's dolls and plays dress-up with her. Should we be concerned?

DR. KERNBERG: Part of imaginary play at this age involves a child's exploring other people's roles and discovering what it's like to be the other person. This can mean a child occasionally crosses sex-bound roles and plays games usually associated with children of the other sex. Instances of a boy's playing such games need not be anything to worry about. However, if a four-year-old boy plays exclusively with girls and plays only with dolls, or plays dress-up all the time, there is some cause for concern.

Of course, boys and girls today play with various sex-typed toys, often crossing over from one role or toy to another. Girls sometimes play cowboys, whereas boys can occasionally play with dolls. This can be an enriching experience for children of both sexes. It's really a question of quantity, and whether or not a child engages exclusively in a certain kind of crossover play, that determines whether or not a child has a problem about being a girl or a boy. (See in Chapter 2, "Boys and Girls Together: The Differences Between the Sexes.")

Too Much Too Soon?

Our four-year-old is beginning preschool, and I've learned that this school places a great deal of emphasis on reading and other skills. Is this doing too much too soon, and is it really necessary?

DR. KERNBERG: There is an ethos in the United States that says the earlier you start, the better it is. But, in my opinion, earlier does not necessarily mean better. A child of four years may be very interested in letters, and, of course, a parent or teacher can help the child explore his curiosity and play with letters. But formal teaching at this time can be detrimental.

Studies clearly show that formal teaching of reading to very young children detracts from their curiosity and from their capacity to explore creatively. Children this age can be taught to parrot what they hear and see, but not much else, because they have not yet mastered the concept of symbols. Symbolic thinking must be developed organically, over time, and there's no sense in trying to rush it. I think that exposing a child to a very rich *play* environment is the best way to stimulate a child's mind and capacities. Such play is the best teaching that a four-year-old can ever get. (See in Chapter 2, "Reading to a Child.")

Irrational Fears

My five-year-old daughter has frequent bad dreams and is frightened of bogeymen in the night. What causes this?

DR. KERNBERG: Such fears among five-year-old girls are virtually universal. This is due to a combination of a little girl's imagination and her own hostile feelings toward mother during the Oedipal phase of development. A little girl who wants daddy all for herself may dream of witches who come for her in the night. The five-year-old boy who wants to get rid of his father may dream of bogeymen. In his dream he is punished for having "bad" thoughts.

These dreams are perfectly normal during the Oedipal phase. They will most likely subside and come to an end when your child passes through this period.

Ready for First Grade

Our five-year-old son seems a little immature for a child in kindergarten. How can we determine if he's ready to move on to the first grade?

DR. KERNBERG: In this situation, you can probably count on the advice of your child's teacher. A teacher has a very good sense of a child's capacity. This input may be particularly necessary with boys, who tend to be very active during the kindergarten year. Girls find the task of attending kindergarten much easier than boys; they're more able to sit quietly and be attentive to the teacher. While there are some psychological developmental reasons for this, there also seem to be innate sex differences between boys and girls, regardless of what the women's movement says.

Consult with your child's kindergarten teacher. She will be able to tell you how your son plays by himself and how he interacts with other children. She'll be able to describe how he reacts to the usual rough-and-tumble activities of children of this age. She can probably give you insight into other issues as well: How does your son deal with small responsibilities such as putting on his coat and galoshes? How does he organize his belongings? How does he speak and communicate verbally? It is important to assess this ability because when he moves to the first grade, he will be part of a larger class in which he'll have to communicate effectively. So there are clear criteria you can explore with the teacher to determine if your son is ready to move on to the first grade.

Remember, at so young an age even a six-month age difference can be enormously important. A child may be literally half a year younger than other children in his class; six months of development is a long time at this age.

Worries of a Full-Time Mother

I'm a full-time mother and have been with my four-year-old daughter since she was born. Some of my working-mother friends say that nursery school has made their children friendlier, brighter, and better able to deal with people. Am I depriving my daughter by being a full-time mother?

DR. KERNBERG: This can be a difficult question. My response depends upon how much you allow your child to play with other children and have experiences outside the home, even though she does not attend a nursery school. Some mothers are quite shy and have few social contacts themselves; the child becomes the mother's full-time companion. Such mothers tend to view a small child as an extension of themselves. In such an arrangement, a child can be deprived of the company and exploration afforded by being with other children and engaging in creative play.

However, if your daughter has various experiences with other children, there is no deprivation in her not attending a preschool. A formal preschool or nursery-school experience is not mandatory for a child to develop healthfully, to become socially active, and to learn to deal effectively with other children.

A Shy Child

Our five-year-old is shy. She hesitates to approach other children and get acquainted. We're worrying that this can limit her development. What causes shyness and how can we help her overcome it?

DR. KERNBERG: Shyness may be no more than a question of temperament. Some children simply require more time than others to warm up to a situation, to learn what to expect and to feel reasonably at ease with others. What some people call a "temperamentally-slow-to-warm-up child" is actually quite a common phenomenon.

When evaluating any child or situation, my approach is to consider both the child and the parents. Because parents regulate and modulate a child's behavior, my first question is, how ready are you to relinquish hold of your child, to allow her to interact with others?

Some mothers, though allowing a child to socialize, communicate to the child on some level that mother is the most important figure in the child's life. A child in this position may develop a reluctance to meet new people or develop friendships with other children. Some parents are reluctant to allow a child to expand her universe because it means "losing" the child. This of course emanates from a particular parent's anxiety and has little to do with a child's shyness. It is important to keep these two issues in mind: the temperament of the child, and the interaction between child and parent. Both factors are vital in determining how a child relates to others.

Bribing a Four-Year-Old

My husband bribes our four-year-old son to get him to do everything. He gives him presents for virtually anything he does. Am I right to disapprove of this kind of "bribery"?

DR. KERNBERG: Children most often want to do the right thing when they are having fun doing it and when they are rewarded for it. Let's explore what is meant by the notion of "reward." Often, the reward that a child derives from a task is his feeling competent and developing a sense of mastery over the task. This sense of accomplishment lends an intrinsic value to the task itself.

In your situation, it's important to empathize with your husband and help him understand that he seems to lack confidence in his child's willingness to perform tasks for the intrinsic value they provide and for the feelings of mastery and confidence they may evoke in your son. Your child very much wants to know that he has such capacities and will ultimately feel a sense of self-esteem because he successfully completes various tasks.

A parent's positive reinforcement is also very valuable. You may occasionally want to provide a reward that is more concrete than approval or even more demonstrative than a loving hug. But it isn't necessary to give gifts, which may indeed seem to be a form of bribery. Some parents find it useful to paste gold stars on a board when a child does well or accomplishes something. This can concretely give the child the feeling of a symbolic reward for a task well done. Paradoxically however, too many concrete gifts can convey that a parent thinks the child must be "bought" or bribed to do the right thing. Such a subtle message does little to enhance a child's self-esteem.

Above all, a child needs a *relationship* with the parents. A poverty-stricken parent can give a child something so simple as a lollipop, or may not give anything but a hug and earnest praise. This can still have enormous meaning to a child, enhancing his self-esteem and feelings of mastery. A wealthy parent can give a child terribly expensive gifts, and they may lack true meaning. Rich or poor, if you give gifts instead of having a real relationship with your child, you are not helping your child. Children easily see through such transparencies. A parent who gives promiscuously may lack confidence in his or her ability to form a good and meaningful relationship with a child.

Enhancing a Child's Language

I would like my four-year-old daughter to have the best chance possible for her language ability to develop. How can I enhance her use of language and its growth?

DR. KERNBERG: There are many ways to enhance your child's ability to use language. First, you can talk with your child in dialogue. This means asking questions and giving your child sufficient time to answer. It also means making provocative comments that stimulate the child to want to say more and elaborate on whatever has been said. This is an open-ended dialogue. Ask your child about school, what she did that day, whom she saw. Ask about any friends that she mentions, what she saw on the way to school, and a variety of other stimulating questions. Showing such interest and allowing your child the time to think about the questions and to make responses to them can greatly encourage and enrich her use of language. It is also part of a stimulating and caring relationship with your child.

A four-year-old is very interested in play, and play is the rule of this age period. Playing with words can be very helpful. There are various word games, especially on television, that allow a child's vocabulary to expand. Playing with words, puns, and jokes can be an excellent way to teach the value of words and encourage the use of language. Singing and reading to your child are also excellent ways to enhance your child's facility with, and love of, words.

Most important of all is the simple fact that all of development occurs in the context of an ongoing relationship. This is especially true of language development. This may be why we sometimes say mother tongue when describing the language that is closest to the heart. (See in Chapter 2, "Reading to a Child.")

Chapter 4: The School-Age Youngster — Ages Six to Twelve

◇ YOUR DEVELOPING CHILD

Having struggled through the Oedipal phase of development, a six-year-old has resolved many conflicts and fears. The child has gained a solid identity as a boy or girl, has achieved a sense of right and wrong (although the conscience is harsh and demanding at this age), and is able to place a great deal of emphasis on learning. This chapter will describe a period of six years in your child's life—a period of time that may begin with the first-grader who still believes in Santa Claus, and ends with the junior-high-school girl going to her first dance.

The first day of school heralds a new era in your child's life, and you may uncomfortably feel you are "handing your child over" to the world. Although most children have attended nursery school and kindergarten, the schoolchild encounters new roles and expectations.

With the beginning of school, your child's energies are directed outside the family. He must deal with a greatly expanded world, one that will require the maturing of his emotional and mental capabilities if he is to succeed. Although parents will still be the child's emotional lifelines for years to come, his life now becomes far more complicated.

Within the family, the child is loved and accepted simply because he is your child, nothing more and nothing less. But school mates (and children outside school) won't automatically bestow this kind of familial affection on him. They won't particularly care if your child is a younger brother or older sister. They won't bother to understand any quirks or preferences, and if the child has any strange mannerisms, he may be teased or taunted.

Both in and out of the classroom, your child must deal with a variety of new people and situations, without your direct guidance or reassurance. In time, your child comes to realize that some children will like him and want him as a friend or a member of their team. Others may avoid him or spurn him, sometimes for reasons he cannot fathom. The child must evaluate and respond to this, and must make his own social judgments in turn. This may involve his rethinking certain basic assumptions about himself and his family, self-examination he may be performing for the first time in his life.

Your youngster learns about achievement and competition, about his strengths and limitations, and about cooperation with other children. He learns that others expect things from him, and he comes to expect things from himself. With the beginning of school, a child lives in several parallel environments—the home, schoolroom, play group, religious school, and others. He takes on new values and tries out different roles. In one setting, he or she may be a leader, the best athlete, the brightest, the prettiest, the most assertive and best-liked. In another setting, things may not go so well. The child begins seeing himself and the world from varying and widened perspectives, all the while moving beyond the family-centeredness of childhood to a widening and many-faceted world.

With peers, a youngster learns skills for living. The group becomes all-important and a crucial regulator of behavior, even a form of self-government. Learning value systems that are totally different from those at home, your youngster discovers a variety of new roles and an array of heroes and villains. In this growing arena of experiences, your child acquires intellectual, personal, and social skills that will be vital determinants of success throughout the rest of his life.

When the home is stable and when there is no serious family strife, most children this age are relatively free of most burdens and responsibilities, except for the demands of school. Spending many hours each day with friends, they enjoy an expanding repertoire of activities with very little meddling by adults.

Boys and Girls Apart

For many middle-class children, life is highly organized, scheduled around Little League, music lessons, dance or singing lessons, visits to the orthodontist or doctor, school or after-school programs of many kinds. During the summer months, many school-age children go to camp or attend summer study programs. Even during unstructured time, many hours are spent watching television, playing board games, with collections, or with other children, so that the school-age youngster's life brims with activities. No matter how structured or organized youngsters' lives may be, a quick glimpse at their activities reveals a very striking characteristic: boys tend to associate with boys, and girls with girls, each group pursuing interests and identities very much apart from the other.

This segregation by sex becomes quite pronounced by about the third grade, and may continue into early adolescence. While not absolute, this separation of the sexes is important, especially for the boy. With friends, he finds a new "society," or subculture, outside the home or school, and for the first time in his life, his activities are not directed or controlled by a woman (his mother or a female teacher).

The boy now acts as if girls are to be avoided, no matter what. In fact, girls are to be teased, chased, picked on, and are completely disavowed as worthwhile companions or partners in anything. A boy between six and eleven would rarely admit to enjoying the company of a girl, and being called a "sissy" by other boys can impel a youngster to daring (and dangerous) feats of behavior. Girls are rejected, except perhaps for the occasional tomboy who acts like and can compete with the boys.

There are several reasons for this. First, the boy this age is trying valiantly to separate himself from his mother. In attempting to weaken this attachment, he radically removes himself from anything remotely reminiscent of mother, including, of course, girls. Second, the boy is trying to consolidate his masculine identity. To a certain extent, he becomes a caricature of what he considers masculine; he exaggerates every so-called masculine trait he thinks important. We often see this in the young boy's choice of heroes. Superman has a girlfriend, but it's common knowledge that nothing serious will ever develop with Lois Lane. Batman has Robin and the Batmobile, nothing else. Hulk Hogan has Mr. T, or perhaps Cyndi Lauper (but it's nothing romantic), and he conquers the bad guys. The important heroes for the young boy have no serious connections with women; they battle evil and do good (often with magical or supernatural powers) but have little or no romantic involvement with women.

A third reason the school-age boy avoids contact with girls has to do with the anxiety of the developmental period through which the boy has only recently passed. While not necessarily consciously, the boy is anxiously aware of the girl's lack of a penis, and because this can make the boy quite uncomfortable, young girls are generally avoided.

The cleavage of boys and girls into distinct groups is partly a matter of different interests and activities, and in spite of changing sex roles today, the play patterns of boys and girls are very different. Girls still play house, nurse, and teacher, and still love games like hopscotch, jacks, and jump rope. Boys wrestle, fight, play whatever sports are in season, roam far from home, and often get into "trouble." Each group expresses contempt for the other, the boys fantasizing that they will become superheroes, astronauts, football or baseball players, and other action-oriented figures, the girls nourishing dreams of romance, love, marriage, and other roles having to do with domestic life.

While girls have traditionally moved smoothly from childhood into their accepted and expected adult roles as wife, parent, and homemaker, nowadays more and more young girls aspire to careers and professions. By contrast, throughout their early school years boys learn and have reinforced in their behaviors the roles of warrior, conqueror, and two-fisted hero, attitudes that have little bearing on or resemblance to the life a boy will eventually lead as a husband, parent, and worker.

The boy's situation is a bit stormy. Mother and teacher (in grade school, usually a woman) expect him to behave properly, exhibiting decorum and restraint at school and elsewhere. Yet the culture actually expects a certain rebelliousness and aggressivity from the young boy. If a youngster doesn't exhibit some of these traits, adults—men *and* women—may become worried that the boy is a bit of a "sissy." The boy is taught obedience, tolerance, and kindness, yet, if he doesn't "stand up like a man" or "fight for his rights," he may be labeled a "chicken," a "faggot," or a "sissy," especially if he dares enjoy the company of girls, or if he prefers reading as compared to the rough-and-tumble company of other boys.

Often, we think we are witnessing the "natural" unfolding of "male and female" traits in these emerging sex roles and different ways of behaving. Actually, without realizing it, most adults participate in continuing a kind of sex-typing that begins at the very outset of a child's life; they teach their boys and girls to think, feel, and behave in ways that are labeled "male" and "female."

As mentioned in Chapter 2 ("Boys and Girls Together: The Differences Between The Sexes"), these stereotypes of male and female roles are now undergoing a slow process of change. Some experts question the wisdom of encouraging separation of boys and girls during the school-age years, maintaining that this fosters deeply held resentments and stereotypes, influencing how men and women perceive each other throughout their lives. There is probably much truth in this position.

It seems unlikely, however, that sex-role differences will ever be completely abolished. No doubt, boys will always be taught to act like boys, and girls like girls. But the long-term effects of education and of consciousness about "maleness" and "femaleness" in our culture may actually bring about meaningful long-term changes, making men more "feminine" and women more "masculine." More accurately stated, this means that men may become more interested in domestic activities and in nurturing their children and that they may find it easier to express tender, loving feelings. It may eventually result in men changing their views of women and of their abilities. It means that women may become more comfortable entering what have been traditionally "masculine" fields and occupations, that women may become less "helpless" or dependent and will exhibit more competitive, "masculine" traits.

Despite cultural changes in how we view sex-appropriate roles and behaviors, boys and girls spend most of the time between the ages of six and twelve very much separate and apart. Let's look briefly at some of the traditional activities of boys and girls during the school-age years.

The Girl's Activities

Girls' activities have traditionally been less "aggressive" than those of boys. The young girl spends a good deal of time pursuing games such as jacks, hopscotch, jump rope, playing teacher or nurse, bouncing a ball (A, My Name Is Alice . . .), and other activities that place a premium on social interchanges and talking. The girl spends plenty of time out of doors: riding a bicycle, ice-skating, roller-skating, going to parks and playgrounds where she participates in various activities, very few being competitive team sports. She will learn to play cards and board games, will most likely enjoy school and diligently do her homework, and will probably do better (both behaviorally and academically) than the boys. The young girl often discovers a role model in some favorite grade-school teacher, and at this age, many a young girl wants to become a schoolteacher.

Friends become increasingly important as the girl approaches ten, and your child may join a club and appear to crave constant companionship. She may part with her best friend after hours of furtive whispering, talking, and giggling, only to dash for the telephone to continue the conversation the moment she arrives home. Group excursions to parks, to an ice-skating or roller-skating rink, to the movies, or to a friend's house become important activities, although she may spend a good deal of time alone tending to a doll collection, poring through movie and television magazines, reading, or simply fantasizing in her private world.

The Boy's Activities

As with girls, boys' activities vary depending on whether they live in a city, the suburbs, or the country. Early games may involve Hide-and-Seek (by no means limited to boys); Cops and Robbers; Cowboys and Indians; Monkey in the Middle; war; tag; kite-flying; bicycle-riding;

skate-boarding; roller-skating; marbles; flipping baseball, football, or any other kind of cards; and other action-oriented pursuits, all involving some combination of competition and vigorous use of the body.

At eight or nine years of age, boys place more importance on team games requiring some organization, although this varies depending on the amount of parental guidance for such things as Little League. Baseball, football, basketball, and other games are played. All involve passionate arguments about rules and regulations, about choosing sides, scoring and playing fairly, and all place a premium on competition and on winning or losing. Nearly all boys emulate their sports idols during these games.

There are quarrels between friends; fights; threats; bets; dares (double dares and triple dares); and stentorian howls of protest when a rule is broken ("No fair!") or when the exact ritual of the game and its rules aren't stringently followed. There is prodigious boasting, shouting, and intimidation, an endless array of insults, nicknames, catcalls and countercalls, and inevitable comparisons between one boy and another, or between one group of boys and another (who is stronger, bigger, who can run faster, jump higher, or throw farther).

Time indoors is spent playing board games, card games, watching television, reading and trading comic books, going to the movies (usually in a group that often gets into "trouble"), building models, and engaging in various activities that may lead to physical contact, where furniture and household fixtures fall prey to the boisterous drama of a war game. There seems no end to a young boy's energy except when he is exhausted at the day's end.

Collections

Both boys and girls tend to be avid collectors. At first, the collecting may have very little organization; a child simply accumulates a wide variety of miscellaneous objects ranging from scraps of paper to pebbles, marbles, or bubble gum prizes. As the child matures, however, the collecting takes on a more organized and specialized quality, and becomes a hobby or an expansive collection that reflects the child's interests. Stamps and coins have traditionally been favorites of children during the school-age years, and many children collect comic books, baseball cards, dolls, movie magazines, autographs, tropical fish, or miniature cars, depending on the child's gender, interests, and on the availability of the objects to be collected.

Collections serve a deep psychological purpose for the child: they help the child gain a sense of mastery and organization over a rapidly expanding world, and during the school years many children take solace in the belief that the world's menaces and anxieties can be controlled or dampened by keeping everything in order.

Magic and Ritual

These are the years during which a sense of magical ritual pervades many children's activities, even though they no longer think in the magical ways of preschool children. Kids this age are fascinated by ritualistic codes and "secret" languages such as pig Latin or other "indecipherable" means of "private" communication. The code or language excludes others and is meant to be understood by only a select few. The function of the language is largely ritualistic; the child who has mastered it can sometimes barely think of anything worth saying, but the satisfaction gained by simply being able to participate, by being "in the know," is of crucial importance.

Ritual and formula are especially obvious if you watch a group of kids choosing sides or deciding who will go first or who will be It in a particular game. "One-potato, two-potato, three-potato, four . . ."; "Eeny, Meeny, Miney, Mo . . ."; "One, two, three, shoot . . ."; "Ink-a-bink, a bottle of ink, the cork fell out and you stink!" After one child is selected as It, the entire group joins in the choral chant: "Susie's it, caught a fit, doesn't know how to get out of it!" These chants are recited the same way each and every time, without change, lest the validity of the process be undermined by some unacceptable deviation from the norm. At times, it seems that the game itself hardly matters; rather, the rules must be strictly followed and all experience must be organized, categorized, and bound by ritualistic rules.

Some ritualistic chants are reserved for special occasions or situations: "I scream, you scream, we all scream for ice cream!"; "Last one in is a rotten egg!"; "Ladybug, ladybug, fly away home . . ."; "It's raining, it's pouring, the old man is snoring . . ."; "Step on a crack, break your mother's back!"

Structure and controls are important, and kids this age often form clubs and organizations in which the rules are everything. A group of children meets and draws up sets of rules: how one becomes a member, what each member must or must not do to remain a member, where and how often the club will meet, who can and cannot belong, all for no real purpose other than the feelings of structure and organization that the very existence of the club provides.

Individual rituals abound during the school-age years. Steeped in a kind of magic, they're meant to ward off imagined menaces and the threat of the unknown. Touching every third telephone pole, not stepping on sidewalk cracks, counting every station wagon, obsessively humming or singing a special song or chant are some of the magically steeped rituals of this period of development. Synchronizing one's steps to those of a stranger walking down the street, stepping off the curb with the left or right foot, and hundreds more are parts of virtually every child's daily routine.

The child must scamper into the bedroom and be under the covers before the hallway toilet stops flushing lest the frightening troll lurking beneath his bed clutch his ankle and drag him down. The same route must be taken to school each day, lest some unnamed and unknown misfortune befall the child. A certain article of clothing (a blouse, sweater, whatever) or some charm must be worn or carried to school on the morning of a test if the child is going to be "lucky" and do well.

The school years mark a time when the child's world expands far beyond the cloistered environs of the family and its protective shell. It's a time when the child visits other children's homes, when he hears parents (both his own and other kids') arguing, when he discovers that adults lie, can be dishonest, and are sometimes cruel. He learns that adults use foul language, or that they have sex. In short, he learns that his parents, and all adults, are far from perfect.

The child learns to read, comprehending increasing doses of what he sees and hears, both in daily life and in the various media (radio, newspapers, magazines, and television). He learns that the world is a far larger, more disorganized, less predictable, and more frightening place than he ever imagined; he comes to know that countries go to war, that people move away, may be untrustworthy, and may disappoint him. The innocent and magical world of childhood begins to crumble, giving way to the disappointing, sometimes harsh and frightening realities of adult life.

The host of rituals and magic are, above all, attempts to make all this controllable, allowing the child to deal with a predictable, self-manufactured kind of anxiety, one that will rarely escalate beyond his powers of control. He may not be able to control or predict what will happen between the U.S. and Russia, or how a baseball game or tomorrow's test will turn out, but he can surely prevent the ogre beneath his bed from getting him—if he slips under the covers in time.

The Stresses and Meanings of School

At about the age of six, school becomes a major factor in your child's life. While preschool and kindergarten were important, they were not as central as school will soon become. The school must teach your child the knowledge and skills that will be necessary for her to become a self-sufficient adult. But it also becomes a kind of social system for the child.

Beginning school is often stressful for any child. Your child will be treated as part of a group, rarely receiving the individualized attention that was available at home or at preschool. The child may feel lost among so many new children or overwhelmed by all the new procedures. She may not know how to respond to the teacher, who is very different from mother. For the first time, the child will be scrutinized by an adult stranger who evaluates her on her merits in relation to other children. She will be judged by her achievements rather than for simply being.

In school, your child will learn about achievement and competition, about her assets and limitations in relation to children as bright as she, or brighter. The child may discover that a trait her parents consider adorable, such as a peculiarity of speaking, is something that the teacher tries to correct. She learns that the teacher expects a certain level of performance from her, and she comes to expect things of herself. She must deal with inconsistencies, with occasional harshness, and sometimes with minor (and not so minor) forms of cruelty. Perhaps for the first time, your child learns that the world is not always fair.

Linda, a bright, enthusiastic girl, was far ahead of the other children in her class. One day, the teacher gave out alphabet kits. Each child received a box containing flat tiles; each tile had a printed letter of the alphabet on its surface. There were also numbered tiles, from 0 through 10.

The teacher announced a contest to see who would be the first to arrange the tiles across his or her desk so that the entire alphabet was correctly spelled out. Dumping the contents of their kits onto their desks, the children began eagerly arranging tiles.

Linda sped through her tiles, suddenly realizing that her kit was missing the letter Q. Thinking quickly, she seized the 0 tile and with a pencil, turned it into a Q by adding the diagonal slash. She then raised her hand, indicating that she had finished. She was first in the class.

The teacher approached her desk and stared down at Linda's tiles neatly arranged in correct order. "You cheated!" snapped the teacher. "That's not a Q. It's a zero!"

With tears welling in her eyes, Linda tried to explain that the Q tile had been missing, and she had simply made the correct substitution.

"Cheaters can't win," the teacher announced with finality. She then commanded Linda to stand in the corner of the room for the rest of the morning, the usual punishment for a child who had done wrong.

Early in her school career, Linda learned that sometimes ingenuity and creative quick-thinking may not be highly valued in a world in which the best and the brightest do not always prevail.

Of course, a good teacher should be warm, objective, and treat children fairly, but such fairness and equanimity are not always the case. Actually, sometimes the differences between teacher and parent may not be so great, particularly in the early grades when a teacher treats children in an openly maternal way, becoming very much a mothering figure to the child. However, a teacher tends to be much more objective in evaluating a child's achievement, because she lacks the intense emotional investment of the parents.

Most parents convey their hopes and expectations that their child will strive to do well in school. Some parents, without realizing it, communicate that their satisfaction with the child depends on how well or poorly she does in school. When the child senses that a parent's love is contingent upon school performance, the road is paved for serious learning and emotional problems.

In addition to being evaluated by the teacher, your child is evaluated by her classmates. Children judge each other by different standards than those of the teacher, and the children with whom your child will compete (or be compared) are those whose acceptance and company she seeks at school. The society of classmates may or may not be as personal and meaningful as her own neighborhood group. This varies for different children. The group of classmates differs from the neighborhood group because it is subject to adult supervision and authority, while the neighborhood group has a life of its own, most often away from adults. Your child must adroitly learn to relate simultaneously to a number of different groups, satisfying the requirements of them all: the family; the school group, comprised of children and the teacher; and the neighborhood peer group.

A child whose personality is developing effectively can reasonably balance the different, and sometimes competing, forces of these various groups in his life. He has friends in the neighborhood (some of whom may be classmates), satisfies his parents, functions well as a student, is liked by his teacher, and is reasonably well liked by most classmates.

Being liked by classmates does not mean your child must befriend every student in the class. There may be one or two children from the neighborhood peer group in the class, but often the child's classmates are not neighborhood children, and classmates form an important new group in which your child must now function. From the first day of school onward, a child begins sorting through classmates and finds a few with whom he or she feels comfortable. Such choices may be made on the basis of a compatible intellect, on common interests, on an ethnic similarity, or any of a number of personality factors.

With the beginning of school, your child must balance the various forces within the parallel environments in her life, using social skills and emotional maturity not required during the preschool years. When the balance between these different environments is too heavily weighted in any one direction—such as when a child is too attached to his parents, or when there are enemies at school—problems can rear their heads, as will be discussed in the section "Dealing with School Phobia," later in this chapter.

At school, a child must perform in various ways: intellectually, socially, and sometimes athletically. A child's ability to perform in any of these areas is an important basis of his acceptance by teacher and classmates, and a great deal depends on a child's motivation to succeed. The youngster who is motivated and who achieves in school has a sense of being able to function well, making for important feelings of self-esteem.

Many children do not achieve in school, not because they lack ability, but because of emotional problems that were not obvious before the demands and stresses of school entered their lives. The painfully shy child may have difficulty participating in class. The child who is overly attached to his parents may find that school makes her nervous. A child may become nervous when being tested or when she feels that she is being scrutinized in some way. The youngster who craves the individual attention formerly available at home may be disappointed by the classroom experience; his poor performance may be a way of asking to return home. Another child may perform poorly as a way of gaining attention from parents or a teacher, while another needs constant attention in order to function adequately. There are dozens of reasons why a child performs poorly at school. Some may clear up with time and understanding; some may require more individual, tailored attention; others may require psychological counseling.

Many children function poorly at school because of earlier experiences of deprivation. If a child grows up in a barren intellectual environment, one in which little or no emphasis or value is placed on learning, reading, problem-solving, or intellectual curiosity, the child is disadvantaged in relation to school. Such a child will likely lack the prerequisite intellectual tools (or the motivation to use his or her innate tools) to be a good student and eventually to become a productive, self-sufficient adult member of society.

In general, a young girl is likely to do better at school than a boy of the same age. While this isn't universally true, girls are developmentally more advanced than boys of this age; they are more mature, more able and willing to concentrate on schoolwork, have more desire to please the teacher, and are less restless. This usually pertains throughout the early school years. A young boy is trying to separate himself from mother and from most things maternal; to some extent, this can include a teacher and the classroom.

Some young boys have a stormy time in school; disruptive or restless, they may be labeled as having a conduct disorder. Such a child may actually be quite normal, despite his rebelliousness. He has conflicts dealing with the structure and organization the classroom imposes on him. He simply cannot sit for hours on end without stimulating teaching, frequent breaks in the schedule, and ample opportunity for athletics and other physical activities. Such children are frequently misdiagnosed as being hyperactive or as suffering from an attention deficit disorder, a topic that will be discussed in Chapter 16, "The Child with Learning Problems."

A good school program is one that takes such possibilities into account and tries to keep the classroom an interesting and stimulating place for the child to nurture intellectual curiosity. As part of such a program, ample time must be provided for youngsters to participate in physical activities, so that their restlessness can be dissipated and they can turn their attention to learning.

The Society of Children

School-age children live in a psychologically separate world from adults. Though there is intermingling and while parents often take an active interest in their children, much of a child's daily experiences and concerns focus outside the family, within the peer group or "gang." By the age of eight or nine, the transition to the peer group is quite complete, and the child takes on the group's attitudes and values, much to the distress of many parents, who often grow concerned because their child seems to have become less affectionate, confiding in them less and seeming in some ways a stranger.

The society of playmates (or peers), a subculture of its own, exerts a powerful socializing influence on any child. Its values and mores are transmitted independently of family or school, passed on from child to child in a constant succession. There is constant movement into and out of the age group, each child remaining within the group for about six years. The ways of the peer group are learned from the older children, who move on as they become adolescents. The younger ones move up in stature, as new youngsters hang on the periphery of the group, waiting their turns.

The peer group has a number of purposes: It serves as an arena in which your child learns the necessary skills for living with others. The group becomes a regulator of behavior, even a form of self-government for children. It becomes a vehicle by which youngsters learn to find meaning and stability within themselves, away from parents, who, the children are beginning to realize, have imperfections and frailties. The prospect of becoming more independent and of finding one's own identity can seem frightening to a youngster; the group serves as a meaningful intermediate reference point. Each member reinforces the others' sense of growing independence and separate sense of self-identity.

Childhood peer-group activities seem to remain stable over many generations. Many common children's games date back to antiquity: checkers, marbles, games of tag, Johnny-on-the Pony, and others can be seen in paintings that are hundreds of years old. While the names and specific details of these activities change with time, they remain essentially as they were centuries ago. So, too, with jokes and riddles; generation after generation of children guffaw at "new" jokes, rushing to tell them to their parents ("Why does the chicken cross the road?"; "Why did the moron throw the clock out the window?"; "What's black and white and red all over?"). In truth, many of the "new" jokes children find uproariously funny are older than their parents.

Through group activities in the society of children, your child learns essential tasks for living, and for eventually becoming a member of the larger society outside the home.

HOW THE GROUP IS ORGANIZED. The juvenile group or "gang" may vary from being a loosely organized cluster of children playing in a schoolyard to well-defined clubs, teams, or school-related organizations. At first, the group may be haphazard in its membership, but by age ten, groups are likely to be organized around such specific activities. This is a time when a child may belong to many different groups, formally or informally, and these varying affiliations lead to multiple identifications.

As a rule, children who live close together play together. If they attend the same neighborhood school, this commonality reinforces the geographic basis for the peer group's structure and meaning. The neighborhood play group may include a variety of kids playing together (depending on the number available) or may break down into subgroups, divided according to sex and age.

A neighborhood grouping may be diluted by many factors: after-school activities organized by adults; adult-sponsored activities such as Little League teams; private schools with different hours than those of the neighborhood schools; a thinly populated suburban or rural area, which may not be conducive to the formation of a neighborhood street group. As a result, suburban children, who largely depend on their parents for transportation, have many adult-sponsored and organized activities. Even then, youngsters manage to form their own peer-group culture, away from the adult world.

Generally, each group has a leader, usually a youngster who is energetic, outgoing, athletically endowed, or blessed with whatever characteristic is valued by the specific group. Different groups value different assets, and your child may be the leader in one group (let's say, a baseball team) yet be relegated to a more passive position in another (such as a school drama club). Often, a youngster who is popular and a leader in one area is also a leader in others. Athletic ability, a striking asset for a boy, may make him very sought after by other boys.

Belonging to a group provides its members with a sense of "we-ness." Excluding others ("them") seems to be as important to school-age youngsters as the stated purpose of the group, club, or organization. The sense of being separate and apart (from parents and from other kids) provides a basis for an emerging sense of identity, away from parents and other adults.

WHAT THE PEER GROUP DOES.   The peer group helps a youngster begin to break free of adult authority and domination. In a general way, the entire adult world is challenged by the group. This is especially easy to see when a teacher unwisely asks a class of children to identify some wrongdoer; the curtain of silence that quickly descends indicates the group's reluctance to violate an unspoken code against "telling" or "snitching."

The group has its own weight and authority, one often used by the child to convince a parent of something or to counterweight a parent's authority. "Why can't I go to the movies? All the other kids are going"; or "Billy's mother said *he* can go roller-skating"; and a host of other pointed comparisons universally impel parents to assert their indifference about the workings of another child's family: "In this house, we do things *our* way!"

The group provides each youngster with certain codes and standards. It becomes a self-governing body, a regulator, of sorts, of each child's behavior. A sense of egalitarian selflessness, crucial to the group's functioning, is observable in the group's (often unspoken) codes of conduct. A youngster who gets along well in the group isn't afraid to stick up for another child; he's fair and willing to share; he's willing to compromise; he isn't a bully who picks on younger or smaller kids; he tolerates defeat graciously and isn't a "sore loser"; if teased or wronged, he doesn't run to his parents and isn't a "crybaby"; he keeps his mouth shut and won't "snitch" or "rat" on the others; he keeps a secret; he'll take a chance; he isn't a "chicken"; he doesn't complain; he plays by the rules; he doesn't cheat; he's not a "goody-goody," a "sissy," or a "faggot," and above all, he's loyal to the group's values and ways of doing things.

Honesty is important, especially in dealing with one another. Standards of dishonesty concerning the adult world, however, are flexible. Swiping a comic book or some inexpensive item from a store may occasionally be permitted. Often, such behavior is a testing of limits, and if a child never dares to flout adult (parental) standards or authority, he is apt to be labeled a "baby," a "sissy," or "chicken." The threat of being so labeled can impel a boy to act in ways he would never dare on his own, but the threat of losing stature (or acceptability) in the group can be a powerful source of motivation for youngsters.

Within the limits of the group, each child learns what constitutes acceptable behavior. Each learns about the rules and regulations of life. In dealing with the group's mores and standards and learning how to accommodate to the group's expectations, the child practices fitting into the larger society, beyond the family and the group. Through the group, each child learns which challenges he can accept and confront without coming to physical harm and without experiencing guilt or moral discomfort.

This necessary proving ground, in which your child learns how to get along without parents and to find his way in the larger world, presents certain dangers: It can generate subservient conformity to the group's standards, sometimes leading to inappropriate or even dangerous behavior. The occasional foray into minor stealing, the furtive attempts to smoke cigarettes, and anxious sexual explorations are to be expected. But sometimes a group can be carried away by a mischievous spirit, one that leads it to throw stones at passing trains or snowballs at passing cars; behaviors that can have disastrous consequences far beyond anything the group imagined.

A gang or group of youngsters is usually quick to seize on an individual child's idiosyncrasies or deficits, and many children willingly endure a variety of degrading nicknames for the sake of belonging to the group. Four-Eyes, Bugs, Shorty; Cootie, Flab, Dumbo, Bones, and other unflattering nicknames are borne as proud badges of belonging. Recognition for any skill, quirk, trait, or bodily deviation is preferable to exclusion from the group. Feelings of some personal power, of being acceptable, and of being able to deal with others are vital if a child is to have reasonable feelings of self-worth. The group provides these feelings. When a child feels unwanted by his peers, his sense of self and of self-worth is thrown into jeopardy.

BEING LEFT OUT.   Occasionally, a youngster may be excluded by other children. He or she may be completely left out, or partially excluded from certain activities. A child who is deliberately excluded from all activities becomes a scapegoat and may be mercilessly picked on by other youngsters. This situation evolves for various reasons, usually having to do with a combination of the child's traits mixed with some basic violation of the group's code of ethics.

Richard, ten years old, was a shy boy and a poor athlete. In addition, it was common knowledge among the kids that he was a bed-wetter, and he occasionally smelled of urine. Nicknamed "Roach," he was the object of considerable taunting. Yet a certain fondness seemed to prevail, and within limits Richard was included by the boys in their various games.

One day, the group (all boys ten and eleven years old) began playing Monkey in the Middle with Richard's hat. Tossing it back and forth, they refused to return it. Frustrated, Richard finally ran into his house.

Moments later, Richard's father appeared, angry and threatening. Retrieving his son's hat, he yelled at the boys, having fumed for months at the scapegoating his son endured. One of the boys responded with a verbal provocation and Richard's father slapped him soundly across the face.

Richard had violated a basic group code in going to his parents. By his angry outburst and poor judgment, Richard's father had condemned his son to being an eternal outcast. No one ever played with Richard again. The following year, Richard's parents enrolled him in a private school, hoping their son would make new friends.

It's wise to allow the social code and mores of the group to prevail. Children usually work out their own pecking orders and ways of dealing with each other. The sands of loyalty can shift with amazing capriciousness, and the child who is left out today may be part of the "in" group tomorrow. Parental meddling (trying to cajole or coerce the other kids into playing with a child, becoming a disciplinarian, and other unwanted intrusions) can spell trouble for a child's acceptability within the group.

Within any large group of children, there is sometimes a child who, for one or more reasons, is left out. It's not unusual for such children to form an exclusive club or group of their own, allowing them to have a sense of belonging and to reap the benefits that a peer group provides. Once in a great while, a child may not be acceptable to any group; in such a case, professional counseling may be in order.

The Best Friend

At about the age of ten, your child may form a relationship with someone who becomes a "best friend," a youngster who is held in special esteem by the child. Many parents grow concerned by this intense relationship and by what appears to be a constant need to be with this particular friend. A child may have more than one "best" friend at a time or may form an intense chumship with one youngster, only to replace this friend with another at a later time.

This intense attachment to a best friend is important in your child's developmental progress. The sharing of interests, intimate secrets, and feelings helps lessen the child's sense that she is unique or the only child perplexed or occasionally troubled by various problems. The friendship helps her learn how someone else manages the very same feelings and problems. This relationship represents your child's stepping beyond the "self." She is developing empathy and the capacity to relate closely to another person, not because the friend is a family member but because of shared interests and ideals.

The friend is of the same sex because at this age the sharing of feelings and empathy can only comfortable occur with a child of the same sex. This is not an indication of homosexuality; rather, it indicates that your child is developing the healthy capacity for intimacy beyond the confines of the family.

Your Child's Views Change

During the school years, a child's exposure to different peer groups exposes him to new sets of values. Some of them may not comfortably fit with the values of his family or with her previous assumptions about the world. During the first six years, parents are central in his life. They are the primary repository of all wisdom; they are the ultimate authorities and have set all values, however right or wrong.

During these years, a youngster comes into ongoing contact with the values of companions. He eats at friends' homes and realizes that there are different styles of preparing food, various ways of eating, different kinds of households and families, and different relationships between family members. The child learns that friends' parents are different from his own (for better or worse), that some households are tumultuous, others are calm, some are barren, others rich in values and traditions. No matter what, he is now exposed to families who are very different from his own.

A youngster develops a basis for comparing his own parents and home life to those of his friends. In other words, the family-centeredness of earlier years begins to break down, and the child begins judging his parents as real people rather than the presumed bedrock of wisdom and the enduring core of all that's good and right in the world.

This can be an eye-opening process for any child, and his experiences with different people may expose him to social cruelty. He may be surprised to learn that other people (adults and children) can be stupid. They can be scornful, deciding who is "good" and "not good," who is acceptable or unacceptable. The youngster discovers that such decisions are based on the most insubstantial of facts and sometimes on nothing more than prejudicial thinking. In other words, with increased exposure to different groups of people at school, in the neighborhood, and elsewhere, your child encounters the varied influences of the world at large.

A child's view of himself and his family may undergo radical alterations during this eye-opening process. While parents remain the primary emotional figures in a youngster's life, there can be sudden disillusionment as the child discovers that he is "different" or unacceptable to others. A child grows up in a family with loving, kind parents. They are good and reasonable, and he loves them. Moving out into the larger world of school and various peer groups, the youngster learns that his parents are fallible and may not be part of the larger, more acceptable social group.

He and his family may be the "wrong" color, "wrong" ethnic group, "wrong" religion, or may not have the "proper" socioeconomic status to satisfy the requisites of those "in the know." The child is exposed, perhaps for the first time in his life, to prejudice and a devaluation of himself and his family. This can cause a great deal of distress and turmoil, calling into question a youngster's view of himself and his family. He must eventually come to terms with himself, with his position in the community of his peers, and with where he belongs in the larger society.

Most children, while upset and even confused by such exposure, eventually succeed in this psychological task. On occasion, a child may become so upset by prejudice that he begins not only questioning himself, but devaluing himself and his family. If your relationship with your youngster has been open and communicative, you can reinforce your family's basic values to your child, telling him that some people are judgmental and will always look to devalue others. These can be harsh lessons in life, but a youngster who feels genuinely loved by his parents, who has a relatively strife-free home life, and whose parents communicate feelings of basic worth about themselves and their children, will not be "scarred" by such encounters. This may be a long process in which a child must eventually learn, with your help, to live in a complex and always imperfect world.

Heroes and Heroines

During these years, new ideals are established by the peer group. The group's values are different from those of the family, and various models become crucial to the child, serving as a basis for the child's image of the person he would like to become. This is the age of hero worship.

Heroes and heroines—all models for the child—are taken from life, from the movies, television, newspapers and from books. Such a figure may be the older adolescent boy or girl: the high-school athlete or the beautiful sixteen-year-old whom a ten-year-old girl would like to emulate. Professional athletes of every sport become models for boys during these years. A girl may develop an intense attachment to a particular teacher or admire a girlfriend's older sister who seems strikingly glamorous.

New heroes, heroines, and roles are taken on with almost frightening speed, and a parent may see abrupt changes in a child's behavior and role-playing; the changes can have a chameleonlike quality, but they are very normal. A boy may be consumed by football or by some other sport, emulating a particular hero day and night. Without warning, he may find a new hero in another sport or field of interest. Within a week, he may capriciously shift from being a basketball hero to a hockey star (depending on the season and on the availability of models to emulate), then to a passionate interest in becoming an astronaut. This varies depending on current trends and events: during the Super Bowl he may eat, drink, and sleep the Refrigerator, at election time it can be a top-ranked politician, and so on. Choices of heroic figures and roles are also influenced by the whims and fads of the peer group, a potent force in setting values to be admired and emulated.

Whether it's a rock star, an actress, an athlete, or some other figure, these idols seem virtually interchangeable, as the youngster tries out different social roles. The child is experimenting, trying to determine through active fantasy how well he or she fits in with the range of potential roles the larger society offers. The heroes and heroines, the constant role-playing and -modeling, are healthy ways for your child to modify his view of himself and eventually to move toward independence.

Despite these fluctuations in roles and role models, the school-age years are a time when most children seem untroubled. Generally happy with life, children enjoy a multitude of activities; they are eager to expand their worlds, are willing to learn, and are curious about people and the world at large. They function well in groups, choosing ones in which they can play the various roles about which they fantasize.

This is a time of mastery, of learning, of intellectual and physical growth. If the developmental tasks of this period are mastered relatively well, if the child takes to school, enjoys learning and expanding her world, she develops a sense of industry and the wish to meet new developmental challenges, growth that is readily reflected in school activities and the classroom. However, if a child does not consolidate these developmental tasks during the school-age years, she develops a pervasive sense of inferiority and inadequacy, which can have profound repercussions throughout the rest of life. See "Counseling and Child Guidance," "Signs of Trouble," and "What a Parent Can Do," later in this chapter.

What's Happened to Your Child's Sexual Interests?

Many parents incorrectly believe that children have no sexual interests during the school-age years. This perception is largely a matter of how our society has become structured; we view certain areas and interests, including sexuality, as the exclusive domain of adults. In fact, sexual interests have not evaporated, although they are somewhat muted and rarely expressed directly.

There was a time when children worked, earned money, and contributed to their families' incomes, and when they were more directly exposed to experiences of sexuality, birth, and death. When our society became more technologically advanced, children were shielded from such experiences. Birth and death now take place in hospitals, rather than in the home. And children learn that they are not expected to know about these matters, including sex. Children often smother their direct interest in sexual matters in response to adult expectations, but these interests are still present.

Children of this age tell stories and jokes that are overtly sexual, even if some of the details are beyond their understanding. Such tales and excursions into sexuality are partly a way for children to share in the forbidden, and by ignoring parental prohibitions about sex, they further establish a sense of growing independence. They often pore through sexy magazines and other materials to satisfy their enormous curiosity. Whether looking at pictures, reading racy descriptions of sexual activity, or perusing the dictionary for sex-related anatomical terms, youngsters share with each other their secret fantasies about sex, often contributing information (as well as myth and misinformation) to each other's expanding fund of knowledge.

Certain overt sexual behavior may occur during this period, too, especially as children approach age eleven. Boys often compare the size of their genitals, have contests to see who can urinate farther, and may masturbate with each other. Physical exploration of each other (the famous doctor game), which includes exploring children of the opposite sex, is common, and may occur at home with a sibling of the opposite or same sex. This is all quite normal and to be expected.

Some parents grow particularly concerned if they discover that a child engages in sexual activity with another child of the same sex. This is not necessarily homosexual activity or a forerunner of homosexuality. Rather, it's part of the curious sexual exploration that takes place during this period, undertaken with a child of the same sex because it is less emotionally threatening (and seems less forbidden) than physical exploration with a youngster of the opposite sex. It isn't uncommon for youngsters (let's say, two boys) to share their heterosexual fantasies, to leer at various photographs, and to demonstrate heterosexual interests, and to then engage in sexual activity between themselves. Generally, a homosexual orientation, if it does occur, becomes more apparent during mid-to-late adolescence. However, many normal boys engage in some sexual activity with another boy during the school-age years.

Your Child's Mind

Throughout these years, your child's mind advances in a variety of ways. It is no accident that the period between seven and eleven years of age is filled with concentrated teaching and learning, both in and out of school.

A school-age child now has the ability to view a situation, take note of several features of the interrelated parts, and choose to focus on one feature at a time. The child can understand that a change in one dimension can be offset or compensated for by a change in another dimension, and he understands that changing the spatial configuration of something does not necessarily change its quantity. In other words, the child can maintain the idea of constancy over apparent change.

Recall that the preschool child could not understand that the volume of liquid in a container remained the same whether the liquid was contained in a tall thin container or a short wide one. A school-age child can understand that the amount of liquid is unchanged, that nothing has been added or taken away by the change in shape of the container. In other words, the child can integrate these different dimensions, understanding that they compensate for each other in a reciprocal way.

A school-age child is capable of solving complex problems. If John is taller than Joe, and Joe is taller than Bob, then John is taller than Bob. In other words, the child can now deduce a new relationship from a set of earlier ones. This is an important step in logical thinking and in understanding various relationships in the world.

A school-age child has developed the ability to classify things, and kids this age love to classify everything; rock, coin, stamp, baseball card, doll, and other collections amply demonstrate this capacity. The ability to classify things is important, and as the youngster advances intellectually he can make more subtle distinctions among people, places, ideas, and things.

During this period of development, the child develops a crucial mental capacity to reverse processes. If you flatten out a clay ball, you can reshape it into a round ball again. If you lengthen the clay, you can then shorten it. Operations of one kind or another can be reversed mentally and in actual fact. This is an important logical capability; for instance, subtraction reverses the process of addition; division reverses the process of multiplication.

This capacity for reversing ideas and concepts has certain practical and emotional implications. A preschool child cannot truly fathom that if a bone is broken, it can eventually heal. The younger child's ability to conceptualize healing (a kind of reversibility) is very limited; a bone once broken remains (in fantasy) forever broken. For the younger child, the prospect of a parent's anger carries with it fantastically frightening implications: the parent will always be angry. Recall that the Oedipal child struggles with feelings of competition and hostility, with envy and love, all mixed with the overriding feeling of needing both parents. The child doesn't yet have the capacity to integrate these opposite (ambivalent) feelings; because of a limited ability to mentally reverse a situation (or an idea), he becomes terrified at the fantasy of the parent's anger. Angry for a moment means angry forever.

The school-age child's newfound ability to classify things, to appreciate categories and degrees, and to realize that things can be grouped in various ways or can occupy two or more classifications is very important. A preschool child has not yet achieved the ability to appreciate subtle differences between seemingly similar events. For instance, he cannot appreciate that there are varying degrees of illness. To a preschooler, the common cold, pneumonia, and a life-threatening illness such as cancer, are all the same. Sick is sick!

But the school-age child of seven, eight, or nine years of age appreciates that illness can be classified in different ways, especially in terms of seriousness. There are minor conditions, moderate ones, and serious illnesses. Of course, children vary in the ability to make these distinctions, and in their ability to understand the finality of death.

Other major changes occur in your child's ability to think logically during this period of time. As your youngster's thinking becomes more logical, it becomes less magical. This is amply demonstrated by children's responses to magic shows. Many well-intentioned parents arrange for a magician to appear at a party for preschoolers. Parents are dismayed when they realize that the children (aged three, four, and five years) aren't startled by the magician's incredible feats of prestidigitation. To the magical-thinking preschooler, everything is possible, and the hundred multicolored ribbons snaking from the magician's palm is no remarkable feat. But the school-aged child is amazed at this display. Having advanced beyond the preschooler's magical thinking, the youngster marvels at the incongruous violations of logic and expectation the magician's trickery provides. For this youngster, the show is a source of amazement and delight, and the child will beg to know how each trick is done.

During this period, your child's thinking becomes less egocentric, and she develops the capacity to more completely put herself in another person's place, to more fully appreciate that person's thoughts and feelings. This opens up a new realm of possibilities for relationships.

During these years, your child develops a heightened awareness of the body and its processes. She comes to realize that the heart pumps ceaselessly, that she always breathes, that the mind always thinks, that bacteria and viruses (germs!) exist and can cause illness, and that the body is a growing and changing thing. The child realizes that squinting can sharpen the eye's focus, that baby teeth are lost, overused muscles become stiff, you can gain or lose weight, you can hold your breath for just so long, some people are "double-jointed," a lucky few can wiggle their ears, and a host of other revelations about the world, and about space and its relation to the body. The idea of weightlessness is particularly fascinating to children and becomes a topic of rich fantasy; school-age youngsters are avid audiences for intergalactic films and fantasies.

A child this age appreciates the concept of time, knowing that people and events (indeed, the whole world) existed before she did and will continue on beyond her existence. The child learns to tell time and is capable of organizing and scheduling activities in a complex and efficient way. Age differences are no longer a mystery, and age-specific relationships are understood: mother and father are older than their child; grandparents are the parents of the parents, and are older than the child's parents.

At this time, the child becomes aware of the mysteries of birth and of life, often evolving complicated (and usually incorrect) notions about how babies are produced, confusing the role of sexuality with reproduction. The child also ponders the mystery and finality of death.

With all these advances, a child's thinking is still deeply colored by fantasy. Despite the capacity to read complex passages, despite the ability to deal with addition, subtraction, complex calculations, and subtle comparison, and though he can appreciate many concepts and subtleties, a child this age often thinks illogically, will occasionally regress to using a concrete form of reasoning, is capable of making the most obvious mistakes in judgment, and may even make up "facts" to substantiate an opinion. In other words, the child has not yet made a complete transition to true higher logical thinking, a change that takes place during adolescence. Even after such thinking occurs, all people's thinking is often colored by emotion and fantasy.

The most striking thing about the intellectual development of children at this age is that they have insatiable appetites for knowledge, wanting to explore everything and know as much as possible. This is a period of remarkable intellectual growth, a time during which your child may consolidate mental skills and capacities that will accompany him for the rest of his life. If nurtured and encouraged, your child's intellectual curiosity can become a formidable tool for knowing the world, and can lay the groundwork for later intellectual accomplishments.

The Maturing Conscience

Your child emerges from the Oedipal phase with a harsh and strict set of internalized standards. These are akin to internal commandments to which the child rigidly adheres, rather than being well-thought-out ethical values. A six-to-nine-year-old child follows inflexible internal "rules" or guidelines; he cannot deviate even slightly from them, as evidenced in his adherence to immutable game rules. A child this age considers the rules an inherent part of the game; they cannot be changed. The rules are the rules!

Similarly, a six-to-nine-year-old child cannot discriminate between a lie told to obtain personal gain and a "white lie" told to spare someone's feelings. To the child, a lie is a lie. He cannot judge an act according to its intent. In the same vein, a child who accidently breaks a window is judged as guilty as one who maliciously hurls a stone through a window.

Ethical development depends on a child's gaining experience by dealing with different people in various situations over a period of time, beginning with the first regular exposure to others outside the home, at six years. The child must move beyond accepting his parents' notions about right and wrong; he must move beyond internalizing these values as infallible moral edicts. By relating to other adults and peers, your child gradually modifies ideas of right and wrong, learning to consider the subtleties of a person's intent, and learning to make fine distinctions about a situation and its circumstances.

In addition, your child learns to understand the concept of punishment in a more sophisticated way. A young child expects that punishment will fit the crime; he will be deprived of going outdoors in proportion to the number of poor grades he brings home. As he grows older, he can understand punishment by reciprocity; if he refuses to help his mother wash the dishes, he can expect that she will refuse to drive him to the movies.

The neighborhood peer group plays a crucial role in a child's ethical development. Within the group, children learn how to play and get along with each other; they must make up rules; they arbitrate among themselves; they must take each other's shortcomings and intentions into account. Teachers, too, exert an important influence in helping a child refine the ability to make moral judgments. Rigid or arbitrary teachers and parents, those who insist on rigorously following inflexible rules and standards, will hinder a child from defining moral and ethical values beyond the more primitive stage of development.

◊ PRACTICAL ISSUES DURING THE SCHOOL-AGE YEARS

Certain difficulties, such as bed-wetting, may persist during the school-age years. They will be discussed in this section along with issues that are unique to the child who attends school. A special area of concern to some parents is the subject of learning problems. This topic is so important that Chapter 16, *The Child with Learning Problems*, is devoted to it.

When Your Child Doesn't Want to Go to School

The reluctance to attend school (technically called "school refusal") may be the result of a school phobia or of truancy. A child who has a school phobia has a fear or dread of going to school. The fear may be of the entire school environment and experience, or may be focused on some specific factor, such as a teacher, tests, a particular subject, or school toilets.

School phobia can occur in every grade; the peak occurrences are at the beginning of kindergarten, first grade, and junior high school. A child's phobia can begin suddenly as a transient episode of fear or reluctance to attend school or may be a long-standing problem in which the child attends school despite feelings of discomfort and anxiety. Usually, such a child has a poor attendance record.

It's important to realize that not all refusal to attend school is due to a school phobia. For some children, there may be realistic reasons for fearing school; for example, there may be threats to a child's physical safety. In such a case, a change of school or class usually resolves the problem.

Another important distinction should be made between the child who has a school phobia and the one who is truant. The truant young-ster experiences no anxiety about leaving home or attending school. The truant openly dislikes school and simply prefers not being there. He also avoids home when not attending school, while the phobic child enjoys being home and is afraid of leaving the house. Generally, a truant child has done poorly at school, while the phobic child has consistently done well.

An episode of school refusal may occur because of an acute stress at home, such as the birth of a sibling, which causes the schoolchild to regress and want to stay at home with mother. This is usually transient, and a parent must take a firm position with the child, yet be supportive and understand the child's fear of losing love or attention. However, the child must not be allowed to stay away from school.

The symptoms of school phobia vary. They are usually worse on Sunday evening and Monday morning, and intensify after Christmas or Easter vacation or summer recess. The child becomes more anxious as the time for school approaches, and may complain of illness: abdominal pains or cramps, diarrhea, or nausea and vomiting. If parents pressure the child to go to school, he may become panicky and then physically resist. As soon as the child is allowed to remain home, anxiety fades and the physical complaints disappear.

School phobia is a problem of separation and individuation. Although it is often precipitated by an occurrence at school, it is actually based on a conflict that takes place at home. The central problem for parent and child is one of separation. For some children, home is simply too attractive a place to leave. For others, an intensely dependent, resentful, and ambivalent relationship exists between parent and child. Many experts believe that the child deals with angry and resentful feelings toward mother by viewing her as "all good," while the teacher or school becomes "all bad." This allows the child to deny or "pretend away" any bad feelings toward mother.

DEALING WITH SCHOOL PHOBIA.   Most child psychiatrists view school phobia as a psychiatric emergency. It must be quickly treated. A child with a phobia should *not* be kept out of school; it becomes more difficult for him to return the longer he stays at home. If physical symptoms such as nausea and vomiting are part of the picture, a thorough medical evaluation should be made by the family pediatrician. If nothing is wrong, the child should be told so and returned to school without delay. It's crucial that your youngster realize that he is expected to stay in school and that you are committed to this course of action. Should the child sense your ambivalence about his returning to school, he may press harder to remain at home.

School phobia is a very common problem. Counseling is indispensable if the fear persists longer than a few weeks, or if it worsens. As a parent, you must understand that you play a part in the problem and in the treatment. Most child psychiatrists prefer to go beyond individual sessions with the child, and to have family sessions as well. These can be very helpful.

Getting a child to return to school can be done in a number of ways. Desensitization may be used; for example, the child may be returned to school, but not immediately to the classroom. The youngster may attend class for a short time, with each visit prolonged until a full day is spent in class. The child may be helped to make the transition by spending a brief period of time with a guidance counselor each day before class begins.

Some therapists feel that medication (imipramine) helps quell the child's separation anxiety. Such treatment has been helpful in many cases.

It's important to realize that when your child returns to school, professional treatment must continue. Often, the sessions then focus on various aspects of the parent-child relationship. Successful therapy depends on parents participating equally in treatment.

Bed-wetting

As described in chapters 2 ("Bladder Training") and 3 ("Bedwetting"), most children achieve both bowel and bladder control by about three and a half years years of age. However, about 7 percent of children wet the bed after the age of seven years. Physical problems are present in only about 5 percent of such children. Psychological factors and developmental immaturity are considered the most important causes of bed-wetting, and a complete evaluation (physical and emotional) must be made before appropriate steps can be taken.

Many parents are reluctant to acknowledge that a child who persistently wets the bed has a problem. Parents are often embarrassed by this symptom, feeling that it must be hidden or kept secret from the outside world. This presents a psychological danger for the youngster, because the need to hide the symptom often means he can't stay overnight at a friend's home, that he cannot go on an overnight trip to a relative's house, or that he can't go to overnight camp. He is forced to renounce or avoid certain activities that could help expand his world beyond that of the family. The child must also live with a dreaded "secret" about himself, one implying that he must hide some "bad" part of himself or his behavior. This is never good for a child's self-esteem or sense of self worth.

A school-age child with a bed-wetting problem may become the object of jokes and name-calling by other children; such ostracism and denigration are obviously damaging to any youngster's self-esteem. This can have far-ranging consequences because such a child becomes inhibited in his relationships with other children. Fearful of being "discovered," he may constrict his activities and interests, avoiding those that could possibly lead to embarrassment.

A complete discussion is found in the section "Bedwetting" in Chapter 3, along with a description of the various treatments for this problem. Bed-wetting is a common problem. It's completely appropriate to get professional help for a school-age youngster, for the price of letting the "secret" continue is simply much too high.

Stealing

Many parents become very upset when they discover that a child has stolen something. There are different kinds of stealing, and a child can have many motivations for taking something that does not belong to him.

A child may occasionally take money (usually small amounts of change) from a parent's coat or pocketbook. Or the child may take a toy or some minor item belonging to a friend or classmate: trading cards, a penknife, a pen or pencil, crayons, or a comic book. Usually, the item is minor and, more striking, is something the child doesn't really want or need. Rather, he seems to be satisfying some other urge by the act of stealing.

Surprisingly, many a child who steals in this fashion actually craves more attention from his parents; the stealing represents a way of "getting more" and sometimes the child unconsciously wishes to be caught. In this way, he receives attention, bad attention being better than none at all.

Danny, an eight-year-old-boy, was frequently caught stealing. He would swipe comic books from stores (sometimes taking three or four of the *same* book), took candy bars, and stole toys that he never used. In fact, he often gave them away. On a few occasions, he gave stolen toys to younger children, who then told their parents. This eventually led to Danny's being "caught."

After a series of incidents involving irate storekeepers who caught the boy stealing, it became clear to Danny's parents that he stole in order to be caught. The attention he then received was in some way very important to him. Danny was taken to a child psychiatrist and counseling was begun.

Danny's stealing had erupted two years earlier, soon after he began school, and coincided with the birth of a sister. The combination of the new baby and Danny's being "sent away" to school made him feel unimportant and unwanted. He soon began stealing for the attention that being caught provided. It was a plea for love.

Danny and his parents met with the psychiatrist for a few months and these issues became very clear. Soon afterward, Danny's stealing stopped.

If you are certain that your child has stolen something, tell him so and insist on knowing the truth. There's no point in heaping moral condemnation on the child, and it makes no sense to devalue him as a person. You want him to know that *stealing* is morally reprehensible, not that *he* is bad.

Insist that he take the item back, but try to avoid making this a humiliating experience. Accompany him to the friend or classmates's house. If he is returning something to a store, go with your child and tell the owner that your youngster wants to return an item that he took without paying for it. Most reasonable storekeepers will understand and won't make a major issue of it. It's important to insist that the item be returned; otherwise, your maintaining that stealing is wrong constitutes a decided double message, one that "winks" at the act of stealing.

Try to understand the reasons for a child's stealing. Is your youngster feeling deprived in some way? Is he getting less of something (attention, allowance, etc.) than other kids his age? Does the stealing occur repeatedly? Does it fit into a pattern, as in the case of Danny? Try to determine if the youngster is giving you a not-so-subtle message that he craves attention or affection.

Another kind of stealing is more related to a child's wish to be part of the peer group than to any maladjustment or emotional difficulty. Many children, whether responding to a dare or vying to be accepted by the other kids, occasionally swipe something from a store. This usually is an isolated incident and should not be viewed as anything more than an indication of the power of the group and the child's wish to be accepted.

If stealing persists or takes on a pattern, guidance and counseling must be considered. Usually, such a child feels lonely, unwanted, or unloved in some way, and the stealing is a symptom of these underlying emotional difficulties.

The Tomboy

Many parents are aware that certain girls are tomboys; they prefer to join boys in their activities during the early and middle school years. Sometimes, a tomboy excels to the point that she performs better than boys her own age. While this is only a temporary reversal of a girl's sex-role identification, some parents grow concerned if their daughter isn't "acting like a girl."

The young girl who is a tomboy is often hard-pressed to keep pace with her male playmates, and she is usually doomed to the fate of having the more athletically endowed boys eventually outstrip her in physical prowess. Tomboyishness is usually outgrown, and eventually a girl who favored athletic activities and playing with boys assumes a female role, especially as adolescence approaches.

Some parents worry that tomboyish behavior is a forerunner of female homosexuality, but this is rarely the case. In fact, today there is a blurring of role distinctions and activities designated "male" or "female," and children of both sexes often take part in activities that were traditionally labeled the province of one sex or the other. Schools today stress the importance of athletics for girls, and the athletically endowed young girl is encouraged to participate in volleyball, basketball, softball, swimming, and a variety of sports that some years ago were the sole domain of boys. Today, girls are also exposed to activities such as shop and other crafts once thought to be the restricted privilege of boys.

While some tomboys may have feelings of preferring to be a boy, this is usually temporary and can be viewed as a corollary of the young boy's envy of girls. This does not indicate emotional maladjustment. Rather, it is a route by which some girls eventually develop a complete sense of themselves.

The "Sissy"

Parents sometimes worry when a young boy shows interest in "girl's" activities. The situation for a boy can be complicated. A boy's mother expects him to be gentle and kind, to share and be fair, yet if he doesn't demonstrate a good deal of boisterous aggressivity (even ruthless aggression), a parent may worry that the boy is a "sissy." In other words, the role expectations for boys include elements of being rebellious and assertively physical, along with other traits that are quite the opposite. And the boy's eventual role as an adult is rarely a physical, two-fisted one, even though the early years focus on models of physical prowess and aggression.

Traditionally, boys are expected to be ambitious and push for achievement. While this is becoming a more acceptable model for young girls, too, boys are still expected to disavow interests and activities that are deemed to be "female" (even though the greatest chefs have traditionally been men). This is a form of role-modeling, not the natural unfolding of inherent male traits.

While a girl who demonstrates tomboyish characteristics is rarely thought to be in danger of becoming a lesbian, many parents worry that a boy who takes an interest in girls' activities will become a homosexual in adult life. This is by no means necessarily true, and many boys who take interest in girls' activities develop into healthy heterosexual adults. In truth, adults are often less tolerant of a boy's demonstrating interest in girls' activities than they are of a girl being interested in activities designated as "masculine."

Our society is now becoming more sophisticated about these matters. There is less demand for sheer muscle power, and men are now allowed to be more interested in so-called feminine things (home life, children, art, music, and so on). Women are now becoming more interested in "masculine things" (work, professions, ambition, and competition). With these changes, men can be interested in aesthetics, while women can be interested in athletics. As a parent, it is understandable for you to become concerned that your son may be indicating a tendency toward homosexuality if he shows no interest in friendships with other boys; if he plays almost exclusively with girls and shares their interests while ignoring male interests; or if his gestures, mannerisms, and general demeanor seem feminine. However, a boy's occasional interest in girls' activities does not indicate such a tendency.

The Child with Few Playmates

The peer group is usually very important during the school years but isn't a vital part of every childhood. Not every child can have an available pool of playmates; there may be many reasons for a child having very few companions during these years.

In rural areas, great distances may account for a certain isolation. A youngster may not be able to participate in various activities because of health or because of some handicap. A child may be a member of a minority group and can be excluded from the society of his peers. Some children are "loners" by disposition and may only partially join in the peer group's activities. The child of a schoolteacher, a principal, or a clergyman may be deemed "different" from the other children and may find it difficult to make friends.

As a parent, you may wish to make efforts to help your child find a peer group. You may encourage your youngster to take part in after-school activities. Such organized group situations are common in rural and other exurban areas where a neighborhood play group is not easily available. For some children, even organized efforts may not provide a readily available group.

This need not be an important deprivation. Most children of this age can readily occupy themselves. A child can use a great deal of fantasy and imagination, and very creative people often report that as youngsters they experienced a certain loneliness and the need to rely on fantasy. The child who grows up with less exposure to peers may not have some of the advantages of a ready-made group, but this child may develop an active and creative fantasy life.

Books can provide a form of companionship for a child. Though certainly not a substitute for real people, the characters and stories that books provide can be a welcome retreat for a youngster who needs to fill the emptiness of a long day or who needs to discover new worlds, ones far away from that of everyday existence. Books can provide compelling models for a child to form important identifications, in addition to their being an important source of entertainment and intellectual enrichment. It is during the grade-school years that an enduring love of books often develops. (See "A Loner," later in this chapter.)

Tics

A tic is a rapid, repeated, and purposeless movement of various muscles, usually facial. Such a gesture can be voluntarily suppressed for a time, but the child eventually repeats it. The most common tics involve facial grimacing, raising the eyebrows, eye-blinking, winking, mouth-twitching, twisting of the neck and other movements. Other kinds of bodily movements, such as repeated shaking of the arm, hand, or foot, are regarded as tics. Other repetitive purposeless symptoms include throat-clearing, sniffling, sighing, and yawning.

A tic may suddenly appear, last for a few days or weeks, and then disappear. It may reappear with more or less intensity and then go away, never to appear again.

Tics are generally a sign of psychological stress, and during this period of development many children develop transient mild tics which disappear in a matter of weeks. A tic may be caused by a traumatic experience but more often is an indication of inner tension and stress in a child's life. These tensions can be associated with school, with peers, either at school or in the neighborhood, or within the family. Tics tend to increase in frequency and intensity when a child is emotionally excited, and decrease or disappear when the child is distracted or concentrating on something else. They disappear completely during sleep.

Most tics or nervous movements occurring during a child's development are transient and will have no long-range consequences.

A child may copy a tic from another youngster, and then go on to display his own variation of the symptom. This simply indicates that the child was struggling with inner tensions and stress before being exposed to the other youngster.

If your child develops a tic, it's best to minimize her focus on this nervous habit. Most likely, it will disappear in a matter of weeks. The more her attention is directed toward the movement, the more intense it may become, which is of course an undesirable development. When tics begin, it's best to think about your child's school and home environment, trying to pinpoint any areas that are sources of undue stress. This may be difficult to do, and often no clear-cut source of anxiety can be observed.

If the tic persists, the youngster should be evaluated by a child psychiatrist. The doctor will interview the child and parents to assess any tensions or problems that are contributing to the nervous movement. The doctor may also consider recommending a medical and neurological evaluation, if this is indicated by the nature and intensity of the symptom.

Gilles de la Tourette's Disorder

This syndrome (a group of signs and symptoms) is called Tourette's disorder. The symptoms begin in childhood, anywhere between the ages of two and twelve years. A child with this disorder begins to display a variety of motor tics that involve grimaces and stereotyped (that is, repetitive and complicated) tics of various kinds. Spasmodic movements of the upper body occur, and may spread to involve most of the body until the ticlike movements involve skipping, jumping, and other sudden motor movements. In addition, a patient with this disorder feels a compulsion to suddenly and explosively call out various profanities, which may be accompanied by coughing, spitting, or even barking sounds. The patient may also repeat words or phrases immediately after hearing other people say them (technically called echolalia). These outbursts of motor and verbal behaviors occur spontaneously and are completely unpredictable, although the symptoms worsen when the child is experiencing emotional stress or fatigue.

Certain tics of childhood (see above) may be mistaken for Tourette's disorder, and other rare degenerative diseases of the nervous system may also be confused with this disorder. However, none of the other diseases are characterized by the characteristic sounds of Tourette's disorder, and the onset of these diseases (Sydenham's chorea; Huntington's chorea) is usually later than for Tourette's disorder.

While no specific cause has been demonstrated for Tourette's disorder, most experts agree that a neurochemical or neurologic abnormality exists in patients who suffer from this disease. Until recently, no known treatment was available for this relatively rare disorder, but treatment with a psychiatric drug named haloperidol began in the 1970s. In most patients treated with this medication, reduction in symptoms of 90 percent have been reported. In addition, behavioral therapy (in which the patient "learns" to control certain tics) combined with verbal psychotherapy and medication has been helpful.

Stuttering

Stuttering, or stammering, is a disturbance of rhythm and fluency of speech caused by intermittent blocking, convulsive repetition, or prolongation of sounds, syllables, words, or phrases. The most recent research indicates that psychological stress or anxiety can worsen stuttering, but it is not the basic cause of the problem.

Between one-half and 1 percent of children have stuttering problems. It is found more frequently in boys than girls, and studies have shown that 50 percent of the relatives of a child who stutters have speech problems themselves. There is little doubt that stuttering tends to run in certain families.

Various theories have been proposed to explain the causes of stuttering. A variety of psychological causes have been proposed, emphasizing either the child's problems or those of the family as a whole. Some experts consider stuttering to be caused by problems in learning language, while others have focused on failures in brain feedback mechanisms or on various organic problems resulting in failure to coordinate speech patterns, hand movements, and other subtle, brain-controlled behaviors. Studies of twins and of genetic, family patterns strongly suggest that most stuttering is a genetically inherited neurologic disorder, but more research on brain functioning is needed to clarify the cause or causes of stuttering.

There is no doubt that emotional stress worsens the problem, and it is clear that stuttering can bring on a variety of emotional difficulties for the child.

Stuttering may appear at any age, but it usually starts in childhood. It tends to peak at two or three years of age, without necessarily progressing to become a real problem. A child may occasionally stutter, then the symptom disappears. The next peak period when stuttering appears is between five and seven years, and a child who habitually stutters in elementary school is likely to become a stutterer.

Stuttering usually develops slowly, over a period of weeks or months. Even after it develops, it may be absent during oral reading, singing, or when a child talks to a pet.

A full description of the onset of stuttering and of the various ways this problem presents itself is beyond the scope of this book. There is little doubt, however, that a child who stutters can become anxious about those situations that precipitate or worsen stuttering: classwork, oral recitations in front of the class, having attention focused on one's self, speaking to strangers, using the telephone, and others. Many stutters tend to develop poor self-esteem, are less willing to risk failures, and are more hostile or anxious than people who do not stutter.

Psychotherapy should be considered if it becomes clear that your child stutters only in certain anxiety-provoking situations, such as the birth of a sibling, in the presence of a specific person, or when the child meets a new person. Counseling may be helpful, as a way of dealing with the anxiety or stress that worsens or even starts the stuttering.

It's also important to consider psychotherapy if a child's emotional and social functioning are impaired because of the stuttering problem, as happens when a child develops a poor self-image or feelings of insecurity, anxiety, or depression because of the stuttering. Certain family situations may contribute to a child's stuttering, or there may be discord and stress within the family, brought on because other family members become frustrated in trying to cope with or help the child who stutters. If this is the case, it can be helpful for the family to meet with a child psychiatrist to discuss the problem.

Treatment for stuttering is offered by speech clinics and in special classes conducted by qualified speech therapists. Most modern treatments are based on the view that stuttering is a learned form of behavior, and not a psychiatric disorder. If there is a neurological problem, it cannot be reversed or changed; therefore, the emphasis in treatment is on compensating for, or minimizing, the problem.

Parents interested in learning more about stuttering and its various treatments can contact the Center for Communication Disorders located at the Department of Otolaryngology of the Eastern Virginia Medical School, 825 Fairfax Avenue, Norfolk, Virginia 23507. Telephone (804) 446-5934. The center will supply interested parents with pamphlets and literature about speech disorders, and will also refer you to a center for speech disorders in your area, anywhere in the U.S.

Compulsions

Some parents become worried when they notice their child developing certain do's and don'ts of everyday life. These "habits," "mannerisms," or little rituals are technically called compulsions, and you may very well remember some of them from your own childhood. A common one is either avoiding or making sure you step on sidewalk cracks. There are many others, such as touching every third lamppost, repeating some phrase or sequence of words before doing something, and hundreds more.

As discussed in the section "Magic and Ritual," earlier in this chapter, your child uses these actions to deal with anxiety about the world. There are many compulsions and rituals during the early school years because your child's conscience is still very strict. For one reason or another, she may have angry feelings toward mother, father, sister, or brother. These repetitive acts (like not stepping on the sidewalk cracks) are a way of turning hostile thoughts into little games that deflect the underlying wish, thought, or feeling that the child's conscience finds unacceptable. Later, when her conscience is more flexible and mature, the older child will be more able to tolerate her own ambivalence toward someone, knowing that she can both love and resent mother, father, or a sister, that such feelings often coexist side by side.

Another reason these minor compulsions appear at this time is that a child of nine or ten years is struggling to keep sexual thoughts and feelings to a minimum. The repetitive ritual or compulsion focuses the child's attention, keeping thoughts about sex away from consciousness. During this period, a child is absorbed by school and learning, as well as by peer activities. Later, with pubertal changes and the onset of adolescence, sexual interests will surge to the surface. The adolescent is far more capable of dealing with these feelings than is the elementary-school youngster.

Daily compulsions and minor rituals are so common among kids that they are considered a normal part of growing up. Yet there are important exceptions: if your child's compulsion begins taking up too much time, interferes with her social or family life, or inhibits or interrupts school work, help should be obtained.

Let's say your daughter feels she must wash her hands before dinner. That's fine. She may then feel the need to again wash after dinner, and then washes her hands a half hour later. Let's say she then must wash her hands before going to bed; then she gets out of bed to again wash, and then once again. If washing, or any other compulsive ritual, gets to this point, counseling is needed. A youngster whose rituals or compulsions become so overwhelming is struggling to contain very powerful (and unacceptable) sexual or hostile feelings. The child should be helped to deal with them in a more reasonable way.

Teaching Your Child About Sex

School-age children learn to hide their sexual interests from what they think will be the disapproving eyes of adults. Parents who think that elementary-school children have no sexual interests are incorrectly taking children's behavior at face value. While it's true that a major developmental emphasis at this time concerns learning and mastering the social and intellectual skills needed in the larger society, a child's sexual curiosity hasn't faded into oblivion.

Children often struggle to smother their sexual thoughts and feelings through rituals and compulsions. But these very struggles are further evidence of children's interest in sex, as forbidden and frightening as these concerns may be to them. Sexuality is one of the great mysteries of childhood, and most parents are aware of their child's sexual curiosity as early as age three. During the elementary- and junior-high-school years, children are eager to acquire information about sex, and though it may not be obvious, kids are often absorbed by sexual curiosity.

Nine-, ten-, and eleven-year-olds giggle and laugh at "dirty" jokes; these often involve references to the body, especially sexual anatomy. Youngsters can be found poring through the dictionary, through library books and medical texts in a quest for words and descriptions detailing sexual anatomy and functions. Children seem always able to obtain sex magazines and "dirty" pictures; many of today's publications are far more revealing than those of years ago. And during this period, children engage in curious sexual exploration with members of the same and opposite sexes, with friends, relatives, and even with siblings.

A great deal of information, including myth and misinformation, is transmitted from one youngster to another. For better or worse, your child has been picking up information from a variety of sources through-out all of childhood.

Above all, your child's perceptions about the relationships between men and women are deeply influenced by a mother and father's relation-ship to each other and to their children. Parents are always the primary educators of their children, and no matter how much sexual information is actually provided to a child by various people, a youngster's views about sex are colored by what is seen, heard, felt, and sensed at home.

If a boy's father is abusive and violent, the child's ultimate views of what it means to be a "man" will reflect something of these experiences. The child will carry these emotional and mental images in his mind, and they will help determine the kind of man he becomes, including his sexuality. He may grow up to think that a man rules the house with an iron fist, threatens and abuses others, and acts violently when his anger is aroused. His views of sex will probably take on the same tone.

If a girl's parents are cold and indifferent to her, if she is made to feel unwanted and unloved while her younger brother is the obvious favorite, she will most likely grow up with a devalued self-image. She will probably resent men, feeling that they get all the privileges and pleas-ures, while a girl (and eventually a woman) receives none. These distor-tions in her view of herself and in her views of men will become part of her overall set of expectations, and she will bring resentful, devalued feelings to her relationships with men, including her sexual relation-ships.

Children ask about the "facts of life" at quite an early age. A parent can and should provide simple, clear explanations about "where babies come from" without burdening the child with more details than he or she asks for or can understand. One step at a time is a sensible way of dealing with sexual issues.

Some parents feel that their children never ask, but they are probably incorrect. Most three-, four- or five-year-old children ask about sex and about babies quite directly. During the school-age years, these questions come in a more indirect way, especially if a child senses that parents are made uncomfortable or embarrassed, or are reluctant to discuss anatomy and sexuality.

During the toddler and preschool years, ample opportunity presents itself for parents to openly and naturally give a child sexual information. When your daughter sees her brother's penis, she may make subtle (and not so subtle) inquiries. She may try to urinate while standing, imitating brother and father. This provides an excellent opportunity to tell her about the differences between boys and girls. This helps her understand what she sees and helps avoid frightening fantasies if she draws the wrong conclusions (such as that she is damaged or has had her penis removed). Many other opportunities arise for telling a girl or boy a great deal about sex and about the differences between boys and girls.

The preschool and elementary-school settings present other opportunities for sex education. A child may watch or care for an animal: a dog, cat, hamsters, mice, tropical fish, and other forms of animal life. The animals and their lives are rich topics for discussion (and fantasy). This can be supplemented by what a child sees in films and on television, since many programs deal with animal life. A child can learn about reproduction, mating, babies, suckling, and other aspects of animals' sexual and nurturing lives. Everyday life provides ready-made opportunities for a parent to discuss human sexuality on a level that a child can understand.

Many parents feel uncomfortable discussing sex with their children. They don't know what to tell a child, how to tell it, and when to discuss such matters. One thing is certain: you can be sure that your child is picking up information, right or wrong, as well as attitudes about sexuality, from members of the peer group. If you want your own views about sex to prevail, it's best to give information sooner rather than later.

Of course, sex education can be given at school, but as a parent you have no direct control over what is being told to your child. Even assuming that the teacher is well informed and transmits information without bias or distortion, a sex-education course can't be timed to suit the varying needs of individual children. Children differ in what they want to know, in how they can best deal with what they are taught, in the details they require, and in when they want to hear it. They also need different lengths of time to think about what they've been taught.

Books can be helpful if they are selected carefully by a parent. However, they vary in quality, and a book alone may confuse a child. If you use a book, it should be in conjunction with helpful advice and explanations, to ensure that solid, sound information is available to your child.

Telling a child about sex is often an emotionally loaded issue for parents and children alike. Some parents can't bring themselves to discuss sex with their children, and some children refuse to accept sexual information from their parents. It's best to proceed gradually, beginning with the direct questions of a preschool child, and then picking up on the subtle cues you hear from your child later on. At some point, you may feel comfortable enough to openly discuss sex with your child. This is best done when the youngster is ten or eleven years old, when puberty is right around the corner.

A father will probably feel more comfortable discussing sex with a son; a mother will find it easier with a daughter. This cleavage makes sense, and there is no need to force a discussion with a child of the opposite sex if it makes you feel embarrassed or uncomfortable.

TALKING WITH YOUR DAUGHTER.   A girl should be told by ten years of age that within the next few years her body will change. She should know about breast development, about her menstrual periods, and about the function of her uterus. When discussing these details with your daughter, emphasize that these are natural functions and that her body will be preparing her to eventually have a baby.

Some mothers wrongly convey negative feelings about the menstrual period, making it seem as though a period is a burden or a "curse." Some mothers tell a prepubertal girl that during her periods she won't be able to participate in various activities and that her life must change or will be somehow altered. This is a mistake and conveys to a girl that her body is somehow "unhealthy" or "unclean." Such a message can have especially negative meanings for the girl who as a young child felt somehow "damaged" or devalued because she didn't have a penis. It's clear that the menstrual cycle need not mean a girl must alter her life or avoid most activities, even though some girls may eventually develop menstrual cramps. Again, your feelings and attitudes about your own body and sexuality will come across to your child when you discuss these important issues.

TALKING WITH YOUR SON.   A ten- or eleven-year-old boy is rapidly approaching puberty. He needs to be told about erections and nocturnal emissions, that they are natural and expected and are part of growing up to be a man. Like the girl, the boy should be told about sexual anatomy and the details of reproduction and sexuality.

TALKING ABOUT MASTURBATION.   A youngster, boy or girl, should be told that masturbation is a natural part of life. Never propagate myths about it. Masturbation isn't "unnatural" or "wrong"; it is not "immoral"; it doesn't cause pimples; it doesn't "weaken" the body; it doesn't "thin" the blood; it won't harm future sexual functioning; and it won't make anyone sterile. Masturbation is perfectly normal and causes no harm of any kind.

ABOUT YOUR ATTITUDE.   Discuss sexuality with your youngster in as natural a way as you can. Approach such a series of conversations as an important parental function, keeping in mind that the discussion will be helpful to your child if you can be interested, casual, and informative. After all, your child is not only interested in sex but is also wondering whether these are normal and acceptable concerns. Assure your youngster that sex is a part of life, and that all children wonder and occasionally worry about it.

Don't idealize sexuality with platitudes about love or claims that sex only occurs when people love each other and want to have a baby. Remember, your child knows much more than you think; he or she hears, reads, and learns about sexual matters throughout childhood. Today, television, films, and the mass media expose children to a variety of sexual topics from an early age. Even before your child understands everything, he or she reads or hears about abortion, AIDS, venereal disease, homosexuality, gay rights, prostitution, unwed mothers, adoption and unwanted babies, sex abuse, and other topics that directly or indirectly make an impact on how a child thinks and feels about sexual matters.

Your warmth and acceptance of sexuality as part of life and your interest and honesty can play a vital role in your child's perceptions of and attitudes about sexuality.

Counseling and Child Guidance

During the elementary-school years many parents consider getting advice or guidance for themselves or for their child. This occurs because a youngster may first show adjustment problems at this time when his world is enlarging and when various demands are made by parents, teachers, peers, and others. Academic or behavioral problems may crop up at this time; parents are often uncertain whether a child is truly having a problem, and if a problem does exist, they may not know how to obtain a professional consultation.

If a child is having difficulties at school, the most logical place to begin consulting is with the teacher. An interested teacher can be a valuable source of information about a child and may very much want to speak with you. The teacher may make helpful suggestions or even recommend that a child be seen by a psychiatrist for a consultation. Parents are sometimes disbelieving when a teacher describes behavior that the parents have never seen their child exhibit, and some parents question the validity of a teacher's observations and comments. However, an experienced teacher is not only a good judge of a child's capacities and behavior but is usually able to provide intelligent feedback to parents.

Many schools have a guidance counselor on staff. On a teacher's recommendation, this counselor may request a meeting with a child, and with parents, too. If the counselor feels the child needs further guidance or help, he or she may make a recommendation.

Many parents with questions about a child's school performance or behavior prefer a private consultation with a qualified professional. This is probably the most direct and effective way to get an opinion about whether or not a child is having problems.

Following is a brief description of the mental-health professionals most qualified to diagnose and treat emotional problems during a child's development:

- A *child psychiatrist* is a physician, an M.D., who, having gone through medical school and an internship, has become a specialist in psychiatry (the diagnosis and treatment of mental and emotional disorders). This psychiatrist then has undertaken a course of training to become a specialist in dealing with children's problems. As is the case with any physician, this doctor can prescribe medication if it is necessary.
- A *psychologist* is a mental-health professional trained in any one of the various branches of psychology. This person is not a physician but is qualified to perform intelligence and aptitude tests and personality tests, and can administer tests used to determine the causes of learning and behavior problems in school or at home. A child psychologist is also trained in treating childhood problems. (See the next section, "About Counseling and Therapy," for a description of treatment.)

If you don't know a child psychiatrist or psychologist, there are various ways to locate one for a private consultation or for an appointment through a psychiatric clinic or child guidance center. Here are the easiest ways to locate qualified professional help:

- Ask your family doctor or pediatrician for a referral to a child psychiatrist or licensed child psychologist. It's best if this is not a "blind" referral; that is, it's preferable that your doctor actually know the doctor to whom the referral is made.
- Contact your local medical society or local Council on Child Psychiatry, if there is one. Virtually every city and county has a medical society to which physicians of all specialties belong. The society will provide you with a list of qualified physicians in your area who specialize in child psychiatry.
- Contact a local hospital that maintains a child psychiatry clinic. Such clinics provide a wide range of services, at varying fees, including diagnosis and treatment of children's problems. Usually psychiatrists and psychologists work together to diagnose and treat children's problems. They are assisted by psychiatric social workers and nurses who will occasionally visit a child's school or interview family members.
- Physician referral services are often maintained by local hospitals. Such a service will provide you with the names of specialists who belong to the hospital staff and who are able to accept referrals for private consultations and treatment.

About Counseling and Therapy

Only rarely do people *easily* seek out counseling or psychotherapy. Despite our living in a very sophisticated society, many people still view the need for professional help as a sign of weakness or deficiency. This unenlightened attitude can lead to unnecessary suffering for both parent and child.

A younger child is simply not mature enough to know when she needs help. She may not be aware of feeling troubled by any particular problem but may instead have a general sense of distress or tension. A youngster of ten or eleven years may simply keep her feelings to herself, even though she knows she is troubled. This is because of her emerging feelings of self-sufficiency and the need to diminish her dependency on parents. In general, the troubled child will most likely indicate the need for help by various behaviors ranging from "acting up" to isolation and withdrawal. As a parent, it's important to be aware of the signs of trouble so you can effectively help your child, should the need arise.

SIGNS OF TROUBLE.   Some behaviors are such clear indicators of a child's troubles that they seem obvious. Help is clearly necessary when a youngster's behavior is harmful to himself, other people, and to property. The child who cannot control his temper, who acts violently, who smashes windows, who persistently steals, who cannot get along with other children or adults, who is withdrawn, who fails to do well in school despite a good intellect, or who tortures animals is clearly in need of professional evaluation and, if indicated, psychological counseling.

Certain events that threaten a child's security and sense of well-being may trigger the need for help. Severe injury or loss of health; parental separation or divorce; the death of a parent, brother, or sister; moving to a new neighborhood; and other important life changes may cause so much emotional turmoil that help is required. The signs of a troubled child are many and varied. In general, a noticeable change in a child's mood or behavior that cannot be explained by some important event may indicate trouble. Even if such a mood or behavioral change can be understood as a reaction to an event, the persistence of this change beyond two or three weeks may indicate trouble and should alert you that help may be needed.

Crying, sleeplessness, appetite changes, withdrawal, loss of interest in formerly enjoyed pastimes and activities, feelings of guilt, worthlessness, helplessness, and hopelessness are all signs of depression. But depression presents other faces, too: overactivity, restlessness, irritability, sudden outbursts of temper and destructiveness or delinquency may all mask a child or preteenager's underlying depression.

Anxiety, too, presents itself in many ways, including restlessness, tension, irritability, moodiness, unreasonable fears and phobias, fatigue, nail-biting, tics, stuttering, problems in concentration, compulsive rituals such as hand-washing, explosively rapid speech, and frequent, unexplained illnesses. They indicate that a child has problems that may require diagnosis and treatment. As a child approaches puberty, different signs of trouble may appear; they can include use of alcohol or drugs, sexual promiscuity or acts of delinquency.

Whenever a child complains of physical symptoms, a pediatrician or family practitioner should be consulted to first rule out the existence of a medical problem. Only when such a possibility has been completely eliminated can you assume that underlying emotional difficulties are causing the symptoms.

WHAT A PARENT CAN DO.   If you are convinced that your child has emotional problems, you are best off telling him you are concerned about his troubles, whether they are difficulties with school, general unhappiness, trouble with friends, or whatever has been going badly. It's important to convey both your concern and your wish that he feel better. While you cannot force your child to get help, you can make it very clear that you would very much like him to do so.

A child may be reluctant at first. If this happens, be patient and wait, but continue to gently insist that he visit a trained professional and, if necessary, begin counseling. A young child will most likely consent, while an older child may balk at first, but then accept the idea of counseling if you continue to point our that you very much want to see him feeling better.

Occasionally, the parents of a troubled child feel guilty about what has happened, even thinking that they caused the child's problems. While understandable, such feelings rarely reflect the truth, and may be harmful because they can cause you not to get help for your child. It is best to focus your emotional energies on helping your child get the best counseling available.

PSYCHOTHERAPY WITH CHILDREN. While a complete description of psychotherpy is beyond the scope of this book, we will present a brief description of this process.

Generally, a child does not initiate the request for counseling or psychotherapy; usually, parents are anxious for a child to receive counseling, but the situation may be fueled by a great deal of parental frustration and even anger at a child who has been "a problem." Therefore, the psychiatrist's first task is to help motivate the child for counseling sessions and to do so in a way that fosters a trusting, therapeutic alliance with the child.

Because the child is brought into treatment by the parents and because the therapist is an adult, it's easy for a child to view the therapist as a "parent" who is part of the adult world. The child may expect that the therapist will act like a parent, making judgmental observations, and may even expect the psychiatrist to "take the side" of the parents. The therapist refrains from judging the child's behaviors as "good" or "bad," but rather is interested in the child's thoughts and feelings and in how the child interacts during counseling sessions.

Most child psychiatrists use interactive play and a few simple toys to help the child communicate fantasies, fears, and conflicts during their sessions together. This is called play therapy, which can help the child reveal a great deal about himself. For instance, a seven-year-old girl who is very jealous of a newborn brother, when presented with boy and girl dolls, may use the dolls to play out her angry thoughts and fantasies during the session with the psychiatrist. Or a five-year-old boy who has developed a phobia of the kindergarten bathrooms, when presented with "mother," "father" and "child" dolls, enacts his concerns about separating from his parents while in session with the psychiatrist.

Therapy involves the psychiatrist's learning as much as possible about the child's conflicts and the psychological processes that have led to behavioral difficulties or symptoms, such as phobias, anxieties, compulsions, etc. In turn, the therapist helps the child understand himself by relating these fears, wishes, and conflicts back to the youngster in a way that the child can understand. This allows the child to begin making changes in his behavior.

Psychotherapy with children usually requires parental involvement because the child lives with his parents in a completely dependent way. The psychiatrist usually provides parents with guidance, including specific do's and don'ts, for dealing with their child. In addition, the psychiatrist may meet with the parents to focus on their own needs and difficulties, and continue meeting separately with the child. Sometimes, it is preferable for the psychiatrist to meet with the entire family, focusing on problems that involve their living and functioning together.

There are various techniques in psychotherapy, and each therapy must be somewhat tailored to suit the child and family. No matter which variation is used, the goal of treatment is to help a child and family make emotional and behavioral adjustments when there have been difficulties in either school performance or relations with siblings or peers, or where there have been symptoms such as depression, anxieties, unwarranted fears, withdrawal, repeated stealing, or other behavioral problems.

◊ A CONSULTATION—QUESTIONS AND ANSWERS

In discussing the school-age child, we will hear from two consultants: Aaron H. Esman, M.D., and Margaret E. Hertzig, M.D.

Dr. Esman is a Professor of Clinical Psychiatry at Cornell University Medical College and is the Director of Adolescent Services at the Payne Whitney Clinic of The New York Hospital.

Dr. Hertzig is an Associate Professor of Psychiatry at Cornell University Medical College and is the Director of Child Outpatient Services at the Payne Whitney Clinic of The New York Hospital.

Reading Score Is Only Average

Our eight-year-old son is in the third grade. His reading scores are "average," but we know he's bright and capable of more. His older sister was reading at a more advanced level when she was in his grade. We're worried.

DR. HERTZIG: There are individual differences between children. They may differ in many respects: physically, intellectually, and in the ways they handle their environments. When facing new situations, some children move into them with gusto, while others hang back. Some children show pleasure or displeasure very intensely while others are more restrained in expressing feelings.

Children also differ in how they approach problems of all kinds. Some have more stick-to-itiveness than others, and once their interest is captured, they work on a problem until it is mastered. Others with broader interests may focus their attention on many different problems over a shorter period of time. Children achieve various mental abilities in different ways and at different rates. In other words, individual children have different temperaments and different developmental courses.

As groups, boys and girls usually differ in their rates of development. Girls tend to mature more quickly than boys. They usually develop language and reading skills earlier than do boys, although once boys and girls master these skills, they do equally well. But these milestones appear slightly earlier in girls than in boys. There are cultural reasons for some of this. Girls behave better, and are usually more agreeable, more diligent with schoolwork, more eager to please, and less distractable than boys. These qualities are often reinforced by parents and teachers at an earlier time in girls than in boys.

So I see no need to worry about your son's reading scores as compared to his sister's. Give him time and you may be very pleased as he matures and makes progress over the next few years. (See in Chapter 2, "Reading to a Child.")

A Loner

Our son is a bit of a loner. He's content to be by himself much of the time. What causes this and what should we do?

DR. ESMAN: There are many differences between children. Some are very introspective and reflective, while others are outgoing, social, and athletic. Neither is necessarily right or wrong, nor is one better than the other. There may be nothing wrong at all when a child spends a good deal of time alone; in fact, it may be more of a problem when parents impose their expectations of what is considered "normal" onto a child and his behavior.

Yet this applies only to a degree. If your child is completely avoiding other people or is uncomfortable about his lack of friends, or if he's living a life of social isolation, a professional consultation may be helpful. But we cannot assume that every child should conform to a particular standard of social relationships. If your son seems fairly comfortable with his somewhat solitary life, yet is capable of interacting with others when necessary, then I don't think that anything should be done.

You should also evaluate the quality of the time your son spends by himself. If he spends a good deal of time reading or doing creative or constructive things, he may have an intellectual or even a creative nature, which should not be discouraged. Forcing him into social situations won't necessarily conform to his own individual way of being in the world.

Refuses to Practice the Piano

My daughter is in the sixth grade and is refusing to practice the piano. My husband and I didn't force piano lessons on her, she wanted them. Now she's losing interest. Should we insist that she practice?

DR. HERTZIG: When my daughter was ten years old, she wanted to take piano lessons. I hesitated, anticipating endless hassles about practicing. I recalled that sometime earlier we had bought her a rabbit (at her insistence) with the understanding that she would take care of it. Of course, I not only had to keep after her to feed the rabbit and clean the cage, but I sometimes did it myself. I anticipated a similar problem in her meeting the responsibility of the piano lessons.

At that time, I was talking with a friend who happened to be a child psychiatrist. She said, "You don't *have* to be involved with your daughter's piano lessons. Nothing will happen to the piano if she doesn't *feed* it, or if she refuses to play the thing!"

And that was the basis on which we arranged for her lessons. Our understanding was that our daughter wanted the lessons, and we would love for her to be able to play the piano. But the issue of practicing was strictly between her and the teacher. I would not get involved. At the end of six months, I would meet with them both and we would determine if it was worthwhile to continue. By the way, we eventually decided not to continue with piano lessons.

The general rule, I think, is that certain discretionary activities should not become the focus of conflict or arguments. Other things may be crucial to your child's well-being or future: school, homework, behavior in the class—those should become important issues if problems arise in those areas. But piano lessons are quite discretionary, and I would let events take their course.

Sex Play

We recently discovered our nine-year-old son with his friend (also a nine-year-old boy) playing with each other's genitals. Should we do anything about this?

DR. ESMAN: Sexual activity is so common among children of this age that in itself it has no real negative implications. If this is an isolated incident, it doesn't call for any dramatic or heroic action. I think you might want to talk quietly with your son and suggest to him that this behavior is not really appropriate, but you should avoid sounding critical or punitive or judgmental.

If you become aware that this is a continuing pattern of behavior, then you might be concerned and should think of having a professional evaluation for your youngster. But as a single isolated incident, it doesn't warrant any great concern. Remember, children are very curious about their bodies, and they're curious about other people's as well. At this age, they're likely to engage in a certain amount of exploring and experimenting that has no serious consequences. This would apply, by the way, if your nine-year-old son was involved in this activity with a nine-year-old girl. This behavior and experimentation is so common as to be virtually universal among children.

Can't Say No

Our ten-year-old daughter does everything her "best friend" asks of her, even if it's something she doesn't enjoy. We've told her that she must learn to say no, but she's still passive with this friend. We're a bit troubled. What should we do?

DR. HERTZIG: Kids who are nine, ten, and eleven years old are particularly apt to form close "chumships" and frequently have "best" friends. For girls, these very intense attachments can seem all-encompassing. Boys of this age often develop categorical friends; that is, their friends fall into different categories or groups—they play baseball with some boys, collect comic books or baseball cards with others, or play basketball with still others. Some friends may overlap from one category to another. Girls, on the other hand, tend to form serial friendships that can be completely absorbing; this sometimes worries parents.

Your daughter may have an easy-going temperament and may wish to avoid upsetting or disagreeing with others. Her behavior with this friend may be quite consistent with her behavior in other situations. You might think about helping her expand her opportunities to make other friends in addition to this one girl. But the overwhelming intensity of a friendship is common at this time of life, and it will most likely pass as your daughter develops other areas of interest and finds new friends.

A Favorite Blanket

Our eight-year-old son still has a favorite blanket. This concerns me because it seems babyish. Should I do anything?

DR. ESMAN: Many children have favorite toys or objects that they continue to use for long periods of time. By the way, girls tend to remain attached to these transitional objects longer than boys do. We often see college girls going off to school carrying a favorite teddy bear or blanket as a security device. There is no need to become concerned about this behavior.

A single behavior is very difficult to evaluate outside the context of the child's overall behavior and functioning. If your eight-year-old is doing well in most other respects—he gets along with other people, makes friends, sustains friendships, can tolerate separations without too much anxiety or discomfort—then his attachment to the blanket doesn't warrant any concern.

If, however, this attachment is part of an overall pattern in which he has separation difficulties—he's generally anxious and regularly has difficulty sleeping at night—then the blanket is simply another indication that he has problems with separation. But as an isolated behavior, when everything is going well, it's nothing to worry about and nothing should be done. Simply allow your son to gradually release this object; he undoubtedly will do this as time goes on. (See in Chapter 1, "A Linus Blanket.")

Uses Bad Language

Within the last few months, my eleven-year-old son has been using foul language when he's with his friends. He's now beginning to use it around the house, especially when he's annoyed with anyone in the family. What should we do?

DR. HERTZIG: Parents often worry when they hear their child using bad language. The essential feature here is that your son's use of foul language began when he was talking with his friends. Approaching adolescence, he is entering the adolescent peer-group subculture. It's crucially important for him to feel that he's doing what his friends are doing, and they're all using foul language.

Understanding the peer pressure he experiences does not obligate you to give up your standards and ideas about proper language. If his language is offensive, make sure your son understands your feelings. He must be made aware that in certain situations—at home or in school— he must behave (talk) appropriately. His language when he's alone with his friends is his business.

There's another issue here. Children of this age may have an intense interest in sexual issues, although they don't express it directly. Much of your son's language, especially anal terms, may be a indirect expression of sexual interests, which continue from the Oedipal period and again become noticeable as adolescence begins. (See in Chapter 3, "Uses Bad Language.")

Too Much Television

Our seven-year-old watches television as much as possible. My husband insists that we limit the TV to some extent, but I'm not sure. What should we do?

DR. ESMAN: The place of television in our society and in our children's lives is a major and controversial issue. My personal view is that excessive exposure of children to television is undesirable. It tends to induce a certain passivity of attitude and expectation, and because television is very seductive it can close them off from other healthy and necessary activities. Television can unfortunately take priority over such things as reading and more active play. In addition, it frequently exposes children to stimuli that are, in my view, undesirable, given the enormous amount of aggression that is part of the universal fare of television.

I think that you are correct in wanting to restrict the amount of time your child watches television. It would be perfectly reasonable for you and your husband to agree on a schedule that allows your child a certain amount of television time. By no means do you want your child's intellectual and fantasy life to be limited to this one kind of experience. A balanced living pattern includes social interaction with other children, reading, creative and constructive play, along with television. This is much more desirable than having your child spend all his free time watching television.

Is Music Video a Bad Influence?

I'm concerned about the music video on television these days. It's very sexual, even sadomasochistic, and I worry that our nine-year-old daughter will be adversely influenced. I hate to seem old-fashioned, but should I worry?

DR. ESMAN: Experts do not yet know if music video and television sexuality are harmful to children. Unfortunately, the data are not yet clear on this issue, and no reliable scientific work has demonstrated that exposure to this kind of video is harmful. However, I personally am inclined to agree with your concern about the effects of rock video on your daughter.

I would discourage a preadolescent child from watching this kind of material. I think it exposes her to stimuli that she can neither adequately understand nor make appropriate discriminations about. While we don't know scientifically that this material can distort a youngster's fantasies or "preprogram" a child's fantasy life, you are best off being cautious. For the time being, I would assume that distortions in your child's fantasy life may occur from this exposure.

The issue of limiting television fare, either the amount of time or its quality, is sometimes a difficult one for parents. I think it's best for both parents to present a unified view to their child. Both parents can make it clear that they think certain programs are either undesirable or inappropriate for a preadolescent child. Parents can encourage and even help provide other kinds of entertainment and activities to help a child productively and enjoyably spend time when she might otherwise be passively watching television.

There certainly are television programs that families can watch and enjoy *together*. I think such a shared experience is much better than having a child become completely absorbed in a private, violent, and sexually stimulating fantasy-laden world that excludes involvement with adults and takes the child away from sharing interests with adults and other children.

Exaggerates Too Much

Our ten-year-old son exaggerates about almost everything, especially his own exploits. I'm worried because I don't know what this means or what to do about it. Please advise me.

DR. ESMAN: In the course of their lives, children tend to lie or exaggerate about certain things for a variety of reasons. If your child exaggerates about almost everything, this is a cause of some concern. Such global exaggeration suggests that he's insecure and has a need to aggrandize himself in order to protect himself against an unfavorable self-view. He must have very little self-esteem if he must enhance his self-view by so much exaggeration.

His exaggeration may also be understood as a plea for attention, which would indicate that he feels he isn't acceptable or adequate as he now is, and he must therefore aggrandize himself. If this is a persistent pattern, it may indicate that your child has a serious problem. It shouldn't be dealt with in a disciplinary way. It would be best to obtain professional help to determine your son's worries, needs, and inner concerns. It would probably be helpful for your son to have the opportunity to talk with someone outside the family, so he can discuss as much of this as possible. In a very real way, his exaggeration is really a symptom of a deeper problem that he should have a chance to understand and overcome.

Loves Adult Company

My husband and I entertain often. Our seven-year-old daughter loves to stay up with company. My husband gets annoyed and insists that company is for "adults only." How can we handle this without making our child feel ignored or unwanted?

DR. ESMAN: There are a number of issues involved in the dilemma of a child remaining in the company of adults. First, you don't want to embarrass your child, or make her feel unwanted. Second, you don't want to antagonize your adult guests. And third, you must balance the forces between your daughter and your guests. An appropriate course of action would be to allow your child to have some brief contact with your guests as they first come in. She can have a few words with them and exchange some pleasantries. Then, firmly and politely, it's best to insist that it's time for the adults to do what they do, and for her to do whatever she does.

It's undesirable that the roles between your child and the adults be blurred, or for generational boundaries to be muddied by your daughter encroaching upon adult conversation. This would expose your child to adult matters which she probably would not understand and in which she could not comfortably participate. Such an arrangement places an unfair burden on the adults, who are then forced to monitor what they say and how they say it in the presence of a seven-year-old child. A compromise is the best solution: your daughter can participate to some reasonable extent, but then must busy herself with her own activities away from the adult company.

A Messy Room

Our eleven-year-old is mature enough to keep his room clean. But it's a mess, and I end up nagging. My husband says it's our son's room and I shouldn't get so upset, but I do. Is there a better way to handle this?

DR. ESMAN: "Nagging" and "neatness" are universal issues with virtually every preadolescent or adolescent. This issue can be argued in a number of ways, and the terms of the argument are set in the following way: On the one hand, it's your son's room and he should presumably live in it the way it's congenial for him to do so. On the other hand, it's your home and you're entitled to have your home maintained in a way that you find acceptable.

This issue is a major source of antagonism and conflict in a good many homes. The period of development between ages eleven and thirteen is normally one in which kids tend to regress somewhat and become messy, even when they have previously been quite orderly. And this period of time is often one in which kids tend to be quite rebellious and are most likely to get into battles with parents about issues of autonomy. My feeling is that if you can maintain a sense of humor and a sense of proportion about all this, the issue will probably fade as your youngster approaches adolescence and becomes more concerned about his appearance and neatness.

Parents have some right to establish certain expectations from their youngsters. Some kind of negotiated position is usually the best way to deal with this problem. While you don't have to insist that your son's room be immaculate, you may want to set some minimum standard of cleanliness and orderliness. If you can do this in a reasonable way that allows him an element of autonomy and you an element of orderliness, then that's fine. In most reasonable families, these issues can be worked out as a negotiated understanding. Generally, I would say negotiate, don't nag.

If in spite of negotiations nagging seems to become necessary because your son persistently rebels, you should be alerted to the possibility that he may have deeper problems—difficulties that find an avenue of expression through rebellion and messiness. If things get very much out of hand, you might consider having a professional evaluation to determine the cause and extent of these problems.

"What If . . . ?"

Our seven-year-old-daughter asks, "What if . . . ?" all the time. "What if I get sick and nobody's home?" "What if you and Daddy get divorced?" She's very anxious about these things. Is this normal?

DR. ESMAN: Your daughter's intense concern about these matters indicates anxiety about certain fundamental emotional issues. Children ordinarily have concerns and anxieties about various things, and these are sometimes expressed openly. But if your daughter's worries and anxieties are as persistent as you've described, she has more than the usual amount of anxiety and apprehension.

Her question concerning a possible divorce is one that may have some merit. Her other question concerns the issues of separation, abandonment, and desertion. One must wonder if family tensions exist that are stimulating your daughter's anxieties. A child often picks up on ongoing family conflicts, and the youngster's anxieties and behavior can be a very accurate barometer of these things.

Your daughter is giving you a signal that she is preoccupied by anxieties about the issues of separation and abandonment, which seems to be at a very high pitch in this situation. A professional opinion should be sought to determine whether your child's worries are the result of her own internal turmoils or whether family problems and tensions are instrumental in stimulating your daughter's concerns.

Wants a Dog

Our ten-year-old son has been agitating for a dog. I'm concerned that he won't take care of it, and that I'll get very attached and end up doing everything. How can I teach my son that having a pet is a responsibility he'll have to meet?

DR. ESMAN: Parents commonly have to deal with a child who wants a dog and who then hardly cares for it. You must decide upon the extent to which you're willing to take a certain calculated risk in this situation. Having a pet can be a very important and positive experience for a child. I think you would want to encourage such an arrangement if it's physically and emotionally possible for the family to make reasonable accommodations and handle the situation.

A ten-year-old child is old enough to understand the concept of exchange and reciprocity. In exchange for being given this benefit (the dog), he must assume some responsibility for it. On the other hand, you must be prepared for the possibility that the baseball game, the hockey game, or the piano lessons will make it incumbent on one or another of the parents occasionally to assume responsibility for the dog's care. If nobody other than your son is able or willing to care for the dog occasionally, it might be better to avoid potential conflict by not getting a dog. I think that as a parent you should be prepared to bend somewhat in this regard, because the experience of having a pet is a very valuable one for any child.

A Bright Child

Our eight-year-old is very bright. His IQ was measured at 145. Will telling him his score make him overly confident or affect him in some way? Should we tell him?

DR. ESMAN: I don't think it's a good idea to give your child a "number." He doesn't really know what this number means or where it places him in relation to other children. Such a label only offers a child an instrument that can be used competitively in a very undesirable way.

A child has a right to know that he's bright and that he may be unusual in certain ways. More important than assigning the child a number is the way in which parents use this information in their relationship with their child and in their expectations of him. For some parents, it serves their own selfish emotional needs more than it serves as a reasonable and useful guide to the child's education and as an indication of what they can reasonably expect of him.

My practice is simply one of not providing the child with a number. Nor do I give the parents a number. Many psychologists and schools provide parents with these scores, but I'm not in favor of such a practice. First, these numbers are very ambiguous: like any kind of shorthand information, they don't provide a balanced picture of a child's strengths and weaknesses. I prefer to minimize scores and instead would rather discuss the child's strengths, capacities, what should be expected of him, and the special educational opportunities that should be made available to the child.

Changing Friendships

Our ten-year-old son has had very little contact with his two best friends lately. We think he's upset, but he won't talk about it. Is there a way we can deal with this?

DR. HERTZIG: It's important to realize that children go through periods when they change their friendship patterns. They may drop some friends and pick up others. A question I sometimes ask is, how many friends does one child need? It may not be important to find out what's going on if you have evidence that your child is moving on to new relationships. Perhaps your son has found new friends, or is now interested in other activities. There is a frequent reshuffling of kids' relationships, and this situation may not require any intervention.

Since this just began, it's best to let things take their course. Keep your ears open and listen to your son's communications. You could raise the issue and ask him directly what's going on, although this may not yield productive information. If your son brings the situation up on his own, or if it arises spontaneously in another context, then by all means pursue it.

Keep in mind that your child, like most children, has a clear sense of loyalty, especially to his peer group. Something may indeed have happened, but your son may be reluctant to reveal it for fear of violating the group's principles. Remember, a "good kid" (that is, good according to the peer group) doesn't tattle and doesn't tell.

Parents often ask whether they should intervene by going to the other children's parents. This depends on your relationship to those parents. If you are friendly with them, the issue can come up as part of your usual conversation. A simple statement such as "Have you noticed our kids aren't spending much time together lately?" can be very effective. This can also be done with parents you meet on a casual basis. You may know them because your kids have been in the same class, or you've seen them at a school-related function. However, if you have no real contact with these parents, I would hesitate to arrange a meeting.

All things considered, an important issue is to decide *if* you should become concerned about this. In general, time heals these minor wounds and solves the transient ups and downs within a child's peer group. Above all, there is nothing to worry about if your child is doing well in school, has other friends, and develops new relationships. He may feel regretful at the loss of a friend and may even feel injured. But disappointment is a part of living, and your youngster will become accustomed to occasional disappointments throughout this time, and in his life. (See "The Society of Children" and "The Best Friend," earlier in this chapter.)

Preoccupied with Appearance

Our eleven-year-old daughter now spends an enormous amount of time looking at herself in the mirror. She seems very preoccupied with her looks and her body. Is this usual?

Dr. Hertzig: It is quite usual around the time of puberty for a child to become concerned about her looks. This would apply equally to a boy. While dramatic pubescent changes may not yet have begun in your daughter, they have possibly begun in her friends. She's beginning to think about the changes that will inevitably occur to her body. This concern is to be expected, and interest in the developing body is very important for a young girl. Once pubescent changes begin, they move with remarkable speed. The degree of change a child's body may undergo can be truly astounding, not just to others, but to the child as well.

I have been treating a twelve-year-old boy since he was six years old. He beautifully demonstrates the changes that occur at this point in life, and the sense of wonderment they bring for a child. Since I've been seeing him, he has occasionally fashioned a paper airplane and shot it across the room. The other day he made one and it soared to the top of a nearby cabinet. When he was seven years old, this height was far above his head and his first reaction to the plane landing there last week was, "Uh-oh, what will I do now?" After a brief pause, he gazed at me with a look of realization and said, "You know what? I can *reach* that airplane now." Until actually confronted by this situation, he had no true awareness of how dramatically his body had changed or of his new capabilities.

Your daughter's looking in the mirror, determining how she looks, primping, preening, and concern about her physical self is perfectly normal. Adults often forget what it feels like to experience the body changing, but for your child this dramatic and immediate experience will absorb her for the next few years.

We often think of adolescence occurring at age twelve or thirteen, or even older. While this is often true, pubescent changes often begin earlier for girls, sometimes starting as early as nine or ten years of age. Remember, even if your daughter has not yet begun her pubertal changes, some girls with whom she has daily contact have begun. Your daughter is now comparing her body to those of the other girls. This is all very normal.

Repeating a Grade

We've just learned that our eight-year-old daughter may have to repeat a grade. I'm not sure that this is really necessary. How can I be more certain, and how can this be handled?

DR. HERTZIG: You certainly want to find out what's been going on in school and why it's been occurring. You would want to inquire about two major areas: her academic performance, and her classroom behavior. By inquiring about both areas, you will probably discover the problem.

Your daughter may be doing well academically but may not be participating in school routines. Or she may have an important learning disability. Any child not making good academic progress requires a complete battery of psychological and psychometric tests. These examinations explore her intellectual and cognitive competence to determine whether or not she has a learning disability.

Once you elucidate whether your daughter has an intellectual difficulty or a behavioral problem, such as being oppositional or not participating, you should talk to school personnel. This includes a guidance counselor or psychologist, and should involve a discussion about the best method of addressing the particular problem. Your daughter's having to repeat a grade may very well be an appropriate response to her difficulties. It's impossible to say without knowing more about your child.

Parents commonly react to a child's being left back with the concern that this will be a terrible trauma for the child, that she will be teased, that she will lose self-esteem, and that this will have a negative impact on her development and education. Actually, some children who have had difficulty experience being left back with relief. We occasionally see a child who, once left back or placed in a special class, feels more comfortable, and these problems rapidly come to an end. Such a child's "failure to learn" may really have been a plea for help. In this situation, the long-term effects of the child having to repeat a grade don't have to be negative.

As your question indicated, you're not certain that your daughter should be left back. By all means, take appropriate steps to determine the reasons for this action. By all means, move up the administrative ladder to determine your child's situation and the reasons for the school's decision. Be aware that decisions about leaving a child back are never made by a teacher alone. Invariably, a review process occurs in which a teacher recommends a course of action but is not the exclusive determinant of a child's progress. This is especially true if the child has been having difficulties all along and if at midterm the teacher has given the child and parents notice that something is wrong. This should be a signal to any parent that a systematic investigation of the child's difficulty should be undertaken.

If psychological and psychometric testing [a battery of tests designed to measure intelligence and elicit any perceptual or learning disorders] rule out any significant learning disability, and if the teacher's description of your child's behavior indicates an emotional difficulty, a professional consultation with a child psychiatrist or a child psychologist can help assess the problem. Such emotional difficulties are best investigated by a competent professional who will go beyond testing and provide you with the human dimensions of your child's problems. (See Chapter 16, *The Child with Learning Problems.*)

Too Good to Be True

Our eight-year-old niece visited us, and I couldn't believe her good behavior. She was constantly cleaning up after my kids and helping me all the time. I hope this doesn't sound silly but is there such a thing as a child who is too good?

DR. HERTZIG: It's important to realize that you are describing a child who is in somebody else's home. Most parents have had the experience of hearing another parent describe their child by saying, "He's so wonderful!" The parent of the child often wonders, "Are they talking about my child?"

At six, my own son was an absolute monster. He complained frequently, and was very oppositional at home. At open school week, when the teacher told me about him, I must confess that I didn't recognize the description of my child. He was the first one to hand out the pencils and to erase the blackboard, he was very bright, and above all, he was a "wonderful child." Coming home, I said to him, "Martin, I simply don't understand something. How come you're so good in school, and at home you're a complete horror?" My son looked at me and said in the cutest voice, "All my goodness gets used up at school."

It's very common for children to behave very much better in someone else's home than they do in their own home environment.

This reminds me of a father I recently interviewed who complained bitterly about his son. The boy never helped around the house and never cooperated. They had a knock-down, drag-out battle when the son refused to help his father wash the family car. The father grounded him for the next one hundred years, but you know what the father saw one hour later? His son was helping a neighbor wash *his* car.

On the other hand, some children appear compliant. They never say no, and always do what parents and other people ask them to do. There may be some constriction of such a child's ability to relate to other people or to assertively refuse to do something. These children place more importance on pleasing others than on feeling good about their own activities. Such a child would exhibit a pervasive pattern of behavior in virtually all activities and relationships. If a child exhibits such absolute compliance one might think about a professional consultation to discover the source of this behavior.

In general, however, I would encourage you to view your niece's behavior with some skepticism, keeping in mind that children are often very, very good when visiting other people's homes.

Learning Responsibility

Our kids are seven and nine years of age. I insist that they help around the house, doing dishes, clearing the dinner table, neatening their rooms, and so on, but my husband says that I make too many demands on them. I think it helps them learn responsibility. Who's right?

DR. HERTZIG: There's no question that part of becoming a social human being involves learning responsibility. Parents are important teachers of responsibility, and the question arises about how to help children develop a sense of responsibility throughout various stages of their emotional development.

The first way in which any child learns is by imitation and identification. Therefore, it makes sense to be responsible yourself in those areas about which you want your child to learn responsibility. It's difficult to teach a child to be courteous if parents are discourteous. The ways parents teach responsibility and present themselves as models for identification and the ways responsibilities and chores are apportioned take different forms from one family to another. For instance, some families have clearly assigned chores for each member. In other families, everyone pitches in to do things together. Of course, there is no single right way of doing things. As a child-rearing philosophy, there's no question that you catch more flies with honey than you do with vinegar. Therefore, reasonable rewards and "positive reinforcement" for a child's taking care of responsibilities will probably bring the best results.

It's difficult for a child to carry out responsibilities if he feels that he's the only one doing things while the parents are reading the newspaper or having fun. It's equally difficult for a child to feel good about responsibilities if other children don't have comparable responsibilities. This pertains not only to siblings but to neighborhood children as well. In other words, there's a family style and a community style concerning what is deemed appropriate for teaching responsibility, and for what is expected from a child in a particular setting.

As a learning experience, it's useful for children to have one or two realistic responsibilities rather than being deluged by so many chores that they interfere with other activities. As is often the case in child development, you tread gingerly between overindulgence and overexpectation, wanting to expect neither too much nor too little. You don't want to overburden your child, yet you want to impress upon him the importance of living responsibly with other people.

It's helpful to realize that, when a child comes of school age, one should distinguish between responsibilities that affect the entire family versus those affecting only the child. For instance, there's an enormous difference between a child's strewing his belongings all over the house and leaving his own room a mess. The first situation encroaches on the rights of other people, whereas it's not a big deal for a child to have a somewhat sloppy room. Here the child's lack of responsibility affects only him; it doesn't interfere with household harmony.

Some parents, ever-insistent that a child meet his responsibilities, find themselves constantly nagging. If this is your situation, you should ask yourself certain questions. Is what I'm asking my child to do reasonable? Are his responsibilities part of the social milieu of the family and the community? Does he have too many responsibilities? Is he getting sufficient support in executing these responsibilities? Does he feel overburdened in relation to his siblings or when compared to friends?

It's important to discuss this with your child. You might say, "I find myself nagging, and there seems to be a problem." You may find that while your child balks at certain responsibilities, he is perfectly happy doing other chores. Flexibility about responsibility and chores is important.

The definition of "nagging" is important, since parents' perceptions of what constitutes nagging can vary. Some parents feel they are ceaselessly nagging, simply because they had to remind the child to take out the garbage. Let's remember that school-age children often need reminders. They are not really capable of functioning independently.

If after assessing the situation you determine that you haven't been nagging and haven't been overzealous in assigning responsibilities, then you must ask yourself another question; namely, is an emotional problem causing my child to oppose or disregard me? Oppositional behavior can permeate every area of a child's activities. If your child completely resists cooperating, you are best off getting a professional consultation.

Plays with Younger Kids

Our eleven-year-old son has friends his own age during school hours. However, when he gets home, he plays with younger children. All his friends are eight or nine years old. He seems not to want to make the effort to play with children his own age who live only three blocks away. We're concerned. What should we do?

DR. HERTZIG: A parent may indeed grow concerned when a child plays with others who are younger. It's important that you indicate that your son has age-appropriate friends at school. Generally, children tend to play with children who are at their own cognitive and emotional level of development. It would be an ominous sign if your son played exclusively with children two or three years younger than he and was unable to get along with children his own age while at school.

You raised the issue of availability, which is an important variable in determining a child's friends. If a child leads a relatively isolated life in a rural setting where few age-appropriate friends are available, he may be forced to play with younger children. This can also occur in a city, where a child may be two or three years older than the other children in an apartment building. Generally, any prolonged pattern of behavior that worries a parent, whether it's playing with younger kids or refusing to assume responsibility, should probably become an issue for consultation with a trained professional. It's better for a parent to clarify questions or concerns about a child rather than to ruminate and worry about them.

This raises the issue of children's temperaments, which may play a part in your son's situation. Some children find it difficult to warm up to others; it takes them a long time to feel comfortable in the presence of others, especially strangers, or new situations or relationships. This is the "slow to warm up" child. Or your child's reluctance to find age-appropriate friends who live nearby may indicate problems in separating from his home base. Such a child may be extremely anxious, which is different from the temperamentally "slow to warm up" child. Once the ice has been broken, the "slow to warm up" child feels perfectly comfortable, whereas the tense, overanxious child has difficulties all along.

Consider these possibilities in trying to understand your son's choosing to play with the younger children on his own street.

Right Age for Summer Camp

Our son is six years old, and we think he's ready for summer camp. It's an eight-week stay, and we'll be allowed to visit him three times during the summer. As the time draws close, we're having second thoughts. Is six old enough for summer camp?

DR. HERTZIG: The center of a six-year-old's life is still the family, particularly the father and mother. A six-year-old child is only beginning to move out into the wider world of peers and school and other activities. A child of this age may have friendships with other children, but peers do not yet provide the support, comfort, and guidance that parents do.

In deciding whether or not your child is old enough for summer camp, you must assess certain parameters of his development and behavioral activities. First, has he ever visited away from home? For how long? Has he visited grandparents or other relatives for any length of time? Has he slept over at their house for a night, or perhaps spent a weekend? How have these visits gone? Has your child demonstrated an enormous amount of anxiety at these separations? Has he looked forward to these visits and separations? During these visits, what kind of contacts did your child maintain with you? Was there evidence of a disturbance in his behavior such as trouble sleeping, or an appetite disturbance? You must determine how your child handled previous separations.

You can also assess how your child relates to other children. Does he get along well with them? Does he make friends easily? Does he adapt to new situations with ease? Can he readily turn to another person for comfort and use a camp counselor as a surrogate parent?

Children differ in their ways of handling the world. Some children move readily and quickly into new situations or experiences, while others take longer to adapt.

When you consider sending a young child to summer camp, think about how best to prepare him for this experience. This also applies to an older child if he or she is temperamentally slow to warm up or a bit shy. It is very helpful for a child to live emotionally and mentally through the experience in fantasy before actually departing for camp. It helps to talk about the experience with the child so he can practice relating to other children and prepare to be away from you.

Homesick

Our ten-year-old daughter has always done well. It's her first summer at camp and she's been there for one week. We've already gotten six phone calls. She insists on coming home because she's homesick. What should we do?

DR. HERTZIG: Virtually any child, when separated from her home and from the people she knows and lives with, will at first feel somewhat homesick. It's important to prepare your child for that eventuality. Before leaving, it can help to remind her that she will probably miss you at first, and may feel sad, especially when she thinks about home. Such feelings should not come as a surprise to you or your child. They are quite common and usually fade within a week. It can be helpful for a child to have a special toy or object that reminds her of home. This transitional object can become an important link to you. In my family there's been a little wooden mouse that somebody brought back from Denmark years ago. This mouse has accompanied one child or another on the first day of school for many years. There are other ways to ease the initial separation when a child first leaves for summer camp: Receiving mail is an important reminder of home, and makes the child feel less separated from the familiar. A planned telephone call or two can be very helpful.

During the first week when a child calls home saying that she's homesick, be supportive and remind her that these are the feelings you talked about and that they will fade. Try helping your child focus on positive elements of camp; ask about the activities she enjoys or about new people and friends she's met, or inquire about her counselors. Try to help your child counterbalance her homesick feelings by focusing on the positive aspects of the camp experience.

For most children, feelings of homesickness quickly fade, and they adapt to the camping experience. However, some children adapt slowly; there may be twinges of homesickness, especially at bedtime, which involves separation, since bedtime means that a child must say good night to the external world. Most children experience less homesickness and separation anxiety as time passes.

Occasionally a child may feel truly miserable and refuse to participate in activities. If she continues this way for longer than three weeks and if the intensity of her pleas to return home does not diminish, a parent must think that perhaps the camp experience is not appropriate at this time. It is best to arrange a meeting with the child's counselor to find out how she is doing generally. If you learn that she seems homesick or depressed (her pleas are not manipulations) you must think about allowing her to come home. You must be able to accept such an eventuality. It's unwise to burden your child with the feeling that she has failed herself or has failed her parents.

If your child must return home, be somewhat matter-of-fact about it, and remain unconcerned. Simply view it as a developmental step for which your child is not yet completely ready. Next summer, the experience will probably be much better.

Part II

———————◇———————

Special Issues in
Emotional Development

Chapter 5: Sibling Rivalry

Rivalry among brothers and sisters is so prominent a feature of childhood that we sometimes forget that siblings are also companions and friends. Siblings may feel that they are simultaneously best friends and the worst of enemies. Sibling rivalry will always be a part of family life, because each family has only a certain amount of resources, emotional and material, including everything from parental attention to clothes. By competing with each other, children ask themselves, "Who gets what around here? Am I getting enough?" In the end, each child really wants to know, "Am I loved most of all?"

Because each family's set of relationships is unique, it's difficult to generalize about something as complex as sibling relations. A child's reaction to the birth of a sibling will depend partly on the developmental tasks the child is dealing with when the new baby arrives. The relationship between siblings will be influenced by many things: the age difference; whether siblings are of the same or the opposite sex; the number of children in the family; the position of a particular child (the youngest, middle, oldest); the role of each sibling within the family; the expectations that family members have of each other; and the ways parents deal with each child.

In some very important ways, siblings are partners within a family. During their early years, siblings who are close in age must cope with the fact that they are much less powerful than their parents. It can be a positive and meaningful experience to have someone close who is not quite so powerful, even if it means sharing the parents' love and affection with the other one. Siblings two or three years apart can become good companions. If two siblings are of the same sex and fairly close in age, the older often takes the role of mentor (whether wanted by the younger one or not). When siblings are in different stages of development (such as a three-year-old preschooler and a ten-year-old schoolchild), there may be many important differences that can prevent real closeness.

Of course, there are problems. Feuding and bickering are inevitable, but even these difficulties are part of family life. Because siblings share, care, and interact with each other, deep bonds of loyalty and affection often develop, although they may be masked by the turbulence of the sibling relationship.

Relations between brothers and sisters will always be of great concern to parents. Today, with divorce so common, more and more family situations arise in which stepsiblings enter into the family equation. It's not at all unusual today for a child to have to adjust to "new" brothers or sisters, or to have a half sibling arrive because a divorced parent has remarried and decided to begin a "second" family.

The complexities of family life and of sibling relations result in various outcomes. Many siblings come to realize their closeness and special bonds to each other when they are adults. Unfortunately, some siblings don't like each other, even as adults. This most likely occurs when a family's environment is one of conflict and scapegoating, where the rights and needs of each child are not protected by the parents, and when love, support, loyalty, and cooperation are not encouraged by parents.

The following pages present a roster of questions often posed to our consultant, Theodore Shapiro, M.D. Dr. Shapiro is a Professor of Psychiatry at Cornell University Medical College and is the Director of Child and Adolescent Psychiatry at the Payne Whitney Clinic of The New York Hospital.

Preparing for a New Sibling

We have a three-year-old son, and are now expecting our second child. How can we prepare our son for the arrival of a newcomer?

DR. SHAPIRO: Your three-year-old has the capacity to understand that there are other children in the world besides himself. He has the intellectual capacity to understand that some of his friends may have little brothers and sisters. In that sense, he is already somewhat prepared.

To help prepare him for the arrival of a newcomer, we would need to know the answers to several questions about your three-year-old. How was he brought up? Was he "king baby"? Has his omnipotence ever been tested or curbed? Does he attend nursery school, where he is familiar with the idea of sharing or taking turns with others? A first child has never had to share or take turns with a sibling, and this new arrival will not only live in the house but will also demand parental time that was once exclusively devoted to your three-year-old. Your son's reaction to the arrival of a sibling will depend on how he was brought up and on how much he expects to have exclusive rights to your attention and affection.

When parents begin telling their child about an expected baby, the child may respond with initial excitement. There may even be a proprietary feeling about the newcomer, especially if the older child is a girl. She may tell her friends, "We have a new baby," or "We're going to have a new baby at home," or "I have a new baby at home." When that kind of statement occurs, you know you're on the right path because you are hearing an identification with you, the parents, in the caretaking role. This is a healthy development. On the other hand, when a three-year-old actually sees the new arrival, there may be a regression, especially when the child sees the infant doing the things he himself did not very long ago.

Preparation for a new sibling should take into account some estimate of your child's developmental stage. Is he a mature three-year-old? Has he been very indulged up until this point? It's important to give your child sufficient time to cope with the fact that a newborn is coming. The nine-month pregnancy allows parents to accommodate to the idea and provides time for them to make an emotional investment in the yet-to-be-born baby, and nine months is certainly enough time for a three-year-old child to invest emotionally in a new baby. In fact, it's best not to mention the new baby until the mother begins to show, since the first few months of a pregnancy may be tenuous and there is no need to burden a child with such knowledge when a miscarriage can occur. Also, until mother is showing, the idea of a new arrival may be little more than a meaningless abstraction for a three-year-old.

A three-year-old will become impatient for the newcomer's arrival; impatience can turn to anger once the baby comes, so that we hear the usual "Let's get rid of him." What you tell a child and how to do it is a personal matter, but in general it's best to enlist your child's participation in things having to do with the new baby. This can include having your child participate in choosing the new arrival's name, so long as he doesn't have the right to choose a name you dislike. The child can also help in getting a room ready for the new baby or help make space in his own room. With all this, it can be helpful to give your three-year-old something that will belong only to him, so he doesn't feel he will be completely usurped by the new arrival. The basic idea involves allowing your child to feel he is part of what's going on, while reassuring him that there is plenty of parental attention to go around.

Jealous of Baby Brother

Our two-and-a-half-year-old daughter is obviously jealous of her newly arrived brother. She makes references to sending him "back" and seems very hostile. Although this is only verbal, we're worried. How should we handle this?

DR. SHAPIRO: Sibling rivalry is blatant in the everyday expressions of children, and it has been around since time began. I cannot imagine a two-and-a-half-year-old child not feeling some jealousy toward the new baby. Rivalrous, antagonistic, and competitive feelings have always coexisted with caring, affectionate, and loving feelings in virtually all sibling relationships.

The fact that human babies are born in small broods and have a long period of dependency creates a problem in terms of the dependent child's need for attachment to parents. A two-and-a-half-year-old has not yet left the developmental phase of feeling she was recently the center of her parents' universe. She will now have to share, where before this time everything belonged to her.

The two-and-a-half-year-old lives in a very egocentric little world. Only recently your daughter experienced herself as absolutely central in the home. Actually, you should welcome your daughter's open expressions of hostility and not try to drive them underground. All too often, parents say to the older child, "Oh, the new baby is so nice. You'll have such a good time together," rather than listening for the hostility and empathizing with the older child's feelings. It's best to acknowledge the rivalry and say, "We know it's hard for you to share, but there's enough here for you both, and we love you very much."

It's best to allow the child to vent some of her hostility while allowing her to accommodate to the newcomer's arrival. Her perception at the moment is simply that the new baby is an intruder. As long as her hostility remains verbal and as long as your infant is protected by sufficient surveillance, you will notice that the older child will show evidence of tenderness as well as hostility. It is very likely that your daughter will soon begin to identify with the parental role and become a "little mother," even becoming a bit "bossy" when she's alone with her younger sibling.

If an older sibling is physically aggressive toward the younger one, this of course can be dangerous. If an aggressive act has not harmed the baby, the act should be forgiven, keeping in mind that your child does not yet have impulse control and could do damage to the baby. Therefore, you must encourage physical restraint, telling your child that while she can say anything she wants, physical expressions of hostility are not permitted. You create a moral injunction by saying "We don't do this to little babies." If an overtly hostile act occurs, you can constructively direct it toward the long-term process of socialization.

Upset at Mom Being Pregnant

We have two daughters: one is nine years old; the older one is eleven. I've recently become pregnant and our older daughter seems upset and angry. She avoids mentioning the new baby and won't talk about it. What's going on, and how can we handle this?

DR. SHAPIRO: This is a question that may appear to be part of sibling rivalry but by and large is not. In fact, it probably indicates some rivalrous feelings with mother. Your eleven-year-old daughter has probably had her first period or is about to have her period, and is entering puberty. She is beginning to experience her body changing. Your pregnancy forces her to take notice of the fact that you, her mother, are a sexual person.

During the preadolescent and adolescent period, the denial of parental sexuality is enormous. A child this age has a self-protective need not to recognize that her parents are sexual beings. In fact, one sometimes hears people who are otherwise quite bright say, "After I was born, my parents never had sex anymore." Many adults have such a blind spot; your daughter's avoiding any mention of your pregnancy should not be too surprising. A preadolescent girl's attitude about sexuality in the family is very ambivalent. Your daughter's embarrassment is understandable. In fact, most parents are nearly always an embarrassment to adolescents, no matter what they do.

Wants the Same Things

Whenever I buy anything for my seven-year-old son, my five-year-old daughter demands the same thing. I'm often tempted to purchase something for her, too, even if it's simply a token, but I'm not sure this is best.

DR. SHAPIRO: This relates to a larger question we often see around birthdays. Parents and grandparents, when bringing a gift to the birthday child, frequently bring a gift for the younger child, too, so that he doesn't feel left out. These are attempts to ameliorate the reality that in the end we all have our birthdays. We simply cannot be rewarded on everyone's birthday. It's also an attempt to deny the fact that there are times when we get things and other times when we do not.

The decision not to give your child a token gift because her older sibling received something is one that must be based on an estimate of your child's capacity to withstand frustration without too much anger.

If you are tempted to buy something in this "me too" atmosphere, you are probably making some judgment that your daughter can't take it if she is "left out." Possibly, you are overreacting to your *own* feelings about being left out in your competition with your own siblings when you were growing up. You may be far too overprotective of your daughter's feelings. I would encourage any parent in this circumstance to ask, "Is the gift for the second child, or is it for the child that still resides within myself?"

Some children cannot tolerate the notion that a sibling receives something while they do not. In this situation, to maintain a semblance of harmony, you might give a token gift to the other child. However, you should not blur differences by giving the same gift. It's a dilemma that parents with twins often face, because twins, and sometimes siblings, must learn to perceive themselves as distinct individuals, separate from each other. Keep in mind that your estimation of "equivalent" gifts may not be the child's idea of equivalency. A young child may regard *size* as the primary determinant of a gift's value.

Above all, it's not that your younger child necessarily wants a gift, or even an equivalent present. The fact is that your younger child wants to be reassured that she is not being emotionally shortchanged. A child like this really wants to be sure she receives some share of love. More important than bringing a token gift to the younger one is the need to assure her that you really love her.

Parent Takes One Sibling's Side

We have two children, a daughter of ten and an eleven-year-old son. They're always at each other, bickering and competing. My husband was an older sibling himself. His sister is two years younger than he, and he always takes our son's side in every dispute. How can I get him to take a more evenhanded approach with the kids?

DR. SHAPIRO: The issue in this question can be viewed from a number of vantage points. One such point is the question of how a parent determines justice in a setting in which he himself has prejudices. This often comes up in parental disputes about how to handle children.

While your husband seems to identify with your son, one must also question to what extent *you* may identify with your daughter. Your husband's taking your son's side may be understood as his supporting the child of the same sex or as his supporting the older child. In some families, this breaks down according to Oedipal attachments: daddy always champions the little girl, while mother champions the boy. The question is, how can you be evenhanded in such circumstances? There can really be no evenhandedness until a parent begins to understand why he views the situation the way he does, and why he rigidly responds as he does.

It's a difficult situation because if you nag your husband about his inflexibly taking one child's side, this could further feed into the problem. If you can enlist your husband's attention and concern by asking him if he has noticed that he always takes your son's side, you may be able to get him to cooperate. This is best done in a questioning rather than a confrontational way. Your husband must be able eventually to understand what led to his skewed way of seeing his children's relationship to each other. He may eventually be able to say, "I guess I'm unfair because I myself was an older sibling, and I know all too well what it feels like." At that juncture, he can understand that his prejudice can create very wrong impressions in both children.

In discussing sibling rivalry, we must really discuss the question of what children compete for. In a parentless circumstance, rivalry between siblings diminishes, because sibling rivalry is always for parental affection and attention. This was noted in a famous study by Anna Freud. During World War II, many children were found wandering through the streets of London during air raids. There was very little rivalry and a great deal of cooperation among the children when they were first brought to an institution. When adult leadership and counselors were present, competition and rivalry among the children suddenly became a prominent part of the picture. Above all, kids are rivals for the emotional resources of the family.

Older Daughter Depressed

My first marriage ended in divorce many years ago. I have a daughter from this marriage who is now sixteen years old. Since then, I've remarried, and my daughter seemed to like my new wife. Everything went well until a few months ago when my new wife gave birth to a baby girl. Since the birth of her half sister, my sixteen-year-old daughter has become very depressed and now says that she wants to drop out of school. I know this has something to do with the new baby, but what's going on?

DR. SHAPIRO: Some of the major researchers of divorce suggest that there are no victimless divorces. That may sound like a harsh overstatement, but it is my view that there are probably no victimless lives.

One of the major issues of development is accepting the notion that you must occasionally give up certain things in order to get other things.

One must survive a series of disappointments in life. Early in life, one is less ready and able to deal with whatever happens, and one must passively accept certain things. But as we grow and develop, we also evolve a greater capacity to cope with life's difficulties. One of the many amazing things about development is the fact that children are extremely resilient. They do get by.

We are more indulgent today in the ways we allow people to express their feelings. The social dictates of shame and guilt are not as prominent a deterrent to such expression as they once were. Given this permissive social climate, your sixteen-year-old daughter is saying exactly what she feels. What is troublesome here is not the fact that your daughter has such feelings but that she is having a breakdown in her school functioning. As a parent, you must try to demonstrate that despite your having a new wife and new baby, you love your sixteen-year-old daughter.

A parent's remarrying or having a baby with a new spouse can be very disturbing to a child from a former marriage. This occurs because such an event can shatter the child's fantasy that her parents will ever get back together. Nearly every child of a divorced couple entertains the notion that the parents may someday reunite. In your daughter's situation, she is deeply upset, and may act in a way that can ultimately harm her. It may be wise to consider professional counseling under these circumstances.

Merging Families

I'm a widow with a ten-year-old daughter. I'm about to marry a widower who has three children, all living with him. I'm concerned that my daughter will have a difficult time being accepted by this tightly knit family. Please advise me.

DR. SHAPIRO: Although these situations usually work out, they may be occasions for some great difficulties. Your daughter will have to deal with a new family. You will have to deal not only with your own daughter but with three new children. Your daughter may feel that this dilutes the amount of attention and love she receives. In turn, the other three children will be asked to accept you and your daughter.

These situations can work well, or there can be many problems. Children will have some difficulty adapting, but the problems are not insurmountable. A good deal will depend on the amount of physical room available; upon how much sharing must occur; on how much time each parent has available; and on how much a blood allegiance makes a difference. Much depends on how well adjusted the parents are, on how well you, as a mother of a greatly expanded family, will be able to open your arms and give personal time to each of the children.

There's one more issue; namely, the death of your husband and of your intended husband's wife. Has mourning taken place? How long ago did these deaths occur? Each of the children will have to deal with feelings involving the grudging acceptance of the parent who will replace the lost father or mother. There will be a good deal of resistance toward accepting a new mother or father. (Most people find it very difficult at first to call their in-laws "Mom" and "Dad.") There is usually but one mother and father in any person's life.

In all, you can expect that everyone will have to make enormous adjustments and accommodations in an effort to merge two families into one harmonious unit. Although problems will no doubt arise at first, they can be overcome by keeping these issues in mind.

Plays with Brother's Friends

Our seven-year-old son insists on being included in everything his older brother does. He makes a pest of himself and tries to force himself on his brother, including playing with his friends. How can I deal with this?

DR. SHAPIRO: This is a frequent occurrence. Very often, the younger sibling will claim adulation for the older one, while the older one feels little more than annoyance at the younger sibling. There are two issues here. One is your older son's right to his privacy and friends. The other is the anguish that the little one feels in being left out, and wanting to be as big, as good, and as acceptable as his older brother. Little siblings are often accepted in such circumstances by being particularly cute or by developing a mascotlike relationship with the older kids. This can eventually color their personalities.

On the other hand, the younger child may feel acutely rejected. Parents must sometimes be firm, allowing the older child to be with his friends, while occupying the younger, or making sure the younger one has friends of his own. This may require having a "play date" with another friend at a different location. We see cross-age friendships in small communities where siblings may be the only available playmates. Here, the younger child may be incorporated into the older child's play setting.

Parents must be cautious about giving each child his due, while at the same time encouraging healthy peer relationships for each one. It's sometimes helpful to discuss with the older child the possibility of occasionally including the younger one in some activities but not all. After all, the older child has the right to some privacy. It would not be good for your younger child to always be permitted to play with his older brother and his friends. He must truly learn to find his own friends, and his own way of being.

Aggressive Playacting

I have two daughters, ages seven and three, and am expecting my third child soon. We've told both children. I've recently noticed that the three-year-old is playacting very aggressively with her doll, hitting it. Her older sister has always been a tease, and I'm worried that my three-year-old will start acting the same way with the new baby as she now does with her dolls. Should I worry?

DR. SHAPIRO: The problem here is universal, and the number of siblings in a family can have enormous effects upon a child's developmental course. Your younger daughter is doing to her baby doll what her sister had done to her. This is called "turning the passive into the active" and is healthy because it promotes being an active participant in one's life, rather than being a passive victim.

You are understandably concerned that your three-year-old may be practicing for the new baby when it arrives. This may be the case, but not necessarily. Actually, your daughter seems to be trying to master her feelings in fantasy, *before* the baby is born. Such playacting in fantasy can be very healthy. Once you notice it, you can discuss it with your child. At three years of age, your daughter can express these fantasies without inhibition; she is also old enough to know that she must share, and that aggressive outbursts are not acceptable. This is all par for the course. Allow it to develop. At some point, you can discuss your child's playacting and use it in the service of helping her accept the inevitable arrival of the new baby.

An Overview

DR. SHAPIRO: Learning to live with siblings is no different from learning to live with anybody else. It's part of a socialization process. The only way in which it is different is when a child is at an immature status very early in his life and must learn to adjust to the fact that he is not king of the roost. Keeping that in mind, a parent must take into account a child's level of intellectual understanding, his emotional ability to grasp situations, or the likelihood of a child regressing in the face of sibling rivalry rather than using the birth of a sibling as an opportunity to gain new skills and become more socialized.

The birth of a sibling forces a child to gain social skills and also helps him develop adaptive capacities for other issues that he will inevitably face in life. This pertains to all human relations. During their preadolescent years, children often develop chumships, in which one can be intimate with another person outside the family. In many respects, a sibling can be a chum as well as a rival, a companion as well as an enemy. Ambivalence runs through all of sibling relationships in a rather unique way, but family life goes on, and kids survive it.

Chapter 6: Separation, Divorce, and the Child

Many experts agree that a couple's decision to divorce or remain together should not be governed by the impact of this event on their children. Though divorce changes the course of a family's life (especially a child's), it need not alter the child's entire outlook or capacity for happiness. But there is no way around it: separation or divorce causes a momentous upheaval in the lives of all involved, one that requires each family member to make changes and adapt to new circumstances and relationships.

Divorce is not a brief, isolated incident; rather, it is a long-range situation often beginning with shifts in family harmony and a lessened sense of security for the children. These changes are followed by separation, by divorce, and then by an emotional reaction to the divorce in which a child experiences uncertainty, loneliness, anxiety, and other feelings.

At some point, there is a restabilization as a single-parent family, which may continue throughout childhood and adolescence. For some children, this process may mean accommodating to a parent's dating and eventually remarrying. The child must then make an adjustment to the stepparent and often, to stepsiblings.

As a parent who is separating or divorcing, you may worry about a variety of issues: how and when you should tell a child about the intent to separate or divorce; how this prospect will affect your child; how you can help a child deal with the inevitable restructuring of relationships that divorce brings; what anxieties and concerns divorce will evoke in your child; how you can avoid blaming your spouse or self; and how you can recognize if your child is having problems dealing with the stress that divorce can cause.

Our consultant for this discussion is Stephen Herman, M. D. Dr. Herman is an Assistant Professor of Psychiatry in Psychiatry and Pediatrics at Cornell University Medical College and an Attending Psychiatrist at the Payne Whitney Clinic of The New York Hospital.

Staying Together for the Kids' Sake

My husband and I have been discussing divorce for a while. Our two children are five and eight, and my husband feels we should stay together until the kids are older. I'm not sure if this is wise. Can you advise me?

DR. HERMAN: This question runs through most couples' minds, especially when they're not completely certain they want to divorce. Under circumstances of doubt, many couples look for some reason to stay together. In my opinion, this consideration should not enter into the decision about whether or not a couple should stay together. This pertains, no matter how old or young the children are, and no matter how many children there may be. The one question that must be answered is: can a couple maintain a fulfilling and reasonably happy life together?

If a couple decides to remain together because of concern about the effect of separation on the children, this can cause many problems. If they truly don't want to live together, resentment and anger will inevitably accumulate to an extent that will be impossible to hide.

Children are exquisitely sensitive to the emotional climate of the house; they will sense that the household smolders with turmoil. Usually, such an arrangement backfires, because the parents are angry at each other, and even worse, resentful of the children. The inevitable feeling of parents who stay together because of these considerations is "I did it for the kids," which complicates the situation and deepens resentment for everyone in the family.

When to Tell the Kids

We've been talking about splitting up, and it may soon become a reality. We have two daughters, ages six and seven. How and when should we break this to them?

DR. HERMAN: Your question states that you've been talking about splitting up, and it *may* soon become a reality. Naturally, one may never be completely certain about so complex an issue, just as when you decide to marry, you're never absolutely certain. This is natural, because any major life step is fraught with mixed feelings. At the outset, it's best to be as certain as possible about your plans *before* telling the children anything. Make certain you've *both* arrived at this important decision.

It's best to have already taken some concrete steps in this direction, such as talking to a lawyer, or one partner preparing to move out of the house. Parents should avoid musing aloud about divorce. Avoid conveying uncertainty by saying, "Dad and I are *thinking* about breaking up." When you're as certain as possible and have begun taking concrete steps, it's time to tell the children.

As a general rule, once the decision to separate or divorce has been made, it's best to discuss it with the children as soon as possible. Some people prefer that one parent tell one child, while the other tells the other at a different time, but I think both parents should tell the children together.

There is no need to shield a child from this reality. Children today know a great deal about divorce. If it hasn't already happened in the family, it's most likely happened in the families of a child's classmates; children have heard the word and know what divorce means.

Couples who are about to separate often create little lies when telling children about their intent to separate or divorce. Honesty is the best policy here. We know from research with children that they live in a very self-centered and egocentric universe. A child can believe that he is the center or cause of things, and may develop a fantasy that his parents are divorcing because of something he did. Therefore, when telling a child about an impending separation or divorce, let him know it's not because of anything he has done, even if you and your spouse have argued about your child. You must convey to your youngster that grown-ups sometimes discover that they cannot live together in harmony and that the decision to separate or divorce was made for that reason, and not because of the child.

A child needs to know that both parents love him or her very much and that they will not abandon the child. Your child needs to hear that although living arrangements will change, you will always be loving parents and will both continue to be involved in your child's life.

Fearing a Traumatic Reaction

We're going to separate soon. We have two kids, ages four and nine. I'm afraid this may be traumatic for them, especially when their father leaves. What kind of a reaction can we expect from them?

DR. HERMAN: Separation or divorce is a trauma for children, but a trauma is not fatal. Human beings must deal with some very trying, even traumatic, events in their lives. You're going through one, and you'll survive it. So will your children.

A child will react in one of many ways to separation or divorce, depending on a number of factors: the child's personality, his basic endowments, the developmental experiences he has undergone, his intelligence and sensitivity, and the manner by which he processes his experiences.

Virtually all children react with at least some symptoms, before, during, or after the breakup of a marriage. A four-year-old child may develop sleep problems: he might have difficulty falling or staying asleep, he may have nightmares or even walk in his sleep, he may wish to come into bed with the remaining parent, or he might suddenly begin fearing monsters more than ever. A child's usual developmental fears and difficulties may become more pronounced or exaggerated during the critical period of separation.

A nine-year-old child may develop school problems when his parents separate. He may suddenly have trouble doing homework. Behavioral and academic difficulties may surface where before this time the youngster was always a fine student whose conduct at school was exemplary.

When reacting to divorce, children tend to "act out" or "act in." A child who acts out is one whose conflicts become very obvious to other people. This is the youngster who nudges the one next to him in the classroom, or the one who continually talks, or who throws spitballs and gets into trouble with teachers. This youngster is making a "statement" that he or she is in conflict.

On the other hand, the child who acts in directs the conflict into the self. She pulls everything inward without showing obvious behavioral problems to others. She may develop a stomachache or become depressed or withdrawn.

A child's reaction to separation or divorce depends on her personality and temperament, and also upon what she has seen in the family. Your child will react in ways similar to those that you and your spouse have habitually reacted to problems. After all, children learn a great deal by imitation and identification, taking on their parents' styles of reacting to life's difficulties.

While it's difficult to know exactly how your children will react, know that they *will* react to the separation. Hoping that your children will not respond to such an event would be unrealistic. If your child develops conflicts or symptoms while going through this traumatic time, don't feel that you've failed or that you are lacking as a parent. Expect that your children will react to this momentous upheaval, just as you are reacting. Separation and divorce is a difficult, even traumatic, process for an entire family, parents and children alike.

Separation is a family crisis, but it can be mastered. The key is to be honest with yourself and with your children. This is a process, one that takes time. There are different stages of separation and divorce—beginning, middle, and end stages—in which everyone eventually adapts to new realities. But it's important to acknowledge that there is no conflict-free or totally smooth method of going through this family crisis.

Does an Aggressive Child Need Help?

Since my husband and I separated, my six-year-old has become hostile and aggressive at school and is getting into trouble. I'm wondering if he needs professional help. Can you advise me?

Dr. Herman: Before making any decisions about your son's behavior, examine your relationship with your husband. Are you hostile and angry with each other? Are you barely civil with each other? Is there acrimony in the relationship, on the telephone or when he comes to visit your child? Was the breakup particularly bitter or aggressive? Examining these facets of your relationship might provide you with important clues about your child's present behavior.

Parents know their children in ways that few other people ever get to know them. If something inside you says, "This problem is growing bigger than I'd anticipated," or "I'm not sure what all this is about, perhaps I should talk to someone," it's probably a good idea to have a professional consultation.

Going to a child psychiatrist for a consultation doesn't mean committing yourself or your child to endless therapy. A trained professional can give you a solid assessment of the problem and an opinion about whether or not therapeutic intervention is reasonably indicated. In an ideal world, every child could probably benefit from guidance when going through a separation or divorce. If you're concerned about your son's behavior, or if you suspect he might need help, it's perfectly reasonable to consult with a professional.

There are certain obvious signs of difficulties. If a youngster is becoming aggressive or hostile at school, or if the child becomes withdrawn or depressed, a consultation is definitely needed. Any behavioral change in eating, sleeping, in school, or at play with other children, may indicate trouble, and warrants discussion with a child psychiatrist.

A consultation can be most helpful when *both* parents agree that it is in order. When parents agree that a consultation is needed, the child receives a clear message that *both* are concerned about him and care enough about his well-being to seek help. I see many situations where one parent says, "I'd like you to evaluate my child, but my husband doesn't agree," or "My husband doesn't want our child to come." When a clandestine consultation occurs, or when parents disagree about its value, the child quickly discerns this discordance and feels that his parents cannot agree about how to help their own child. Under any circumstances, if a child is truly troubled, a consultation is surely indicated.

Doesn't Accept New Husband

I was divorced some years ago and recently remarried. Things are working well, but my ten-year-old daughter hasn't accepted my new husband. She isn't overtly hostile, but she's always talking about how great her father is. My husband is understanding, but I'm worried that this will eventually interfere with our relationship. What can I do?

DR. HERMAN: It may take a few years before a child can accept a live-in stepparent. Developing an acceptance of a stepparent is a process; it doesn't happen overnight, nor is it automatically guaranteed. The way in which a child negotiates this process depends on the youngster's personality and temperament, on previous experiences, on the personality of the stepparent, and on how sensitive the stepparent is to the child's needs and fears. It's a difficult adjustment, one requiring time and sensitivity. It cannot be hurried or slowed.

Your new husband must realize that he can never replace your daughter's father; nor should he try. He should not bend over backward, trying to be a superparent. Nor should he try to compensate in some way for your daughter's emotional turmoil and difficulties. Doing so guarantees that he will become resentful of the situation. He should simply be himself, which can be difficult, because it involves being sensitive and kind to his stepdaughter, who is part of a past to which he does not belong. It's futile for a stepparent to try to "win the child over," since this will incur the parent's resentment.

It is crucial to realize that this process takes time. Be as kind and as sensitive as you can be, and keep lines of communication open. It's helpful if stepfather and daughter can talk and eventually get to know each other. Generally, new families work better as time passes, and as the people involved become more accustomed to the situation and to each other. Above all, try not to delude yourself; your loving your new husband is not an automatic prescription for your daughter to feel the same way.

Letting an Ex-Husband "Stay Over"

I've been divorced for two years and find it difficult to meet new men. Every once in a while, I let my ex-husband "stay over" for the night, and this seems to upset both our kids; they're six and ten years old. Am I making a mistake?

DR. HERMAN: Yes, I think you are making a mistake, both for yourself and for your children. You are slipping back into a situation that you must know is not going to lead anywhere. You are prolonging certain fantasies about you and your ex-husband getting back together again. We know from working with children that *all* children, even adult children, have fantasies that their divorced parents will somehow reunite. Your husband's spending the night rekindles these fantasies for your children, thereby creating even more emotional turmoil for them.

While it's difficult to meet new men, there are many ways to do so. There are groups for single parents. If you don't want to be identified as a single parent, there are adult education courses, health clubs, resorts, and other means by which you can meet new people of your own age with similar interests. By expanding your social life and meeting new people (including men), you will concretize, for yourself and your children, that one chapter of your life is over and a new one has begun.

Feeling Uncomfortable Dating

I've been divorced for four years and recently began dating. My son and daughter, ages eight and eleven, make me feel uncomfortable whenever a man calls on me. It's awkward, and I've noticed that my son ignores my date. How can I deal with this?

DR. HERMAN: This is an unfortunate development. You need to feel comfortable with the fact that you are dating other men. At eight and eleven, your children are old enough to understand this. In the initial stages of a new relationship with a man, it's probably a good idea not to have him visit the house or to have much contact with your children. You can expect that at first your children will not be ecstatic with whatever dating arrangements you work out.

Interestingly, I've noticed that a double standard seems to prevail: both boys and girls tend to be more understanding and accepting of a father meeting new women than of a mother meeting new men. This may be a telling commentary on our perceived sexual roles and on sexism in our lives today.

Be firm with your children; you have a life of your own, and part of that life means dating a man. Your children must deal with this, and eventually accept it. You would want your children to be civil toward *anyone* who visits, just as they should be if your visitor was a woman friend. But don't expect miracles. This is a process, and will take time.

Above all, you must feel comfortable with your dating arrangement. If *you* don't feel guilty about dating, then you'll be better able to tolerate your children's attitudes. Often when a divorced mother begins dating, she may not be certain that she is ready for this step. She may feel guilty about the divorce and its effects on her children. She may then attempt to be a "supermom." Under these circumstances, if a child resists her beginning to date, the mother may feel hurt, even resentful. Feeling comfortable with this new situation can help greatly in dealing with your children's understandable resistance to this important development in your life, one that is fraught with meaning for them as well.

A Sexual Life

I've been divorced for some time now, and I've been seeing a wonderful man for the last few months. Our relationship is becoming intimate, but I'm not certain how to deal with sex because of my two daughters, aged seven and ten. What's the best policy?

DR. HERMAN: You certainly have a right to a fulfilling sexual life. Living with children as a single parent creates some complications. If you've become involved with a man and your relationship has expanded to include being sexual with each other, that, of course, is your business. But in the early stages of the relationship, sex should probably be kept outside your own home. If you want to spend the night with him, it's probably best that this occur somewhere else.

When it appears that you're getting serious with each other, it may happen that he will stay overnight at your house. This should come at a time when you're feeling very sure about the importance of this man in your life. But, as would be the case if you were married, discretion is the best policy. You should be quiet, keep doors locked, and wait until the children are asleep. At ages seven and ten, your daughters can be told that you and this man love each other and want to be part of each other's lives in every possible way.

Dealing with Visitation

I've been divorced for six years. Our kids have adjusted well, but whenever they spend a weekend with my ex-husband, I end up paying the price. He spoils them and gives them everything, so I end up looking like the villain. I resent the inevitable comparisons the kids make between me and him, and I don't know how to handle this.

DR. HERMAN: This situation can occur when a father is peripherally involved with the children and becomes the so-called Sunday afternoon father. In this arrangement, the father engages in fantasy activities with the children: going to movies, the circus, baseball games, or the zoo.

It would be preferable if you and your husband could communicate regularly about how each of you conduct yourselves with the children. Even though you're divorced, it would help to know each other's styles with the kids. You may discover that he's not spoiling them but that your children are reacting to the tension of going between their parents. Or he may be spoiling the children; this can be a problem.

All you can do is continue being the parent you feel you should be with your children. Let them know that you feel comfortable being this way. As for spoiling: most children are more comfortable with limits; they actually want them. Most kids don't want Sunday seven days a week. They understand that part of growing up means sharing responsibility and also having limits set. You need not apologize for setting limits. In the long run, your children will understand.

From talking to children whose parents are divorced, we know that visitation, even in the best of circumstances, can be very stressful. Sometimes, parents use their children as messengers or go-betweens; they may intentionally or inadvertently make negative comments about the ex-spouse in the presence of the children. Or they may say something they know the children will take back with them. This is unproductive and places added burdens and stress on a child. Doing this may make a parent feel better for having gotten something off his or her chest, but the child is being asked to choose sides, which demands something of a child that he or she cannot do.

Sometimes, a child may latch on to a parent's word or comment and use it to get something from the other parent. While this occasionally happens to most separated or divorced parents, it's best not to allow it to become a regular pattern of interaction. If you're angry with your ex-spouse, it's best to express this directly rather than using the children to convey such messages. One can hope that in time all concerned can make visitation as stress-free as possible.

Will Children Be Scarred?

I've been divorced for ten years and my children went through some difficult times. So did my ex-wife and I. My biggest concern is the effect all this had on our children, who seem to have adapted well. Did we scar our kids for the rest of their lives? Will they ever trust anyone or be able to form good relationships?

DR. HERMAN: It is not simply a question of whether divorce per se affects children; it's equally important to consider how a couple divorces. The emotional climate of this process is vitally important in its effect on children. One must consider what led to the divorce and the way in which a couple separates and deals with their disappointment, frustration, resentment, and other feelings, during and after the actual divorce. In discussing whether children are scarred by divorce, one must clarify the issue. Does divorce affect a child? Does it cause certain thoughts and feelings that will persist throughout a child's life? The answer is yes, but this does *not* mean that a child will never have fulfilling relationships or will never trust anyone.

Divorce is undeniably a major event in a child's life, one which the child must negotiate and to which he must make certain adaptive changes. *How* this is conducted is most important. If a husband and wife can divorce in a reasonably humane and caring way, taking into consideration the needs of their children, with minimal fighting or using of the children, then the children can better deal with this process and adapt well.

There's no reason to think your children will never trust again or be unable to develop good relationships. In fact, quite the opposite may occur. Having gone through divorce, many children make profound adaptations, and as adults work very hard at their own marriages so their children won't experience what they themselves went through. While no one would say that separation or divorce is an inherently good development in a child's life, it need not be viewed as something that will scar, inhibit, or limit a child's future or potential for forming good relationships.

Joint Custody

My husband and I are getting a divorce. We are thinking of a joint custody arrangement. Is this advisable?

DR. HERMAN: Joint custody is the buzzword of the 1980s. Under English law, children were considered property, so the father always received custody of the children. In the early 1900s, the idea of the "tender years" held sway. This meant that there was a developmental period of time called the tender years, when children were thought to be best off staying with their mothers. In the last twenty-five years, fathers have become far more vocal in wanting equal access or even sole custody of their children. Now we often hear of people trying to mandate joint custody.

Joint custody can be convenient for parents, lawyers, and the courts, but may or may not work for the children. Joint custody means that parents share as equally as possible in the rearing of the children. The children live with both parents at various times, and decisions about school, vacations, and other major matters are made jointly by the parents. The children have equal access between homes, and in a sense live with both parents, albeit separately.

This can only work when two parents have successfully put their great disappointment and frustration in each other behind them. It can work only when both parents are mature enough to work together in the best interest of the child. It can be successful when two parents can negotiate and still like each other enough to work together for their child's benefit, despite being unable to live together and remain married. In such a case, it probably doesn't matter whether there is joint or sole custody, because the children will be the beneficiaries of the prevailing harmony.

In some unfortunate joint custody arrangements, the parents are at constant odds with each other, and the children are ferried back and forth amid a torrent of acrimony. The parents argue incessantly and the kids, caught in the middle of everything, are severely stressed and utterly miserable. Joint custody can work well under special circumstances, but by no means is it a prescription for harmony.

Chapter 7: When Mother Works

There are 18 million working mothers in the United States today. Even the mothers of preschoolers tend to have jobs; in 1984, more than half of all women with children under six years of age were employed. Some younger children of working mothers are cared for by nannies or babysitters. Others, a little older, spend extra hours in after-school activities, while others (ranging in age from seven years to the teens) come home to empty houses. Called "latchkey kids," they carry their own house keys and develop ways to cope with loneliness.

The mother who stays at home is now the exception rather than the rule. Recent changes in American households have brought more freedoms and additional responsibilities to mothers and fathers than ever before. And they have caused parents to worry about the long-range effects that mothers at work will (or will not) have on their children. Parents question the wisdom of a mother beginning work during a child's infancy; they express concern about a child's attachment to a surrogate care-giver; they worry that they may be emotionally damaging a child by this arrangement; and they worry about children resenting a mother's absence during working hours. All this can cause powerful feelings of guilt in many parents.

Each family's situation is unique and depends on certain specifics: the mother's working arrangement; the availability of outside help; the intactness of the family (whether there is a divorce or not); the reasons for a mother's working; whether or not a mother enjoys work; and many others.

The following pages address the most frequent concerns that working mothers express about themselves and the possible effects their working has on their children.

Our consultant is Margaret E. Hertzig, M.D. Dr. Hertzig is an Associate Professor of Psychiatry at Cornell University Medical College and is the Director of Children's Outpatient Services at the Payne Whitney Clinic of The New York Hospital.

Full-Time or Part-Time

I have a six-month-old daughter and would like to return to work. I have the choice of returning full-time or part-time with an eventual transition to full-time work. Is there an advantage to either way?

DR. HERTZIG: In answering any question about a mother's returning to work, one must consider a variety of issues: family factors, a mother's personal needs, and an understanding of your child's developmental stage. In this situation, we are concerned with providing surrogate care for a six-month-old child. A child this age has probably developed what is called stranger anxiety. (See in Chapter 1, "Stranger Anxiety.") This means that she has developed the beginnings of a real attachment to you, the primary caretaker. She has also become attached to other members of the household: father, siblings, and possibly others.

The important consideration is not whether you should return to work on a full- or part-time basis, but rather the alternative child-care provisions you can make for your baby. In other words, you must provide substitute care that will meet your child's needs so you can return to work feeling confident that you've met your responsibilities. In introducing a surrogate caretaker to your six-month-old baby, it is best to allow an attachment to form between your baby and her care-taker before you return to work, whether on a full- or part-time basis.

A number of options are available to you. You could introduce the caretaker to your household before you return to work, or you could introduce your baby into the caretaker's home before returning to work. This would allow your child to adapt to the new caretaker and begin forming a satisfactory attachment. Once this is done, you have the choice of returning to full-time work or beginning on a part-time basis and gradually making the transition to a full-time situation. The essential consideration is to introduce the caretaker and your baby to each other, whatever your plans for returning to work may be.

Will a Working Mother "Lose" Her Child?

I'm a full-time working mother, and our nanny is great, maybe too good. I'm worried that my seven-month-old daughter will become too attached to her. Is this a possibility?

DR. HERTZIG: The nature of a child's attachment to her mother has been extensively studied by researchers and experts. A great deal has been learned about the importance of early attachment and bonding to a primary caretaker, who is usually the mother.

Humans are social beings. A baby's characteristics at birth successfully evoke caretaking behaviors in adults, whether family members or strangers. Virtually every adult feels compelled to soothe a distressed infant. Very few people can walk by a grinning baby and not respond in kind. The infant's potential for developing a social bond, powerfully present at birth, develops increasing complexity as the child grows older.

The social bond is not an exclusive one. The young infant usually develops a powerful attachment to the primary caretaker but can develop attachments and relationships with other people as well. These are often "special" relationships with significant others in the infant's environment. These relationships take on a more specific tone as the baby grows and develops. For instance, at four months, the baby may play certain games with father as opposed to mother. Interactions may occur with siblings that don't take place with mother. Grandparents and other specific figures in the baby's little world may evoke special reactions from the infant. A crucial developmental task for any infant is to evolve differentiated responses to various people in the environment, and the baby acquires an expanding range of attachments to others as it develops. This expansion eventually culminates in peer relations outside the family when the child enters school.

Your question makes me wonder how you feel about not being a full-time mother. Your concern that your baby may develop too strong an attachment to her nanny may reflect some guilty feelings; such worries are virtually universal among working mothers. When the concept of day-care centers was first developed, many people thought that children who were placed in such centers would be deprived because they wouldn't have the ever-present input of the primary mother for all caretaking. Experts were concerned that there might be differences in the quality of baby's attachment to the primary caretaker once a surrogate-mothering situation arose. However, research does *not* demonstrate significant differences in the attachments that babies of working women develop to their mothers, as compared to babies of full-time mothers. The nature of the primary attachment remains the same no matter what the mother's work situation may be. Children of working mothers become attached to an expanding number of people in their environment, but this does not compete with the powerful primary attachment to mother.

Let me further address this concern. Parenthood involves an enormous amount of responsibility. Many parents are concerned that they may be doing something that is less than optimal when they try to meet a child's physical and emotional needs. A parent must consider a child's needs for any particular stage of the child's emotional and physical development. And a parent must recognize that a *variety* of environmental experiences is available to address a particular child's needs.

Using multiple caretakers or mothering figures is one among a panoply of acceptable choices. It's a variant and an option that has historically occurred since time began. In days gone by, an extended family with grandparents and other relatives was often instrumental in performing many caretaking functions. Older siblings helped out, too. In those days, mothers rarely devoted exclusive attention to newborn infants as they now do; rather, members of the extended family provided a great deal of the caretaking.

The most important consideration about your infant's caretaking is the degree of stability and predictability, and the quality, of your baby's relationships with caretakers. While one can readily empathize with your concern about being a working mother who employs a surrogate caretaker, there is no danger that your infant will become overly attached to that caretaker. She will no doubt develop a "special" relationship with her nanny, but this does not exclude you, nor does it detract from her relatedness to you. Your baby will simply have one variation of many possible choices in her early development.

How to Choose a Surrogate Caretaker

I'm a full-time working mother of a two-year-old boy. We have a nanny. I know that nobody's going to care for my child the way I do. I'm concerned that my child may be deprived of the proper mental and verbal stimulation since I'm not around. In addition, our nanny is from a different background and doesn't speak English very well. Are my concerns valid?

DR. HERTZIG: The real issue in this question is how does one assess the quality of surrogate caretaking? That is, how do you choose someone to care for your child while you work, and what considerations are most important in making this vital decision?

When you think of employing a surrogate caretaker, you must consider your child's specific needs at his stage of development. You must also contemplate this over the course of time, because your child's developmental needs and tasks will change over time. Just as parents can find one stage of child development a great deal of fun while another seems burdensome, so can surrogate caretakers vary in their own preferences. A particular caretaker may be more or less appropriate for your child at one developmental time or another.

If you select a caretaker who develops a genuine attachment for your child, if there is a real basis of affection and responsiveness going both ways, if the caretaker can understand your child's needs and provide a reasonable balance between frustrations and gratifications, then your child and the surrogate caretaker can do very well together. The surrogate does not have to function as an educator and need not provide educative or cognitive stimulation.

Certain practical considerations are crucial when you contemplate hiring a caretaker. Perhaps most important is the degree of comfort you feel with this individual. A parent should learn to trust his or her intuitive feelings in this situation. If this person turns you off despite being highly recommended, even if your feelings of being "turned off" seem irrational or vague, you should regard them as a warning signal of potential problems between your infant and the caretaker, or between you and the caretaker. Trust your basic feelings in this matter. If you sense it will be difficult to work cooperatively with someone, respect your capacity to know intuitively what's best for your baby.

Try to assess, as best you can, this individual's tolerance for your child's behavior. Try to gain a perspective on how this intended caretaker will respond to your child's behavior and relatedness at his specific developmental stage. If your child is two years old, the caretaker will have to deal with plenty of negativism, and with the noes of the so-called terrible twos. If the surrogate seems easily upset by disorder, or by the inevitable reality that the house will often be less than spotless, reconsider the wisdom of choosing this particular person. Equally important, you should observe your child's reaction to this individual and the nanny's response to the baby. Observe their interaction over a period of time, trying to assess whether they respond warmly and positively to each other.

You should not worry about the caretaker's less-than-excellent language skills. Let's think about how children develop language. Certainly, they must have the opportunity to hear language if they are going to learn to speak. However, your child's time with the nanny will hardly be his sole exposure to spoken language. He will evolve increasingly sophisticated language by being exposed to various language sources: television, records, other people, children in the sandbox or park, and, most important, plenty of stimulating verbal input when you and your husband are home. A child this age has a powerful developmental thrust toward verbal communication; it cannot be denied.

More important than the quality of the nanny's speech is her attentiveness to your child's communications. Equally crucial, she should communicate back on an *emotional*, empathic level. The most important qualities for a nanny to possess are warmth and responsiveness in the context of a good relationship between you and the nanny, and between the nanny and your child.

What is Quality Time?

I hear a lot about quality time versus quantity time. Is there any truth in this notion, or is it really hype?

DR. HERTZIG: There is a great deal of truth in this concept if we understand what is meant by the idea of quality time.

There is a myth stating that quality time must be unendingly positive and stimulating for both parent and child. While positive time is, of course, important, one must also remember that part of development involves a child's learning to delay gratification, to manage frustration, and not to become disorganized by negative or by less-than-perfect circumstances when they occur. It's quite unrealistic to expect all experiences to be positive.

A child learns in a social context, and the most important socializing force for any child, whether present all or part of the time, is the parents. Providing your child with quality time means providing a wide range of emotional and learning experiences. One valuable experience for a child to master is the reality of a parent being absent. After all, leave-taking is part of life, and your occasional absence helps your child deal with separation, which ultimately helps him individuate and function on his own. Your child must learn to derive pleasure from social interactions other than with parents, and must learn to handle the inevitable frustrations of living in a very imperfect world.

I am occasionally concerned because some parents think that quality time must never be frustrating and never make demands of the child, that it must be absolutely conflict-free. This is not the case. Quality time is not necessarily free of stress or strain for your child, or for you. Quality time means that you have ongoing, responsive interactions with your child, interchanges that are emotionally rewarding and help your child deal with a variety of situations that take into account the complexities (and frustrations) of the world. This is done in the context of a caring, loving, and responsive relationship. The concept of quality time, in my view, is not a myth. It does exist, but in the ways that I've indicated.

If you take your parental responsibilities seriously and try your best to be responsive and attentive, the chances are very great that you will provide your child with a great deal of quality time, whether you are available on a full- or part-time basis.

Forced to Grow Up Too Fast?

Since I'm a working mother, my children have had to become more self-sufficient. Am I forcing them to grow up too fast?

DR. HERTZIG: There are many roads to your child's becoming a well-integrated adult who copes with the world's demands and who derives satisfaction from personal and work relationships. There is a wide range of good mothering behaviors and environments. When thinking about child care, the important issues are your child's developmental level, his personal characteristics, and his day-to-day life within the family.

Children develop at different rates and in different ways, so it's very difficult to make a statement about a child's being forced to become self-sufficient at too early a stage of life. If your child seems to thrive on responsibility, if he is goal-directed and fulfills reasonable demands, if he takes pride in completing tasks, then you are *not* making too many demands, nor are you forcing the child to grow up "too fast." Your child may capably handle expectations and be more self-sufficient than another child.

For instance, a child may derive pleasure from getting home from school, going to the freezer, taking out the meat for that night's dinner, and defrosting it. Another child may be more easily distracted and less able to assume this responsibility. He might be forgetful and would handle everyday household responsibilities poorly if mother is not available when he arrives home from school. He may still be thinking about a conversation with a friend on the school bus, and he may need someone to remind him of his responsibilities. His own personal development may make so seemingly small a responsibility quite stressful for him. There is a range of responses, and a child copes, depending on his developmental maturity and on the context of the family.

There is no simple answer to this question. You must know your child and her capabilities, her level of development, and how well she deals with responsibilities. You must know your child's capacity to complete any tasks you ask her to perform. This can help you determine *realistic* tasks for your child to accomplish, therefore enhancing her sense of herself and her self-esteem.

You would also want to determine the emotional supports your child may need. A latchkey child may have various environmental supports, depending on who is available, and what the next-door neighbor can do practically to help. There are many ways to help your child function self-sufficiently once you know her capacities and limitations. These relate to the nature of your work, when you return home, your availability to telephone your youngster when she arrives home from school, and many other factors.

It has generally been found that most mothers make demands that are just one step ahead of their children's capabilities. These demands are closely attuned to the child's level, and they help spur him to expand his repertoire of capabilities. This seems to occur spontaneously between parents and their children; parents don't purposely intend it that way.

This general principle can be extended to the school-age child's capabilities and limitations. You can make very reasonable demands that are a half step ahead of your child's capabilities. In other words, a latchkey situation can help a child deal with reasonable and realistic demands, helping him become increasingly social and requiring him to take an active role in household functions. Of course, this can occur whether a child is a latchkey child or not.

There is no question that the life circumstances of the child whose mother works are different from those of the child whose mother is at home. But the developmental tasks placed before each child are very much the same. Any child will develop and become self-sufficient at a reasonable rate when the youngster is given proper emotional support and when realistic demands are made so the child can take pride in his or her accomplishments.

Nanny or a Private Day-Care Center

I have a one-year-old daughter and I'm ready to return to work. I have the option of employing a nanny or of enrolling my child in a private day-care center where she would be cared for by a trained professional who would care for two other children the same age. Which is preferable?

DR. HERTZIG: As always, you must consider the developmental stage to which your child presently belongs. A child of one year is still very much an infant and doesn't require a great deal of socialization in the company of other children. Generally, social interaction begins between two and three years of age. If you're thinking of the possible social interaction provided by a day-care center, such a consideration is not really important at your child's age.

At one year of age, the opportunity for a one-to-one relationship with a good surrogate caretaker would probably be preferable to a day-care situation. If a day-care center is the only option available to you, by all means take advantage of it. You would want to consider the center's ability to individualize a caretaking relationship for your child.

If your daughter were three years old, she would be ready for a preschool or day-care experience. The opportunity to interact with peers and to spend time with various people other than the primary caretaker would become increasingly beneficial. All this involves the beginning of movement away from the family and an evolving range of attachments to other people. This enlarging world will eventually become the world of school and peer relationships and will assume greater importance as your child develops. Day care might be preferable for the three- or four-year-old child because it provides these developmental and social opportunities.

Aside from the question of one-to-one versus group interaction, other considerations greatly influence a working mother's choice of surrogate care. For instance, any working mother must take into account how well an arrangement will work when her child is ill. Some day-care centers handle children with minor illnesses such as colds; others may not. You would want to explore this issue before deciding on a day-care facility or an individual surrogate.

You must consider backup for the surrogate care, and must determine how flexible any arrangement will be. A day-care center is always there! An individual caretaker may have emergencies of her own, and even the most reliable nanny may occasionally become ill or be unavailable. In that event, you may have to miss a few days of work in order to care for your child.

The major considerations in helping a parent decide about child care are: the nature of your work, the flexibility of your hours, the amount of time you will have for various emergencies, the options that each arrangement gives you, your child's specific developmental level, and how effectively any arrangement can deal with any particular developmental issues that may arise.

Consider all these parameters from many vantage points, in order to work out the arrangement that will most satisfactorily meet your child's needs, your needs, and your family's needs, and that will least interfere with the demands of work. No matter which method of surrogate care you choose to provide for your child, some compromise will always be necessary.

Feels Guilty

I quit my job after having my baby, but after some months of being a full-time mother, I began resenting it. I've returned to work and have hired a nanny, but I feel a little guilty. Did I do the right thing?

DR. HERTZIG: Life is full of conflicting demands. Most people struggle to meet them in a way that will generally be most gratifying and least troubling for them. There are times when the demands may seem to be less in conflict. A mother who returns from the hospital with a tiny newborn baby is so absorbed by this infant and by the experience of delivery that there is very little conflict involved in her deciding to remain at home with the baby. This is also seen with fathers; today there is increasing pressure for paternity leave as well as maternity leave.

As this bond becomes established, certain things begin to change. The infant becomes less regulated by physiologic functions alone; the parents learn more about their baby; the mother feels less tentative and learns more about her child's communicative signals; and the mother-child interaction becomes more predictable and stable. At some point, parents begin discovering a resurgence of interest in each other, as they become somewhat less totally absorbed by the child. Their interests in other activities undergo a resurgence as well.

At this point, a mother may find herself wanting something to take up the slack. If she had a meaningful work situation prior to the baby's birth, this may come to the fore again. Some aspects of infant care can make a mother begin feeling resentful, and I do think that some resentment is quite common, especially today, with so much emphasis placed on mothers finding other interests. Caring for a very young infant can be a lonely and isolated experience and can leave a mother feeling trapped. If the weather is bad, a new mother may not even get out to the park; she can begin feeling constricted and suffocated. Some women, having had meaningful work activities before the baby's birth, may indeed begin feeling resentful at this point.

There are peaks and valleys of infant care, and a mother's intense interest in her baby may not stay as totally focused as it was when the baby was new and when mother's constant input was far more necessary.

If you find yourself beginning to feel resentful in a full-time mothering situation, it can be helpful to involve other people in some caretaking tasks. How to bring this about is a problem that a mother must solve on her own, given her own personal and family situation. A mother must be able to get out and do things that cannot be done if she stays with the baby full-time. This may include shopping, getting her hair done, and spending some time with her friends.

A husband can be very helpful, depending on his willingness and ability to share in some caretaking. Even if his job is very demanding and limits his time, a husband can still help with a bottle in the middle of the night. Other chores can be shared. Equally important is the couple's willingness to talk with each other about the baby and its development, along with willingness to share not just concerns, but the pleasures of watching a baby grow and develop. This supportive element can be valuable for any mother.

There is little question that any full-time mother will feel occasional twinges of resentment. Should she return to work, she will most likely experience some pangs of guilt. These normal feelings are part of living in a world where compromises must be made.

An Overview

Dr. Hertzig: Our culture barrages parents with conflicting messages about child-rearing. Mothers are viewed as the principal caretakers and socializers of their children, with vast responsibilities. Yet they are also expected to develop fully as people, to maximize their own potentials and needs.

Most parents worry about the impact of their actions on their children. They wonder whether something they have done will injure, inhibit, or limit a child's development. These feelings often resonate with their own experiences of having been parented, and with their own wishes to perform better or differently than their own parents did with them. To their great horror, most adults discover that they behave toward their children exactly as their own parents did to them when they themselves were children. In all this, parents often ask which method of doing something is better or "best."

The answers to these questions are never simple. Questions about child care are best considered from the perspective of the variety of solutions available. How does a parent begin to think about the implications of a given choice? This must be considered within the context of a parent's life, her choices, her family, and the variables of her child. In other words, life is a negotiable experience. You and your child—together and separately—must negotiate life's demands.

It's important for a mother to consider her options when she thinks about working. She must think about working full-time, part-time, or not at all. The options must be considered in light of the child's developmental needs, the parents' needs, the family's needs, and how all these needs can be reconciled for the benefit of everyone. Arriving at a specific solution does not guarantee that everything will go smoothly. An arrangement may work when a child is two years old but may fail when the child is five. The child will be in a different developmental stage at that point, or family circumstances may have changed. It's an experience of discovery and of negotiation, as time goes by.

Chapter 8: Telling Your Child About Death

Death is a part of life, yet death is a taboo subject for many people. Adults often think they are protecting a child when they avoid mentioning death or when they prevent a child from attending a funeral. But avoiding such topics doesn't prevent a child from feeling grief at the loss of a loved one. In fact, shielding a child from death may prevent the expression of bereavement, which can have long-term consequences, as the following pages will show.

Parents have many questions about helping a child cope with death, whether it's the death of a grandparent, sibling, parent, or another significant person in the child's life. In the following pages, our consultant answers the most frequently asked questions about helping a child deal with concerns about death and dying.

Our consultant is John M. Ross, Ph.D. Dr. Ross is a Clinical Associate Professor of Psychology in Psychiatry at Cornell University Medical College and an Associate Attending Psychologist at the Payne Whitney Clinic of The New York Hospital.

Should You Tell?

Our four-year-old is attached to his grandfather, who recently had a stroke and will probably die soon. Should we tell our child that grandpa is sick and that he may die? How can we handle this without frightening our son?

DR. ROSS: A parent has a far better developed sense of time and of the future than does a four-year-old. A parent can therefore begin the mourning process before a child does. A parent may tend to project his or her own concerns onto the child and burden the child with certain anxieties. If grandpa is living with you and is sick or unresponsive, and if it's obvious to your son that things are not as they used to be, talk with him about grandfather's being ill. But I would not introduce the idea of death before it becomes a reality. To do so at this time is not in step with the child's emotional life, because your child has only a vague appreciation of the future. We don't quite know how a child will respond to such information.

A child perceives things in a very egocentric way, feeling that he is in the center of the universe, sometimes actually believing that his own thoughts and feelings can cause unrelated events to occur. A child may inappropriately think that his own bad thought about grandfather resulted in this illness, and eventually in grandfather's death. If grandfather is acting strangely or is for some reason "not himself," your son will realize this, and could fantasize that *he* caused this strange behavior. If grandfather doesn't respond to your son, the child may feel he's being punished or ignored. Your basic posture should be to explain that this is an illness, one for which neither your son nor anyone else bears any responsibility.

However, if grandfather lives some distance away, and your son has not yet seen him ill, I would not comment on the situation at this time.

Should a Five-Year-Old Attend a Funeral?

My mother-in-law just died and the funeral is in a few days. Should our five-year-old daughter, who was very close to her, attend the funeral?

DR. ROSS: If the casket will not be open and it's not an overwhelmingly frightening experience for the child, then the shared mourning experience can be helpful for everyone, including your child. While a five-year-old does not completely understand the meaning of death, your child can still benefit from attending a funeral. The shared experience of bereavement can be beneficial so long as death is explained in terms that the child can understand. Beyond age six years, the child becomes increasingly able to cope with and more fully understand the concept of death.

There *is* a cut-off point—at about three or four years of age. For so young a child to attend a funeral would confront that child with certain untenable possibilities: the specter of his or her own death, or the child might fantasize about the potential death of her parents. This can be enormously frightening to a three- or four-year-old who needs to feel secure and completely protected.

The factors entering into a decision about allowing a five-year-old to attend a funeral are the child's closeness to the deceased, the nature of the funeral, and the parent's willingness to comprehensibly explain death to the child.

How to Explain Death

Our five-year-old son's uncle recently died, and our son has asked about him since he's been gone. My husband wants to tell him that his uncle went to sleep, but I favor telling him that he died. Who is right?

DR. ROSS: At five years of age, children universally equate sleeping with death. It's not a good idea to aid and abet this childhood fantasy. Nor is it a good idea to prematurely expect a child to fully understand and assimilate the concept of death and its irreversibility. The question is, how do you explain death to a child of five or six years of age?

It's best to compromise in explaining death. This can be done so that you don't lie or mystify a child, yet you don't expect too much comprehension from him either. In other words, I would say, "Uncle Joe has died, and won't be coming back. But we well always remember him, and he'll continue to live in our memories." That's an acceptable solution, one that a child can understand, even if he does so somewhat concretely. It's a reasonable way to explain the reality of death. To tell your child that death is equated with sleep promotes fantasy, can evoke anxiety, and encourages him to use denial.

Denial of death, that is, pretending that someone hasn't died, or helping a child avoid thinking about or dealing with death can, in the long run, lead to problems. Such denial can encourage a child to dis-avow what he actually perceives; the child "sees" and does "not see" the truth (reality) at the same time. Fostering denial in this way can result in a child who never properly mourns the lost person.

Failure to mourn can cause a child to make identifications with the dead person, or it can encourage enduring fantasies of reunion with that person, especially with a dead parent, and can cause distortions in relationships later in life. I treated a woman whose father died when she was six years old. She never truly mourned that loss; instead, she formed a strong masculine identification with her deceased father, and later in life was uncertain how feminine or masculine she perceived herself or wished to be. For her, being masculine meant, in a way, holding on to her father, through an identification with him.

I've seen cases in which children were encouraged to use denial in dealing with death. Never truly acknowledging the death of a parent, these children entertained very powerful reunion fantasies. They re-tained, deep in their minds, the notion of rejoining the deceased parent. Later, as teenagers and adults, they entered into ungratifying relation-ships based on the need to become involved with someone who, in fantasy, represented the dead parent. As adults, they chose romantic partners who always left them; these people repeatedly entered into relationships in which they were abandoned. In other words, they unwittingly repeated the loss of the unmourned person from earlier in their lives.

There are important general principles concerning children's reactions to death. We must understand that a child is at a particular developmental level in terms of understanding the world, whereas adults are at a vastly higher level of understanding. As parents, we must present the world to our children as we understand it, recognizing that they will understand the world in their own childish way. We cannot interfere with a child's process of comprehending the realities of life and death; that is, we cannot hope to completely bridge the gap in understanding between a child and an adult. We best serve a child by truthfully explaining things in a way that the child can grasp, so that he or she can grapple with certain realities and not develop unrealistic or unhealthy fantasies.

When a Pet Dies

Our dog just died. Our children, ages five and eight, are very upset. How long should we wait before getting another dog?

DR. ROSS: A patient of mine was very preoccupied by death. Having had a grandparent die when she was very young, she never resolved certain problems about death and separation. In talking about her early losses, she angrily remembered when as a child her blue parakeet became sick. She recalled going to sleep that night and awakening the next morning to find a green parakeet in the cage instead of the blue one. Her mother then tried to convince her that the parakeet had molted, and though it's color had changed, it was the same parakeet.

Her mother tried to convey to the child a sense that there had actually been no death. This substitution was a denial of the bird's death, and as a child my patient was not given the opportunity to mourn the death of her pet.

Mourning is quite painful, but it is necessary. You must give your children sufficient time to experience the loss of a pet as a distinct individual, one that is not replaceable. You don't want to encourage emotional promiscuity in children, where they learn to simply replace one pet (or person) with another. Children are *entitled* to the experience of loss, despite the considerable pain it brings. Your children should mourn the loss of their pet; after about one year, it is perfectly reasonable to replace the animal with another.

I've been talking about bereavement. It's important to define this process because bereavement is the central issue in dealing with death. In a sense, all of life can be viewed as a mourning process. We lose people who are close to us as we progress through life. Mourning involves a deep, painful reaction to the loss of someone who was close to the survivor. There is a withdrawal of interest from the outside world, and a preoccupation with thoughts of the dead person for a period of time. This is accompanied by a sense of sadness, until the loss is slowly assimilated and accepted over the course of time. This happens through memories, through identification with the dead person, and by other psychological mechanisms. The ultimate purpose of this painful process is to allow the bereaved person to slowly relinquish his or her ties to the deceased, and to then proceed with life.

There are pathological kinds of bereavement. As mentioned before, there can be an overidentification with the dead person. Also, it is quite common for the survivor to feel anger, even rage, toward the person who died. In a sense, the survivor experiences himself as having been "abandoned" by the deceased. If the survivor identifies too strongly with the dead person and is also enraged at that person, he can become angry at himself. This can lead to a depression, a condition in which a person is filled with self-hatred.

Remember, children's magical thinking can lead them to imagine fantastic causes of various events. Children are especially vulnerable to forming fantasies and distortions, especially about death. That is why it's necessary to explain death as carefully and as completely as you can to a child. Children are capable of mourning, even though they don't fully understand life and death. A child should be given the chance to mourn. It is a necessary part of life.

About an Afterlife

My brother recently died, and our six-year-old son misses him terribly. Although we aren't religious, I've heard that it's helpful to instill in a child the belief in an afterlife. Is this true?

DR. ROSS: I don't think you can instill in a child a belief that is not truly your own. To attempt to do so asks that a child disavow his own perceptions of you. However, if your child wishes to believe in an afterlife or in heaven, such a wish should not be disrupted or discouraged. The child may need this notion to maintain a sense of security or to master what might otherwise be incomprehensible. However, telling a child something that you yourself don't believe mystifies the child and beclouds his or her perceptions. You can say, "Uncle Joe has died. He won't be coming back, but we'll remember him and he'll live on in our memories." If the child chooses to construe this as an afterlife, that's his choice. I wouldn't challenge that belief.

Letting Go

My wife died four months ago. My nine-year-old daughter and I have made many adjustments. I now feel that I want to sell the house. From the standpoint of my daughter's adjustment, is this a wise thing to do now?

DR. ROSS: It is probably too early to sell the house at this time. The house and everything in it are transitional objects relating to mother. Her environment—the house, the furniture, and her clothing—are all links to her and part of the attachment to her. (See in Chapter 1, "A Linus Blanket.") In my view, four months is not a sufficient period of time for mourning to have progressed. Your daughter needs the intense emotional involvement with her mother and with mother's proxies: the house, the furniture, the very environment of the house.

Over time, there can be a gradual "letting go" of mother and a reawakened involvement in the outside world. By selling the house too quickly, you may encourage your daughter to use denial, or help her foster too quickly the sense that mourning is "over" now. This could lead to denial of this important loss and to later complications.

One of the tasks in life is to be able to bear intense feelings such as sadness, grief, and anxiety, rather than to pretend these feelings away or deny them. As a young girl of ten whom I treated once said to me, "Don't put your feelings in a box."

Violent Death and Nightmares

My eight-year-old son witnessed his friend's death when struck by a car. Now my son is having nightmares and won't play outdoors. How should I handle this?

DR. ROSS: If your son's nightmares persist or become crippling, and he continues to be phobic of the streets, or if the phobic feeling expands, then a professional consultation may be necessary. However, keep in mind that your son is dealing with a very traumatic situation. The nightmare provides a vivid repetition of this traumatic event, which can be a very useful way of attempting to master the trauma. Many people need to review actively in their minds, even in their sleeping minds, a traumatic event before they come to terms with it.

Keep in mind that a dead friend is not only a beloved figure who was lost. A child can have rivalrous and competitive feelings toward a friend, and a certain amount of hostility can be present along with the good feelings. Unfortunately, a tragic accident can sometimes mean that a child realizes his own hostile wish to "get rid of" or prevail over someone. Your son may slowly have to come to terms with some fantasized version of his own hostility toward his now dead friend.

A parent should not raise this issue unless the child himself raises it. As with sex, so in death: don't go beyond whatever the child is asking. You should address the issue at the level appropriate to the question being asked by the child. In a traumatic death, you can reassure a child by saying, "Yes, this is very frightening. These things are rare, and it's unlikely that this will happen again or that it will happen to you. It was a terrible experience and it makes you feel sad. But people must go on living." If your son's symptoms persist or multiply, or if your son's functioning at school or with peers becomes compromised, a consultation may be in order.

Having a Reaction to Father's Death

My husband suddenly died six months ago. My six-year-old son seemed to withdraw at the time. Now, six months later, he's become angry and pushy at school, and I'm concerned that he's having a bad reaction to his father's death. What can I expect in the future?

DR. ROSS: Six years of age is a traumatic age for a young boy to lose his father. At this age, your son had conflicting feelings toward his father, since he was going through the Oedipal phase of development. On one hand, he loved his father dearly, wanting to identify with him, to grow up to be like him, and learn from him what it's like to be a man. On the other hand, a six-year-old boy has hostile and competitive feelings toward his father, wanting to be "rid" of him and take whatever belongs to father. Thus, the death of his father is, at the same time, a terrible loss and an imagined triumph for a six-year-old boy. This unusual circumstance is unlike a grandparent's death or the death of a relative such as an aunt or an uncle. The loss of a boy's father when the child is six years old is developmentally traumatic, and can be very fertile soil for conflict, which may become evident in your son's behavior at school and elsewhere.

We live in an era of expertise, where parents often turn to people who are credentialed. Parents look to experts to guide them in certain matters in which a parent may have a great deal of intuitive knowledge. In fact, parents are sometimes more effective at gauging a child's feelings and conflicts than all the experts in the world. This is partly because of the intimate bonding between parent and child, and results also from the profound empathy that a parent has for his or her own child. A sensitive parent can do a great deal for a child without necessarily seeking professional help.

In this unusual situation, however, it seems that your son could benefit from a consultation with an expert. If you yourself have questions or feel overwhelmed, or don't quite understand your son's behavior, you can seek out professional help as an additional resource in trying to help your child.

Another point should be made here: we sometimes seem to assume that parents have no conflicts, needs, and longings of their own. Remember, when a child's father has died, the dead man's wife has lost her husband. She has deep feelings and reacts to this event in her own way. Death is a family matter, and mourning is a shared experience. A parent and child can be brought together through the tragedy of a death such as this one. Despite all the sorrow, death can eventually become a source of communication between parent and child.

A Suicide

My husband recently committed suicide. How do I handle this with my nine-year-old son?

Dr. Ross: Suicide is a very complex issue. Your dealings with your child depend on the circumstances of your husband's death, and on how much your child actually knows about these circumstances. You should not overburden the child with too many details, yet you do not want to mystify him. If it is obvious that your husband committed suicide, you must convey to your son that parents can sometimes become emotionally sick and can be burdened by feelings they cannot control.

It is helpful to communicate to your son the very valid thought that when a person kills himself, the people closest to him may sometimes blame themselves, even though they did not cause the suicide. In this exquisitely terrible circumstance, a child may, in fantasy, blame himself for the parent's death. This could easily happen if the child and the deceased parent argued at any time prior to the parent's death. You must clarify to your son that your husband did not commit suicide because of anything that your child may imagine he did.

Be alert to your son's rage: rage toward the parent who abandoned the child by deciding not to continue living. A death such as this can evoke enormous rage in a child, much more than does a natural or accidental death. Your child may try to deny this tragic death by suicide, believing instead that his father died a natural death. If that is the case, then you must respect your son's defense, because we sometimes need our illusions. The blow may simply be too much for your child to bear at this time, and he may have to wait until he's older before he integrates and finally accepts his father's action in bringing about his own death.

One other issue is crucial: you must acknowledge your own intense feelings of anger, sadness, and loss. Try to help your child understand that you, too, are in the midst of reacting to your husband's death and that you are not now feeling as though you are your usual self. Try to reassure your child that you will *both* go through these difficult times together. After all, death is a family affair.

Chapter 9: The Gifted Child

Your child walked at ten months and was talking by one year of age. When he was eighteen months old, he had an amazing vocabulary. As a toddler, his memory was astounding and he could recall everything: people, places, things, and events. They seemed indelibly etched in his memory.

Now, at four years of age, he's interested in everything: cars, baseball, numbers, drawing, books (he already reads), and he has an enormous attention span for so young a child. You've begun wondering just how smart he really is, thinking to yourself that he may be gifted. But just what does "gifted" mean? Is it the same as "genius," or does it merely mean your child is very bright?

"Gifted" does not mean genius, although some geniuses are indeed gifted. Only one child in thirty thousand is considered a genius (IQ of 160 or above) but as many as 3 percent of children may be gifted.

According to the U.S. Office of Education, gifted and talented children are capable of high performance in any of five areas: general intellectual ability, specific academic aptitude (for instance, outstanding ability in writing, or using language or mathematics), creative or productive thinking, leadership ability, or talent in the visual and performing arts.

Most gifted children have IQs of 130 or above, but IQ is only one (and an incomplete) way of identifying the gifted child. Most educators and mental-health professionals hear about gifted children in a variety of everyday descriptions given by parents and others:

"He taught himself how to do multiplication in the first grade."

"She could draw things incredibly well—even using perspective as though she'd taken art lessons—before she was five years old."

"She could hear a tune once, and then play it on the piano."

"I recited a long poem to him, and he was able to recite it back the next day, without a mistake."

Parents who suspect that their child may be gifted should look for certain signs, some appearing before two years of age. They include:

- Walking and talking at an early age.
- Highly developed verbal skills. A gifted child may use complete sentences, have an advanced vocabulary, and may learn to read before entering school.
- Persistent curiosity. A gifted child often asks challenging, provocative, and imaginative questions.
- The ability to retain information. The gifted child usually has an excellent memory, easily recalling past experiences very accurately.
- An unusually long attention span as compared to other children the same age.
- A wide variety of interests, some dominating at one time and receding at another period of time.
- A vivid imagination along with a tendency to fantasize. The gifted child may read more into a situation than is actually occurring.

Few children actually exhibit all these signs, but most gifted children show more than one of them. Parents often suspect very early in a child's life that he or she is gifted. Most parents seem to recognize the signs of giftedness during the first two years of a child's life, but giftedness often goes unrecognized (or doesn't fully blossom) until the child is well into the school years.

Some parents, suspecting giftedness, have a child tested very early in life. There is no harm in this, but bear in mind that IQ tests are only one measure of giftedness. It's also important to remember that such tests have a great deal of variability and are not necessarily valid when administered to a child younger than four years of age.

A gifted child often has special needs and problems. As the parents of a gifted child, you play a central role in guiding your child's efforts, whether at school, at home, or with peers. Your knowledge about giftedness and your understanding can help your child make the most of his or her gifts.

Our consultant for this topic is Aaron H. Esman, M.D. Dr. Esman is a Professor of Clinical Psychiatry at Cornell University Medical College and is Director of Adolescent Services at the Payne Whitney Clinic of The New York Hospital.

Doesn't Feel Challenged

Our seven-year-old daughter has an IQ of 145. She's a fine student but doesn't feel challenged by her schoolwork. How can we make sure that school remains an exciting and rewarding experience for her?

DR. ESMAN: Providing a gifted child with a rewarding school curriculum can be a challenge for both the school and the parents. It may require a cooperative effort.

Your daughter's curriculum will depend on the extent to which the school is able or willing to modify its program for your daughter in order to meet her capacities and interests. You should consult with the responsible people at school, including the principal, guidance personnel, and the teacher. In discussing this problem, point out that your child needs a more stimulating and challenging program. They might be able to provide such a curriculum by modifying her class assignments, or by introducing additional or novel elements into her program to engage and challenge her intellect. If the school cooperates, things can work very well.

If the school cannot modify its program, you may have to find another school setting, one pitched at a higher level and experienced in dealing with gifted kids. Such a school could offer a more stimulating and energizing curriculum for your daughter.

In addition to any school program, consider supplementing your daughter's program with other activities. Foreign language courses, creative arts experiences, special summer camps, and other activities can be pursued outside the school program and can provide your child with greater stimulation and more challenging learning experiences than her present school situation. These can all help in meeting the special needs of a gifted child.

Hops from One Thing to Another

Our six-year-old son could read by age four and has been labeled "gifted" by his teachers. Yet he seems disorganized. He often reads through two or three books at one time, and doesn't focus his energies. He hops from one project to another. Should we be concerned?

DR. ESMAN: An extraordinary range of interests is not unusual for gifted children. If, in hopping from one project to another, your son derives satisfaction from what he's doing, and is absorbed by each project, there is no need to be concerned about it, at his age. If he were doing this sort of thing at fifteen, you might have cause to worry. One would expect an older child or adolescent to focus his energies more consistently, but a six-year-old child is beginning to learn what the world is about. His hopping from one thing to another indicates his fascination with the many things impinging on his world. He is completely caught up in it.

You might try to promote his engagement in a particular area by encouraging him to read further in one subject, or perhaps guide him into collecting things. He might become interested in a collection that could focus his interest in one area.

But this is not at all uncommon in a very gifted six-year-old. In fact, one of the indications of giftedness is such an extraordinary ability to hop from one thing to another. Your son is excited by, and receptive to, the many stimuli he encounters. This is an excellent sign of his intellectual curiosity and his intelligence.

Won't Develop Her Talent

My daughter has been called a gifted dancer, but she doesn't seem motivated to use this talent. This has become an issue at home. What can we do?

DR. ESMAN: A gifted child is not obligated to pursue an interest in the area of her giftedness, and such lack of motivation should not become an issue with parents. Your concern about this matter seems to reflect your own interests, aspirations, and expectations for your child, but may not be what truly engages her. If she is gifted, her "gifts" will doubtless express themselves in some other area that may be more to her taste. It's best not to thrust upon a child a sphere of interest or activity that doesn't emerge from her own tastes or motivations.

We occasionally see parents with unfulfilled aspirations of their own who belatedly try to live out those aspirations through their children. They sometimes push a youngster into activities that are more gratifying for the parent than for the child. This rarely works to the child's advantage.

Avoids Responsibility

Our nine-year-old is quite gifted. I expect him to have certain responsibilities around the house, such as taking out the trash, but he's always reading or involved in some special project at school. I'm concerned that he's using his intellectual gifts as an escape hatch to avoid responsibility and sharing things with other people. Should I be concerned?

DR. ESMAN: No matter how gifted a child may be, he must live in the real world. Parents' expectations for the ways in which the family operates together should apply to a gifted child as well as to an ungifted one. Though I'm not sure you should be overly concerned, you have every right to expect your child to participate in family life, as do other family members. If you expect your son to shoulder certain responsibilities, you should pursue this expectation. While promoting your son's interests along the intellectual lines to which his giftedness applies, you should encourage him to carry out all reasonable responsibilities.

While he may or may not be using his intellectual ability as an "escape hatch," he certainly must find his books more interesting than carrying out the trash. That's understandable, but his interests and intellectual potential should not take precedence over relationships with other people and with family. After all, while his intellectual pursuits are important, equally vital areas of life should not be ignored.

Could Do Better

Our ten-year-old daughter is intellectually gifted, but her motivation doesn't seem to match her intellect. She brings home A-minuses instead of A's. My husband always tells her that she could "do better," and I'm a little worried she's getting the message that she could be better, that he's chipping away at her feelings about herself. Is this possible?

DR. ESMAN: A gifted child may occasionally fail to live up to a parent's inflated expectations. This can set the stage for a child's actually feeling somewhat victimized by his or her own gifts. If a child is frequently told that she should bring home A's instead of A-minuses, and if a consistently fine performance is met with disapproval, she may eventually feel that she is failing herself and failing to live up to parental expectations. As a result, she could come to regard her very high performance level as inadequate and begin feeling that she herself is inadequate because she's not doing as well as expected. Her feelings about herself could eventually be eroded. I would be less concerned about your gifted child's bringing home A-minuses than about the possible effects of repeatedly being told that she's not living up to expectations. I would encourage your husband to praise her for the A-minus rather than criticizing her for not bringing home A's.

The parents of a child who has been labeled "gifted" may expect the child to perform in superhuman ways. Some parents attempt to live out their own frustrated wishes through a child; a parent who has underachieved may seek to have the child perform at spectacular levels to achieve vicariously what the parent never achieved. This is rarely a good development. Parents should be realistic in their expectations and not demand that a child compensate their own thwarted dreams and wishes.

Parents should not ask more of a child than is reasonable or within the child's capacity. In other words, don't measure a foot with a thirteen-inch ruler.

Wants to Be with Friends

Our son is gifted in math but doesn't want to attend a special school. He'd rather stay with his friends. What can or should we do?

DR. ESMAN: Gifted children may have difficulties finding age-appropriate friends; a gifted child who feels comfortable with certain peers may be considered quite lucky. I would not consider your son's wanting to stay with his friends to be a problem. If he is mathematically gifted and cannot get the intellectual challenge he requires, it may be possible to supplement the school program by offering him tutoring or instruction in some other setting. This could allow his intellectual curiosity and gift to be promoted, while he remains at school with friends or with familiar kids.

It's not unusual for a child to want to remain with his friends or to be reluctant to enter an entirely new peer group. Assuming that his present school is satisfactory, explore the possibility of extracurricular stimulation and special instruction in math. That would be wiser than imposing on a child a change for which he may not be ready.

An Enriched Environment

I've been told that our gifted son could benefit from an enriched learning environment to maximize his gifts. But providing maximal learning opportunities puts a burden on his teacher, and I'm not sure that he should be treated as though he's "different." Am I right or wrong?

DR. ESMAN: Providing maximum learning opportunities for a gifted child can bring a number of challenging issues to the surface. An enriched environment can be provided without necessarily disrupting a child's life or having him labeled "different." If your son's present school is unable to challenge him to a sufficient extent, then an enriched environment might be appropriate. If, however, he is satisfied by the current school curriculum, it may be unnecessary to make any major changes.

When encouraged and supported, a very bright child can do a great deal of independent learning; he can read books outside of school and can pick up many things from various sources, including the communications media and other avenues. He may very well fulfill his intellectual promise, even in a conventional school setting. Without knowing more about your child's interests, needs, and talents, it's difficult to answer this question completely.

In principle, one wants to provide every child with a program conducive to the maximal use of his or her capacities. If a stimulating, enriched school program is available in the community, you might want to make use of it. However, I would not recommend disrupting a child's life and stamping him as "exceptional" if he can make use of the currently available resources.

Is Labeled an "Oddball"

Our son is exceptionally brilliant in mathematics. He's viewed as a bit of an "oddball" by the other kids at school and hasn't been able to find suitable friends. We're concerned. What can we do?

DR. ESMAN: Many very gifted children have a difficult time socially. In a real way, an exceptionally brilliant child *is* different. Gifted children's ways of thinking can be different than those of other kids. They may not share their interests with less gifted children. Their ways of perceiving things are different from those of regular kids, and less gifted kids may view the exceptional child as an "oddball."

A possible solution is to find other kids who are similarly gifted, which means placing your child in a special school if he can't become engaged in a conventional peer group. Special classes or schools pitched at a higher level than the local public school may be a very good answer to the problem of socialization for the exceptional child. This provides such a child with an alternative peer group. Or a special peer group setting can be found in an after-school situation or a recreational program that meets with a brilliant child's particular interest. But the fact is that many especially gifted children find it difficult to socialize throughout elementary and secondary school.

When they arrive at college, gifted kids frequently find peers who share their interests and their styles of thinking. At that time, they can more easily enter into a suitable peer group and have good peer relationships. There is no facile answer to this issue.

Gifted in One Area Only

Our son is brilliant in science. However, his reading and verbal skills are poor. We're a bit concerned by this and don't really understand it. Please advise us.

DR. ESMAN: There are various domains or areas of intelligence and of intellectual possibilities. A child may be gifted in one sphere of the mind and yet be perfectly ordinary in others. It's not unusual for a child to have extraordinary mathematical talents but to be a conventional reader or have ordinary language skills. There are also children with exceptional music talent who in the more conventional, intellectual areas are quite ordinary.

A child should not be expected to achieve in every area what he can accomplish in the sphere of his greatest gift. A parent's expectations should be in tune with the child's capabilities, and a parent should not feel disappointed because a child's gift is limited to one or two areas.

Chapter 10: The Only Child

The only child is both privileged and disadvantaged. Only children tend to take charge easily, to advance their own interests, and to expect rewards for their efforts. Often successful, they may not even be aware of their competitors. But many only children must spend long hours alone, and some experts feel that unless parents make special efforts to provide opportunities for friendships with other children, the only child misses out on the give-and-take of having siblings.

Some parents worry that by having only one child, they may lavish too much attention on a youngster, that an only child may somehow feel "special" and never truly learn to share with others. While there are no simple answers to these questions or concerns, it seems that the only child may occasionally have certain particular difficulties.

Our consultant for this topic is Cynthia P. Pfeffer, M.D. Dr. Pfeffer is an Associate Professor of Clinical Psychiatry at Cornell University Medical College and is the Director of Child Inpatient Services at the Westchester Division of The New York Hospital.

Asks for a Brother

Our five-year-old son, an only child, occasionally asks for a younger brother. We don't plan on having any more children. How can we deal with our child's concerns?

DR. PFEFFER: Your child seems to be asking for company, which is understandable. A child of this age is beginning to have relationships with other children in nursery school or kindergarten. This can stimulate your son's concern about who else could or should be in the family, and what it would be like to share family resources with a sibling. Your son must be aware that most other children his age have brothers and sisters, and he could very well want one as well.

At five years of age, your son is at the height of his Oedipal period and may indirectly be asking about babies and where they come from. At this time, he would naturally be curious about how his parents spend their private time in the bedroom.

There are many complex issues at work in this question, and it's difficult to provide one all-inclusive answer about what may be occupying your child's mind. In general, when a child poses such a question to a parent, it has something to do with concerns about the body, about sexuality, and about birth. To best answer such questions, parents must know how they feel about such issues, which is not always easy. Your child is posing an intriguing and challenging question, but not one that should make you feel defensive.

Talk is a very valuable commodity with children. It's best to talk at your child's level, and not divulge all your thoughts and feelings about having another baby. I would encourage him to talk about this, asking how long it has been on his mind. I would ask how he would feel about having a baby brother or sister, what he would like or dislike about it, and would encourage him to talk about any worries he may have.

It is best to leave this an open issue with the child; there is no need to answer the question in one fell swoop, or close the issue with a single answer. This question does not necessarily require a direct yes-or-no answer. Remember, we never know what will happen at some time in the future, and you may yet have another child. Your child's curiosity about babies and siblings is quite healthy. You and your child should be able to explore these issues over a period of time.

Spends Time with Adults

Our seven-year-old daughter is our only child. She spends a great deal of time in the company of adults and seems not to relate too well to children her own age. What can we do?

DR. PFEFFER: Parents of an only child may grow quite concerned by this issue. Children should have plenty of interaction with adults because it gives them models to emulate, and it helps them develop a sense of security about someone being available to care for them. During the school-age years, a child will naturally look to adults when she has questions or concerns.

It's also very important for a child to have involvements with peers. While the younger child is only capable of parallel play, a seven-year-old child can have far more meaningful interactions with children her own age. Spending much of each day in school, a seven-year-old is often away from parents and must develop ongoing relationships with peers. Having friends and peers is important, and a parent may occasionally have to orchestrate certain peer relationships for a child. This can sometimes be difficult with an only child, but we occasionally see such problems in the child with siblings who spends a great deal of time with the siblings and rarely relates to peers. This can be a disadvantage because it tends to create a very circumscribed view of the world.

An only child may be more vulnerable to being alone and may not easily venture forth for peer relationships. This can have a great deal to do with the youngster's personality, with how much or how little parents encourage other attachments, and with the presence or absence of siblings.

I think this is a universal issue; it is not strictly limited to the only child. As a parent, it's important to try to motivate your child to have peer involvements. It's best for a child to avoid restricting herself to the home setting and to not be limited to the company of adults. This is why birthday parties can be so valuable. A birthday party marks time and also helps concretize a child's peer relationships. This may partly account for today's parents placing so much importance on birthday parties for their children. It can be an extremely important means of socialization for children, especially in some urban settings where children are not readily available to each other.

A variety of activities provide opportunities for socializing with other children. They include scouts, after-school activities, religious groups, community centers, and courses and programs geared for children. No doubt, this can be carried to the extreme and a child can be overprogrammed and overexposed to activities. A balance between social activities and home activities must be reached.

The only child may occasionally feel unique or very special and can become quite possessive of family relationships. Therefore, it's very important for the parent of an only child to help the child develop a sense of being outwardly directed so that energies can be routed away from the family. Again, this does not mean that the child should be in constant motion or overly exposed to social programs and settings. But it is in any child's best interests for parents to help the youngster relate to people, both adults and children, outside the home.

Getting Spoiled

Our six-year-old son is our only child. Both sets of grandparents lavish attention on him, and we're worried that he'll be spoiled by being the only one. How can we change this?

DR. PFEFFER: My sense is that no child can be spoiled by too much attention. Attention and praise foster a child's self-esteem. A problem can arise when attention is given without a true sense of feeling, or when commodities become the main interaction with the child, rather than affection. When that happens, a child is not being spoiled so much as being deprived—deprived of the emotional component of the interchange. This can be a problem in child-rearing and may appear more pronounced for an only child because such a child is the sole object of focus.

Every family has its own pattern of relating to children, and each child within any family is unique. We rarely see two siblings treated in the very same way. An only child may be the only one onto whom parents project their feelings, and there can be a great deal of exclusive parental interaction with an only child, but that doesn't mean the child is being spoiled. The manner in which attention is given can be a spoiling influence. Promiscuous and meaningless gifts or commodities can spoil a child, not too much attention or affection.

Learning to Share

Our four-year-old is an only child. We're concerned that she won't learn to share or get along with others. Is this true?

DR. PFEFFER: The only child is the only one on whom parents can project their feelings, both positive and more complicated ones. Parents usually have a more intense relationship with an only child than they have with two or more children, and this can make for some difficulties in sharing or in learning to deal effectively with others. The only child may be more vulnerable to having a slightly skewed approach to relationships with other people. When a second child enters the family, some of this intensity lessens.

This doesn't have to become a problem. Today, the media provide many opportunities for a child to share and to interact with other children. When a child watches certain education-oriented television programs, peers are brought into the living room, even though the child may be alone. Many children's programs encourage viewer participation, and in a vicarious sense the child must interact and share with others.

Today, children attend preschool at a very early age. This enables the only child to develop an early awareness of other children and helps the child learn how to share with and relate to others. Teachers usually notice a child who is very possessive or who cannot share or relate well; they will usually bring this to parents' attention.

Some children—not just only children—may strike people as though they have a sense of "entitlement," as though they are the proverbial princess or prince. They may push peers aside and seem not to realize that there is the need to share. Such a child may indeed be selfish and quite self-centered, but we see this in children other than the only child.

The only child may have to fantasize or imagine what it's like to have a sibling. He or she may have to imagine what it's like to be challenged by the need to share, or by the possibility of having to compete for the parents' attention. In this sense, the only child may be considered at a slight disadvantage since he has to work at imagining the give-and-take that is ordinarily a part of sibling relationships.

Much of how a child relates to others is based on his view of his parents. A parent can help a child learn to share by being a good model of sharing. As a parent, you can also bring other children into your home, exposing your child to the give-and-take he might otherwise miss. If a parent never encourages the presence of other children in the home and does not attempt to foster a willingness to share with the child's peers, then the youngster can indeed become the only one. He or she may be the only child ever present in the home, and may have difficulty learning to share or compete or deal with other children. By emphasizing sharing and by encouraging contact with other children, parents can help an only child learn to share and relate well to others.

Great Expectations

We're the parents of an eight-year-old daughter. She's our only child. My husband wants her to become a doctor, and I'm worried that he has too many expectations and makes too many demands of her. Please advise me.

DR. PFEFFER: For every parent, having a child is something like having a blank canvas on which the parent can paint his or her own picture. Each parent may try to write his own story or spin out his own fantasy through the child. However, children are very resilient and usually challenge these parental expectations. It's quite rare for a child to conform to a parent's wishes, expectations, and fantasies. Up to a point, it is desirable for a parent to have certain expectations of a child; this promotes socialization and familiarizes her with certain cultural roles and expectations. It also presents a child with a model that can be very helpful in identity formation.

Whether parents have one child or several children, they must eventually come to grips with their expectations as compared to the child's goals, wishes, and limitations. Every parent wishes to have some feeling of lineage, even a sense of immortality, and this is often accomplished (in reality and in fantasy) through children. Your husband must attempt to become more flexible in his expectations; all concerned will be better served if he can accept your daughter's identity and her own wishes for herself and her future. A parent who cannot relinquish his own inflexible expectations or fantasies about a child will eventually become frustrated, disappointed, and unhappy with his child's accomplishments. This in turn can profoundly affect the child. You and your husband should discuss his demands and expectations. Hopefully, he can learn to become more flexible.

Parent Fights Son's Battles

We're in our early forties and have an only child, a five-year-old son. My husband is very protective of him, even fighting battles for the boy. My concern is that this overprotective attitude will stifle our child's independence and sense of himself.

DR. PFEFFER: This is a common question concerning both the only child and the child with siblings. In a family with more than one child, such overprotectiveness may focus on one particular child. An only child can become a parent's primary focus because, simply put, there is no other child available for such attention. In addition, an only child may seem to be a parent's one chance at immortality. This is more a quality of a certain kind of parent than it is of the only child. Certainly, an only child may be perceived as somewhat special; but so is a firstborn, middle, or youngest child. Each child is special in a *particular* way, and each will have certain characteristics and will have to deal with certain issues based upon his or her position in the family. An only child may be viewed as special and may be more likely to be overprotected. This can be especially true if parents have unsuccessfully tried to have a child for some time. When one finally arrives, he may be viewed with a particularly intense sense of specialness.

Such a parent can have a very potent effect on an only child. The child can become especially sheltered and even become constricted in his ability to deal effectively with others. It would be best if you could help your husband understand that part of your son's life must involve healthy competition, and even an occasional battle for his own rights. If you cannot convince your husband to take a more flexible and less suffocating approach toward your child, a discussion with a child psychiatrist may prove helpful.

Child Upset by Miscarriage

We have a seven-year-old son. We tried having another child, but on one occasion I had a miscarriage, and another time I gave birth to a stillborn child. Our son seems upset and preoccupied by this. Please advise us.

DR. PFEFFER: A miscarriage can raise profound issues between parents and children. When an aborted pregnancy or stillbirth occurs, a child has a distinct sense that something is wrong in the family. Aside from any concern about the birth of a sibling, your child is aware that there have been losses. It is important to consider how much of this your seven-year-old is able to understand and to be aware of how easily a child can distort reality. If you are upset or depressed, your son could develop the idea that *he* is responsible for the loss of the expected baby. This can be especially compelling for the only child, who has no siblings with whom he can share these thoughts and feelings.

When there has been a stillbirth, family members have gone through the experience of the pregnancy, having anticipated your returning from the hospital with a baby. The loss is far more obvious, and the child must deal with having been told about a sibling who, in fact, never arrives. You can expect that a seven-year-old child will evolve some theory or explanation for this, one that partly holds himself to blame for what happened.

It's very important for you and your husband to heal yourselves. You must talk with each other, arriving at some understanding of all this. You may be forced to accept the reality of not being able to have another child. Here it would be helpful to discuss as much as possible with your obstetrician so you have a realistic idea of your future options for having another baby.

As parents, you and your husband must separate yourselves from your own needs, and address your son's concerns. You must speak with your child. In the case of a miscarriage that never went to a full pregnancy, there was less external evidence of the pregnancy; your child does not have the concrete validation or external evidence of what happened. If your child did not know you were expecting, and there was no evidence of the pregnancy, there is no need to inform him of the miscarriage. However, in the case of the stillborn child, you cannot and should not try to hide the obvious reality of what has happened.

In talking with your child, it is best to explain that you wanted a brother or sister for him but that you could not carry the baby in your womb. Be aware of any evidence that your son is blaming himself for what happened and make certain to explain that such things are no one's fault.

Wants a Sibling for Daughter

We had our first child when I was thirty-eight. I'm content with an only child, and now that I'm forty, I don't want to try again. My husband feels that it's not fair to our daughter for us not to have another child. Please advise.

DR. PFEFFER: This is a common concern. Parents often want companions for their children. This can be especially true if a parent comes from a family with many children; this parent may wish to have many children, too. If you feel unsure or ambivalent about having another child, it would be wise to discuss these doubts; after all, you will be the primary caretaker—at least at first—and a mother's feelings about pregnancy and a new child are crucial for the growth and emotional development of any child.

Feelings about the number of children a parent prefers have a great deal to do with the parent's wishes, concerns, fantasies, and her own past development. If a mother is extremely adamant and would be upset by having another child, caution should be exercised when considering this issue. If the arrival of a new baby will create only minor tensions, they can probably be worked out between the parents. There is no need to feel that you are "depriving" your daughter by choosing not to have another child. Many opportunities exist for your daughter to have companionship and a healthy give-and-take with others, if you promote and encourage these opportunities. The number of children you wish to have is an important life-style choice and must be made with a genuine consideration of all the people and factors involved in such a choice.

An Overview

DR. PFEFFER: The only child is a special child, but no more so than one of many children in another family. Every child in a family needs to be considered "special," and in that sense "only," because every child is truly unique. It's delightful to have one child, and delightful to have more than one. If parents can be emotionally available and supportive of a child, if they can have empathy for a child's needs, then the child-rearing experience will be wonderful, no matter how many children are in the family.

If parents feel that having one child is sufficient and they feel comfortable about this choice, the only child will do wonderfully well. In the future, we will probably see more and more families with one child; this arrangement will no longer be considered unusual or something that requires special consideration or concern.

Chapter 11: The Adopted Child

The parents of an adopted child must deal with many issues. If they have not been able to have a child of their own, they must come to terms with that fact. Once they have decided to adopt, they must then deal with the rigors of the adoption process, which can be very trying.

The greatest hurdle that parents must face is how and when to tell the child that she was adopted. Some parents, when revealing this emotionally charged fact to their child, say, "Other parents had to accept the child born to them, but we *chose you.*" In hoping to counter any possible feelings of being inferior or unwanted, these parents place an unfair burden on their child by making her feel "special" or chosen above all others, which in fact, is not true. What *should* be communicated to an adopted child is that the parents very much wanted a child and that they chose to adopt. This conveys that the child was wanted, while not burdening her with the fantasy of being somehow "special" or "chosen" in preference to others.

It doesn't take very long for a youngster to figure out that to have been chosen, she first had to be *given up* by someone else. To spare a child the trouble of having to deal with this unsettling knowledge, some adoptive parents have handled the issue of revelation by keeping it a secret, living in fear that someday the truth would emerge. Indeed, it usually does, and many an adopted child learns about being adopted from a friend or relative, sometimes after the adoptive parents have died. Others tell of having learned they were adopted when, as children, they accidentally came upon adoption documents while rummaging through a forbidden drawer or closet.

Over the past few years, candor has been the rule, and parents usually tell children about their adoption while the child is still a toddler or during the preschool years. Most experts feel there *is* a time to tell a child that he or she is adopted, and they agree that this information will be distressing to any child. But distress is a normal life experience, especially when dealing with an issue as important as one's origins.

Distress must be distinguished from trauma, which is not a normal experience, and there are ways to reveal the adoption without traumatizing a child.

No matter how a child is told about being adopted, he or she must master this information, and the family must deal with it for the rest of its life together. The following questions deal with issues frequently raised by parents who have adopted or who have seriously thought of adopting a child.

Our consultant for this topic is Paulina F. Kernberg, M.D. Dr. Kernberg is an Associate Professor of Psychiatry at Cornell University Medical College and is the Director of Child Psychiatry at the Westchester Division of The New York Hospital.

When to Tell

When should I tell my child she was adopted?

DR. KERNBERG: When to tell a child he or she is adopted is a major issue for parents and for the child. Some people think that a child should never know, while others feel that a child should know as early as one year of age. Such controversies don't help parents determine when to tell the child. This question must be answered in terms of two determinants: when the parents feel comfortable enough to do so, and when the child is able to understand this information without feeling threatened or frightened.

The first step toward feeling comfortable involves the parents, either by themselves or with the help of a professional, coming to grips with the psychological impact of their decision to adopt. They must become aware of their very mixed and complicated feelings about adopting a child. They may desperately wish to adopt and may deeply love an adopted child, but such a child is a reminder that they did not have one of their own. In a sense, parents who adopt, though dealing with positive and loving feelings, must also grieve for the fact that they did not or could not have a child of their own.

In other words, the parents have to work at psychologically adopting the child. There are two facets of adoption: one is the legal adoption, while the other is the emotional adoption. The emotional adoption occurs after the legal process, something like the sound of thunder occurring after lightning. It is a two-way street: parents adopt the child emotionally, and the child adopts the parents emotionally.

The second determinant of when to tell involves the child's being able to understand the adoption process and not be frightened by it. This occurs when a child is four to five years old. While some experts suggest that a child be told as early as possible, even mentioning it before the age of one year, this is more in the service of helping the parent *practice* at telling the child than of actually conveying information.

One cannot hide adoption from a child because children have a way of sensing a secret. It's impossible truly to keep such a family secret. Secrecy erodes the parent-child relationship, because, once sensing it, a child develops a feeling of being excluded. One of the worst things that can happen is for a child to learn from others that he or she is adopted.

One must also consider the time dimension when telling a child about adoption. A child has a different level of understanding at each developmental phase throughout life. For instance, it's one thing to tell a four-year-old about college and another to discuss college with a twelve-year-old. Keeping this in mind, one must realize that telling your child about adoption is really an evolving process more than providing information at one point in time.

Any parent telling a child about adoption must be prepared for repeated questions about this issue over a period of years. Some parents unrealistically believe that it will suffice to tell a child once, that the knowledge will "sink in" to the child's awareness, and then the child "knows." Such complex, important, and emotionally charged information cannot be retained and fully understood by the child in one fell swoop. Rather, this information must be conveyed as part of an ongoing process. The child will understand different implications of the knowledge throughout his or her emotional development.

How to Tell

Our child is adopted, and we're planning to tell her soon. How should we tell her?

DR. KERNBERG: Another important issue is how to tell a child she was adopted. A fine way of telling is simply to present the situation as one in which mother very much wanted to have a baby; because she could not carry the baby herself, another woman carried it.

Parents who anticipate telling a child about adoption are best off practicing how to comfortably communicate this information. There are many ways of approaching this: some parents choose to discuss this with a counselor to understand more clearly what feelings this situation

288 The Growing Years

evokes within them. Above all, adoptive parents should know that they can tell their child about being adopted in a way that promotes closeness rather than distance.

Where Babies Come From

Our son is four years old. We adopted him when he was one month old and have yet to tell him. He's now beginning to ask where babies come from. Is this a good time to begin telling him about being adopted?

DR. KERNBERG: A child's concern about the origins of babies can present a possible window for telling the child about adoption. A mother can say, "Babies come from mommy's tummy, and some ladies cannot carry the baby. Therefore they have another lady who carries the baby for them, and then the baby goes to the real mother." Certainly, when your child poses the inevitable questions about birth and mother's body, an excellent opportunity is provided for beginning the process of communicating this vital information to your child.

Is Mother Too Sensitive?

I'm the mother of an adopted three-year-old. I resent the idea of calling my daughter's biological mother her "real" or "natural" mother. Am I being too sensitive? Is there a better term for these relationships?

DR. KERNBERG: There is no doubt that the physiological mother is the "real" mother of the child. The *psychological mother*, however, is the *adoptive* mother. This concern may arise when adoptive parents idealize and overvalue the blood tie between the biological mother and the child. Anyone belonging to a family knows that while we have blood ties, they do not necessarily denote good relationships.

Parents of an adopted child may find this a difficult issue. Indeed, the process of adoption is a psychologically difficult one because it may involve the feeling of having "stolen" a baby, or of having "cheated" nature. There may be a great deal of guilt involved in adoption, although in my opinion, adoptive parents have their rightful place in heaven. Most experts concur that if a child's natural parents cannot care for him, the best thing that could happen is for the child to be adopted by people who truly want a child.

There is no doubt that the person who *takes care* of the child is the child's psychological parent. The term "biological mother" is technically correct, but the true mother and the emotional mother of a child is the psychological mother, the person who is actually the caretaker.

Didn't Come from Mommy's Womb

Our five-year-old daughter is adopted. We've told her about babies and that she didn't grow inside my womb. This seems to upset her. How can I help her deal with this?

DR. KERNBERG: This question relates to how best to tell a child that she is adopted. Your child seems to feel that "You didn't come from my womb" constitutes a rejection. Your child is asking, "Why couldn't I have come from your womb?" or "Why didn't you carry me in your womb?" It is perfectly appropriate to respond to this question by saying, "I would have loved to carry you, but my womb was not made in the right way, and I could not carry a baby until it was ready to be born. I had to have another lady carry you until you were ready to be born."

The quality of that communication is loving and is genuinely sensitive to a child's needs. This can be difficult for a mother to say because it involves her acknowledging what may be an unpleasant reality: that she did not or could not bear a child of her own. The general message to your child should be: "I very much wanted to carry you, but I couldn't. I wanted a child very much, so I did it this way. I did it the best way I could."

Doesn't Look Like Her Parents

Our adopted seven-year-old doesn't look like either one of us. She knows she's adopted, but I find it distressing when strangers ask her where she got her blond hair from. How can we handle this?

DR. KERNBERG: When dealing with adoption, as with many other issues in life, one should not try to deny the obvious. Your daughter knows that she's adopted and is asked about her obvious physical characteristics by strangers. She must be her own advocate in this matter. She must say, "I am adopted, and while I don't know my parents, they may have blond hair." This issue must be addressed at face value.

Appearing like one's parents is not the crucial issue. Adoptive parents often underestimate the fact that their child grows to be very much like them because the child takes on many attributes of their personalities. The child undergoes a profound identification with the adoptive parents. An adopted child may actually say, "I'm not blond like mommy, but I like to cook like mommy," or "I like the color red, just like mommy does." The boy may say, "I like to play soccer like my daddy," or "I walk just like daddy." There are literally thousands of ways in which a child identifies with his or her parents, whether they are biological or adoptive parents.

When I deal with adoptive parents and their child, I make it a practice of pointing out identifications and similarities between the parents and child. I stress the positive and important meanings of these likenesses. These identifications and similarities indicate a successful emotional adoption. While we can never underestimate the power of genetics, we must not undervalue the crucial importance of the family setting in a child's emotional development. The family setting is a powerful determinant of a person's thinking, feeling, and behavior throughout life.

Wants to Find "Real" Parents

Our daughter is twelve years old. We adopted her when she was seven months old, and she's long known that we aren't her biological parents. We thought these issues had been ironed out, but she's developed an intense interest in locating her "real" parents. What is all this, and how should we handle it?

DR. KERNBERG: Many adoptive children do search for their biological parents, and the outcome of these encounters is often very mixed. I've seen cases where a child locates one or both parents and is struck by the thunderous realization that the parents want nothing to do with the child. On some occasions, the child and parents may have sporadic contact. In other instances, a child develops relationships with some of the biological relatives but not with the parents themselves. It's very difficult to predict the outcome of such encounters.

It is certainly a child's right to seek out her natural parents, and there is often a deep emotional need to know "Where do I come from?" Adoptive parents may feel that something like a romance occurs between the child and the biological parents, which causes some adoptive parents to worry. However, it is very unlikely that adoptive parents will be psychologically replaced by the biological parents. A child has been with her adoptive parents most of her life, and, in the truest psychological sense, they are the parents. An adoptive parent must realize that the child will always have two sets of parents. That reality cannot be denied.

An adoptive family always lives with the ghost of the biological parents, and their presence, real or imagined, is always a fact. Adoptive parents must accept that and not allow themselves to idealize the biological parents or be fearful that the biological parents could have "done better" than they did or could have "rescued" the child. A child's searching out her biological parents is not a criticism or rejection of the adoptive parents. The quest for these ghostlike figures is really no more than the question so many people understandably ask themselves—"Where do I come from?" A sign of being a good parent would be for you, as an adoptive parent, to facilitate your daughter's quest.

Adopting an Older Child

We will be adopting a ten-year-old girl. Are there any special considerations when adopting an older child?

DR. KERNBERG: There are indeed special considerations when adopting an older child. It would be important to know as much as possible about an older child's past. It's likely that such a child will have been transferred from one foster home to another and may have been in various institutional settings. The child can benefit enormously from an adoption but may also put the adoptive parents to a great test. This can occur because the child may have difficulty believing that she will actually be allowed to stay in your house. In fact, the adoptive parents of an older child have a right to rescind the adoption if they change their minds.

In your case, an initial honeymoon may be followed by a great deal of testing of your intentions and good will. If the child eventually begins to develop feelings that she does belong and will be allowed to stay, the anger and resentment felt toward earlier foster parents may finally surface and be expressed toward you as adoptive parents.

A ten-year-old child may be very tentative in readily expressing warmth, or in feeling truly accepted by any new parents. She may express this by aggression and hostility. In testing the new parents, the child says, "If you really care for me, you'll put up with almost anything and allow me to stay." All the usual issues of adoption are present but are complicated by the child's traumatic history of being transferred from one home to another.

Unfortunately, older adoptive children may have severe behavioral problems involving lying, stealing, and other troubles encountered in emotionally deprived children. Parents who consider adopting an older child must deal with these realities, and it's my feeling that all three of you could probably benefit from counseling with a sensitive professional.

An Interracial Adoption

We're thinking of adopting an Asian baby because we can't easily get an infant. What special issues should we know about before we do this?

DR. KERNBERG: An interracial adoption may involve differences of culture as well as of race. Such an adoption also brings a child into a setting where he looks very different from his adoptive parents.

Some parents may feel more comfortable adopting a child from another race, one who is *clearly* not theirs. In a sense, they can then make a statement that they have rescued the child, and sometimes they *are* rescuing a child. In this way, racial differences can facilitate some of the more complicated elements of the adoption process.

Do not be surprised if, as your child grows older, he or she wishes to find the real parents. The issue of "ghosting" (where the adopted child retains an "image" or fantasy about the biological parents) may become a real one, even for a child from another country. I know a few American families who have traveled with their adopted children to Vietnam, or in one case, to a small village in Brazil, in search of the biological parents. Most children want to know "Where did I come from?" A child's wish to identify with his or her roots and birth culture is very important.

In working with a young adopted boy from Mexico, I was once confronted with this issue. Nothing was known about his natural parents, or even about the village of his origins. Unable to return to Mexico to search for his biological parents, he made what was for him a psychologically important substitution: he kept and cherished certain articles of clothing from Mexico. These items provided enough of an image of his biological parents and of his roots to be meaningful to him.

As the child grows older, he may develop increasing interest in the culture of his birthland. This should not be deterred. The child comes from two cultures, the adoptive *and* the natural culture, and must, in the long run, form a viable synthesis of the two, creating a special blending of his own, in his own way.

Any adopted child's wish to seek out his natural parents can make adoptive parents feel insecure, and even a bit resentful. Adoptive parents often feel that they must prove they are "perfect," or far better than other parents. They may even feel that they are somehow "less" than regular parents. The process of adoption, especially through agencies, is often quite protracted and, in a sense, somewhat painful. Because adoptive parents sometimes endure great difficulties in adopting a child, they may feel resentful of the child's wish to then locate his natural parents. Despite years of having raised the child, the parents may feel inordinately threatened by the existence of the "real" parents.

Adoptive parents need to know that their work has not been in vain. A good relationship with their child cannot be supplanted or replaced. It cannot be diminished. Adoptive parents must be content that they did as good a job in raising their child as they could, perhaps better than could have been done by anyone else.

An Adoptive Child Joins a Family with Children

We've recently adopted a three-year-old girl. We have two children of our own, an eight-year-old girl and a nine-year-old boy. What can we expect in this arrangement?

DR. KERNBERG: When adopting a child into a family that already has biological children, the question must inevitably arise about why the parents want another child. It would be important to include the older children in the decision-making process regarding the adoption of another child. Ironically, the biological children could begin to feel that the adopted child is preferred, in contrast to the usual assumption that the adopted child would feel unpreferred. To promote family unity, the biological children should be involved in planning the practical issues concerning the newly adopted baby. Such participation by the biological children can help them feel that this is truly an addition to the family and not an exclusion of them.

About Being "Chosen"

We are about to tell our child she was adopted. My husband wants to tell her that we chose her above all others. Is this the way to go about it?

DR. KERNBERG: In telling a child that she was adopted, it is best simply to tell the unadorned truth. Your child was not chosen above all others and will eventually see through this transparency. In fact, your child was adopted because she was the one who came along, and you were available for each other. If anything, most adoptive parents don't have much of a choice.

It's best to tell your child the truth, which need not be inordinately painful for your youngster. You can say, "We were very lucky that you happened to come along," which is a positive and true statement, and shows how very much you wanted a child. But it's a mistruth to tell your adopted child that you chose her above all others.

Other Considerations

DR. KERNBERG: Adoption is a *process*, sometimes a difficult and conflictual one. Sometimes, one spouse wants to adopt more intensely than the other. This can create problems. In a biological family, when a child is behaving poorly, one spouse may say to the other, "This is *your* child." Of course, when the child is being good, he is "*my* child." Such dichotomization can also occur with adoptive parents. When a child is being good he is "our child," and when he is bad or not doing well, he is "their child," namely the child of biological parents. If one spouse has decided to adopt and the other is not quite so eager, this unhealthy dichotomization is made easier. One spouse may say to the other, "This child is being difficult, and he's *yours.*"

It's important for both parents to feel that the adopted child is *their* child, no matter how well or poorly the child does. As a general rule, when a couple think about adopting, the partners should fully explore this issue between themselves. They should decide that they *both* very much want to adopt a child and that for better or worse the child will belong to them both. Then, no matter what happens, it's all in the family.

Chapter 12: Twins

_____

The birth of twins has inspired awe, wonder, and speculation for thousands of years. Twins have been the subjects of myth and legend throughout history, and the parents of twins must often separate superstition from fact.

While some parents worry about having limited financial resources, most feel that the birth of twins makes them twice blessed. The birth of twins is an event that brings great joy, and a good deal of upheaval. First-time parents may feel overwhelmed by the responsibilities of caring for two newborns, but they usually accommodate well, discovering shortcuts in child care to make their lives a bit easier.

Whether identical or fraternal, twins raise certain crucial psychological and developmental issues for parents.

Our consultant for this topic is Muriel C. Winestine, Ph.D. Dr. Winestine is a Clinical Associate Professor of Psychology in Psychiatry at Cornell University Medical College and an Associate Attending Psychologist at the Payne Whitney Clinic of The New York Hospital.

Dividing Time Between Twins

We have six-month-old fraternal twins, and it's difficult to keep up with feeding, changing, washing, and caring for them both. I'm concerned that I'm giving each one less individual stimulation and caretaking than would otherwise be the case. Could their emotional development be affected?

DR. WINESTINE: Having two babies in the same stage of development inevitably confronts you with the reality of having to divide your time. With very young babies, you may feel that you are missing opportunities for the leisurely pleasure of relating to only one baby at a time. As twins, your babies, whether fraternal or identical, are in the very same stage of development at the same time. This presents you with a situation in which you must compromise so your babies can receive the kind of

295

stimulation and caretaking you want to provide for them. You must be receptive to obtaining as much help from others as you can.

If you do not have everyday help, you must then make other compromises. For instance, at six months of age, your babies are well regulated, and you would want to establish a bathing schedule. Should you bathe your babies simultaneously or separately? I would not compromise on the opportunity to have a one-to-one relationship with a child at any one time. Therefore, I would compromise on the *frequency* of bathing, and bathe each baby every other day or night, thereby allowing the opportunity to spend individual time with each baby alone. One hopes that this would enhance each infant's growth and individuation as a person over a course of time.

Certain activities allow little choice or compromise. One important area is that of feeding. It would be best if you had some help, either paid help or that of someone else in your family. By six months of age, certain consistent patterns will be established, and you can regulate certain activities according to your babies' patterns. As fraternal twins, your infants' endowments will be quite different, and by six months you will have already noted differences in their rhythms and patterns. This can make feeding the babies easier to accomplish.

No matter how much you attempt to provide the babies with individual attention, the fact of their twinship cannot be denied. It is a potent force in the infants' relationship with each other and in each baby's relatedness to you. The presence of another baby, both for you and each twin, is undeniably a source of great stimulation. Twins are a source of mutual stimulation. The danger inherent in this situation is that some mothers become content to leave their twin babies in the company of each other, where there are mutual movements, and mutual cuing and handling of each other's limbs.

The danger with twins is that too many daily activities can occur simultaneously, with both twins receiving maternal care at the same time, and always in each other's company. For twins, this may serve to enhance a feeling of being part of a unit of two, of being only part of a greater whole, namely, the twinship. This can detract from each child developing a discrete sense of self.

If allowed to continue, this situation could foster in each twin the indelible idea that any relationship with or comfort derived from mother must include the physical and emotional presence of the other sibling. The developmental danger can be an interference in a close relationship with mother, as well as difficulty forming an individual sense of self.

Dressing Twins Alike

Our identical twin daughters are four years old. My husband likes to see them dressed identically and thinks it's cute that no one can tell them apart. I've heard it's best to dress twins differently from each other. What should I do?

DR. WINESTINE: It is indisputably true that when parents learn they will be having twins, the father's reaction may be to feel doubly special, as though his potency somehow accounts for this miracle. Both parents may be very gratified by presenting this unique duality to everyone. To some extent, such pleasure comes to virtually any parent who can "show off" a new baby, but for many parents of twins, the two babies can be a double dose of self-regard and enhanced good feelings. They may wish to maintain both children in an identical way so that everyone can clearly view this miracle of nature. This can become too dominant an emotional investment for some parents, who feel they must always present both babies together, as a unit, rather than simply acknowledging what is little more than an embryologic turn of events.

This can result in a process known as "twinning." Twinning is defined as a mutual interdependence that may result in a failure of twins to become properly individuated from each other. This interdependence may cause a blurring of self-images, with a confusion in each child of the sense of separate identity. A child who has a twin has an environment at birth that is very different from that of a nontwin child, whose individuation is enhanced by different sequences of birth and development among siblings, and by a different status for each sibling within the family.

Twinships may vary in certain important characteristics: whether the twins are of the same sex, their comparative physical conditions and birth experiences, parental attitudes toward each twin, and the presence or absence of other siblings within the family. While these and other factors affect the twinship, one vital characteristic distinguishes twins from nontwins: the intense physical and emotional proximity to another individual in the same phase of development.

If fostered too intensely by parents, this twinship can cause profound personality disturbances in the children. The children may develop the idea that devoid of this fluke of nature that has them looking identical, each twin on his own is less interesting and not "worth" as much as he is valued as part of the twinship.

Your husband's wish to present the twins identically dressed and indistinguishable from each other fosters in the children's minds the need always to include the presence or the idea of the other twin in order to feel complete and worthwhile. I emphatically recommend that from the very outset parents of twins do as much as they can to foster and maintain the children's sense of individuality. I also recommend that parents avoid the pitfall of choosing names that rhyme or couple. It's best not to allow the sense of twinship to totally pervade the children's lives.

Of course, a certain amount of pleasure is involved in twinning. To see someone exactly like oneself provides a great deal of gratification. To some extent, we all tend to choose people in our lives who represent something we would like to be, or we choose someone very much in our own image. Such choices minimize the need to adapt or adjust to another person's different needs and ways of doing things. The notion of having a "mirror image" or of being part of the twinship can really extend too far for some children.

I know of two boys who are twins; they choose to be identical because of these early influences of twinning. They so prefer to be perceived as identical that they even answer for one another. When questioned why they do this, one twin says, "It doesn't really matter who answers because my brother will have the same answer as I do." If their mother doesn't have two matching pairs of socks, but instead has one pair of brown and one pair of blue, each boy wears one blue and one brown sock so they can remain identical! It's obvious that these boys have very little sense of individual identity.

In contrast, I know of a pair of twin boys who have a much healthier attitude about themselves and their twinship. They feel that being a twin is quite convenient in some respects, but it doesn't define them. As one boy put it, "It's really nice to have a kid my own age, and if nobody else is around to play tennis, I can always count on him." However, if one twin is invited to a birthday party and the other is not, the uninvited boy doesn't get upset. The boys recognize and accept the fact that they are different and have lives of their own. Actually, they become somewhat resentful if they detect that someone feels one twin can serve as a substitute or alternate for the other. They regard such a view as an incursion into their own individual identities. These boys do not dress in the same way; they don't have names that couple or rhyme; and they truly experience themselves as discrete individuals. Their parents have made a point of fostering as many differences between them as possible. As a result, the boys are psychologically healthy; they simply happen to be twins.

Help your daughters evolve their own individuality and a sense of being separate from each other. Avoid dressing them identically and do not foster their twinship so that they engage in the process of "twinning." Instead, consider yourself doubly lucky to have two daughters, but provide them with separate things and foster their differences so they each evolve a discrete and unique sense of individuality.

Are Twins More Independent?

I'm the mother of identical twin daughters who are now two years old. I've been told that twins become more independent of their parents than other children. Is this really true?

DR. WINESTINE: Under some circumstances, a twin may find constant company in the co-twin. Some twins even develop a kind of gibberish or mutual language that only *they* can understand. It becomes a special form of communication that excludes all other people. The parents of twins should be alert to any behavior that begins to look like pseudo-independence in their children, especially if this begins very early in their development, such as at two years of age.

There are some healthy aspects to this interaction. For instance, the maturational rate may be more accelerated in one twin as compared to the other. One may walk before the other. The second child may learn from the first, and to some extent may experience a slight acceleration in response to the more quickly developing child.

However, twins should not be more independent than other children. The danger signal should sound if your twins seem very independent because they spend so much time with each other that they have less need of their parents. It's far more beneficial for any child to have a solid image of the parents and of other people, and not just an image of the co-twin.

Should Twins Be Separated?

Our four-year-old identical twin boys have been together from the very beginning of their lives. I've heard that it's best to separate twins when they begin preschool. Is this true?

DR. WINESTINE: Ideally, if the school setting allows the children to be separated, and all things being equal, separation of the children is best. Separation allows each child to experience other children and adults without the constant presence of the other child. The ever-present co-twin may cause each child to feel unable to relate to others as a complete person without the physical presence or mental image of the twin sibling. This can also affect each twin's relationship with other children. Separating the twins allows other children to relate to each child individually rather than as part of a constant pair.

Parents may be very energetic in carrying out such a separation and may needlessly deprive one child or the other of an optimum education. It is unwise to send one child to preschool while keeping the other at home, unless one child is ready for preschool and the other is not. Another problem may arise if the twins are gifted and there is only one special class for gifted children. It would be unwise to deprive one child by sending him or her out of the class. Such insistence on separation at any cost can be detrimental to one of the children, and in such a matter a parent must use commonon sense.

Separation of twins should be accomplished gradually over a long period of time, rather than as a sudden separation later in development. I've seen a number of cases in which at age ten twins were suddenly separated after the pair had spent all the previous years together. Both children had difficulty concentrating on schoolwork in the absence of the cotwin. Once they were brought back together, the children could again function very well. Here again, the parents of twins must allow their children to individuate as separate people so that each develops a sense of being a real person, even in the absence of the other child. This doesn't preclude one twin's thinking about the other in the cotwin's absence, which simply indicates that a child can miss a sibling. But a parent must avoid allowing a child to foster the notion that the other twin is essential in order for the child to function.

Parents must help a child learn to tolerate a certain amount of conflict and frustration. For instance, one twin may be invited to a party, while the other is not. Should this occur, parents can be very helpful. While any child may find not being invited to a party painful, a parent can point out that the children are separate and unique individuals; they don't automatically participate in each other's lives. They are not Tweedledum and Tweedledee.

A parent does not have to try to artificially create these frustrations; life will deal them out. Such frustrations and social slights, while sometimes painful, can be used to help the children grow and individuate as separate people with meaningful and independent lives. As a parent of twins, you should become concerned if your children have a mutual pool of friends, and neither has separate relationships or activities that indicate an individual life.

Forming Sexual Identity

We have a seven-year-old son and daughter who are fraternal twins. I've heard that because they're twins they may have difficulty forming male and female identities. Is this true?

DR. WINESTINE: All siblings, in any family, whether twins or not, have the opportunity to observe the behavioral as well as bodily differences between the sexes. This is all for the good. Anatomical differences are bewildering and psychologically stimulating to children. No matter what is said or done, a certain amount of penis envy occurs in any little girl. The fact is that she sees someone who has something that she does not have. Similarly, we know that a little boy will be envious of what the girl can have and grow up to have; namely, breasts and babies. Put succinctly, biological, social, and cultural differences exist between boys and girls.

With fraternal twins of the opposite sex, a boy and girl grow up in the same home while they are in the same stage of development. A seven-year-old girl's maturation rate is usually faster than that of a boy; she may be talking better, writing better, performing better at school, and may even be taller than her brother. They are probably in separate classes and have different friends, both in and out of school. All these factors tend to encourage the formation of separate and distinct individual and sexual identities.

Fraternal twin brother and sisters may develop a blurred sense of sexual identity if the children have been inculcated with too great a feeling that each is part of the other, if there has been a great deal of "twinning" in their development. There can be an enhanced bisexual feeling if the children feel that both members of the twinship must be present for either sibling to function as a person.

Parents of a boy-girl twin pair should be cautious about bathing the children together at an early age. There should not be constant physical exposure of one naked twin to the other. For the young boy, the naked girl's constant presence is a reminder that she looks very different than he does. This can by psychologically metabolized into a belief that she has lost her penis, which can cause a small boy to worry that he too will lose his penis. While some anxiety about this issue is normal for a boy, the constant and needless exposure to the naked girl could unduly increase his anxiety about his own penis.

For the little girl, constant exposure to a naked boy can lead to thoughts that she, too, has a penis, since after all, her twin brother is a part of her. She may develop the notion that her own penis is just hidden from view. If this belief persists, she may never resolve a very important childhood conflict concerning her eventual acceptance of the bodily differences between boys and girls. So it is quite important for the parents of fraternal twins of the opposite sex not to overly expose their naked children to each other. (See in Chapter 3, "Worries About the Body" and "The Oedipal Phase.")

Children of five and six years of age must accept the reality that the parents are a couple who have a relationship that does not always include the children. This means resolving the Oedipal phase, which helps the child develop a sense of right and wrong, as well as a sense of himself or herself. If a set of twins—a boy and girl—can too easily believe that just as mommy and daddy are a couple, *we* are a couple, and if the parents enhance such a belief by bathing the children together and by promoting their constant companionship, the children can bypass having to accept their own roles and identities as a boy and a girl who must respectively grow up to be like father and mother. Such a boy-girl pair of twins may be forced to deal with special problems in resolving the Oedipal phase of development.

Will Twins Be Loners?

I'm the mother of twin daughters who are now three years old. They're very close to each other and sometimes tend to exclude other children. Will they become loners who don't get along with others?

DR. WINESTINE: Twins can sometimes have a tendency to gang up against other children, and even gang up against their parents. Some twins can actually develop a certain sense of omnipotence. For a twin, there is not only the need to separate and individuate from mother but also the need to separate and individuate from the co-twin. A twin or twin pair that excludes others may be suffering from a lack of sufficient differentiation from *each other.* Such a sign is a very powerful indication that the parents should get busy providing their children with different playmates, and help them separate and individuate.

Being twins does not necessarily mean that your children will be loners or fail to get along well with others. The most crucial consideration is the degree to which parents provide an opportunity for the children to learn to relate to people beyond the twinship. Twinning is not a disease. Most things that happen in twinning happen in normal sibling relationships. However, twinship can create difficulties when it comes to each child forming a separate sense of self.

Ideally, you must try to provide your children with as much a sense of separate selfhood as possible. This includes, if possible, names that do not couple, and providing them with opportunities to form separate lives and interests.

Competitive Twins

As the parents of five-year-old twins, we're worried because we've heard that twins are usually intensely competitive and can have very hostile relationships with each other. Is this true?

DR. WINESTINE: Yes. It is not only true, but I would say that if some competitiveness and some hostility are *not* present, I would be concerned. The competition is only natural; after all, you have two children at the same stage of development who must negotiate the same intellectual, emotional, psychological, and social tasks. Why wouldn't they be competitive? Competition always breeds some degree of hostility. Some competition and some hostility should be music to twins parents' ears. It is in the service of differentiation of one twin from the other, and is quite healthy.

Virtually any set of twins will compete and experience some hostility and, at times, aggression. These feelings should be acknowledged and not denied. Ambivalent feelings about each other can be more difficult for twins than for other siblings because despite hostility, twins truly love each other and love to be with each other.

You should be able to communicate to your twins that it's quite understandable to be hostile and angry at someone with whom he or she experiences so much throughout the early years. All in all, ambivalent feelings between twins is quite natural.

Resents Twin Sisters

I have a seven-year-old daughter and a set of three-year-old twin girls. The older child seems very jealous of the twins and feels that we pay too much attention to them. How can I handle this?

DR. WINESTINE: Your seven-year-old may be acutely jealous of the fact that you must spend so much time with the twins. You should do everything you can to make especially clear to your daughter that the "specialness" of the twins does not make her less important or less special than the other two. She should not feel that the twins serve some very special narcissistic or exhibitionistic gratification for the parents. Any child in a family will, of course, develop some sibling rivalry. In this case, your daughter has a double dose. It would help to make her feel as unique as her twin sisters.

Chapter 13: The Selfish Child

Selfishness comes in many forms. A child cannot share toys or possessions with others. A child must always have things his or her way, or a child must be the center of attention. A child occasionally seems not to realize that other children have needs and feelings, or that an entire world exists beyond the youngster's own desires.

What we adults would call "selfishness" is a normal and expected way of being for the toddler and young preschool child. However, as children approach the school-age years, they have increasing contact with others. The egocentric and self-oriented ways of early childhood must give way to the realities of life: a child must share a teacher's attention with others and must relate to others as part of a group. As with many developmental tasks, some children master this one quite well, whereas others have difficulty renouncing the ways of childhood.

Our consultant for this topic is Ladd Spiegel, M.D. Dr. Spiegel is an Instructor in Psychiatry at the Cornell University Medical College and an Assistant Attending Psychiatrist at the Payne Whitney Clinic of The New York Hospital.

Refuses to Share

Our five-year-old daughter refuses to share anything with her seven-year-old sister. How can we handle this?

DR. SPIEGEL: You must first determine if this refusal to share is only occurring at home, or is this a problem at school as well? The first step, then, is to ask your daughter's teacher if she is having trouble sharing with children in her kindergarten class.

If we assume that your daughter has only recently begun having trouble sharing with her sister—and that the problem is limited to home—then there are certain directions to take.

A five-year-old is just beginning to experience the wider world outside the family. A child of this age is emotionally and mentally discovering the world of peers, particularly friends of the same sex. A major life task for a five-year-old is that of trying out different ways of relating to people, different ways of having friends, of discovering how angry one can become at friends or how angry they may become at her. All this involves a form of experimentation in which the child learns about the world.

A natural, normal, and healthy way of going about this is for a child to engage in practicing with her own family. The child will make certain mistakes and will be repeatedly challenged by the task of learning to share and discover how selfish she may or may not be. It is preferable that some of these mistakes be made with family members who will tolerate what nonfamily people would not.

There are specific factors at work in your situation. A five-year-old is just beginning to discover the world, while a seven-year-old has dealt with the outside world for some time. Your five-year-old may be very jealous of her older sister. While two years seems like a small difference, it is a great leap for the five-year-old child. A very common problem we see with children this age is that of a five-year-old appropriating the toys of a seven-year-old in an attempt to become more adult.

This situation can be converted into one that fosters learning. It can be turned into an opportunity to teach your five-year-old how to share. This must be done slowly and kindly, keeping in mind that the younger child feels very insecure. Helping a child learn how to share is a challenge. A practical way to go about doing this is to compliment your child each time she shares something with someone else. This will imbue her with positive feelings about sharing; the experience can become one of gaining reward (your compliments and indications of affection) rather than be one which is perceived by the child as a "giving up" of something. In other words, the experience can become one in which positive reinforcement is used to foster a willingness to share. Equally important is the fact that parents can present role models for their children. If the parents willingly share and if sharing is openly valued by family members, a child can be helped to learn how to share. This is a slow process, and cannot be accomplished quickly.

It would also be helpful to talk with your seven-year-old to determine if she has been contributing to the rivalry. The situation can also help the older child if you explain to her that her younger sister probably admires her and is envious of her. You can tell your seven-year-old that she probably has a great deal to teach her younger sister, which is no doubt true, and help her put all this in perspective.

Won't Let Kids Play with His Things

Our three-and-a-half-year old son refuses to let other children at preschool play with his things. Should we worry, and what is this all about?

DR. SPIEGEL: As our society has changed, children who some years ago would have remained at home with mother are exposed to preschool settings. Therefore, we begin seeing new kinds of problems.

Child psychiatrists are aware of an enormously wide range of behaviors that can be considered normal during the preschool period; there is no narrow definition of normality. Much of this depends on the nature of your child's prior experiences with other children. If he is an only child with few experiences relating to others, and for the first time finds himself surrounded by other children, his response is completely normal. However, if he has had earlier experiences in a nursery, or has been with other children, his behavior may be the first indication that he relates to others in a way that will not be terribly successful.

Once a child has settled into a preschool setting, one expects him to be able to play reasonably well with other children. Most preschools advise parents not to allow a child to bring toys from home. Such items can create difficulties because a child often feels possessive of toys from home and may not be able to share them successfully with others. Your first approach should probably be to discuss with school personnel whether or not children should bring toys from home. Generally, the school has a collections of toys available for all the children, which obviates this sort of problem.

Let us assume that this has been a consistent pattern, and that your child has had plenty of opportunity to play and share with other children. Let's also assume that your son is having this difficulty with virtually any toy that comes into his hands, not only those he brings from home. In this situation, it would be best to have the teacher intervene. A teacher knows how to gently tempt a child into sharing toys and playing with other children. It's very difficult for a parent to intervene in this way because, generally, parents feel loyal to a child, are usually protective, and often take their child's side. Therefore, it's best for a neutral person—the teacher—to become involved and begin educating the child to share more effectively.

When a child has problems sharing at home, an effective partial remedy is to purchase two or three toys that are clearly identified as belonging solely to the child; they need not be shared with anyone. Similarly, other toys should be defined as being meant for sharing with others.

Birthday parties are an exceptionally good way to establish such a principle. The child can feel special and receive presents on his birthday. However, on another child's birthday, he observes the other child receiving presents, which can be instructive because it confronts the child with issues of possession and entitlement, and indicates he cannot always be the center of things. A parent may have to purchase a small token item for a very jealous child when buying a birthday present for another child.

Wants Things Her Own Way

Our eight-year-old daughter seems very self-centered and always wants things her own way. If she doesn't get her way, she becomes upset. What can we do?

DR. SPIEGEL: By eight years of age, a child understands that other people have lives and feelings of their own. A child of this age should be able to balance her desires and needs with those of others. Your question states that your daughter wants things her own way. Children go through different phases of development; each phase entails a different way of relating. There is something we call temperament which actually forms the basis of a child's personality. Temperament remains as a steady characteristic, regardless of the child's developmental phase. It seems that your daughter is temperamentally self-centered. If this is true, then it is unlikely she will alter her way of relating to others. Her personality traits will tend to be somewhat fixed by eight years of age and will most likely persist throughout her life. The question is, how can she be helped to adjust her ways of relating so that her temperament is not a stumbling block to developing good relationships, both now and throughout her adult life?

You must carefully explore whether this occurs only at home or prevails as well when your daughter relates to other people. It would be best to observe or inquire about her when she is with her friends and when she is at school. Ask her friend's parents if they have observed your daughter behaving in a selfish way. If she is not as self-centered and is more flexible with others, then her seemingly self-centered demeanor may not reflect her basic temperament so much as it would indicate some problem in the home. In such a case, you must establish the important household rules, whether they are bedtime rules, household responsibilities, or others. You may simply have to be prepared to struggle with your child in implementing these basic rules.

If, however, your daughter is self-centered with friends as well as with the family, you have additional reason for concern. It would help to determine whether or not some family situation is causing your child to be self-centered. For example, a sibling who receives an unusual amount of parental attention could be at the root of your daughter's behavior. Is there a brother or sister who suffers from a physical illness? Is there a handicapped child at home? Is there a stepchild who receives a great deal of attention? Is there an unusually gifted child? Is there a slow child at home who must receive special privileges or tutoring?

If something is occurring at home that has caused or heightened your daughter's self-centeredness, try talking with her about this. A child of eight is capable of discussing her thoughts, feelings, preferences, and complaints. Discussing this issue will convey to her that her feelings are understood and respected.

If no family situation accounts for your daughter's feeling neglected and if she is consistently self-centered with family and others outside the home, then she is temperamentally self-centered. You should consider consulting with a school counselor, psychologist or child psychiatrist in an effort to determine if your daughter could benefit from counseling or from a play-group situation.

Brags About Exploits

Our ten-year-old son has always tended to brag a bit, but recently, for reasons we don't know, he's begun bragging about everything. We're getting concerned. Please advise us.

DR. SPIEGEL: Children today are maturing faster and faster. We now see puberty beginning at younger ages, and today problems previously faced by teenagers are often found among ten-year-olds. This occurs more often with girls but is seen in children of both sexes. Today, we may consider a ten-year-old boy to be on the threshold of puberty.

For a boy of this age, physical size and attributes become paramount. Bragging usually suggests that a child is fabricating accomplishments or exaggerating them in a way that is unusual or excessive. There is a difference between a child who feels proud of his accomplishments and wants his parents to respond positively to them, and a child who brags. The child who brags does not feel good about himself. He feels inadequate in some way, and my guess is that a ten-year-old boy may feel badly about being somewhat small, awkward, or lacking physical prowess.

In its own way, this may actually be a great opportunity for a parent. As your child approaches the teenage years, the door between you and your son's inner emotional life will close very tightly. Once your son reaches adolescence, you will have few hints about his feelings or concerns. Therefore, take this opportunity to discover your son's preoccupation. Most likely, the very things he brags about are those about which he feels most inadequate.

If he's bragging about success with girls, the chances are that he feels uncomfortable with girls, or about his looks. If he brags about his daredevil exploits, the chances are he's a bit frightened. If a child feels inadequate, it is unlikely that he will express these feelings directly. However, this is an excellent opportunity to let your youngster know that you understand that he doesn't feel good about himself. You need not get into his specific concerns, but you can let him know that you understand he would want these things to be true even though they are not.

You can take this opportunity to bring out and make him more aware of his own positive points. For instance, if your son is small and some of his friends are beginning to show signs of puberty, he may be painfully aware of this discrepancy. However, let's assume that he's an outgoing youngster and that other kids and teachers like him very much. While a ten-year-old may not value "personality" greatly, he would certainly appreciate your letting him know all the good things that people have said about him.

Bragging can sometimes become a problem when a child is boasting in order to please a parent. This usually indicates unrealistic or inflated expectations of the child by the parent, and the child is merely trying to live up to his fantasy of the parent's expectations. It would be helpful if you can assess if your son is, in his own way, picking up and reflecting on your own disappointment in his lack of physical prowess. Kids, of course, are incredibly sensitive barometers of parents' feelings and concerns. If, after reflective soul-searching, you determine that this is partly true, you should sit down and discuss all this with your son.

Wants to Be the Center of Attention

Our eleven-year-old daughter wants always to be the center of attention. If she feels that others are not paying enough attention, she gets very upset and becomes depressed. We're concerned. Please advise us.

DR. SPIEGEL: Your daughter is about to discover that the real world is very different from the world of children. If a girl is attractive and has a captivating personality, she may easily be the center of attention at home or within a small group of friends. There is little doubt that some children possess a certain magnetism and appearance that can lead to their being at the center of attention in a particular setting. This can be a telling indicator that a child has certain highly valued social gifts.

The fact is that no one can ever be the center of attention at all times. Most reasonably confident people can step back out of the limelight and let someone else shine. If your daughter cannot do that, she will inevitably be disappointed.

As a parent, you may feel tempted to go to great lengths to prevent your child from getting depressed. While that is understandable, it is not the best thing to do. If your daughter is going to negotiate her teenage years successfully, she must eventually learn to feel good about herself without being the center of attention at all times. Allow your daughter to become upset and depressed within the safety of the family, before she encounters difficulties with other people. She will learn that these feelings are transitory and that life goes on.

On a practical level, you must feel free to tell your daughter that she cannot always be the center of attention and cannot always have everything she wants. Try not to sound too preachy when you do this; say something like, "We know how much you want to be liked and admired, but you can't always be in the middle of everything. Because we can't always pay complete attention to you doesn't mean that we don't love you."

It may also be helpful to foster your daughter's learning to be more self-sufficient; that is, she should learn to undertake activities and derive pleasure from them without necessarily having the approval or attention of others. Encourage her to begin a collection or to begin some project, activity, or hobby that she can accomplish alone, away from the limelight. Reward her with approval when she has completed the task, but try to encourage her to derive pleasure from the task or hobby itself, without needing to bask in the light of others' approval.

The vast majority of children can handle feelings of being upset and depressed for short periods of time, providing the family responds to the child's needs. Your daughter must learn that disappointment is a part of life. She must eventually develop her own inner resources and her own sources of self-esteem.

An Overview

Dr. Spiegel: We live in a period during which self-involvement seems to be the course for most people. Children generally reflect the trend of the society at large. During the 1960s there was a societal turning away from selfishness and from concerns about money and pleasure in the self. Competition seemed to be fading and altruism was very much in the forefront.

However, our culture has changed greatly since then. Adults are now more concerned about appearance, about their careers and self-interests, and spend enormous emotional energy in pursuit of material things, all of which has become quite acceptable. Our children reflect this self-centered and somewhat narcissistic turn of societal events. Families are smaller; there are increasing numbers of older parents with only one child; and there are more households than ever in which both parents work. Therefore, the child of the 1980s is likely to spend a great deal of time alone or with surrogate-parent figures. All this may create or enhance a certain degree of self-centeredness in our children.

It was once believed that infants are completely absorbed by their own needs and were totally selfish. However, modern research indicates that the infant is very much aware of people in the environment, especially of mother. Today, researchers are aware that newborns and infants are *not* completely self-involved, but rather have an enormous amount of critical interaction with parental figures from the very beginning of their lives.

While the young child requires a great deal of unselfish attention to be paid to it, we know that children evolve and develop away from their early overwhelming dependence upon parents. As the child grows older, he expands his repertoire of contacts, becoming more involved with other children in the peer group. Under such circumstances, the child must be able to put aside some of his own selfish needs for a period of time. The child who feels genuinely loved and cared for at home will more readily be able to put aside some of his own needs. The neglected child will constantly seek out others to attend to or satisfy his needs.

There are really three kinds of selfishness among children. One involves a personality trait in which a child enjoys being the center of attention and wishes to be on top. Such traits often coincide with and are responsible for a good deal of success in our society and are not necessarily a problem, so long as the child develops reasonable social skills.

The second form of selfishness among children occurs in response to a change or family crisis: the birth of a sibling, physical illness, a family's moving, some difficulty at school, or some other stress that evokes an upsurge in selfishness. During this crisis or stress, a child may undergo some developmental regression, become "needy," and temporarily need some form of special attention.

There is a third child who can demonstrate selfishness, and this is the child about whom we occasionally worry. It is the child who seems unable to understand that other people have feelings or needs. This is the child who may be cruel to animals, who consistently takes things from other children, and who repeatedly cheats, lies, and steals. This child causes concern among psychiatrists because, as a teenager, he or she may have drug problems and have trouble with the law because the youngster feels that rules apply only to others, not to the self. This child will, in all liklihood, require professional help if he or she is to avoid emotional and other troubles in later years. The child must be helped to understand that other people have needs and feelings.

Generally, selfishness in its many forms will occasionally rear its head in any child's behavior, and need not be considered a problem unless it becomes a predominant and persistent mode of relating to other people. As with so many other things in human behavior, there is a fairly wide range of behaviors that can be termed normal. The extent to which something can be considered abnormal or out of the ordinary is the extent to which it predominates in a child's thinking, feelings, and behavior.

Chapter 14: The Overweight Child

Eating is such a basic and repeated function that it may become the focus for many problems between parents and children. Obesity is defined as weighing 20 percent or more above the ideal body weight for a person's height and frame. The number of fat tissue cells a person has throughout life may be partly influenced by nutrition during infancy, and overfed babies (infants who are fed many more calories than are nutritionally needed) may actually develop more fat cells throughout their body tissues.

Experts have concluded that the experience of hunger is not completely innate; it also contains important elements of learning. While genetic factors may play some role in obesity, they are complicated by the effects of the environment, by faulty eating habits, psychological influences, and emotional traumas.

Obesity in children is rarely caused by underactive thyroid or pituitary glands. Over the years, many physicians have prescribed thyroid or other hormones for certain obese children, even though the children's hormone levels are completely normal. Such inappropriate treatment for obesity has fostered the myth that an overweight child has "glandular" troubles, and some physicians have prescribed hormones because of their own frustration when dealing with a child's obesity or because the parents have coerced the doctor into "doing something" about a child's weight problem.

Overfeeding and a parent's inability to recognize a child's cues about hunger and satiety are usually seen in the families of very obese children. Such a pattern may be quite subtle or very obvious and usually persists throughout a child's life. In fact, most very obese children have been overweight all their lives, even as babies. Yet studies have shown that even severe obesity up to the toddler stage does not necessarily result in permanent obesity unless the pathological parent-child interaction continues. Parents encouraging too much dependency and discouraging independence in a child seem to be the most important psychological factors contributing to obesity.

Even when obesity persists throughout a child's life, a good accepting relationship between an obese child and the family can make a child's life fairly normal, despite the adverse reactions of outsiders toward the obese child. But when an obese child is not accepted by the family and when his weight problem becomes a focus of conflict in the house, the child may develop into an obese and unhappy adolescent.

Our consultant for this topic is Theodore Shapiro, M. D. Dr. Shapiro is a Professor of Psychiatry at Cornell University Medical College and is the Director of Child and Adolescent Psychiatry at the Payne Whitney Clinic of The New York Hospital.

A New Baby

Our five-year-old never had a weight problem until the birth of her younger sister last year. Since then, she's become very overweight and eats voraciously. No one else in the family is overweight. What's going on, and what can we do?

DR SHAPIRO: Are you certain that your daughter "eats voraciously" and is not in a growth spurt? I ask because, very often, reports concerning the quantities of food someone eats are not entirely accurate. Also, there are familial tendencies toward obesity, and there are metabolic differences from person to person.

However, let's assume that your daughter has been eating voraciously and gaining weight in response to the new baby's arrival. Then, certain things seem fairly obvious. This activity is a regression for your daughter, a regression toward a more primitive means of taking in love. She is showing her anxiety about the fact that love and attention must now be shared with her younger sibling. Instead of directly asking for affection, she is eating more. She makes a bid for attention and affection in a way that may be acceptable in your household, rather than by whining or crying, or rather than by saying, "I need some love, too."

Your daughter's voracious eating may also be an important symbolic transformation of the desire for attention and caring. In your complaining about her eating, there's an excellent chance that your daughter is getting exactly what she wants, namely, your attention because she is doing something which you feel is to her detriment and of which you disapprove.

Before saying more about all this, I would need to know more about your family and about its eating patterns. Does obesity tend to run in your family? One must also consider that other things are going on in a five-year-old child's life. Your daughter has recently begun kindergarten and may be leaving home for the first time. It is likely that more stresses are present than simply the birth of a younger sibling. It would be best if all these factors could be taken into consideration by a child psychiatrist, who could then sensibly make a specific recommendation.

Weight-Reducing Camp

Our ten-year-old son has always been overweight, which has concerned us. Over the last year, his weight gain has become excessive. We've had him medically evaluated and nothing is wrong. We're considering sending him to a weight-reduction summer camp. Is this reasonable?

Dr. Shapiro: A weight-reducing camp is fine if your son is unhappy about his excessive weight gain and if he wishes to participate in the camp. When a child is willing, group activities are generally useful in an effort to lose weight and change eating patterns. Such efforts are the basis of the success of many groups, including Weight Watchers, Alcoholics Anonymous, and others.

At ten years of age, your son may simply be in a prepubertal growth spurt, and he may in the long run "string out." You must also consider what significance and social implications his weight gain may hold for him. Does it cause him to be the subject of ostracism and teasing by other kids? Are his sports and social activities impaired because of his being overweight? If your son is unhappy about his situaion, there may be a great deal to motivate him to lose weight. However, a parent should not become directly involved in the conflict. A parent should not be the person to restrict the child; nor is it good for a parent to become frustrated, angry, and resentful at the difficulty in controlling a child's eating habits. Offering your son the opportunity to participate in a weight-reducing camp may be very helpful. In a setting where everyone is in the same boat (among peers), he may do very well.

Binges When Teased

Our nine-year-old son is very overweight. The other kids call him nicknames and make him feel unwanted. We've noticed that after these encounters he comes home and goes on an eating binge. We have always accepted his weight situation, but we are now getting worried. What can we do?

Dr. Shapiro: We usually associate binge eating with female psychology, but that is not always the case. The very thing for which your son is being teased becomes the instrument of his further downfall. The more your son is teased, the angrier and more anxious he becomes. With increasing anger, he manages to tell himself: "I don't care anymore. Everybody can go to hell. I'm going to eat even more and get fatter. I'd better not look for gratification from my peers. I'm going to take care of it myself." At this point, he goes home and eats.

This self-defeating scenario suggests a failure of hope that things can change. It also suggests a failure to discover more appropriate ways of getting other people's attention, and indicates a withdrawal from social stresses and an attempt to achieve gratification in a very self-destructive way. This all becomes a vicious cycle with few positive consequences.

A very important issue is the quality of your reaction as you watch your son enter into this vicious cycle. You must refrain from punitive action, or from anything that will make all this worse for your son. After all, he is looking for caring love, for appreciation and for attention, despite his obesity and the derision that it brings down on him from others. His core sense of self is being threatened. If this cycle has continued for a long time, I would suggest that you seek professional help.

You should also be sensitive for signs of depression in your son's feelings and behavior. He seems to be renouncing a reasonable social life, and his psychological well-being seems quite impaired. I would want to explore with your son whether or not he has friends, whether he feels he can rely on anyone, whether he feels he has anyone he can talk with, and I would want to learn more about what is eating him. It's no accident that I use the expression "what is *eating* him." We often see that people try to resolve conflicts by eating, which is usually quite unsuccessful. All in all, if your son is unhappy with his circumstances, he would most likely benefit from counseling.

Girlfriends Are Interested in Boys

Our daughter is eleven years old and very heavy. This has always been the case and it never bothered her. Now that her girlfriends are getting interested in boys, her weight seems to trouble her. But she still eats too much and has not lost weight. What should we do?

DR. SHAPIRO: In our culture, the twelfth year of life is at best a difficult time, perhaps more so for girls than boys. This is partly because puberty occurs about two years earlier in girls than boys, and with the onset of puberty, secondary sexual characteristics become prominent. With these emerging characteristics, the issue of attractiveness to the opposite sex arises. Youngsters begin to have parties together, and they date and flirt with each other.

Different rates of maturation play an important role in whether or not children become popular. We have a good deal of data concerning this, about both boys and girls. The evidence clearly suggests that the earlier a youngster's onset of physical maturity, the better and earlier will be the socialization with the opposite sex. The later a child physically matures, the later the socialization and the later the popularity with members of the opposite sex. This is also a period of time for young girls when fantasies are driven by crushes and unattainable love. This accounts for the popularity of so many rock stars.

If your daughter's friends are beginning to leave the peer group, your daughter may indeed become more and more isolated. By complaining about this, she indicates her unhappiness with this situation, yet she seems to do very little to become more attractive to boys. Therefore, her obesity may be a screen that successfully prevents her from engaging boys, which may be anxiety-provoking for her.

If your daughter's overeating has become a self-defeating guarantee that she will not be popular, you must be concerned about certain aspects of her personality functioning. Is she retreating from contact with boys or from any opportunity to become involved in certain normal social activities of children her age?

It sounds as though your daughter is engaging in a self-defeating course of behavior that narrows her options for popularity and for some happiness. If she does long to be with her friends—and therefore to be with boys, too—you must encourage her to restrain herself and to control her eating by participating in an appropriate diet program. This can be accomplished together with mother, providing your daughter with a common goal. The two of you can study food-calorie charts, take a course together, and actually use the experience as something you have in common with each other. Or this can be done in a group setting such as Weight Watchers, which provides a common goal as well as a sense of community and belonging. Weight Watchers accepts children as young as ten years; the child must have a doctor's note of approval. Children who belong to the group have their own programs within a peer group. If none of these measures is successful, you must then consider getting professional help for your daughter. It may very well be that her overeating is a neurotic symptom that can be helped by counseling.

Food as Love

Whenever our six-year-old son is upset, my wife gives him something to eat. I disapprove, but this has persisted. What can I do?

DR. SHAPIRO: We live in a symbolic world, and we don't have to translate all our symbols. Sometimes, we find our symbols very gratifying. So long as your child is not made ill by what is being done, the rewards he receives are important and are part of his knowing that he is loved and cared about.

If rewards of food, gifts, or money become the sole or primary expression of love, there may be trouble. Are you concerned that your wife is spoiling your son? Are you envious that your child is getting things you are not? Or does this represent a conflict between you and your wife? There are many things to consider in your question. I must infer that you are concerned that your child might develop a conditioned reflex which says, "I feel needy at this moment. Where's the next éclair?" Certainly, if this becomes a habitual way of dealing with strivings and cravings, and if such conditioning occurs, then such a pattern can lead to lifelong habituation to food, and to an unsuccessful way of relating to people.

Just "Baby Fat"

Our eight-year-old son has always been overweight. I've always been unhappy with this, but my husband, who is also overweight, says that this is just "baby fat." He takes our son out for junk food and encourages poor eating habits. I don't know what to do. Please advise me.

DR. SHAPIRO: Current information suggests that there are certain familial tendencies towards weightiness. We've known for years that some strains of laboratory mice are fat, and some are thin. So, too, with people. People use calories differently and have different caloric requirements. In short, there may be a certain genetic predisposition toward weightiness in both your husband and your son.

Equally important is your understandable concern that your husband is creating circumstances in which your son can identify with overweightedness and with an overattentiveness to food. Your concern has a sound foundation in relation to health and longevity issues and should not be lightly discarded. Your husband's insistence that this is no more than your son's "baby fat" is little more than a rationalization and should not be treated as a serious or responsible rebuttal of your concern about your son's weight. As children approach adolescence, obesity becomes a social deficit and a potent deterrent to a child's feeling well integrated. Obese children often develop certain personality quirks, such as clowning, when they actually feel quite depressed and dissatisfied with themselves.

Another potential problem in this situation is that you and your husband may have different views as to whether your son is still a baby or is a preadolescent. Your husband may view him as very much a child, whereas you may want him to become more mature. When such a situation arises, a child may be playing out a battle between his parents. It becomes very important in this situation for all three of you to seek a consultation so these issues may be discussed and better understood by all concerned.

Hiding Junk Food

Our seven-year-old daughter has always been on the heavy side. Recently we've noticed that she's gained even more weight, and we discovered that she's hiding food—cookies and candies—in her bedroom. What should we do?

DR. SHAPIRO: A child's hiding something rather than showing it openly indicates her awareness of the fact that somebody disapproves of this behavior. Your daughter has no doubt heard certain prohibitions and has tried to control her appetite. Hiding the food becomes a way of not revealing her slippage. Such behavior is similar to that of the sneak drinker or the smoker who slips off into the bathroom for a secret cigarette. Your daughter's behavior clearly exemplifies the war that so many of us wage within ourselves between indulging our wishes and the understanding that we're supposed to have control and act in a way that is best for ourselves. On the other hand, to do only what is right can make life quite boring, and most of us have secret little vices of one kind or another.

Your daughter undoubtedly knows that overeating is bad for her and will meet with disapproval. She therefore resorts to secret indulging rather than using restraint or openly defying you. Her being "caught" may be viewed as a partial wish to be caught. This indicates guilty feelings, and in her own way she is asking you to impose external limits and prohibitions on her. She may need to engage you this way because her own internal constraints are insufficient and do not prevent her from overeating.

Your interaction with your daughter should not be punitive. Rather, try to enlist your child's cooperation by indicating that you understand her wish occasionally to indulge her cravings. Avoid making this issue a maelstrom of conflict in the house. Try to help your child understand the consequences of her actions, consequences that will be more serious and apparent as she approaches adolescence and the need to appear attractive to boys assumes greater prominence for her and her peers. It would be most helpful if you could provide your daughter with consistent encouragement, which can help her when her own resources fail or when temptation is too great.

If your efforts meet with persistent failure, some group activity, such as that provided at Weight Watchers or a summer weight-reduction camp may be helpful. If these measures fail, a professional consultation would certainly be indicated.

An Overview

DR. SHAPIRO: The notion that eating is a separate function to be looked at apart from other matters in one's psychological life is probably wrong. Every study of mammalian activity indicates that survival depends upon physiological sustenance. Sustenance depends, of course, upon taking in adequate amounts of food.

Sustenance (nurturing) is the way infants become attached to caretakers. Our need for an early nurturing relationship is such that we of the human species have a very prolonged childhood. During this prolonged childhood, the human infant depends upon the parent or caretaker, which means that the infant must be provided with the breast or bottle, and eventually other kinds of food.

Finally, after a very long time, the human being can feed himself. During all the early years, the most intense and meaningful socialization with vitally important figures in life takes place around the feeding situation. Many experts feel that this earliest feeding and socializing situation is one of the most influential factors in any child's future developmental course. It is considered to be a crucial determinant of a great deal of later behavior throughout all of life. Therefore, it is inevitable that for human beings eating becomes a symbolically loaded situation, one having a great deal to do with the disposition of love and caring between people.

We see evidence of the emotional meanings of food throughout the life cycle. During toddlerhood, the child begins to want to choose food for himself. A bit later, we see children who become junk-food addicts, whereas others, especially during adolescence, go on selective diets. Others rebel by overeating or by undereating. Some people are disgusted by a particular kind of food, whereas others are made rapturous by that dish. Food maintains a loaded, highly charged, and rich variety of symbolic meanings throughout life. Adults construct a great deal of their social lives around the dining table. They have people over for dinner, go to other people's homes, and are quite concerned about what they will serve, how they will be received, and about the quality of the dining experience. It should be no surprise that throughout the childhood years the issues of food and of eating can become the center of conflicts for both child and parent, and can sometimes become the dominant issue in their relationship with each other.

Chapter 15: The Chronically Ill Child

Illness can dominate a child's life and a family's life. Certain childhood diseases, although having physical causes, are greatly influenced by emotional factors. In addition, they can alter the relationship between parents and a child. The two most well known and important such diseases are asthma and diabetes (discussed in the following pages), although this chapter applies to a variety of other conditions, such as colitis, hemophilia, hypertension, skin disorders, and severe allergies.

◊ ASTHMA

An asthmatic attack is terrifying, not only to a child, but to parents and siblings as well. The child feels as though he is choking to death; he gasps for breath, inhaling deeply, then wheezes as he tries to expel air. He feels as though he can barely take in enough air to stay alive.

Everyone in the home is affected by the attack. Inhalants, needles and syringes, and various medications are always at the ready. Pets are banned from the house. Furniture must be vinyl, not cloth, and dust is kept to a minimum. In the event of a severe asthmatic attack, a trip to a hospital emergency room may be necessary. Hospitalization may sometimes be unavoidable.

Asthma accounts for nearly one-fourth of all days lost in school by children and ranks third among chronic illnesses as a cause of visits to a physician. Because of the terrifying nature of the symptoms, asthma can produce profound psychological reactions in both child and parents. While there is little evidence that asthma begins as a reaction to emotional conflicts, evidence clearly indicates that emotional factors play an important role in prolonging the disease and in triggering attacks

in some children. Emotional factors almost always influence the relationship between the asthmatic child and his or her parents.

Our consultant for this topic is Norman L. Straker, M. D. Dr.
Straker is a Clinical Associate Professor of Psychiatry at the Cornell
University Medical College and an Associate Attending Psychiatrist at
the Payne Whitney Clinic of The New York Hospital. He is also an
Attending Psychiatrist at Memorial Sloan-Kettering Cancer Center.

Asthmatic Attacks Worsen with School

*Our six-year-old son is asthmatic. His asthmatic attacks have worsened
now that he must attend school. We don't want this to become a pattern. What
do you suggest we do?*

DR. STRAKER: First, you should consult with your pediatrician to
make certain that your child is not having a recurrent infection or
allergic reaction that causes his asthmatic attacks. If an examination
proves to be negative, the important issue is one of psychology.

The central problem for many asthmatic children is that of separation from their families. Very often, separation precipitates an asthmatic
attack. Some experts feel that an asthmatic child becomes extremely
dependent because the asthmatic attacks are so frightening and the
parents become overprotective. The child learns that an asthmatic attack is an effective antidote to separation and that his parents will treat
him very much like a child when an attack occurs. Parents may become
conditioned to regard the youngster in a more childlike way, especially
when separation is the issue. This can instill a lack of confidence in both
child and parents. Separation is difficult for any child, especially with the
beginning of school. But some asthmatic children find leaving home for
school especially stressful, and the mere threat of separation can precipitate an attack.

Other experts feel that an enormous amount of separation anxiety
predates the onset of asthma. Such a child has had problems separating
from his parents all along and then becomes asthmatic. As a result of
his attacks, the child develops an even deeper problem when trying to
separate from the parents. In either view, separation and dependency
issues can play an important role in an asthmatic child's life and in his
relationship to his parents.

In this situation, your son is having more asthmatic attacks with the
beginning of school. This clearly involves separation. It is best to speak
with your child about his worries concerning leaving home. In a non-

judgmental, understanding, and accepting way, inquire about school; ask how he feels about his teachers; his friends; and what it feels like to be away from home. It's particularly important to inquire if he has any concerns about his relationship with you, his parents. A very common concern among asthmatic children involves the child's worrying whether his parents will be home when he returns from school. Again, the child's concern involves fear of separation and fear of losing the parents. Some discussion about where mother or father can be reached during the school day may help your child realize that you are both available. It can also provide your son with a greater sense of security if he's worried about having an asthmatic attack while at school.

Another way of lessening your child's anxiety about separating from home is to meet with his teacher and the school nurse. Let your son know that this is being done. This is important because you should detail your child's special needs in regard to his asthma, while avoiding being overprotective. Your son should feel more comfortable knowing that his teacher and nurse can function as surrogate parents, should the need arise. They should also be familiar with your youngster's medications or nebulizer, if used, and should be alert to the occasional need for medication. A central issue in all this, however, is that your son's increasingly frequent asthmatic attacks are a symptom of his underlying concern about being away from home.

Manipulates Family

Our eight-year-old daughter is asthmatic. The pattern of her attacks is becoming very clear. She has one whenever she's distressed or doesn't get what she wants. What is this, and what can we do about it?

DR. STRAKER: Your child has a serious illness and seems to be having symptoms in response to something she prefers not doing. This can make others in the family angry. The angrier you get, the more her attacks will escalate. This places everyone in a difficult position. Your daughter's attacks may be more than a way of getting what she wants; they may be a form of anger that she cannot direct at you. The escalation of angry interchanges is not fruitful in this difficult situation.

A reasonable approach is to try to understand the nature of the communication between you and your youngster. You must arrive at an understanding of what is expected of the child and also explore why your daughter cannot express herself in a more verbal, direct way. Many asthmatic children cannot express angry feelings directly, in words. A compromise way for such a child both to express anger and still be "good" is for the youngster to begin wheezing. Your child should learn to express herself through verbal communication rather than through asthmatic attacks.

It is very important to let your daughter know that you are aware of her tendency to express anger, fears, and wishes in wheezing symptoms rather than by the direct use of words. Help her find a better way to express these feelings. Wheezing, or getting "sick" serves no one well.

Too Much Coddling

I'm the father of a ten-year-old asthmatic boy. My wife treats him as though he's fragile. She coddles him, spends a great deal of time with him, and treats him like a baby. I think this will make things worse in the long run. Please advise me.

DR. STRAKER: As a parent, you no doubt want your boy to develop into a robust young man. Coddling and overprotectiveness must evoke concerns that your son will not develop sufficient independence and maturity. It's very important to determine why your wife treats him as though he's an infant, which can stifle his independence as well as his sense of being able to master his illness.

You must arrive at an understanding of your wife's concern about your son. She may coddle him out of fear that he will have an asthmatic attack. She may have little confidence in your youngster's ability to manage without having an attack. She may lack confidence in the medications. She may doubt your son's ability or willingness to report his symptoms or to take the proper medications. She may even fear that your son may die, a fear that is heightened when he has an attack.

A discussion with your wife seems very much in order. You could explore these issues, together, in counseling. The problem may be as simple as your wife's not knowing enough about the medication or about how asthma is best managed. Or she may not feel free to fully inquire about the disease, because she and your son's pediatrician may communicate poorly. Counseling can help ensure that neither your son nor your wife become an emotional prisoner of his illness.

Off to Camp

Our nine-year-old daughter has asthma. She's the youngest of four children, and we haven't sent her to summer camp because of her disease. She wants to go, but we're not sure. Please advise.

DR. STRAKER: I would suggest that you first have a consultation with your allergist or pediatrician to determine if your daughter's asthmatic condition could tolerate a summer in the country. You should then determine if adequate medical coverage exists at the camp, learning if the medical personnel are familiar with asthmatic children and their management. If you are satisfied on both grounds, you must then face your own concerns and allow your child to go to camp and do what the other children do. This requires a certain degree of confidence in your child, in your doctor, and in the camp's medical facilities.

Allowing your child to go to camp, if this is possible, helps her accomplish one of the most important tasks in dealing with asthma: to live as normal a life as possible while handling the illness. Asthma should not be considered a "disability" and should not set a child aside as being "different." Nor should your child's life orbit around the notion of her illness. Sending your child to camp is in the interest of fostering normal emotional development. Children with asthma often tend to cling and have difficulty separating from their parents. A camp experience can be an excellent vehicle for helping your daughter move toward adolescence, which means developing her own separate identity.

Interestingly, many youngsters have fewer asthmatic attacks once they settle into a camp situation. In fact, many asthmatic youngsters— with no change in medication—quickly improve as soon as they are *away* from home. This may occur because conflicts *at home* often precipitate or worsen asthmatic attacks. Many asthmatic children are reassured when they realize that camp counselors can be excellent surrogate parents. Therefore, the quality of the camp counselor is an important determination when you consider sending you child to camp.

I've worked at a camp for asthmatic children. These were severely asthmatic kids who, when home during the summer, spent entire days indoors, in air-conditioned rooms. Yet they did extraordinarily well in the country air, which was filled with allergens. Removed from the constraints of home and allowed to "misbehave" just a little bit, they functioned beautifully and thoroughly enjoyed themselves. The psychological freedom and the lessening of family tensions can be valuable benefits for a child who spends a summer away from home.

The severity of your child's condition would determine whether she should go to a camp for asthmatic children or to a regular camp. An intractably asthmatic child should probably go to a special camp, simply because it is best equipped to handle the situation medically. An asthmatic youngster who does not have frequent attacks can certainly thrive in a regular camp.

◊ DIABETES

Childhood diabetes presents a formidable coping problem for the child and her family. Although diabetes is a serious disease of unknown causes, when the child and family adapt to the demands of the disease's management, the child can lead a productive and rewarding life. However, when the child, the family, emotional factors, and the demands of the disease are not in reasonable harmony, the disease can become poorly controlled and crippling.

The availability of insulin in 1922 converted what had been a fatal disease into a manageable disorder. Since the actual cause of diabetes is not fully understood, many youngsters have difficulty accepting and coping with a disorder that has no known cause. A young child may feel that she is being punished for being "bad" or for having done something wrong. Since hereditary factors are partly implicated in the cause of diabetes, parents may feel guilty and blame themselves for a child's disease.

Diabetes is a disease with complicated daily and lifelong treatment requirements. The child must cope with daily insulin injections. She must learn to monitor her own blood sugar levels and understand the effects of various foods, exercise, and emotional stress on the course of her disease. Enormous demands are placed on the diabetic child: she must eat regularly, take insulin injections, avoid sweets, carry sugar in case of a hypoglycemic episode, and, above all, be emotionally prepared to make a lifelong commitment to sensible disease management.

The family, too, must cope with the child's diabetes. Some variables in determining the course of the disease are: the age of onset, the ways the parents deal with emotional stress and their child, and the interactions between parents, siblings, and the child in relation to her disease.

Because of these complicated variables, the child with diabetes is vulnerable to having her disease slip out of control. The following questions deal with important emotional issues concerning how a child, and family, deal with diabetes mellitus.

Responsibility for Own Health

Our eight-year-old son is diabetic. My wife insists that he's too young to have complete responsibility over his disease management, but I think he should be able to handle this responsibility within the next year or two. Am I right?

DR. STRAKER: The issue of managing a diabetic child's illness is very important. There is no question that a child must be made to feel that the disease is part and parcel of his life, and that *he* is ultimately responsible for its management. I believe that a young child can begin to have certain responsibilities for the disease, although total responsibility must evolve over a period of time.

The management of diabetes involves regulating blood sugar and modifying diet to keep the blood sugar within reasonable limits. While certain technical details may at first be difficult for an eight-year-old boy, he will eventually master them. It's very important that a child understand something about the disease and its control.

You need not deluge your son with *all* the information necessary to understand his disease; this would be far too much for an eight-year-old boy to understand and integrate at one time. However, you can begin with small steps; over time, he can learn more and more about his disease and its proper control. Each increment of responsibility can be presented as a reward; the child's eventual taking over complete responsibility should be viewed as a major accomplishment, about which he can feel quite proud.

It's important that a child learn to control the disease before the onset of adolescence. During adolescence, a youngster may begin to rebel in a variety of ways. It's best that the child's diabetes not become incorporated into this rebellion, but rather that it was accepted long ago and considered by the child to be part and parcel of his life. It's one thing for a fifteen-year-old to rebel about issues such as friends or staying out late; it's potentially dangerous for an adolescent to rebel by not taking insulin or by eating incorrectly and throwing the disease into disarray. The life-and-death implications of such a rebellion must be avoided. Therefore, between the ages of eight and twelve, your son should learn to manage his disease and assume the responsibility for his own well-being.

Eats Junk Food

Our nine-year-old son has diabetes. He's very bright and knows exactly what he should and should not eat, but he eats junk food and throws his system off. How can we handle this?

DR. STRAKER: It's particularly difficult to ask a nine-year old to think of the future and conceptualize his disease in adult terms. A child this age has less understanding of the long-term effects of improper diet than an adult. He is being asked to anticipate problems and to think abstractly about "disease control."

A nine-year-old child can *directly* experience the symptoms of not complying with disease-management measures. Overindulgence or having a blood sugar level that's too high provide him with an *immediate* experience about his disease, one he would wish to avoid. This provides an awareness of the dangers of overeating. However, it's very common for youngsters to eat junk food—even when they are aware of the immediate consequences. You must explore why this problem persists.

A simple reason for noncompliance could be that your son has become fed up with the rules. He may be envious of his siblings or of other youngsters who eat junk food. This may happen after a party, or after a situation in which the child feels deprived because of not being treated like other children. This may warrant some greater flexibility on your part. Your son should be allowed some sweets and a certain amount of dietary indiscretion on special occasions. This would require alterations in his insulin dose, but it can reasonably be done.

On another level, your son's not complying with dietary restrictions may reflect serious underlying problems. A youngster's persistently eating junk food and making himself ill can indicate that anger is being indirectly and self-defeatingly expressed. Your son may have problems relating to mother or father. Or he may have problems with school.

Another possibility that could account for your son's eating junk food is that of depression. Nine-year-old children do get depressed, which can result in overeating. You would want to search for other signs of depression: feelings of sadness, helplessness, hopelessness, or withdrawal.

Another important reason for eating junk food can be a child's unwillingness to accept his illness. Although he may know about and understand the disease intellectually, he may not have accepted his situation emotionally. This may require further exploration with the pediatrician. Many people find it helpful for a child to get emotional support from other diabetic children.

Generally, whether dealing with diabetes or asthma, a rule of thumb is that if any unsuccessful pattern of disease control becomes repetitive and causes discomfort for a child or the family, it probably indicates that counselling is warranted.

Ideally, upon learning that their child has any chronic disease, a family must make that illness a major focus of family life. This intense focus should eventually dissipate to some extent, and the disease should become a more peripheral matter as time goes by and everyone accommodates to the disease. The youngster should become like other kids, but one who, in addition, requires some extra care because of the disease. The child should not primarily be considered a "diabetic."

Such an adaptation is accomplished by the family's gaining familiarity with the disease and eventually developing a certain degree of mastery over it. Over time, parents must transfer responsibilities for disease management to their child. They must have confidence in the child and not become overly worried about losing control over their youngster. It can be difficult for parents to develop such confidence, but this must eventually be achieved. Should parents become overzealous or too involved in disease management, their relationship with their child can orbit completely around illness. This is best avoided.

Defining Herself as Diabetic

Our eleven-year-old daughter has had diabetes for a few years. I don't want this disease to become her way of defining or seeing herself, and I try to encourage her to be as much like other children as possible. Am I fooling myself by this attitude?

Dr. Straker: While you don't want to convey that your daughter does not have a serious problem, your basic view is correct. Your daughter's life should *not* orbit around the notion of illness and "disability." Some children, viewing themselves as "ill," regard all their difficulties as resulting from their disease. It's crucial for your youngster to be able to define herself in a variety of nondiabetic ways: by her family, her work, her achievements, her interests, her religion, and various other factors by which people define themselves and their lives. While diabetes should be a part of her self-definition, it should be a very small component.

Some children find it emotionally convenient to attribute many feelings and reasons for doing or not doing things to a disease such as diabetes. If a youngster has school problems or has been rejected by another child, she may say she feels bad because "my sugar is off." A shy youngster who is reluctant to attend a party or a school dance might convince herself that she is best off staying at home because of her diabetes. It is an ominous development when a child "uses" the disease to "explain" or rationalize feelings or failures or when the disease becomes a means of avoiding challenges or of sidestepping important developmental milestones. Diabetes should not become the cornerstone of a child's identity.

An Overview

Dr. Straker: The reality of having a chronically ill child, whether the illness be asthma, diabetes, colitis, hemophilia, hypertension, or any serious disorder, can be a devasting blow to parents. The initial shock of such a realization can be profound. It takes a great deal of time and effort to assimilate and then effectively deal with such information.

Learning that a child has a chronic disease can profoundly affect a parent's view of a child's future life and well-being. Parents may feel that their hopes for themselves and their youngster have been shattered when they first learn of the disease. From that moment on, the family's emotional resources may be under great stress. Therefore, the parents of a sick child must meet a number of important challenges.

Parents must first understand their child's illness. This requires talking with the doctor and making an effort to learn as much about the disease as is possible. It may require reading and other efforts to understand intellectually and to cope with the disease.

A wide range of feelings accompanies parent's realizations that they have a sick child. First is the realization that the child must face a lifelong situation. Inevitably, parents are shocked when they realize that their child cannot be carefree and that he or she is imperfect. To some degree, all parents wish for a perfect child. This fantasy is, of course, shattered. The reality of the illness can cause the parents of a sick child to have a variety of profound and disturbing feelings.

These feelings often include anger at what has happened: anger at doctors, anger at fate, anger at the child, and anger at each other. Anger at a spouse can be especially compelling because some diseases have a hereditary component. Marriages sometimes become unhinged because one spouse is angry at the other for having passed on the trait for the disease. Along with these feelings, parents often feel sadness, depression, and a good deal of guilt.

Ideally, parents can deal with these feelings through talking and by emotionally supporting each other. Emotional support can also be provided by a pediatrician, by other family members, and sometimes through counseling. It's crucial that parents not vent their negative feelings on the child, who is an innocent victim of the illness. This can be difficult for some parents, who may resent the child, feeling that he or she is a disappointment. This is dangerous because, in time, such feelings can be internalized by the child, who comes to view himself as a disappointment, as a family spoiler, as imperfect, devalued, and defective. One task for any parent is to understand these feelings and to realize that they are universal among the parents of sick children.

Of particular importance is the way parents deal with their day-to-day anxieties about a sick child. This includes concerns about the child's safety, his health, and his dealings with peers. The degree to which parents manifest their anxiety will affect how a child feels about himself. An overly anxious parent will have an overly anxious, timid, and dependent youngster. A parent who overcompensates in the other direction, expressing no concern about the child's illness, can lead to the youngster denying that his illness requires any concern or management. The parents of a sick child must strive for a balance between the two extremes of overanxiousness or lack of concern.

There are ways of achieving this balance. This must involve the support of the child's doctor. A parent must have an open and trusting relationship with the child's doctor. You must feel free enough to ask *any* question, even one that may seem "stupid" or "simpleminded."

Parents must eventually learn not to overreact to situations their child will encounter. For example, a night spent at a friend's house can be an important developmental milestone for a chronically ill child. This experience can provide your child with a feeling that you have confidence in him and promotes a certain degree of confidence. It's important to consult your child's physician about such issues, whether an overnight stay at a friend's house or something having to do with medication. In time, parents must learn the amount of latitude a child's condition permits them to have.

The degree of comfort that you can achieve with your child's illness serves as a framework for your child's perceptions of his condition and can promote his positive adaptation to the situation. If you've come to terms with the challenge of your youngster's illness and have helped him become an integral part of your family and community, he will become a more integrated person in his life at large. This happens when parents have successfully dealt with their own psychological reactions to the child's illness and have mastered the educational requirements the illness imposes upon them. Parents can in turn use *their own* mastery of the situation to help their child go through the same steps to master the illness.

Parents and the child must maintain an open pipeline of communication, because the child often experiences the same feelings that parents do: feelings of inferiority, devaluation, defectiveness, and of being a disappointment to the family. If open lines of communication exist, you can then convey to your child that he is *not* a disappointment. Yes, chronic illness is an inconvenience and is not what anyone would have wanted. The illness means that you must have a close involvement with the school and with your child's physician. The disease imposes this upon you. It also means that you and your child will have to deal with concern about the possibility of early death, and other difficult issues. All these complexities demand that you and your child communicate openly with each other. When this occurs, your child can deal successfully with his or her condition and lead a full and satisfying life.

Chapter 16: The Child with Learning Problems

One of the most troublesome situations is that of a child who has problems in learning or in mastering certain school subjects. A child is considered to have a learning problem if his achievement lags significantly behind that which would be expected on the basis of his IQ.

The causes of learning problems fall within certain broad categories:

- *Congenital* causes, such as mental retardation.
- *Organic* (physical) causes that may or may not involve the brain. For example, hypothyroidism is a physical cause in which the brain in not involved. Blindness and deafness are two physical causes of learning problems in which the brain is involved.
- *Psychological* causes, such as when a child's emotional conflicts interfere with learning.
- *Social or family* causes, such as poor school facilities, poor instruction, or parents who interfere with a child's attending school.

◊ LEARNING DISABILITIES

In the last few years, attention has focused on a large group of children with normal or above-normal intelligence, who have excellent hearing, vision, and coordination, who are not environmentally disadvantaged, and who have no recognizable emotional disturbances, yet who do not learn well even though they receive excellent schooling. While they have no obvious brain damage, these children have a gap in their presumed capacity to learn and their actual learning performance. These children have a *learning disability*. The learning disability is a disorder in one or more of the basic processes involved in learning, or in understanding or using spoken or written language. This may appear as a disorder of reading, writing, arithmetic, spelling, or talking. A child may have visual difficulties (such as confusing *b* and *d*), hearing problems, or other difficulties with perception. There may be a memory impairment in a specific perceptual area (for instance, the child has difficulty remembering what she reads, but can recall information she has heard). A child may have problems integrating information or may have trouble using language.

Children with learning disabilities present one or more of the following characteristics:

- *Hyperactivity.* Some children with learning disabilities are hyperactive. A hyperactive child engages in random, purposeless, and excessive activity. A hyperactive youngster generally does better on a one-to-one basis than in a classroom.
- *Difficulties in attention.* Many children with learning difficulties have what is called an attention deficit disorder. In this disorder, a child fails to synthesize new information and has trouble separating an object from its background. For example, when looking at one object among others, the child "loses" the configuration of the object and must redirect attention to it again and again, as though it is an entirely new stimulus. Such a child may have his attention effectively held by moving objects, so he is able to concentrate on a television screen but not on his homework.
- *Impulsivity.* Some learning-disabled children are quite impulsive and accident-prone. Projects are done in a sloppy way, with easy items frequently overlooked.
- *Volatile emotions.* Some (but not all) children with learning disabilities are often impatient, quick to anger, and have difficulty inhibiting displays of emotion.
- *Poor motor control.* Some children with learning disabilities may have problems with subtle or fine motor control of their hands or fingers. Somewhat clumsy, the youngster may have trouble tying shoelaces, using a pencil, or performing other tasks that require fine coordinated movements.

Children with learning disabilities often develop emotional problems as a result of the failures and frustrations they experience when trying to master academic subjects.

Our consultant for this important topic is Margaret E. Snow, Ph.D. Dr. Snow is an Assistant Professor of Psychology in Psychiatry at Cornell University Medical College and is an Assistant Attending Psychologist at the Payne Whitney Clinic of The New York Hospital.

A New School

We've just moved to a new neighborhood and our nine-year-old son has begun at a new school. He has always performed very well in all subjects, but for the last month he has had trouble with arithmetic. It's gotten so bad that he receives special attention from the teacher. We're concerned about what's going on. Please advise us.

DR. SNOW. The most important thing parents can do is to make certain they have open channels of communication with their child's school. Presumably, you heard of this problem through the school or from your son's teacher. It's far better to find out in this way than to discover later from the report card that there is a difficulty. Fortunately, you have discovered the problem early on.

In virtually all circumstances, the school is on your side and will work diligently to discover the causes of your son's difficulties. We would hope that the school has a clear record of your son's functioning at his former school. If not, such records should be provided, because it's important for school personnel to know that your son did well until recently.

Teachers often see such problems with children who have difficulty adjusting to a new school setting, to new peers, and to a completely new environment. Your son's teacher can probably make an informed judgment as to whether or not this problem will fade as your son becomes better adjusted to his new environment.

I am not surprised to hear that the difficulty is with mathematics. Math is a subject that demands a good deal of attention and concentration for performance to remain at an optimal level. A child who is preoccupied with an adjustment problem can easily have compromised concentration in a classroom setting. Therefore, certain questions become crucial in attempting to understand your son's math difficulty. Is it equally compromised at home when doing homework? Can he successfully deal with math at home, where he is not distracted by the school setting or by peer pressures?

Beginning at a new school, especially in the middle of a school term, can cause pressures for any child. There's little doubt that, above all, your son wants to be accepted by the other children and would want to avoid being singled out as requiring special attention from the teacher. Such attention could very well hinder his beginning to feel more comfortable in a new school setting. While your son may need help, it would be preferable for it to be given in an after-school setting so that he is not isolated from the other children or made to feel "different." He could probably benefit from some tutorial help, which could be accomplished by employing a private tutor at home.

Since your son is doing well in other subjects and has always done well generally, this is most likely an adjustment reaction to his new school setting. It is likely these difficulties will fade. Should his problem with mathematics persist for more than six months, you may then want to consider testing.

Evaluating a Learning Disability

Our eight-year-old son is behind in reading but not in other subjects. He makes many mistakes when reading, and often confuses b and d. He's doing poorly and his teacher suggests that he may have a learning disability. What tests should he be given to find out if this is true?

DR. SNOW: It is not uncommon for such a problem to be brought to parents' attention when their child is seven or eight years of age. Often, the problem has been present for some time, but becomes obvious at this point. By eight years of age, teachers expect children to acquire certain basic reading skills. If a child is still reversing letters or cannot phonetically discern certain words, the problem must be thoroughly evaluated.

An evaluation can be done through the school or on a private basis. It entails psychological testing, which includes a general test of intelligence as well as tests of specific academic skills. It may also include other measures of cognitive abilities and various perceptual abilities, and tests of specific verbal capabilities.

Children of this age are traditionally given the Wechsler Intelligence Scale for Children (WISC), the most commonly used intelligence test for children at the elementary-school level. This test is divided into two sections: a section measuring verbal abilities and one measuring verbal-motor abilities. Through this test, the evaluator, a psychologist, develops a full picture of a child's intellectual profile. The test determines the child's cognitive strengths and weaknesses, and how they vary in these two areas of functioning.

Once a profile of the child's ability is obtained, the evaluator then determines if academic progress is developing at the expected rate, given the child's intellectual abilities. In your son's situation, it appears that most areas of academic achievement (arithmetic and others) are progressing well but that reading is progressing at a noticeably slower rate.

A learning-disability evaluation will attempt to pinpoint your son's difficulties: specifically, if he is still reversing certain letters. This problem will affect the orientation of certain letters, and may also affect the orientation of parts of words or the positioning of words within a sentence. If your son has a visual-sequencing problem, testing will pinpoint the difficulty so it may be properly addressed.

A learning-disability evaluation must develop a complete, across-the-board profile of your child's abilities, and provide specific information about his reading problem. The evaluation should yield a specific set of recommendations for helping your child deal with his reading problem. A reading problem tends to be a *very specific* difficulty; the term "reading problem" (or "dyslexia") is a catch-all term. It is a nonspecific way of indicating that a child is having difficulty learning to read, write, or spell, and is not achieving those skills at the expected rate, given the child's general intelligence.

A parent must obtain a complete report of the evaluation's results. The report should contain an accurate description of the child's problem and should make very specific recommendations for dealing with the problem. Many individual methods are available to help the child with a reading disability. Typically, a child is offered help in what is called a resource room, usually located in the school. During part of the school day, he receives individually tailored remedial instruction from a reading specialist.

It is vital that your child benefit from a targeted approach geared to evaluating his difficulty. The problem must then be addressed specifically; if this is not done, the disability could spread to other areas of learning. If a child's functioning becomes compromised in a global, across-the-board way, behavioral problems may follow. A targeted remedial approach can prevent such a problem.

Hyperactivity

Our six-year-old daughter has been doing very poorly at school. Her IQ seems normal, but she's just passing. She's easily distracted, has difficulty paying attention, and at times seems hyperactive. We're convinced that something's wrong. I'm not sure what to do. Please advise us.

DR. SNOW: I would recommend a team approach to determine your daughter's difficulty and then to provide specific recommendations. The coordinator of an evaluation team would most likely be a child psychiatrist.

The psychiatrist would take a very careful developmental history of your child. It's extremely important for a parent to be able to provide a detailed history to any professional who is evaluating the child, one that goes beyond presenting a picture of the child's present functioning to encompass an account of her entire developmental history.

Such a history begins with pregnancy. It would include details about the nature of the pregnancy; what occurred prenatally; whether or not there was anything unusual about delivery; your child's postnatal course in the hospital and beyond; a documented history of your child's early development, including major motor milestones; the early course of language and cognitive development; and a view of your child's early temperament. Was the child highly active? Did she have difficulties focusing on activities as a very young child? This important historical data becomes part of the overall evaluation.

Your daughter's evaluation would most likely include psychological testing. This will provide a rounded picture of her general level of functioning, indicating whether or not specific areas of cognitive functioning are compromised because of difficulties in attention and concentration. The intelligence test contains various subtests specifically designed to elicit any such problems. In addition, testing should be performed to evaluate your daughter's academic-readiness skills.

In some instances, consultation with a neurologist might be requested. This would occur if there is evidence of gross motor problems or coordination difficulties. However, most evaluating professionals will not routinely call in a neurologist unless the child's developmental history contains a clue that there may be a neurological disorder. Keep in mind that most hyperactive children are neurologically normal. In addition to testing, the evaluation includes an observation of the child by a child psychiatrist, a psychologist, or a learning specialist, while the youngster is at school.

In all likelihood your daughter has an attention deficit disorder, with hyperactivity. This means that your child is highly distractable and has difficulty sustaining attention and concentration. If she is hyperactive as well, then it's likely she is physically very restless and cannot easily remain still. This may have escaped notice before she entered school because enormous activity and a high level of energy are quite normal for four- and five-year-olds. But by six years of age, children can be reasonably expected to remain at a desk for extended periods of time during the school day. By this age, a child is also expected to function capably as a member of a class or in a goal-oriented group. A hyperactive child has great difficulty sustaining attention in a group setting where there are many distracting stimuli.

A child with an attention deficit disorder does not have problems focusing attention in all circumstances. Frequently, a parent will comment, "My daughter can watch television for an hour and doesn't fidget." This doesn't mean the child does not have an attention deficit disorder. Different stimuli and different stresses encountered in varying situations will evoke symptoms of the attention deficit disorder, and the problem may not appear in every situation.

A complete evaluation is recommended for any child who is presumed to have normal intelligence but seems unable to focus on school lessons and is not integrating and mastering sufficient information to get on with the business of schooling.

If your daughter has an attention deficit disorder with hyperactivity, various treatments are possible. Many such children are successfully treated with medication. Such treatment may be accompanied by behavioral intervention, which can be very helpful. A hyperactive child needs a great deal of structure. Rules and regulations must be made especially clear, and limits and allowances must constantly be defined. Counseling for parents can help them understand the child's needs, so a home environment can be provided to help the child focus attention and better control hyperactivity.

Ideally, the teacher should be aware that a hyperactive child requires a great deal of support and encouragement, as well as clearly defined structure, to help accomplish things during the school day. Parents and teachers alike should be alerted to the possibility that a hyperactive child may have poor impulse control, low frustration tolerance, may have volatile emotions, and may be unable to tolerate long delays in obtaining gratification. Through no deliberate action or intent, a hyperactive child may antagonize other children and may have difficulty forming satisfying peer relationships.

When appropriately treated with a combination of pharmacologic agents and behavioral techniques, a child with an attention deficit disorder and hyperactivity can function well in a school setting. When the child has been given proper opportunities, and when parents and teachers are attuned to the child's needs, the youngster can remain in a mainstream school setting. The child may be able to capitalize on a variety of strengths once attention and concentration can be focused on school subjects.

Will She Grow Up Normal?

Our daughter has an attention deficit disorder with hyperactivity. She's being treated, and so far, is doing very well. Will she grow up normal?

DR. SNOW: When identified and treated early on in their lives, most children with attention deficit disorder have a good chance of having a positive school experience. Many such children have development on their side: in time, they naturally develop out of this problem. Their abilities to pay attention and concentrate improve year by year, even with minimal treatment. If treated early on and appropriately, a child with attention deficit disorder will not necessarily suffer long-term ill effects from the disorder. The youngster can continue to attend school, can learn at the expected rate, and can acquire the skills needed to go on to higher learning.

There is every reason to be optimistic about the child with an attention deficit disorder. An attention deficit disorder need not preclude a child from becoming a high achiever, especially in areas that don't rely heavily on the ability to focus and sustain attention. When treated early enough so that the disorder does not cause secondary difficulties, the ultimate prognosis is excellent.

Bear in mind that the pharmacologic treatment of attention deficit disorder does not "cure" the problem. The medication merely smothers the symptoms until development progresses sufficiently for the child to grow out of the difficulty. Again, development is on the child's side, and in time, treatment can be stopped when sufficient maturation has taken place.

Avoids School

Our eight-year-old son wakes up in the morning with a stomachache whenever there's a new assignment in school or there's a test. We know that his ailment has something to do with anxiety about school, and he sometimes refuses to go. What should we do?

DR. SNOW: When a child refuses to attend school, and when that refusal is based on anxiety, a parent must make certain the child attends school. The child who stays home from school, even once, because he cannot confront a test, will find the situation so tempting that he will want to repeat it whenever he must deal with an anxiety-producing activity at school. The behavior can become self-rewarding, gratifying, and positively reinforced. While a parent may sympathize with a child's difficulty, the parent's task is to ensure that the child attends school, since school is not only right for a child, it is necessary. Convey to your child that you understand school can be stressful, but his attendance is still required. School is a child's job.

It's very important to explore the basis of your child's refusal or avoidance. While probing your son's concern about school, it can be helpful to make a comment such as, "I know you feel bad today, but you have a math test, and it's very important to take the test." Avoid a debate about whether or not the child is truly ill, providing you are certain he is in good physical health.

A child who manages to avoid school can easily slip into a pattern of school refusal as a way of avoiding anxiety. A parent must encourage a child to attend school, which sometimes requires considerable energy, but ultimately your child must master the problem responsible for his anxiety. If a pattern of anxiety and school avoidance persists, you should seriously consider counseling for your child. (See in Chapter 4, "When Your Child Doesn't Want to Go to School.")

An Overview

A child's learning problem is discovered in one of a variety of ways. It may be acknowledged by the child himself, who comes home from school one day and says, "I'm not doing well in school. I'm unhappy and I'm not understanding what's going on." Or acknowledgment may come from the teacher who informs the parents that their child is having difficulty with a particular subject. In some unfortunate instances, parents learn of the difficulty when the child brings home an unsatisfactory report card at the end of the term. At that point, it is somewhat late in what is clearly an ongoing process. No matter how it comes to their attention, at some point parents must acknowledge that their child has a learning problem.

Parents must then attempt to do something about the learning problem. It is crucial for parents to open up any channels of communication they can. All too often, antagonism develops between parents and school personnel. This should not be an adversarial situation, however, because in most instances the school has the child's interests in mind. It is important for parents to work through the school, keeping in close communication with the child's teacher, with the psychologist, and with any other specialists who may be involved. A parent must then decide about an evaluation for the child. Should it be done at the school or on a private basis? This can be decided when a parent has discussed the child's situation with the team of professionals who have had contact with the youngster.

An evaluation attempts to discern the exact nature of the problem. Is the difficulty caused by emotional factors, by social issues, by behavioral or motivational problems, or does the child have specific cognitive difficulties? If the child has cognitive difficulties, are they an attention deficit disorder, or is there a specific perceptual problem leading to a learning disability?

A comprehensive and skilled evaluation should provide answers to these questions. The child should be seen and observed a number of times and in varying circumstances, so that a wide range of revealing information is amassed. A thorough evaluation should provide information about the child's intellectual ability. It should provide a revealing profile of the child's functioning across a broad spectrum of intellectual domains. It should also indicate the child's level of achievement in various areas of academic performance and development.

A good evaluation specifically pinpoints the child's learning problem rather than providing global, nonspecific information. Each child's individual difficulty will be different. Many evaluations reveal that a youngster does not have a single, clearly circumscribed area of difficulty. Rather, one difficulty affects other areas of learning, so that various areas of learning problems finally emerge. A child who is very anxious and emotionally overwrought may at first appear to have cognitive problems or a learning disability. A child with cognitive problems or an attention deficit disorder may appear to be anxious or have emotional problems. A thorough evaluation will probe those factors contributing to the child's difficulty, providing a solid basis for making specific treatment recommendations.

When a child's learning problem has been thoroughly evaluated, a parent needs a clear and explicit explanation of the problem. Parents should come away from the evaluation knowing exactly what was done, and knowing the specific conclusions provided by the testing, including the exact recommendations made.

The next step is critical. As their child's advocate, parents must be ready and able to bring the testing information to the professional who will treat the child, whether this person is a tutor, teacher, school psychologist, pediatrician, or child psychiatrist.

Parental counseling is sometimes helpful because it can equip parents with methods for dealing with a child's difficulties. Parents may also need to deal with their own feelings about their child and how the youngster's difficulties affect the family and family life.

Most important, however, is that parents completely understand a child's difficulty; there should be no gray zones. Parents should remain in close communication with the professionals who are working with their child. This contact must be maintained over a period of years while the child's progress is carefully monitored. Parents should feel reassured by the knowledge of exactly what is being done for their child. My model for dealing with the child with learning problems is built on cooperation and open lines of communication among parents and professionals, plus close monitoring of the child over time, with the implementation of appropriate intervention.

While no parent would want a child to have a learning disability, it can become a catch-all term that "takes the blame" and negates other factors that cause school problems. Parents must be aware of today's tendency to overdiagnose children as having a "learning disability." This diagnosis can be made all too frequently, excluding other important factors such as emotional problems or social issues that may interfere with the child's capacity to learn.

Chapter 17: The Bully and the Victim

A bully succeeds in getting his way by throwing his weight around. A bully is often larger and stronger than most of his companions and therefore succeeds in bullying. Such success is hardly surprising in light of the value many parents place on physical size. Comments such as "How big you are!" or "My, you're getting bigger every day!" and other declarations that size is a virtue, are rarely overlooked by children.

A child's abusive behavior is learned from what he sees and experiences within the family: the child does unto others what is done to him. Bullies may feel powerful, but they rarely feel accepted or even liked. In fact, most often, bullies are quite insecure and their bullying ways can be partially understood as a means of overcoming feelings of worthlessness.

Parents grow concerned if their child encounters a bully, especially if such a child is a fixture on the block or in the playground. Do you get involved or not? If you do, does your child learn to handle his own problems and fight his own battles? If you don't, will your child think you don't care enough? Or will your child be hurt, physically or psychologically?

Dealing with the neighborhood bully is a concern that parents find compelling, since it can affect a child during school hours, or the way he spends his spare time. It can also raise questions about whether or not a child has grown accustomed to being a "victim." The following questions are those most frequently asked by parents who are concerned about this troubling situation.

Our consultant for this topic is Robert C. Ascher, M.D. Dr. Ascher is a Clinical Associate Professor of Psychiatry at Cornell University Medical College and an Associate Attending Psychiatrist at the Payne Whitney Clinic of The New York Hospital.

Getting Picked On

Our nine-year-old son has been getting picked on by one particular boy. This happens every day on the way to school. It's gotten to the point where our son is reluctant to go to school. We know we must do something—but what?

DR. ASCHER: In order to make any comments about either a bully or a child who is picked on, it's probably best to start with some generalities. First, there are genetic and dispositional differences among children. Some children are naturally quite aggressive and active, and stay that way from the very beginnings of their lives. Other children are sweet, amiable, and somewhat submissive throughout their lives. And there may be intermittent periods during which a sweet, amiable child is the terror of the sandbox, biting other children and causing mother a great deal of worry. This is usually quite time-limited, occurring between eighteen and twenty-four months of age, usually fading by the age of three.

After these early toddler experiences, the child becomes involved with social relations and peer groups. A bully usually reflects in his behavior whatever is going on at home. Whether a youngster is a bully or a victim, he plays out a specific behavioral role that has been learned in the home. After all, the home is a child's primary socializing experience.

When a parent asks advice about any situation involving a bully or a victim, I find it useful to make certain specific inquiries before offering a recommendation. What is your child's situation at home? Is he the last child, the middle, or the oldest? It's also important to know a great deal about the parents and their relationship. Is there violence or bullying going on at home between the parents? Is the boy identifying with one parent or another, be it a submissive or a bullying role? Are mixed messages being given to the child? We frequently see parents who insist that a child be cooperative and obedient, that he never fight or use violence, and yet the very same parents become very vociferous if the child is submissive or is bullied by another child.

All too frequently, the parents of a child who bullies provide tacit encouragement of bullying behavior. Such invitations can be so subtle that on the surface the parents' reaction seems to condemn the bullying. However, when explored and probed, parents' reactions to a child's bullying may contain, among other things, a somewhat veiled nod of approval for the child who uses physical force to get his own way.

There are other considerations when your youngster is the victim of a bully. Is your son small for his age? Is he nearsighted and wearing thick glasses? Does he have an obvious physical characteristic that may invite cruelty from children who are so inclined? Is your son a provocative boy? Is your family new on the block or in the neighborhood? Are you of a minority ethnic or racial group that sets certain social forces into motion that result in a child's being picked upon? All these questions about any child—either bully or victim—must be answered before a specific recommendation can be made.

I often discover that a child's father objects most strenuously to a boy's passive or submissive ways. I'm now treating a youngster whose father cannot tolerate his son's peaceable ways; I recently learned that the father carries a gun. This man will never surrender any territory at all. Actually, this boy is in more trouble at home, for not being aggressive, than he is with the neighborhood bully.

Different fathers provide different advice as to the best way to handle the situation. One man, having learned long ago that it's best to avoid fights, teaches his son to walk away. Another advises his son to befriend the biggest boy in school so he has ready-made protection. Another tells his boy to walk to school in the company of three other boys. All these issues must be explored: the child's family, and the school and neighborhood situations, as well as the parents' reaction to the child's behavior either as a bully or a victim.

In your situation, assuming that no unusual circumstances prevail, I would recommend that a parent accompany your child to school. The aggressor must be identified and his parents must be approached, but this must be done peaceably. It would also be wise to talk with your son's teacher, who may know the bully quite well. You may discover that this youngster has caused problems for a number of other children or has even had some encounters with the police.

The bully may in fact be a very troubled child who is frequently beaten at home and who feels the need to do the same thing to others. Perhaps the bully can be helped, once he is identified. A very important element in this situation is to determine the receptivity of the bully's parents. Can they tolerate being approached and told that their son is causing trouble? It's axiomatic among child psychiatrists that parents rarely hear what they are unprepared to hear or do not wish to acknowledge. To some extent, the outcome will depend on your ability to establish quickly and effectively a relationship with the bully's parents, and it depends, too, on the quality of their relationship with one another and with their child.

Because your son has become reluctant to go to school, it is imperative that you take quick and effective action to determine exactly what's going on and put an end to this unacceptable incursion into your child's school life.

Three Bullies

Our ten-year-old son is having trouble with three bullies in his class. They've been picking on him and on some other kids. I'm tempted to speak to his teacher or do something, but our son insists he will take care of it. I'm worried he'll get hurt. What should we do?

DR. ASCHER: The first thing to establish is that your child is not the only one in school who is being picked on and that he is not the sole victim of these three bullies.

At times, there is a curious alliance between the bully and the victim. In addition, there is a near-universal taboo, among kids, against "snitching." This powerful peer pressure has its roots in the fact that during the school-age years, a child slowly relinquishes dependency on his parents, shifting a good deal of the dependence onto peers. To a ten-year-old child, satisfying the peer group's requirements has the same force and meaning as pleasing one's parents had at an earlier time in life. A child of this age actually needs the respect, admiration, and even "love" of his peers.

Don't underestimate the powerful meanings of the peer group to a child. While you don't "tell" on mommy and daddy, you don't "tell" on your peers either, even if some of them tend to be bullies. There is an interesting correlation between not "snitching" on parents and not "telling" on members of the peer group when violence occurs. In fact, children who are battered by their parents rarely tell authorities about this. In the same way, because the peer group becomes so dominant a force in a child's life, a youngster who is being picked on by a few children in the peer group has a difficult time letting adults know about it. This occurs because the group is so necessary for the child's self-esteem.

Your son does not want to snitch on these three bullies. Providing that he is not physically injured and continues to attend class, he is best off taking care of the situation on his own. If the problem escalates, you may be forced to contact the teacher or other school authorities. At this point, however, the best policy seems to be one of supporting your son with encouragement and respect, and hoping that he can negotiate his way through this difficulty on his own.

A Constant Target

Our son is eleven years old. He's not terribly athletic and he's been the target of two bullies who have been taunting him for the last two years. My concern runs deeper than this, however, because this is only one of many times he has had this trouble. What's going on, and what can we do?

DR. ASCHER: A child may become a convenient target for other children for a variety of reasons. For instance, he may be grossly over-weight, miserable with his self-image, awkward or bashful, and may unwittingly invite aggression by other children. Such a child manages to find an aggressor wherever he goes. It would be important for your son to talk with a child psychiatrist who could derive some understanding of your son's role in this repetitive scenario.

It's fair to say that in all human reactions there is the one who puts forward his cheek, and the one who does the kissing. It always takes two to tango. Because your son evidently participates in bringing about the repeated bullying, your attention must turn to your son's needs and conflicts. Barring some unusual social circumstances that breed aggression, one must assume that your son is a constant target because he has a powerful inner need to play such a role. In all likelihood, he could benefit from a consultation or from counseling with a child psychiatrist.

Son's a Bully

We recently received a telephone call from the principal of our son's school. Our eleven-year-old has been accused of bullying a number of children. We've seen him behave aggressively before, but it's getting out of hand. What should we do?

DR. ASCHER: Children who become bullies have overtly or secretly been encouraged to use physical force to get what they want. Often, the bully's home is a hotbed of conflict. There may be discord between the parents; there may be physical fights; there may be drinking, and the atmosphere seethes with violence or with the threat of violence. Father may be unemployed or about to lose his job. One parent may be threatening to leave, or there may be some terrible family secret. In most such situations, prevailing family difficulties operate, causing a child to smolder with anger and resentment. Your son's behavior most likely reflects turmoil within the family.

An important consideration when dealing with the bully is to explore the youngster's environment. This can be very telling for urban children who may have relatively few opportunities for physical activity and exercise. Young boys between the ages of nine and eleven need an enormous amount of physical exercise, at least an hour or two each day. Many schools, public and private, allow kids a total of only one or two hours of physical activity per week! A great deal of restless energy is never depleted by these children and some is ventilated as aggression. Many parents, especially in households in which both parents work, recognize this and enroll their children in a variety of after-school activities so this energy can be expended. While this tends to be highly orchestrated, it's best that a child have adequate opportunities to vent frustration and expend energy.

The role of television as facilitator of violence should not be omitted. Beginning in early childhood, youngsters enter into a trancelike state in front of the television set rather than being involved in robust activity. Children can sit in front of the set for hours, which is, no doubt, neurologically disturbing. I've noticed that even after the set is turned off, youngsters continue staring into space, apparently having momentarily departed from ordinary levels of consciousness. Such passive watching has in large measure supplanted the baby-sitter or the grandmother and often replaces physical activity, much to the potential peril of children's healthy physical and emotional development. I truly believe that prolonged television-viewing can be an impediment to proper neuromuscular development and can prevent a child from expending inner tensions and excess energy in a healthy, physical way.

Added to this passivity is the undeniable fact that kids view a great deal of violence on television. They may then experience the need to master their own aggressive impulses by actively participating in those very impulses. Children can feel overwhelmed by constantly viewing victims, as they do on television. They often feel the need to reassure themselves that they will not be victimized; they accomplish this by becoming aggressive themselves. If a child can have healthy outlets for physical aggression, if he can play baseball, football, ride a bicycle, or engage in some other physical activity, he can achieve mastery over his own physical tensions. However, if he is limited to one or two hours of gym class each week, he has inadequate opportunity for the expression of these impulses, and they may emerge somewhere else.

In my experience, a child brought in for a consultation because of bullying behavior often lives in an urban setting and has few opportunities for discharging physical tensions. I sometimes advise parents that such a child may be better off in a boarding-school situation, or that he needs more activity out of doors, perhaps in sports. A remarkable change in behavior may result from such a change. When the youngster is taken to the country or given ample opportunity to participate in sports, violent and hostile behavior often dramatically decreases.

In other situations, I've recommended that parents sharply curtail the youngster's television-watching and encourage more organized physical activity. This can help diminish hostile and aggressive behavior toward others. This may not work, however, when both parents work and where the television has become an electronic baby-sitter. Sadly, many parents feel that by giving a child his very own television set in his room, they are helping the child. In fact, they are adding to the physically stultifying atmosphere in which the youngster is already mired. This also provides increasing doses of television violence, while not helping the child find reasonable avenues for expressing pent-up tensions.

If your son continues to act aggressively, I would recommend a professional consultation for you and your child so that these important issues and determinants of aggression can be explored.

A Bully in the Making

Our son is nine years old and is very big for his age. My husband encourages him to use his size to his advantage. I'm worried we may have a bully on our hands. Please advise us.

DR. ASCHER: Your question foreshadows the problem. You said, "My husband encourages . . ." The real question is, what does a parent admire in a child? A great deal of American myth—and reality—would disagree with a psychiatrist's viewpoint about bringing up a child. Many fathers would say, "To promote peaceableness is to promote cowardice. Good guys finish last. I'm the CEO of my corporation because I push, and I want my kid to push, and I'm proud when he does." While you worry that you may have a bully in the making, your son may be identifying with his father. One can never overestimate the role of identification and modeling for all forms of children's behavior, including bullying.

It is well known that most parents want a child to become whatever they themselves are. Both you and your husband would probably benefit from a consultation with a professional. After all, while you may regret some of your son's bullying, to an extent it may excite you. After all, you married a man who seems to have some bullying propensities. Both you and your husband should obtain a consultation and discuss your son's behavior.

Scapegoating

Our eight-year-old daughter attends an all-girl school. She's very tall and somewhat clumsy, and gets picked on at recess by a particular group of girls. This upsets her, and I'm not sure what to do. Please advise me.

DR. ASCHER: The problem of a girl being scapegoated by other girls occurs more commonly than most parents realize. Parents usually expect bullying to occur at the hands of boys, but it frequently occurs among girls' groups. Young girls of eight, nine, and ten years are busy forming cliques and finding best friends. This may be capricious and there can be a great deal of shifting from one friend to another. A good deal of cruelty may prevail, with one child being left out or with another being scapegoated. Of course, two months later, a girl who was something of an "enemy" is now a best friend. Schoolteachers and other adults who work with children are quite aware of the social cruelty that can pervade girls' peer groups.

In fact, childhood is not the dreamy time that so many adults fondly recall. It can be filled with untamed aggression that finds expression in a variety of cruel ways. If your daughter is overweight, or clumsy, or if she's unusually tall, she may find herself the object of considerable taunting and cruelty.

Another important element in this situation is the possibility that a nine-year-old girl may be experiencing her first period. Menarche aften appears as early as ages eight or nine, and the sudden onset of menstruation for a child this age can be very upsetting. A menstrual period may seem to be a defeat of all the tidiness training that a child has only recently undergone. A young girl having her first period may seem "different" to her friends, and as in all primitive groups, anyone who is deemed different may be treated unkindly.

You may find it helpful to visit your daughter's teacher. Perhaps a change of section or some other intervention will be helpful. However, your daughter may have to negotiate a long and difficult course, especially if she is clumsy or very tall, or somewhat overweight. Such a child may be scapegoated simply for being "different" or because her size is an uncomfortable reminder of parents and teachers to the other girls.

A child who is scapegoated for these reasons needs a great deal of extra love and reassurance from her parents. She needs to know that she is fine, that she is good-looking, and that she is accepted and valued, even if she is not particularly athletic. Perhaps she has some talent in music, singing, acting, drawing, or in some other sphere where she can excel. Such activities should be heartily encouraged. Excellence in any area can be helpful and can infuse your daughter with feelings of self-esteem.

An Overview

Youngsters should be helped to discern the differences between useful aggression and violent aggression. Historically, Americans admire, respect, and need aggression, in the sense that we like to get things done. Yet it is most helpful to encourage children to distinguish between useful aggressiveness and hostile aggression.

Our children are flooded with violence and with the threat of annihilation in the visual and print media. In addition, many urban children lack adequate opportunities for the expression of their physical tensions, instead watching television, which further promotes fantasies of violence. For the child whose home life is in turmoil, this is a ripe milieu for hostility and for aggressive, bullying behavior. Again, parents should help their children appreciate the differences between healthy assertiveness and aggression that is violent and destructive.

Chapter 18: New Kid on the Block

When a family moves from one neighborhood or city to another, its ordinary patterns of living are disrupted. This pertains to children as well as adults, and more so to the school-age youngster than to a very young child. The school-age child must adjust to a new home; new environs; a new school with different teachers, methods, and classmates; and to new peers outside the classroom, which include scout troops, Little Leagues, and others. If the child attends religious or other classes, the adjustment to new children and teachers must be made in this setting as well.

Most children make these multiple transitions with no great difficulty. However, more and more families today move with great frequency, multiplying the variety and number of adjustments that a child must make throughout the childhood years.

Our consultant for this topic is Fady Hajal, M.D. Dr. Hajal is an Assistant Professor of Psychiatry at Cornell University Medical College and an Assistant Attending Psychiatrist at the Westchester Division of The New York Hospital.

Preparing for the Transition

Our family is moving to another state over the summer. Our children are seven and eleven years old. How can we best prepare them for a smooth transition?

DR. HAJAL: The best way to help children make a smooth transition is to inform them about the move as early as possible and to involve them in the decision itself. It can be helpful to discuss with your children the reasons for the move, eliciting from them their feelings about changing friends and schools, and getting as much input from them as possible. As an axiom, it's reasonable to say that if both parents feel good about the move, the children, too, will have positive feelings.

A smooth transition is promoted by helping the children learn as much as possible about the new area, their new home, and the new school. This would include a few preplanned visits before the actual date of the move.

As the move approaches, it is useful to help your children deal with their feelings about leaving the familiar behind: their house, friends, and the old neighborhood. When moving, children must deal with losses; this involves an element of bereavement, and parents must expect that any child will have strong feelings about leaving behind the familiar world. When children express grieving feelings about losing contact with the old neighborhood and friends, it helps to let them know that you understand and that these are completely normal feelings.

After you have moved, it is a good idea to actively help your children make new connections, both at school and in the neighborhood peer group. While children need some time to make connections and adjustments to their new environment, it can be helpful to encourage their making contact with other children. You may want to introduce yourself to the neighbors, inquire about groups or clubs in which your child will take an interest, ask if the child wishes to join the Boy Scouts or Girl Scouts, and generally help your child make the transition once the move has been made.

Relocates Frequently

My husband's business requires relocation every three years. I'm concerned about the effects of these moves on my daughters, ages four and eight, and their capacity to form good relationships and make healthy adjustments.

DR. HAJAL: Any move will tend to be less traumatic for a four-year-old child than for an eight-year-old. Your older child has already made important linkups with other children, both at school and in the neighborhood. Generally, peer relations are more important for an eight-year-old than for a four-year-old. Therefore, your eight-year-old's relationships will be severed and the frequency of moves every three years will create some problems.

As the child deals with the moving process every two or three years, she may begin holding back and become wary of establishing friendships, especially if she has had difficulty renouncing friendships and relationships in the past. To prevent reexperiencing such sadness, she may tend to become less involved with children in a new environment. If frequent relocations continue, this may become an emotional pattern to protect herself from painful feelings.

If you are not moving far from your old neighborhood, it would be wise to help your eight-year-old continue relationships with her old friends through visits, writing, and telephoning. This helps curtail the child's feeling that all old relationships have been completely ruptured.

Your four-year-old will not encounter the same difficulties. At this age, a child rarely has stable friendships or relationships. Younger children go through sets of friends, rarely having the intense relationships that eight-year-olds do. A four-year-old relates mostly to people within the family, but that will change in a few years. Eventually, the family's moving every three years will begin to affect the younger child's relationships as well.

You are obviously concerned about these moves affecting your children's capacities to form good relationships throughout later childhood, into adolescence and adulthood. A child's adaptation partly depends on her basic temperament. Some kids thrive on frequent changes and transitions. They derive a great deal of excitement from new experiences and from meeting new people. Such children can also maintain friendships from the old neighborhood, if this is feasible. Frequent relocations need not necessarily be traumatic to a child, and they need not affect a child's capacity to form good relationships later on.

An important determination in how well a child makes the necessary adjustments is the emotional context in which the moves occur. Parents who prepare their children for these moves and who help children deal with the loss of friends and the familiar, help their children make the necessary transitions and form relationships in the new neighborhood. Concern about the impact of many moves on children is really part of the larger issue of helping a child adapt to ongoing changes in life.

A New School

Our ten-year-old son is in the fifth grade. We're moving to a different community with a progressive school system. What steps should we take to help our son adjust to his new school curriculum?

DR. HAJAL: It's very important to provide your child with as much information about the new school curriculum as possible. This includes information about the structure of the curriculum and the nature of the classes, as well as a preparatory visit to the school. You may want to make a visit with your son during the summer prior to the move, so that he can see what the school looks like. While most families prefer making a midsummer move, this is not always the case, and there are advantages and disadvantages to midsummer and midyear moves.

At some point, the youngster should be introduced to the school and should meet the principal and his new teacher. Make certain to obtain all necessary records concerning your child's past academic performance, which should be provided to the new school. Some schools have a "buddy system," in which a particular child is assigned to a new youngster to help orient him to the new environment.

Generally, a parent can help a child make adjustments by learning about the new school and by determining what will be required of the child. Familiarization occurs in many areas, in subtle and not-so-subtle ways. Some areas of familiarization involve an idea about the children, the new school's dress requirements, the neighborhood "culture," and other subtle bits of information your child will accumulate about the new environment. Actually, a certain degree of culture shock is involved in any move from one school to another, and from one neighborhood to another. Any activity promoting familiarization helps a child adjust and make the transition.

You have indicated that your child's new school has a progressive curriculum. Try not to allow too much anticipation to build up about the curriculum and its requirements. Such concern can become so dominant a preoccupation that it interferes with a child's making a smooth transition. While advance preparation is important, overemphasis on the new school's curriculum can interfere with a child's going through some bereavement for the old school.

Ideally, life should continue as normally as possible, even in the face of a new school with a progressive curriculum. Most children make the necessary adjustments to a new program. Any difficulties can be helped by counselors and academic advisors at school, or even by a brief period of tutoring, if it is needed. If any extra work or tutoring is needed, it is best provided in a way that makes the child feel he is being helped and should not foster the feeling that he is being penalized.

It's usually helpful if parents and school personnel have some contact before the move. This should be done in a way that doesn't arouse too much anticipatory anxiety for the child. If one or both parents have negative feelings about the move, they may convey these feelings to a child by exaggerating the potential difficulties they expect him to encounter. This can create anticipatory anxiety within the child, which is actually a reflection of parental dissatisfaction.

Strong Ties to the Old Neighborhood

Although shy, our eleven-year-old daughter had many friends in the old neighborhood. We moved six months ago, but our daughter is still clinging to friends from the old neighborhood. She telephones them every day and visits them on weekends. So far, she's made no attempt to establish new friends. What should we do?

DR. HAJAL: It's important to distinguish whether your daughter's difficulty in making friends is a result of negative feelings about the move or is more a reflection of her basic temperament. If a child tends to be shy, is somewhat family-bound, is not very exploratory and curious, and is slow to develop initiatives with new people, she will be very much the same in a new neighborhood.

Saddled with ambivalent feelings about a move, parents may seek from a child some reassurance that they did the right thing. This may be the situation with your daughter, because you seem to expect that despite her temperament she will make linkups with new peers. During the first six months, your daughter is still making adjustments to the move; this may take a full year to be accomplished. However, it would still be preferable for a child to take some initiative in making new friends, even if close relations have not yet been established.

You may want to consider ways to help your child negotiate this transition more smoothly. To expect a shy child to venture out and establish new relationships may be expecting too much. You can facilitate her meeting new people and making friends without pushing too hard and without artificially bringing children into your home. Such "matchmaking" can occur in the context of your own relationships, such as having your daughter meet the children of your adult acquaintances.

An important consideration in moving is selecting an area where children are available. An ideal neighborhood is one in which your child can mix school friends and neighborhood peers. Of course, these factors can be considered only in those situations in which you have the luxury of time and a certain freedom of choice.

Clinging to friends from the old neighborhood represents a continuation of old relationships and an unwillingness to completely relinquish meaningful past involvements. After eight months, your daughter should be developing relationships with children in the new neighborhood. Clinging solely to old friends beyond this point may indicate that she is rejecting the move, or may mean she is clinging to the fantasy of not having moved. Ideally, some continuing relationships with old friends will parallel her slowly developing relationships with children in the new neighborhood.

If your daughter's reluctance to form new peer relations continues, you must consider the probability that some conflict is being expressed by this unwillingness. You might then help her make the transition by encouraging her to join various after school activities or groups that include children with similar interests. If she opposes this, encourage her to talk about her feelings and discuss her reluctance to meet new people. If you don't feel comfortable with this, you might arrange a consultation with a professional to help you feel more at ease discussing this important issue with your daughter.

Child Is Being Snubbed

We lived in a middle-class urban area. Last year, we moved to an affluent suburban community, and our eight-year-old daughter is being snubbed by the other girls. What can we do?

DR. HAJAL: Feeling snubbed can be difficult for a child. Try to help your child so that she doesn't personalize this very rejecting situation and suffer a loss of self-esteem. Try to explain the other children's reactions to your child. They may pick out certain differences in your daughter's behavior or clothing, or some other inconsequential difference. Explain that this may indicate their discomfort in the presence of a new person.

It would be helpful to facilitate your daughter's finding other children who would be less snobbish and more accepting. Dissuade your daughter from coming to view this problem in terms of material things. Under these circumstances, a child may develop the fantasy "If only you would buy me this kind of clothing, then I'll be accepted, and everything will be fine." As a parent, you must resist the temptation to make up for this imagined deficit by expending money in pursuit of your child's acceptance.

Your daughter's difficulty relates to the newness of the situation. It is to be hoped that, as the children get to know each other, these superficial issues will become secondary and other, more meaningful, matters will emerge. If your daughter has an interest or talent, such as dancing or singing, enrolling her in a class can create a common ground that has nothing to do with material issues. Try viewing this as a transitional difficulty that will probably resolve itself over the course of time.

A child's seeming "different" can be very important when a family moves. If you are less affluent than others in your community, your daughter may be deemed "different," which may merely reflect the fact that some youngsters in the group feel threatened. A particular youngster may feel threatened by a new child or may fear that the established equilibrium will be upset. The new child may then be scapegoated for real or imagined differences, and kids can engage in a form of social meanness that occasionally borders on cruelty. Children this age often pick on each other, form cliques, and take sides for and against each other. Children are generally aware of this and to some extent expect it. Most kids have found themselves in situations in which they have been less than considerate to other children and in which others have been cruel to them.

As will occur in any group, there will be a mixture of responses toward a new child. Some youngsters will react negatively to any new child, while others will extend themselves. One child may individually extend a welcoming hand, even though acting sarcastic in the presence of the group. An initial negative reaction by the group is not cast in stone and need not become the model for all future relationships within the group. In fact, such reactions are usually temporary.

It's understandable for a child to wish for immediate acceptance by the group because such acceptance helps a child overcome the anxiety of moving. However, a completely smooth transition and total group acceptance is quite rare, and most children experience some initial difficulty with a new peer group.

Midyear Move

We must move in the middle of the school year. I'm concerned that this will affect our children. Please advise me.

DR. HAJAL: Some experts consider midyear moves to be better than summer moves. A midyear move permits the child to move rapidly into a social milieu at school and allows for a quick linkup to other kids. The child is thrust into ongoing activity, without having to go through the doldrums of summer, when school is not in session and when most kids are away. Long summer days spent alone can worsen the normal feelings of loss that a child feels after leaving the old neighborhood.

A child who moves into a new school during the school term will probably do as well as he did at the old school. Yes, some adjustments must be made, and for a while there may be additional work that might require some tutoring. Remember, a move ushers major changes into a child's life, and a certain amount of time will be needed for any child to adjust psychologically, socially, and academically. It would be unrealistic to expect an immediate and perfect adjustment in all these important spheres of a child's life.

Be prepared to discuss with your child any aspects of his school curriculum, the school setting, or other "cultural" issues that may differ from the old setting to which your child was accustomed. While a midyear move may mean a sudden disruption in school and in the ordinary comings-and-goings of a child's life, it does have certain advantages because it allows the child to plunge right into an ongoing curriculum.

An Overview

DR. HAJAL: Any move will affect a child. The extent and the way in which it does depend on the developmental stage the child is negotiating at the time of the move. Parents with children at different developmental stages will easily observe different reactions to a move in each one of their children. When embarking on a move, parents must be aware of the individual style as well as the age of each child and should keep in mind that each child will have a reaction to giving up the old, familiar environment.

An entire family must make an adaptation and deal with the move and its many meanings. In a sense, the family may be viewed as a dynamic system when dealing with a move; everyone must adapt and make the transition, and everyone's feelings will resonate with each other's regarding the move.

A child who is about to move will have some anticipatory grief. This is followed by actual grief once the move is made. There is then a transition to the new circumstances. Most children continue having wishes and fantasies of returning to the old neighborhood and of seeing their old friends for a while after the move. This can be mixed with some angry feelings and with feelings of regret. Family members should allow each other to feel and express all this without expecting instant adaptations.

A family moves, not just a child. Every family member has feelings about this event, and parents must be careful not to project their own anxieties and concerns about moving onto a child. In addition, parents must always be aware of having their own ambivalent feelings about a move. They should avoid expecting a child to make a rapid and perfect adjustment. For some parents, a child's quick adjustment serves as dubious reassurance that the move was a good idea. This breeds unrealistic expectations for the child, making him the barometer of family life and of the decision to move. It can also prevent the child from going through or expressing any of the turmoil he or she experiences at the time of the move.

Parents may be overly concerned that any change in the smooth predictability of life will be "traumatic" for a child. They may therefore try to avoid any situation that is somewhat unpredictable and requires a major adaptation. While moving is disruptive, a great deal can be said for this change in a family's life. If a move will improve the lot of the family, it is, of course, a positive experience. In addition, it allows a child to test out social and adaptive skills.

A move may be viewed as a challenge and an opportunity to relinquish the residue of bygone years. The new neighborhood, the new school, and new peers can all represent an opportunity for new and better ways of functioning. A child is challenged to adapt, to learn new things, and to develop new friendships. These can all be very positive childhood experiences and can create an awareness that there is no need to cling to the old and predictable in order to feel comfortable.

As difficult as a move may be, it can be an opportunity for a child to grow and mature emotionally. When a family moves, the change in the lives of its members can be an enriching experience for them all.

Chapter 19: When a Child Goes to the Hospital

Few experiences are as upsetting to parents or child as hospitalization. Though frightening to any child, the trauma of going to a hospital can be minimized. The steps to take depend on the situation. Hospitalization may be elective: a preplanned stay for diagnostic steps or for surgery such as a tonsillectomy. Or it can be for an emergency, such as occurs with an unexpected illness or with a serious injury.

With elective hospitalization, you can prepare both yourself and your child for the experience, while an emergency hospital visit doesn't allow you the opportunity for careful preparation. No matter what the cause of a hospital stay, most parents become concerned about how best to help a child deal with the experience. Questions arise about visiting, about preparing a child for the stay, and about a variety of other issues.

Our consultant for this topic is Miriam Sherman, M.D. Dr. Sherman is an Associate Professor of Clinical Psychiatry in Pediatrics at the Cornell University Medical College and is the Director of Pediatric Consultation Liaison at The New York Hospital.

A Child's Concerns

Our five-year-old son will have a hernia repair next month. What concerns will he have about the hospital stay?

DR. SHERMAN: A child's reaction to any hospitalization depends on his or her age and the stage of development at that time, the nature of the illness, and the treatment required for that condition. In addition, the child's previous experiences and general ability to adjust to new situations also determine his concerns and his reaction at this time. In addition, the parents' response to the child's illness and hospitalization will play a large role in the youngster's experience.

All children, of virtually any age, ask similar questions, although

362

they are voiced in a variety of ways. Every child faced with a hospital stay wants to know: "How long will I be in the hospital?"; "Where will you be while I'm there?"; "What will happen to me?"; "Was it my fault that I got sick?"; "Will it hurt?"; "Will I look different when I get out?"; "Will I come home?"; and other issues largely determined by the nature of the illness for which the child is being hospitalized.

In a very general way, a child younger than six years is most concerned with separation anxiety when he or she is hospitalized. A school-age child (from about six to twelve years) most fears body damage, while adolescents facing a hospital stay become most concerned with issues of appearance.

A very young child may view any illness and its treatment as a form of punishment. A child younger than six needs reassurance from a parent that the hospital stay is not a punishment for some imagined misdeed. Equally important, the level of cognitive development partly determines the child's understanding of the body and its functions, which in turn, influence the child's perception of the hospital stay. Young children have a variety of fantasies about the body, some based on the most unlikely ideas. They also frequently misinterpret what they hear. Therefore, it's important for a parent to try to determine the youngster's level of understanding and the misconceptions that may prevail in the child's mind before going to the hospital.

For instance, any hospitalized patient will have blood drawn for testing. A child may entertain the misconception that all his blood will be drained, and that he will therefore die. A young child's thinking is very concrete; he may not fully understand that a medicine taken by mouth can promote healing in another part of the body.

All this means that a parent should try to understand what the child understands and misperceives. A parent should then explain everything about the illness and its treatment in terms that the child can understand, trying to counteract the misconceptions and explain everything as clearly as possible.

Preparing for Hospitalization

Our seven-year-old son will be going to the hospital for elective surgery. How can we prepare him for this experience?

DR. SHERMAN: When a child is going to have elective surgery, both parents and child have time to prepare for the experience. Many hospitals today allow for a child to be given an introduction to the hospital before the actual stay begins. The child can see the room, the play area, the toys, and meet the staff personnel who will be present during the actual hospital stay. All these preparatory steps help a child achieve a certain kind of mastery over what can be a very frightening experience.

Parents should explain the reasons for hospitalization, taking into account the youngster's level of cognitive development and ability to understand the body and bodily functions. When discussing all this, the question of pain will inevitably arise. Be honest with your child; don't say "It won't hurt" when you know there is bound to be some pain and discomfort. Tell your child there will probably be some pain, but that something will be done to make the pain less. When going to the hospital, a few treasured objects such as a favorite doll or toy should be brought so your child has some contact with home and the familiar.

A school-age child about to undergo a lengthy hospital stay should be aware that he or she will be able to continue with school, even while at the hospital.

Parents, too, must prepare for all this, and should know that they will be able to be involved in their child's care to some degree. This should be discussed with nurses and doctors, along with items such as what the child will eat, where the bathroom is located, and other practical issues that adults take for granted.

Be prepared for your child to have a reaction to hospitalization, even before the day of admission arrives. Many children regress to ways of behaving that are reminiscent of earlier stages of development. A child who no longer sucks his thumb may begin sucking again. A child who is toilet-trained may begin wetting the bed. Other children may not regress but rather will suddenly begin moving ahead when hospitalization is about to occur. For instance, a child who had been clinging and somewhat dependent, may, when hospitalized, begin acting independently, demonstrating a newfound sense of mastery. Some years ago, my son, then three years old, went to the hospital for a hernia repair. When we got to the hospital, he asked for my doctor's bag. In a very adaptive way, he was turning the passive into the assertive by identifying with me.

Parents should be aware that the hospital has people available to help if a child's reaction involves a great deal of regression. These include nurses, social workers, and, if necessary, child psychiatrists. On the whole, properly preparing your child for a hospital stay means providing as much information as possible, so your child can use his own resources to master the experience.

Staying with Your Child

Our nine-year-old daughter will be in the hospital for five days. Should one of us always be with her?

DR. SHERMAN: Generally, hospitals and parents today are very much aware that the child younger than six or seven should have one or another parent at the bedside during the course of a hospital stay. There are, of course, certain exceptions. When a mother works, it may not be possible for her to remain with her child. Ideally, a parent-surrogate is available in such a circumstance. A school-age child can certainly tolerate some periods of time when neither parent is present at the bedside. It's best to structure your absence for the youngster, telling the child where you are going and when you will return. Generally, the younger the child, the more difficult it is for a parent to leave the hospital during the child's stay. In your situation, with a nine-year-old daughter, there is no harm in taking leave when necessary, so long as you assure your daughter you will return and let her know when you will do so.

During a long-term hospital stay, it may become impossible for a parent to remain continuously with a child. A school-age child does not need to have a parent present throughout each day and every night. A child of this age has generally attained a good deal of mastery over separation anxiety and can tolerate occasional separations from her parents.

After a Hospital Stay

Our ten-year-old daughter recently returned from a week-long hospital stay. She's been a bit cranky and seems less mature than usual. Is this normal?

DR. SHERMAN: When a child has spent some time in a hospital, she may become quite comfortable with hospital routines. During a hospital stay, a certain degree of regression is usual, and is even expected of any patient. A hospitalized patient is not required to carry out ordinary daily responsibilities; meals are served to the patient and total dependence on caretakers such as nurses and doctors is expected. Upon arriving home, a child must soon return to the mainstream tasks and responsibilities of daily living. For a while, she may be reluctant to resume normal responsibilities. In some instances, when the hospital stay was difficult for a child, there may be some posthospitalization nightmares and a few behavioral difficulties. This is not terribly unusual, and parents should not become overly concerned about such changes. In a few days, the difficulties will fade completely. Above all, it is helpful to encourage your child to talk about the hospital stay and to discuss any thoughts, feelings, or fantasies he or she has about the experience.

Feeling Guilty

Our six-year-old son is now hospitalized for anemia. Although it makes very little sense, I feel a bit guilty about this. Is my reaction normal?

DR. SHERMAN: When a child goes to the hospital, both the child and the parents need some preparation for the experience. Part of a parent's preparation should involve identifying his feelings about the situation. In my experience, working with parents and children, I've learned that a child's illness always engenders feelings of fear and guilt in parents. A parent may feel, "What could I (or should I) have done differently?" Other guilt-ridden questions often arise: "Did I do all I could have done?"; "Is it my fault that my child is suffering?" Even when a child has an accident such as falling from a bicycle, a parent may actually wonder on some level, "Why wasn't I there?" or "Could I have prevented the accident?"

These are generally quite normal feelings and concerns for parents, and a child's hospitalization is bound to evoke a variety of feelings in a parent, some logical and others seeming somewhat farfetched. One of the most important things a parent can do in such circumstances is simply communicate these feelings to a spouse. Relying on a loved one for emotional support is the most natural thing in the world and can be very helpful. A child's hospitalization is a stress and a challenge for the child and the parents alike.

An Overview

DR. SHERMAN: While most of us would agree that it is best if a child never has to go to a hospital, it becomes clear that hospitals play an ever-increasing role in our lives. This is true from birth until death. Hospitals become part of our experiences in living our lives, and this reality enters into the relationship between parents and children.

Parents are best off knowing and expecting that a hospital stay is likely to become part of a child's life at some point during childhood. Even if a child does not become a hospital patient, it is quite probable that a visit to an emergency room will occur at some time or another.

Today, we live in an era of relative enlightenment, and hospitals usually make provisions for a parent to visit and remain with a young child during a hospital stay. Visitation, playrooms, and other factors help diminish the traumatic impact of hospitalization on a child. If prepared for and handled properly, a hospital stay need not be an all-consuming, traumatic, and horrifying experience for a child, and need not lead to any major emotional consequences. In fact, a hospital stay is a challenge and can actually become an experience in mastery for a child.

GLOSSARY

ANIMISM. A child's tendency to believe that inanimate objects (such as clouds and trees) are capable of thinking, feeling, or behaving in a purposeful or motivated manner.

ASSOCIATIVE PLAY. A form of play in which young toddlers do the same thing at a specific location (such as in a sandbox), but in which there is little interchange and each child acts separately.

AUTONOMY. The state of mastering one's own body, as when the toddler strives to do things for himself. A striving for self-sufficiency and independence.

BASIC TRUST. A sense that is developed when an infant has his physical and psychological needs reliably satisfied by caretakers. The infant learns that the world is a good, reasonably reliable place in which most things are manageable and in which he can feel reasonably secure.

CASTRATION ANXIETY. A small boy's concern about the possibility of losing his genitals. This emerges during the Oedipal period, when the boy sees the female genitals and when his interest in his own genitals is at a peak.

COGNITION. The mental process involved in knowing, perceiving, thinking, and using language.

COLIC. Intestinal spasms that cause discomfort for a baby. A baby experiencing colic screams, refuses to eat, and may have a swollen belly.

COMPULSION. A repeated, stereotyped, and usually trivial action (for example, washing one's hands), the need for which is insistent, forcing the child to act in a certain way. Not performing the act causes anxiety, while completing the act temporarily relieves the tension. Most children have occasional compulsions that are part of their daily lives.

CONDITIONED RESPONSE. In conditioning, the learned response to a specific stimulus.

CONSCIENCE. The part of the mind that prohibits the expression of unacceptable feelings, thoughts, or actions. Conscience relates to a person's moral and ethical standards. Conscience is slowly internalized over the developmental course of the early years and represents the attitudes, prohibitions, and commands of the parents that have become part of the child's

369

own mind. A youngster's conscience tends to mature slowly during the school-age years and has fully matured by adolescence.

COOPERATIVE PLAY. Play in which children truly collaborate for the activity at hand. It involves discussing, planning, and assigning various roles so that the game may be jointly and successfully completed.

DRAMATIC PLAY. Play in which children act out scenes drawn from everyday life, tinged with imagination. Such play allows the child to try out various roles and identities, thereby expanding his or her experience of the world.

DYSLEXIA. A general term that indicates a learning disability involving a wide variety of specific problems in learning to read and spell. The child usually has difficulty associating words and letters with spoken sounds.

EGOCENTRIC THINKING. The young child's inability to appreciate that his outlook is only his own, and his inability to take another person's perspective into account. The child is generally unaware that the world and the self exist at the same time. By the age of five or six, the child's thinking is far less egocentric and continues to become less so until adolescence.

ENURESIS. The inability to maintain bladder control after the time when it should be achieved, generally after three to four years of age. *Primary enuresis* indicates that a child has never attained bladder control. *Secondary enuresis* occurs when a child has attained control but, for any number of reasons, no longer maintains it.

EXTENDED FAMILY. A family unit in which parents, children, and other close relatives (grandparents, aunts, uncles) are available for caretaking and other family functions.

GRASPING REFLEX. A reflex, found in the newborn, that involves the infant's gripping of an object pressed against its palm or finger.

HYPERACTIVITY. A syndrome involving overactivity to the extent that a child cannot remain still. In a learning situation, the child is unable to focus attention on any one thing long enough to absorb the material.

IDENTIFICATION. A psychological process in which a child takes on the behavior patterns, as well as the attitudes and mannerisms, of role models, at first the parents.

IMAGINARY COMPANIONS. An imaginary playmate, human or animal, that has a psychological existence for the child. Most often appearing during the preschool years, such a "companion" can serve many purposes: companionship, excursions into fantasy, and the opportunity for the child to disavow unacceptable thoughts, feelings or behaviors, blaming instead the "companion."

INDIVIDUATION. A process in which a child eventually experiences the self as a distinct and separate person from the parent. Individuation begins during the first year of life. The child truly senses himself as a distinct and separate person by the third year, but individuation continues throughout childhood.

LEARNING DISABILITY. A child with a learning disability usually has normal or above-normal intelligence, has good hearing, vision, and coordination, is not environmentally disadvantaged, and has no recognizable emotional problems. Despite good schooling, the child, who has no obvious brain damage, has a gap in his presumed capacity to learn and his actual learning performance.

LIMIT-SETTING. The means by which a parent inculcates in a toddler an awareness of do's and dont's, and an appreciation that the child cannot freely navigate everywhere or have every wish satisfied. Setting limits is the child's first experience with parentally disapproved behaviors.

NEGATIVISM. Repeated noncompliance with parents' wishes or commands and refusal of offers of help. A quality often noted in toddlers and considered to indicate the child's wish to become autonomous.

NUCLEAR FAMILY. The basic family unit, consisting of parents and their children.

OBJECT IMPERMANENCE. The infant's inability to appreciate that a person or object continues to exist after it can no longer be directly seen. This inability persists from birth until the baby is six to eight months old.

OBJECT PERMANENCE. The baby's capacity, developed by six to eight months, to appreciate that a person or object can still exist even if it cannot be seen or heard.

OEDIPAL PHASE. The phase during the preschool years (from about age three until six) when a child develops romantic feelings about the opposite-sexed parent and begins to have ambivalent feelings of love and resentment toward the parent of the same sex. The phase is resolved when the child renounces these strivings and identifies with the same-sexed parent, taking on a moral code or conscience.

PARALLEL PLAY. Two or more toddlers playing side by side without really interacting, but enjoying the presence of each other.

PEER GROUP. A group of children who are of similar chronological and developmental age.

PHOBIA. An irrational fear of and overpowering wish to avoid a situation, place, or thing. Phobias are quite common during the toddler and preschool years.

POSITIVE REINFORCEMENT. The consistent rewarding of a certain behavior so that it becomes part of a person's repertoire of behavior—for example, praising a child who does well in school.

PRODUCTIVE (ACTIVE) LANGUAGE. The ability to use words to communicate.

PSYCHOMETRIC TESTING. Testing of various psychological and intellectual traits and abilities so that they may be assigned a score and compared to the general population.

RECEPTIVE (PASSIVE) LANGUAGE. The spoken language that a baby understands; it appears before the baby can actually speak.

REGRESSION. The tendency to revert back to ways of thinking, feeling, and behaving that are characteristic of an earlier time in development.

REPRESSION. A defense mechanism in which painful or frightening wishes, impulses, or memories are forced from conscious awareness.

REVERSIBILITY. The concept that certain things can be undone or reversed: construction versus destruction, addition is the opposite of subtraction.

SCAPEGOATING. The act of venting frustrations and resentments on a convenient person, even to the point of blaming the scapegoat.

SECONDARY SEX CHARACTERISTICS. Physical characteristics, other than the sexual organs, that are related to sexual maturing. In the female, these include breast development and a redistribution of body fat. In the male, there is growth of body and facial hair and deepening of the voice. Both sexes have a growth of pubic and armpit hair.

SEPARATION ANXIETY. The distress and anxiety that a child experiences when separated from the parents. During certain periods of development, intense separation anxiety develops.

SOCIAL PLAY. Play involving the participation and interaction of others.

SOCIALIZATION. A lengthy process by which a child learns the normative role that a given culture expects of the child.

STRANGER ANXIETY. The wariness and distress that a baby experiences in the company of unfamiliar people and places. It makes its appearance at about six to eight months of age and subsides by the end of the first year.

SUCKING REFLEX. A reflex present at birth. Stimulation of the lips or cheeks causes the infant to turn its head in the direction of the stimulus so that it can take the object into the mouth and begin sucking.

SWADDLING. Snugly wrapping a young baby.

TODDLERHOOD. The period of development between about fifteen months and two-and-a-half years of age. It is characterized by the rapid development of motor skills and the child's push for autonomy.

TRANSITIONAL OBJECT. Any object or person that, for the baby, has a mental or emotional connection with the primary caretaker.

TWINNING. In twins, a process in which a great deal of interdependency can develop because of the close, ongoing contact with a cotwin. It can result in a feeling that the cotwin is a necessary component of any meaningful interaction with mother or with other people.

WEANING. The transition from breast or bottle to a cup, and from milk to solid foods.

INDEX

abstractions, 66
abuse, physical, 102–103
activities, school-age, 161–166
  boy's, 163–164
  discretionary, 206–207
  gender segregation in, 161–164
  girl's, 163
  magical thinking in, 165–166
  peer-group, 171
adoption, adopted children, 285–294
  biological vs. adoptive mothers and, 288–289
  child told about, 285–288, 293
  interracial, 291–293
  new siblings and, 293
  nursing experience in, 38
  of older child, 291
  physical characteristics in, 289–290
  process involved in, 286, 293–294
  real parents sought by, 290–291, 292–293
  "where babies come from" and, 288, 289
advertisements, 39, 101
affection, see attention, child's need for; nurturing
aggression, child's:
  in boy's vs. girl's play, 107–108
  disciplining, 87–88
  after divorce, 242–243
  parent's approval of, 345, 350
  parent's death and, 266–267
  in sibling rivalry, 87–88, 230–231, 236
  television and, 140, 210, 349–350
  toddler's, 87–88
  see also bullies

animism, 110
anxieties:
  collecting as defense against, 164–165
  genital play and, 94–95, 148–149
  nursing and, 27–28
  rituals and, 166, 194
  school-age child's, 213
  symptoms of, 202
  see also separation anxiety; stranger anxiety
appearance, preoccupation with, 215–216
appetite, loss of, 85
Ascher, Robert C., 344–352
  on bully's homelife, 345, 348–349, 350
  on factors in scapegoating, 345–347
  on girls as bullies, 351–352
  on violent television shows, 349–350
associative play, 106–107
asthmatic children, 322–327
  coddling response to, 325
  emotional factors for, 322–323, 326
  homelife affected by, 322
  incidence of, 322
  manipulation by, 324–325
  normal activities of, 325–326
  school attendance and, 323–324
attachment, child's need for:
  development of, 11–13, 19, 36–37
  infant's, 11–13, 19, 33, 36–37, 250–251
  trust and, 19
attention, child's need for:
  classroom performance and, 169
  degree of, 19

373

insulin, 327
intellectual development, child's:
  classifying groups in, 180–181
  important first lessons in, 42
  infant's, 16–18, 41–43
  language in, 65–68
  maturational timetable in, 48–49
  object permanence in, 17–18, 65–66
  overemphasis on, 41–43
  play in, 34, 42–43, 65
  processes as reversible in, 180–181
  repetitive behavior in, 16–17, 42
  school-age child's, 179–182
  toddler's, 65–68
intuition, parent's, 6
IQ tests, 214, 269, 270

jealousy:
  of mother's friends, 151–152
  of new sibling, 83–84, 230–231
joint custody, 247–248
jokes, 171, 178, 196
junk food, 319–320

Kernberg, Paulina F., 145–158, 286–294
  on adopted child, 286–294
  on adopted child's new siblings, 293
  on adopted child's search for real
    parents, 290–291
  on adopting older child, 291
  on bad language, 149, 151
  on child's jealousy, 151–152
  on crossover play, 153
  on divulging adoption to child,
    286–288
  on father's age, 152–153
  on fears, 154
  on gifts as bribes, 156–157
  on imaginary playmate, 151
  on interracial adoption, 291–293
  on language development, 157–158
  on masturbating, 148–149
  on play vs. instruction, 154
  on readiness for first grade, 154–155
  on role of preschool, 150–151,
    155–156
  on shyness, 156
  on spanking, 146–147
  on sudden dependence needs,
    147–148
  on terms for adoptive mother, 288

language:
  babbling, 10–11, 20, 62–63
  "bad," 65, 133, 149, 151, 208–209

early exposure to, 19–21
  enhancing, 157–158
  games and, 20
  receptive, 21
  see also speech
laughter, infant's, 3, 19–21
leadership qualities, child's, 172
learning problems, 333–343
  attention deficit disorder, 338–340
  categories of, 333
  child's history in, 337–339
  evaluation of, 336–337, 341–342
  hyperactivity in, 337–339
  intelligence testing in, 214, 269, 270,
    336
  learning disability, 333–334
  in math, 335
  medication for, 339, 340
  in new school, 335–336
  overview of, 341–343
  parental counseling for, 342
  parents' role in, 335, 341, 342–343
  prognosis for, 339–340
  in reading, 335–336
  school refusal and, 340–341
lesbianism, *see* homosexuality
lies, child's:
  parent's reaction to, 132
  peer-group's view of, 173
  preschooler's, 111, 131–132
  toddler's, 69–70
limits, setting, 53–62
  alternatives for, 54, 77
  autonomy and, 56–57
  child's growth and, 58–59
  conscience developed by, 57–59
  contrariness and, 54–57
  curiosity and, 54, 55–56, 76–77
  parent's confidence in, 76–77
  taboo items in, 77–78
  testing vs., 77
  in toilet training, 59–60
Linus blanket, 15–16
loners, 190–191, 205–206
  twins as, 302–303
love, food as, 86, 96, 314, 317–318

magical thinking, 165–166, 181–182
mastery, *see* autonomy, child's
masturbation:
  discussing, 199
  feeling states as cause of, 94–95,
    148–149
  parent's reaction to, 133
  preschooler's, 132–133, 148–149

386   *Index*